THE JOURNALS OF
LOUISA MAY ALCOTT

THE JOURNALS OF
Louisa May Alcott

With an Introduction by
MADELEINE B. STERN

Editors
JOEL MYERSON and DANIEL SHEALY

Associate Editor
MADELEINE B. STERN

LITTLE, BROWN AND COMPANY

Boston   Toronto   London

First Edition

Library of Congress Cataloging-in-Publication Data

Alcott, Louisa May, 1832–1882.
    The journals of Louisa May Alcott / editors, Joel Myerson and Daniel Shealy ; associate editor, Madeleine B. Stern ; with an introduction by Madeleine B. Stern. — 1st ed.
        p.   cm.
    Includes index.
    ISBN 0-316-59362-1
    1. Alcott, Louisa May, 1832–1888—Diaries.   2. Authors, American—19th century—Diaries.   I. Myerson, Joel.   II. Shealy, Daniel.   III. Stern, Madeleine B., 1912–   IV. Title.
PS1018.A425   1989
818'.403—dc19
[B]   89-2419
                                                                                  CIP

10 9 8 7 6 5 4 3 2 1

MV PA

Published simultaneously in Canada
by Little, Brown & Company (Canada) Limited
PRINTED IN THE UNITED STATES OF AMERICA

Contents

List of Illustrations

John Bridge Pratt in theatrical costume
Louisa May Alcott Memorial Association

John Bridge Pratt
Louisa May Alcott Memorial Association

Front wrapper from
Merry's Museum (1869)
Concord Free Public Library

May Alcott's frontispiece illustration to the first part of
Little Women
(1868)

Alice Bartlett
Louisa May Alcott Memorial Association

May Alcott Nieriker's drawing of her
sister Louisa as "The Golden Goose"
Louisa May Alcott Memorial Association

Advertising poster for
Little Men
(1871)
Louisa May Alcott Memorial Association

Advertising poster for
Work
(1873)
Louisa May Alcott Memorial Association

Title page of
Work
(1873)

May Alcott Nieriker's drawing
of her father in his study
Louisa May Alcott Memorial Association

Ernest Nieriker
Louisa May Alcott Memorial Association

May Alcott Nieriker's painting of
her husband in their Paris salon
Louisa May Alcott Memorial Association

Louisa May Nieriker ("Lulu")
Louisa May Alcott Memorial Association

Acknowledgments

IN PREPARING this edition we have incurred many debts of gratitude. We are grateful to the following libraries for assistance in using their collections: Boston Public Library, Concord Free Public Library, Fruitlands Museums, Harvard University Libraries (Houghton and Widener), New York Public Library, Orchard House, and University of South Carolina.

Louisa May Alcott's journals are published with the permission of the Estate of Theresa W. Pratt, Fruitlands Museums, and the Houghton Library of Harvard University. We are also indebted to Charles M. Ganson, Jr., William F. Kussin, Jr., Charles W. Pratt, Frederick A. Pratt, John W. Pratt, and the Louisa May Alcott Memorial Association for help.

We are grateful to the following institutions for permission to publish materials in their collections: Concord Free Public Library, Fruitlands Museums, Houghton Library of Harvard University, Massachusetts Historical Society, New-York Historical Society, and University of Virginia (Louisa May Alcott Collection [No. 6255], Manuscripts Division, Special Collections Department).

Among the many people who have helped us, we would especially like to thank Kelly Aherne, Thomas Blanding (who first discovered the manuscript fragment of the Fruitlands diary), Rodney G. Dennis, Jerome McGann, Marcia Moss, Richard S. Reed, and Donald Siebert. Armida Gilbert assisted us by diligently tracking down obscure people and events referred to in the journals. Jayne Gordon and Peggy Clarke provided invaluable help by opening Orchard House for our use.

Christina Ward gave us much help and encouragement in seeing the book through press. We are grateful to Deborah Jacobs for her exemplary copyediting.

Photographic work was done by the staffs of the Concord Free Public Library, Harvard University, University of South Carolina, and University of Virginia. Photographic work at Orchard House was done by Nancy Hill-Joroff.

Finally, each of the editors has individual thanks to offer. Joel Myerson is grateful to the Research and Productive Scholarship Committee and to Dean Carol McGinnis Kay of the College of Humanities and Social Sciences of the University of South Carolina and, for her usual patience and support, to Greta Little. Daniel Shealy acknowledges the support of the Southern Regional Education Board and Frederik N. Smith, Chairman of the Department of English at the University of North Carolina at Charlotte. He is also indebted to his parents, Ruby and Ralph Shealy, and to his brothers, Roger and Clayton, for their kind support and encouragement. Madeleine B. Stern acknowledges the unceasing support of her partner, Dr. Leona Rostenberg, who originally discovered Alcott's pseudonymous works.

Abbreviations of Works Cited

Cheney. Ednah Dow Cheney, *Louisa May Alcott: Her Life, Letters, and Journals* (Boston: Roberts Brothers, 1889).

Journals. The Journals of Bronson Alcott, ed. Odell Shepard (Boston: Little, Brown, 1938).

Letters. The Letters of A. Bronson Alcott, ed. Richard L. Herrnstadt (Ames: Iowa State University Press, 1969).

SL. The Selected Letters of Louisa May Alcott, ed. Joel Myerson and Daniel Shealy (Boston: Little, Brown, 1987).

Notes on the Text

The Journals of Louisa May Alcott presents an eclectic text of all known manuscript journals written by her, as well as all journals for which no manuscript is extant but a printed text exists.[1] Our primary goal has been to present a readable, continuous text that covers the period from August 1843, when Alcott was almost eleven years old, to March 1888, the month of her death.

At various times in her career, most noticeably after her mother's death, in 1877, and the family's move from Concord to Boston in 1885, Alcott went through her papers and destroyed letters and journals to ensure privacy after her death. Although she simply destroyed her letters, the disposition of her journals is more complicated. All available evidence indicates that Alcott kept a daily journal or diary. At a later date, she summarized and greatly condensed the year's events, both in a journal volume and in her "Notes and Memoranda" volume. The daily diaries were then — or at a later date — destroyed. Only the daily diaries from 1885 to 1888 have survived, and the ones for 1885 and 1886 may be compared with the journals for those years to see how determined Alcott was to boil down the events of her daily life into neat, compact monthly units. As she prepared her journal summaries of the daily diaries, Alcott made relatively few cancellations. However, at later dates she would go back through her journals, both to revise by cancellation and insertion and to add retrospective comments on the events described earlier. The surviving journals, then, comprise both contemporaneous entries as well as later revisions and comments. The extant daily diaries show no such later revisions.

The publication history of Alcott's journals is quickly told. Ednah Dow Cheney published selections from the journals in her *Louisa May Alcott: Her Life, Letters, and Journals* (1889), and the Fruitlands diary fragments were edited and reproduced in facsimile in *Transcendental Wild Oats and Fragments from the*

---

1. Even though Alcott's manuscripts are labeled both "journals" and "diaries," we have, following her own practice and for the sake of convenience, used the general term "journals" for all of them.

Fruitlands Diaries (1975; exp. ed., 1981). In editing the journals, Cheney standardized spelling, grammar, and punctuation; removed what she considered potentially awkward references to contemporaries; replaced most proper names with abbreviations or dashes; and generally omitted a great deal of material she felt was unimportant or reflected poorly on her subject. The text of the Fruitlands diaries is complete, but spelling and punctuation have been regularized.

All that remains of Alcott's Fruitlands diary is two leaves of paper, each folded to make four pages, each page measuring 6½ inches by 8 inches. The pages are numbered: pages 3/4 are conjugate with pages 71/72, pages 5/6 conjugate with pages 65/66. Stab holes indicate that the leaves were once part of a sewn or bound larger unit, now lost.

Unfortunately, the manuscript diaries and journals for part of 1843 and all of 1845–1847, 1850–1862, and 1868–1878, from which Cheney made her selections, have disappeared. It seems likely that Alcott did not keep a journal in 1848 and 1849; in a May 1850 entry she wrote that "so long a time has passed since I kept a journal that I hardly know how to begin."

Alcott's journal for the years 1863–1867 is written in a small ledger-type volume bound in half-leather. Each unnumbered page measures 7¾ inches by 10⅛ inches and is ruled horizontally, with vertical column lines to the left and right of the center section. Alcott has written across the entire page. The journal proper is on pages [1–2] and [5–73]. Pages [74] and [105–110] contain lists of her earnings, repeated in the "Notes and Memoranda" volume. Pages [3–4], [75–104], and [111–116] have been cut out.

Alcott's journal for the years 1879–1886 is written in a notebook volume bound in quarter-leather. Each unnumbered page measures 6⅞ inches by 8¼ inches and is ruled horizontally. The journal proper is on pages [3–51], [53–59], [61–72], [74–84], and [86–105]. Pages [1–2], [52], [60], [73], [85], and [106–140] are blank.

Alcott's diary for the year 1885 is written in the *Excelsior Diary for 1885*, bound in full leather, with pages measuring 3½ inches by 5¾ inches. Typical of such yearly diaries, it begins with printed monthly calendars similar to an appointment book, followed by pages with printed headings for each day, followed by pages for names and addresses, memoranda, cash accounts, and additional memoranda. Alcott has made entries at the end only on three of the four pages in the first memoranda section, the January-July pages in the cash accounts section (the pages for August-November have been cut out), and the sole page of the second memoranda section.

Alcott's diary for the year 1886 is written in *The Standard Diary, 1886*, bound in quarter-leather, with pages measuring 6⅞ inches by 8¼ inches. Each page contains spaces for three daily entries, with columns to the right for monies received and spent. Following the daily entries are pages for memoranda, cash accounts, and bills payable. Alcott has made entries at the end only on the December page in the cash accounts section and on the July, August, and October pages in the bills payable section.

Alcott's diary for the year 1887 is written in *The Standard Diary. 1887*, bound in full leather, with pages measuring 2⅞ inches by 4⅝ inches. It is similar in format to the 1885 diary, but following the pages for daily entries are pages for memoranda, cash accounts, summary of cash accounts, bills payable, additional memoranda, addresses, calls, and letters. Alcott has made entries at the end only on one of four pages in the first memoranda section, on all twenty-four pages in the cash accounts section, on one of the two pages in the second memoranda section, on five of the eight pages in the addresses section, and on four of the eight pages in both the calls and letters sections.

Alcott's diary for the year 1888 is written in the *Excelsior Diary for 1888*, bound in full leather, with a pencil attached by a string; its pages measure 3⅜ inches by 5¾ inches. It is similar in format to the 1885 diary. At the end, Alcott has made entries only in the January-March pages of the cash accounts section.

Finally, Alcott's "Notes and Memoranda" is written in a ledger volume bound in half-leather. Each unnumbered page measures 7½ inches by 11⅝ inches and is ruled horizontally, with a vertical rule dividing the page into two columns. A prose summary of the years' activities appears in the left-hand column, a list of Alcott's earnings in the right-hand column. The ledger, less than one quarter of which is filled with writing, covers the years 1850–1880 and 1883. Alcott set up pages for 1881–1882 and 1884–1885 but left them blank.

In our edition of Alcott's journals, we have printed the manuscript journals or diaries; Cheney's text is used only when manuscripts do not exist. Guided by our desire to show a continuous chronological record of Alcott's life and career, we have chosen, whenever a year is documented in more than one manuscript volume, to integrate all the entries for that year from different volumes rather than to present each manuscript volume as a separate entity. For example, what we print as the 1885 and 1886 journals are in fact conflations both of the entries for those years in Alcott's pocket diaries and her summaries of these entries in her journal volume for 1879–1886, with the condensed journal entry for each month placed before the daily diary entries for that month. Similarly, the "Notes and Memoranda" volume is not edited separately; each yearly summary of events and earnings is printed at the end of that respective year's journal entries.

Alcott's script degenerated after she copied *Work* "three pages at once on impression paper" in 1872[2] and during her final illness. Moreover, she was always careless about spelling, paragraphing, and punctuation. In editing Alcott's journals, we have tried to present a text faithful to the writer yet readable by a modern audience. We have let stand her misspellings (she had particular trouble with "ie" and "ei" words), contractions such as "dont" and "does n't," punctuation placed outside of closing quotation marks, and the use of an apostrophe to form plurals ("picnic's"). We have silently regularized paragraphing; supplied opening or closing quotation marks or parentheses, commas where the meaning would otherwise be unclear, and missing final punctuation;[3] printed the "Notes and Memoranda" text with the list of earnings following the prose, rather than in parallel columns; printed the year in display type at the head of each year's entries; regularized datelines for the 1885–1888 diaries; and deleted jottings concerning expenses that are obviously later additions and not part of the journal proper.[4] Alcott's periods and commas are often indeterminate; we have given her the benefit of the doubt according to the context. Incomplete words or confusing abbreviations have been filled out in brackets. Because paragraphing in the later diaries is particularly erratic, we have presented each entry as a single run-on paragraph. Significant revisions made at the time of the original writing or at a later date are reported in notes found at the end of each year's entries. Alcott's later comments in her journals on earlier entries have been printed in notes when our text is taken from the manuscripts; when our text is taken from Cheney's edition, we have let them stand where Cheney printed them. The texts of all the manuscript journals are printed in full; if ellipses are present, it is because they were there in Cheney's text when that text is used. Later comments in a hand other than Alcott's are not reported.

2. See her journal entry for December 1872 and her letter of 6 June [1884?] to Mary Mapes Dodge, *SL*, pp. 282–283. After the journal entry, Alcott later noted that "the paralysis of my thumb" dated from this time.

3. We have, however, used one-em spaces in her Fruitlands diary rather than silently supplying missing terminal punctuation, in order to give the flavor of this youthful work. We have also let stand lowercase letters following periods throughout our edition.

4. In the later diaries, Alcott numbered her visits to doctors or entered the amounts paid them as a way of keeping her accounts with them; we have not included these numbers. She also did the same for household help, listing the dates of their service and the amounts paid; these too are not included.

Chronology

1799
29 November   Bronson Alcott is born

1800
8 October   Abigail May is born

1830
23 May   Bronson Alcott and Abigail May are married in Boston

1831
16 March   Anna Bronson Alcott is born in Philadelphia

1832
29 November   LMA is born in Germantown, Pennsylvania

1834
September   The Alcotts move to Boston; Bronson begins his Temple School

1835
24 June   Elizabeth Sewall Alcott is born in Boston

1839
23 March   The Temple School closes
6 April   A son is born to the Alcotts and dies soon afterward

1840
26 July   Abby May Alcott is born in Concord

1842
8 May   Bronson sails for England
20 October   Bronson returns to America with Charles Lane and Henry Wright

1843
20 May   Lane buys the Wyman Farm at Prospect Hill in Harvard, Massachusetts
1 June   The Alcotts, Lane, and Wright move to Fruitlands

1844

| 14 January | Lane leaves Fruitlands; the Alcotts stay with the Love-joys in Still River, Massachusetts |
| 12 November | The Alcotts board with the Hosmers in Concord |

1845

January	The Alcotts buy the Cogswell House on Lexington Road in Concord (Hillside)
1 April	The Alcotts move into the Cogswell House
Winter	LMA attends John Hosmer's school in Concord

1846

| March | LMA gets her own room for the first time |

1848

| Winter | LMA writes "The Rival Painters. A Tale of Rome," her first story |
| 17 November | The Alcotts move to Dedham Street, Boston |

1849

| Summer | The Alcotts move in with Samuel Joseph May, Atkinson Street, Boston |
| 19 July | "The Olive Leaf," a family newspaper, is "published" |

1850

| January | The Alcotts move to Groton Street, Boston; Anna opens a school |
| Summer | The Alcotts contract smallpox |

1851

| September | LMA's poem "Sunlight," by "Flora Fairfield," is published in *Peterson's Magazine* |
| Winter | The Alcotts move to 50 High Street, Boston; LMA goes out to service in Dedham and earns four dollars for seven weeks, which her family returns |

1852

8 May	"The Rival Painters" is published in the *Olive Branch*
Fall	Hawthorne purchases Hillside and renames it Wayside; the Alcotts move to 20 Pinckney Street, Boston, where LMA and Anna open a school in the parlor
December	LMA hears Theodore Parker preach at the Music Hall

1853

| January-May | LMA keeps a school |

Fall	Anna takes a teaching position in Syracuse, New York
October	Bronson begins his first midwestern lecture tour

1854

February	Bronson returns from lecturing with a dollar profit
Spring	James T. Fields rejects LMA's story about her going out to service
Summer	LMA keeps a school
11 November	"The Rival Prima Donnas" is published in the *Saturday Evening Gazette*
December	*Flower Fables* is published

1855

June	LMA moves to Walpole, New Hampshire, where she organizes plays by the Walpole Amateur Dramatic Company
July	LMA's family joins her in Walpole
Fall	Anna returns to Syracuse to work in Dr. Wilbur's Asylum
November–December	LMA keeps a school in Boston, staying with cousins Samuel E. Sewall in Melrose or Thomas Sewall in Boston

1856

Summer	LMA moves to Walpole; Abby and Lizzie contract scarlet fever
October	LMA boards with Mrs. David Reed, 34 Chauncy Street, Boston
December	LMA tutors Alice Lovering, living with the family

1857

Summer	LMA goes to Walpole
September	The Alcotts purchase the John Moore house in Concord (Orchard House)
October	The Alcotts move to Concord
Fall	LMA regularly visits Frank B. Sanborn's school; she begins the Concord Dramatic Union

1858

14 March	Lizzie Alcott dies
March	The Alcotts move into Wayside while Hawthorne is abroad and repairs are being made to Orchard House
7 April	Anna and John Bridge Pratt announce their engagement

July	The Alcotts move into the refurbished Orchard House (called Apple Slump by LMA)
October	LMA moves to Thomas Sewall's house, 98 Chestnut Street, Boston, again tutoring Alice Lovering

1859

April	Bronson is appointed Concord's superintendent of schools; Abby returns to Concord

1860

March	"Love and Self-Love" appears in the *Atlantic Monthly Magazine*
23 May	Anna and John Pratt are married in Concord
August	LMA writes *Moods* in four weeks
December	Abby goes to work at Dr. Wilbur's Asylum in Syracuse

1861

Early January	LMA begins writing *Success* (later called *Work*)
February	LMA revises *Moods*
July	LMA goes to Gorham, New Hampshire
August	Abby returns to teach in Sanborn's school

1862

January	LMA boards with James T. Fields in Boston; she begins a kindergarten at the Warren Street Chapel
April	LMA gives up her school, returning to Concord while commuting to Boston
6 May	Henry David Thoreau dies
June	LMA writes "Pauline's Passion and Punishment" for a hundred-dollar prize offered by *Frank Leslie's Illustrated Newspaper*
November	LMA applies for a nursing position in a Washington hospital
11 December	LMA is accepted by the Union Hotel Hospital
13 December	LMA arrives in Georgetown
Late December	LMA learns that "Pauline's Passion" has won the prize

1863

3 January	"Pauline's Passion" begins serialization (ends 10 January)
7 January	LMA is struck by a serious illness
16 January	Bronson arrives in Georgetown
24 January	LMA and Bronson return to Concord
22 March	LMA is finally able to leave her room

28 March	Anna gives birth to Frederick Alcott Pratt
April	Sanborn asks for "Hospital Sketches"
22 May	"Hospital Sketches" begins serialization in the *Boston Commonwealth* (ends 26 June)
August	*Hospital Sketches* is published
October	Abby announces that she wants to be called May
December	*The Rose Family* and *On Picket Duty, and Other Tales* are published
14 December	LMA's dramatization of *Scenes from Dickens* opens in Boston

1864

February	LMA finishes *Moods*
August	LMA goes to Gloucester with May
December	*Moods* is published

1865

4 February	"V. V.; or, Plots and Counterplots" begins serialization in *Flag of Our Union* (ends 25 February)
24 June	Anna gives birth to John Sewall Pratt
19 July	LMA leaves for Europe with Anna Weld
November	LMA meets Ladislas Wisniewski in Vevey

1866

19 July	LMA returns home to Boston
August	*Moods* is published in England
3 October	"Behind a Mask; or, A Woman's Power" begins serialization in *Flag of Our Union* (ends 3 November)

1867

5 January	"The Abbot's Ghost; or, Maurice Treherne's Temptation" begins serialization in *Flag of Our Union* (ends 26 January)
August	LMA goes to Clarks Island, Massachusetts
September	Thomas Niles asks LMA to write a girl's book; Horace Fuller asks her to edit *Merry's Museum*
October	LMA agrees to edit *Merry's Museum* for five hundred dollars a year
28 October	LMA moves to 6 Hayward Place, Boston

1868

January	The first number of *Merry's Museum* under LMA's editorship appears
1 January	*Morning-Glories, and Other Stories* is published

March-May	LMA moves to Concord
May	LMA begins *Little Women*
15 July	LMA finishes *Little Women*, Part 1
1 October	*Little Women*, Part 1, is published
26 October	LMA moves to Brookline Street, Boston
1 November	LMA begins *Little Women*, Part 2
December	LMA closes Orchard House for the winter; she and May engage rooms at the Bellevue Hotel, Beacon Street, Boston
December	*Little Women*, Part 1, is published in England

1869

1 January	LMA finishes *Little Women*, Part 2
March	LMA moves to Concord
14 April	*Little Women*, Part 2, is published in America
15 May	*Little Women*, Part 2, is published in England
July	LMA visits the Frothinghams at Rivière du Loup, Quebec, on the St. Lawrence
July	*An Old-Fashioned Girl* begins serialization in *Merry's Museum* (ends December)
August	LMA and May go to Mount Desert, Maine
16 August	*Hospital Sketches and Camp and Fireside Stories* is published
October	LMA moves to 14 Pinckney Street, Boston

1870

April	*An Old-Fashioned Girl* is published in America and England
2 April	LMA leaves for Europe with May and Alice Bartlett
27 November	John Bridge Pratt dies

1871

January	LMA begins *Little Men*
15 May	*Little Men* is published in England
June	*Little Men* is published in America
6 June	LMA returns to Boston
October	LMA moves to a boardinghouse at 23 Beacon Street, Boston
19 November	May returns to America

1872

1 January	*Aunt Jo's Scrap-Bag: My Boys* is published
October	LMA moves to Pamelia May's boardinghouse, 7 Allston Street, Boston

November	LMA revises *Success* as *Work*
28 November	*Aunt Jo's Scrap-Bag: Shawl-Straps* is published
18 December	*Work* begins serialization in the *Christian Union* (ends 18 June 1873)

1873

26 April	May returns to London
2 June	*Work* is published in England
10 June	*Work* is published in America
August-October	LMA is in Concord
November	LMA closes Orchard House for the winter and moves to a boardinghouse at 26 East Brookline Street, Boston
December	*Aunt Jo's Scrap-Bag: Cupid and Chow-Chow* is published in America and England

1874

March	May returns from London on a visit
May	LMA moves to Joy Street, Boston
Summer	LMA visits Conway, New Hampshire, with Anna and her children
October	LMA moves with May to the Bellevue Hotel, Boston
5 December	*Eight Cousins* begins serialization in *Good Things* (ends 27 November 1875)

1875

January	*Eight Cousins* begins serialization in *St. Nicholas* (ends October)
February	LMA finishes *Silver Pitchers*
22 February	LMA attends Vassar's tenth anniversary and goes to New York afterward
March	LMA goes to Concord
25 September	*Eight Cousins* is published in America and England
October	LMA moves to Dr. Eli Peck Miller's Bath Hotel, 39 West Twenty-sixth Street, New York

1876

Early January	LMA goes to Philadelphia
February	LMA goes to Boston
June	*Silver Pitchers* is published in America and England
July	LMA starts *Rose in Bloom*
September	LMA finishes *Rose in Bloom*
4 September	May returns to Europe
November	*Rose in Bloom* is published in America and England

1877

January	LMA moves to the Bellevue Hotel, Boston, and writes *A Modern Mephistopheles*
28 April	*A Modern Mephistopheles* is published
May	Anna and LMA purchase the Thoreau House for $4,500 (LMA supplies $2,500)
July	The Alcotts begin moving into the Thoreau House
August	LMA begins *Under the Lilacs*
7 September	Mrs. Alcott's final illness begins
14 November	Orchard House is closed and the Thoreau House is opened
25 November	Mrs. Alcott dies
December	*Under the Lilacs* begins serialization in *St. Nicholas* (ends October 1878)
1 December	*Aunt Jo's Scrap-Bag: My Girls* is published

1878

February	May's engagement to Ernest Nieriker is announced
22 March	May is married in London
June	LMA and Bronson read Mrs. Alcott's letters and diaries
15 October	*Under the Lilacs* is published in America
November	*Under the Lilacs* is published in England

1879

January	LMA moves to the Bellevue Hotel, Boston
Spring	LMA moves to Concord
15 July	The Concord School of Philosophy opens
August	LMA goes to Magnolia, Massachusetts
September	LMA goes to Concord
18 October	*Aunt Jo's Scrap-Bag: Jimmy's Cruise in the Pinafore* is published
8 November	May gives birth to Louisa May Nieriker in Paris
December	*Jack and Jill* begins serialization in *St. Nicholas* (ends October 1880)
29 December	May dies in Paris

1880

April	LMA moves to the Bellevue Hotel, Boston
June	LMA goes to Concord
July-August	LMA goes to New York with Fred and John

August	LMA moves to Concord
19 September	Lulu Nieriker arrives in Boston
9 October	*Jack and Jill* is published
Winter	LMA moves to Elizabeth Sewall Willis Wells's house, 81 Pinckney Street, Boston, on Louisburg Square

1881

Spring	LMA moves to Concord
July	LMA and Lulu go to Nonquitt, Massachusetts

1882

27 April	Ralph Waldo Emerson dies
Summer	LMA goes to Nonquitt
Autumn	LMA moves to the Bellevue Hotel, Boston, with John; she begins *Jo's Boys*
14 October	*Aunt Jo's Scrap-Bag: An Old-Fashioned Thanksgiving* is published
24 October	Bronson suffers a stroke

1883

March	LMA moves to the Bellevue Hotel, Boston, with Lulu
April	LMA goes to Concord
July	LMA and Lulu go to Nonquitt
10 August	LMA moves to Concord
27 November	LMA moves to Boylston Street, Boston, with Lulu

1884

June	LMA sells Orchard House to W. T. Harris; she buys a cottage at Nonquitt
24 June	LMA goes to Nonquitt with Lulu and John
7 August	LMA moves to Concord
October	LMA moves to the Bellevue Hotel, Boston, with John
November	LMA moves to 31 Chestnut Street, Boston, with John and Fred
8 November	*Spinning-Wheel Stories* is published
December	LMA works to exhaustion on *Jo's Boys* and is forbidden to write for six months

1885

February	LMA undergoes mind-cure treatments
Summer	LMA goes to Nonquitt; she begins *Lulu's Library*
8 August	LMA moves to Concord

1 October	LMA moves to 10 Louisburg Square, Boston, with Lulu, Anna, John, and Fred
20 November	*Lulu's Library*, Volume 1, is published

1886

January	LMA begins treatments with Dr. Rhoda Lawrence; she continues work on *Jo's Boys*
Early Summer	LMA goes to Concord
June	LMA goes to Princeton, Massachusetts
4 July	LMA finishes *Jo's Boys*
September	LMA moves to Boston
18 September	*Jo's Boys* is published in England
9 October	*Jo's Boys* is published in America
December	LMA moves to Dr. Lawrence's, Dunreath Place, Roxbury, Massachusetts

1887

June	LMA and the family move to Melrose, Massachusetts; she works on *A Garland for Girls*
July-August	LMA goes to Princeton
10 July	LMA makes and signs her will
1 September	LMA moves to Roxbury
25 October	*Lulu's Library*, Volume 2, is published
November	*A Garland for Girls* is published

1888

8 February	Fred Pratt marries Jessica L. Cate
1 March	LMA visits Bronson at Louisburg Square
4 March	Bronson dies
6 March	LMA dies

1889

5 October	*Lulu's Library*, Volume 3, and Ednah Dow Cheney's *Louisa May Alcott: Her Life, Letters, and Journals* are published

1893

17 July	Anna Pratt dies
October	*Comic Tragedies* is published

1975

1 July	*Behind a Mask: The Unknown Thrillers of Louisa May Alcott* is published

1976

1 July	*Plots and Counterplots: More Unknown Thrillers of Louisa May Alcott* is published

1987
 September   *The Selected Letters of Louisa May Alcott* is published

1988
 July   *A Double Life: Newly Discovered Thrillers of Louisa May Alcott* is published

THE JOURNALS OF
LOUISA MAY ALCOTT

Introduction

Madeleine B. Stern

FOR LOUISA May Alcott the journal (or diary) was a room of her own. Often it was the only room in which she could collect the days of her life, witness her time and her place, record her struggles and her triumphs, exorcise her demons. There she chronicled her experiences and confronted her self. There she played the double role of witness and of subject. From childhood she knew what a journal should be, for when she was eleven her mother, having commented upon Louisa's improved penmanship, wrote on a page of her daughter's journal: "Remember, dear girl, that a diary should be an epitome of your life."[1] And of all the multitudinous definitions of the journal-diary, that was probably the best.

Louisa Alcott's journal is indeed an epitome of her life. Here she has chronicled her days, made her inward journeys, and set her sights on the world. In these journals, together with the annual "Notes and Memoranda" summing up the year's events, the writer revealed herself and her world, her family relationships, her poverty and her wealth, her education and her reading, her writing and her fame, her strengths and her weaknesses. Here, in effect, is the web spun by a storyteller who tells her own extraordinary story.

In a family of journal writers (Bronson Alcott would leave thirty thousand pages of journals by the time he died, in 1888) Louisa Alcott, early instructed in the art, would make it the habit of a lifetime. Although she herself later destroyed much that she regarded as too personal,[2] great riches remain. From the earliest struggles with her turbulent persona to the pitiful,

1. Throughout, all quotations, unless otherwise indicated, are from the Alcott journals.
2. In a letter to Louise Chandler Moulton, 18 January 1883, Alcott exaggerated: "My journals were all burnt long ago in terror of gossip when I depart & on unwise use of my very frank records of people & events" (*SL*, p. 267).

3

almost monosyllabic jottings of her last years, Louisa Alcott reconstructed herself and her world in these journals.

Primarily she reconstructed herself. Born 29 November 1832 in Germantown, Pennsylvania, to Bronson and Abigail ("Abba") May Alcott, Louisa was early introduced to the discipline of journal keeping. In his journals her father recorded his philosophical soarings and his pedagogical purposes, as well as the births of his children: Anna, who preceded Louisa, in 1831; Elizabeth, who followed, in 1835. By that time the family had moved to Boston, where Bronson taught the mysteries of God and birth at the Temple School until that school failed and the schoolmaster was castigated as obscene. Abby May, the child of summer, was born in 1840 in Concord, Massachusetts, to which the family had removed. In her own journals Mother recorded struggles with poverty and with her soul poignant enough for Louisa to destroy the majority after she died. Louisa herself, who spent the first ten years of her life alternating between boisterous hoydenism and quiet witnessing from an observation corner, began the serious keeping of a journal in 1843. By that time the Alcotts had moved once again, to a community called — miscalled — Fruitlands.

Located on the slope of Prospect Hill in Harvard, Massachusetts, Fruitlands had been designed (or rather envisioned) by Bronson Alcott and his associates Charles Lane and Henry Wright as a New Eden for a "Consociate Family." The New Eden was to be realized by various forms of self-denial, including the wearing of linen tunics (cotton being a product of slavery and wool the natural clothing of the sheep), a pure and bloodless diet, early rising, cold baths, and lessons in universal good and abnegation of self.

For all the instruction in self-denial, Louisa May Alcott at age ten had already begun searching for her self, analyzing her self, describing her self. In one of the first extant journal entries (of 1 September 1843) she wrote, after recording the day's activities at Fruitlands: "As I went to bed the moon came up very brightly and looked at me. I felt sad because I have been cross today, and did not mind Mother. I cried, and then I felt better, and said that piece from Mrs. Sigourney, 'I must not tease my mother.' I get to sleep saying poetry, — I know a great deal."

The sentiments were repeated frequently at Fruitlands: "I was cross today, and I cried when I went to bed. I made good resolutions, and felt better in my heart. If I only *kept* all I make. . . . But I don't." The future recorder of fictional passions began early to examine her own. As her character was shaping she witnessed and described the shaping. "Father asked us . . . what fault troubled us most. I said my bad temper." Over a year later, after the six-month stay at Fruitlands had ended and the family had moved back

4

to Concord, Louisa's search for self continued. "I am so cross I wish I had never been born." When asked what virtues she wished more of, which vices less of, she placed among the former patience, obedience, and self-denial; among the latter impatience, selfishness, willfulness, impudence, activity, vanity, pride, and love of cats.

Whether her incipient desire for fame was to be counted among the virtues or the vices, it manifested itself early. When her sister Anna sent her a picture of the "great singer" Jenny Lind, Louisa confessed: "I should like to be famous as she is." Thus far the path to fame had not been defined. In 1846, when at last she "got the little room I have wanted so long," she expanded her self-analysis in her journal:

> It does me good to be alone, . . . The door that opens into the garden will be very pretty in summer, and I can run off to the woods when I like.
>
> I have made a plan for my life, as I am in my teens, and no more a child. I am old for my age, and don't care much for girl's things. People think I'm wild and queer; but Mother understands and helps me. I have not told any one about my plan; but I'm going to *be* good. I've made so many resolutions, and written sad notes, and cried over my sins, and it does n't seem to do any good! Now I'm going to *work really*, for I feel a true desire to improve, and be a help and comfort, not a care and sorrow, to my dear mother.

The character of Louisa Alcott — and of Jo March — was taking recognizable shape.

Louisa's journal, especially in the early days, was not strictly or altogether private. The lack of complete privacy did not inhibit Louisa's analysis of self. On the contrary, it probably spurred her on, for she was already becoming a writer in search of an audience.

"I told mother I liked to have her write in my book," she recorded, and the diary became a medium for their notes to one another. Mother confessed: "I often peep into your diary, hoping to see some record of more happy days. 'Hope, and keep busy,' dear daughter, and in all perplexity or trouble come freely to your Mother," to which twelve-year-old Louisa responded: "Dear Mother, — You *shall* see more happy days, and I *will* come to you with my worries, for you are the best woman in the world." Five years later, in July 1850, she wrote: "I found one of mother's notes in my journal, so like those she used to write me when she had more time. It always encourages me; and I wish some one would write as helpfully to her, for she needs cheering up with all the care she has." Father too looked over her journals, concluding that while older sister Anna's journal was "about

5

other people, Louisa's [was] about herself." To this she agreed: "That is true, for I don't *talk* about myself; yet must always think of the wilful, moody girl I try to manage, and in my journal I write of her to see how she gets on."

The progress of that "moody girl" was influenced by the cleavage between her own natural exuberance and the midcentury emphasis upon the virtues of self-denial and repression. Her desire to "improve," to become famous, to become in effect the family breadwinner, was predicated upon the Alcott poverty, which intensified during the 1850s as Bronson Alcott, who could envision utopia, found it increasingly difficult to support his family in a nonutopian world. By 1850, after the family had moved to Boston, when Anna was teaching school and seventeen-year-old Louisa had begun to write stories for the family newspaper (to which Abby May and Lizzie also contributed), aspirations for character development still dominated Louisa's journal. The future writer was already observing herself objectively:

> If I look in my glass, I try to keep down vanity about my long hair, my well-shaped head, and my good nose. In the street I try not to covet fine things. My quick tongue is always getting me into trouble, and my moodiness makes it hard to be cheerful when I think how poor we are, how much worry it is to live, and how many things I long to do I never can. . . . In the quiet I see my faults, . . . I used to imagine my mind a room in confusion, and I was to put it in order.

By 1856 her attempts at breadwinning included a brief term in the drudgery of domestic service, schoolkeeping, and writing, at which she would persist despite James T. Fields's later advice that she "stick to . . . teaching" since she could not write. "The Rival Painters. A Tale of Rome" had appeared in the *Olive Branch*, "The Masked Marriage" in *Dodge's Literary Museum*, and "The Rival Prima Donnas" in the *Saturday Evening Gazette*.[3] For these stories she had earned some five dollars a tale. *Flower Fables*, her first book, published in December 1854, netted the author a bit more than thirty dollars. Louisa was convinced that she had talent. In her journal she wrote: "I was born with a boy's spirit under my bib and tucker. I *can't wait* when I *can work;* so I took my little talent in my hand and forced the world again."

Until 1868–1869, when the spirit under Jo March's bib and tucker would bring fame and fortune to the author of *Little Women*, Louisa continued to force the world and to record the forcing in her journal. Her love of "freedom and independence" was frequently thwarted by events at home. When Lizzie contracted scarlet fever and began a slow decline, Louisa wrote: "I

3. "The Rival Painters. A Tale of Rome," *Olive Branch* (8 May 1852); "The Masked Marriage," *Dodge's Literary Museum* (18 December 1852); "The Rival Prima Donnas," *Saturday Evening Gazette* (11 November 1854).

feel my quarter of a century rather heavy on my shoulders just now. I lead two lives. One seems gay with plays, etc., the other very sad, — in Betty's [Lizzie's] room."

The death of her younger sister Elizabeth, the betrothal of her older sister, Anna, to John Pratt, were described in Louisa's journal as they affected herself. She wrote of 1858 as the year of "two events that change my life. I can see that these experiences have taken a deep hold, and changed or developed me. . . . [I] am learning that work of head and hand is my salvation when disappointment or weariness burden and darken my soul. . . . I hope I shall yet do my great book, for that seems to be my work, and I am growing up to it."

The "growing up to it" is traceable in the journals. All the early exuberance that would be transferred to Jo March is here: the girl who "ran in the wind and played be a horse," who "sang for joy, my heart was so bright," at twenty-six walked from Concord to Boston "one day, twenty miles, in five hours, and went to a party in the evening. Not very tired. Well done for a vegetable production!" Louisa is clearly beginning to know and appreciate herself. Her direction toward spinsterhood is almost self-determined: "Saw Nan in her nest. . . . Very sweet and pretty, but I'd rather be a free spinster and paddle my own canoe."

By 1861 the paddling was, by her own admission, difficult. "The constant thumping Fate gives me may be a mellowing process; so I shall be a ripe and sweet old pippin before I die." After her devastating experience as nurse in an army hospital during the Civil War, when she was stricken with typhoid pneumonia, the occasional self-pity that filters through the journals is combined with a moral tone. It is as if Louisa Alcott were trying to teach herself resignation as her parents had tried to teach her self-denial. These were hard lessons for one who had run "in the wind and played be a horse." "To go very near to death teaches one to value life," but already, at age thirty-one, she regards herself as aging: "Nan & I sat in the gallery & watched the young people dance the old year out, the new year in." She is getting "used to disappointment"; on her birthday she "never seem[s] to have many presents." The antiphonal threads are woven through the fabric of the journals: resignation contrasts with rebellion in "fitful changes of sunshine & shade."

After Alcott's great success with *Little Women* the self-examination that persists in her journals becomes more and more philosophical, if not moralistic. In 1874, at the height of her popularity as America's best-loved author of juvenile fiction, she commented: "When I had the youth I had no money; now I have the money I have no time; and when I get the time, if I ever do, I shall have no health to enjoy life." The remark was prophetic. When

she added: "I suppose it's the discipline I need; but it's rather hard to love the things I do and see them go by because duty chains me to my galley," the analyst must wonder if that "duty" was not in large measure self-inflicted. A few years later, when Anna Pratt, with her sister's help, was able to purchase the Thoreau house, Louisa mused: "So she has *her* wish, and is happy. When shall I have mine? Ought to be contented with knowing I help both sisters by my brains. But I'm selfish, and want to go away and rest in Europe. Never shall." And again: "I doubt if I ever find time to lead my own life, or health to try it." The lessons of her childhood and the ethical standards of nineteenth-century America on the one hand, and her own early exuberance and rebellious longings on the other, stirred the forces of conflict within her. The attempt to reconcile them could never be successful, and so Louisa Alcott was doomed by her own volition. Her awareness of this is apparent in the journals that paint the self-portrait.

The conflict that punctuates the journals through the years was basically the result of Alcott's emotional relationships with the members of her immediate family. As she searched for self-understanding she searched also for understanding of them. And since the Alcott family would be transformed into perhaps the best-known American family of the century, their sketches in these journals take on a literary as well as a psychological significance.

The Marmee of the March family is, so to speak, previewed in the journals but without the gloss that protects the fictive version. The threat of family separation that loomed in Fruitlands ("Father asked us if *we* saw any reason for us to separate. Mother wanted to, she is so tired. . . . I prayed God to keep us all together.") is delineated in a few lines of the early journals, along with Louisa's anguished love for her mother. Filtered through objective sketches are the subjective feelings of the writer, as when, in Boston in 1850, Louisa cogitated about her mother: "What a hard life she has had since she married, — so full of wandering and all sorts of worry! so different from her early easy days, the youngest and most petted of her family. I think she is a very brave, good woman; and my dream is to have a lovely, quiet home for her, with no debts or troubles to burden her."

The novelist was looking at a life in which her own life was inextricably involved. A decade later, in Concord, Louisa regarded her mother with the same combination of passion and dispassion: "All the philosophy in our house is not in the study; a good deal is in the kitchen, where a fine old lady thinks high thoughts and does kind deeds while she cooks and scrubs." In 1866 Louisa wrote: "I never expect to see the strong, energetic 'marmee' of old times, but, thank the Lord, she is still here though, pale & weak, quiet & sad. All her fine hair gone & face full of wrinkles, bowed back & every sign of age. Life has been so hard for her & she so brave, so glad to spend herself for others." Louisa watched and reported the ineluctable decline. Returning from her grand tour abroad she wrote in 1871: "Mother feeble and much aged by this year of trouble. I shall never go far away from her again." Nor did she. She had a furnace installed in Orchard House, and the successful author basked in the knowledge of the bounty she had spread: "Mother is to be cosey if money can do it. She seems to be now, and my long-cherished dream has come true; for she sits in a pleasant room, with no work, no care, no poverty to worry, but peace and comfort all about her."

Nonetheless, by 1877 Mother's final decline had begun. Her words were reported in the journal: " 'Stay by, Louy, and help me if I suffer too much.' " When, on 25 November 1877, Abigail May Alcott died, the deathbed scene was depicted, the last words, the last breath. The professional writer was witness to this tragedy, but so too was the loving daughter: "A great warmth seems gone out of life, and there is no motive to go on now." The following year, as Louisa went through her mother's papers, her subjective emotions overcame her professionalism: "Tried to write a memoir of Marmee; but it is too soon." It was still "too soon" four years later when, in April 1882, Louisa "read over & destroyed Mother's Diaries as she wished me to do. A wonderfully interesting record of her life from her delicate, cherished girlhood through her long, hard, romantic married years, old age & death. Some time I will write a story or a Memoir of it." She would never write such a memoir. In a sense, she had already done so — in *Little Women*.

It is interesting that despite, or perhaps because of, Louisa's abiding and deep-seated love of her mother, there are far more references in the journals to her father. The relationship between Louisa and her father has been the subject of much scholarly and psychological investigation.[4] If that relationship can be elucidated with any degree of accuracy, the key must lie in these journals.

As reflected here, Louisa's attitude toward her father was neither baleful nor unquestioningly adoring, but rather a combination of both, a love-hate viewpoint in which exasperation and admiration, impatience and understanding, were most humanly commingled. In 1853 when Father went West "to try his luck" as a lecturer, his twenty-one-year-old daughter described

4. See, for example, Sarah Elbert, *A Hunger for Home: Louisa May Alcott and Little Women* (Philadelphia: Temple University Press, 1984); Carol Gay, "The Philosopher and His Daughter: Amos Bronson Alcott and Louisa," *Essays in Literature* (Fall 1975): pp. 181–191; Joel Myerson, " 'Our Children Are Our Best Works': Bronson and Louisa May Alcott," in *Critical Essays on Louisa May Alcott*, ed. Madeleine B. Stern (Boston: G. K. Hall, 1984), pp. 261–264; Charles Strickland, *Victorian Domesticity: Families in the Life and Art of Louisa May Alcott* (University: University of Alabama Press, 1985).

him with compassion as "so poor, so hopeful, so serene." The next year Bronson Alcott's return from a similar trip was recounted graphically, poignantly, and memorably:

> In February Father came home. Paid his way, but no more. A dramatic scene when he arrived in the night. We were waked by hearing the bell. Mother flew down, crying "My husband!" We rushed after, and five white figures embraced the half-frozen wanderer who came in hungry, tired, cold, and disappointed, but smiling bravely and as serene as ever. We fed and warmed and brooded over him, longing to ask if he had made any money, but no one did till little May said, . . . "Well, did people pay you?" Then, with a queer look, he opened his pocket-book and showed one dollar, saying with a smile . . . "Only that! My overcoat was stolen, and I had to buy a shawl. Many promises were not kept, and travelling is costly; but I have opened the way, and another year shall do better."
>
> I shall never forget how beautifully Mother answered him, though the dear, hopeful soul had built much on his success; . . . she kissed him, saying, "I call that doing *very* well. Since you are safely home, dear, we don't ask anything more."

The scene epitomizes not only Bronson Alcott's ineptitudes but a marital relationship, not to mention Louisa's perceptive and already protective attitude toward her father.

She knew him well. While "Mother looked after her boarders, and tried to help everybody," "Father talked." Yet Louisa was well aware that some people profited from his talk, and she wondered, "Why don't rich people who enjoy his talk pay for it? Philosophers are always poor, and too modest to pass round their own hats." When, in 1879, the School of Philosophy was opened in Concord with Bronson Alcott as dean, Louisa wrote: "He has *his* dream realized at last, & is in glory with plenty of talk to swim in." A year later, having "got the Dean a new suit of clothes," she commented: "Plato's toga was not so costly but even he did not look better than my handsome old philosofer."

The novelist's pen sketched a portrait of her father as early as July 1857:

> Grandma Alcott came to visit us. . . . I am glad to know her, and see where Father got his nature. . . . As we sat talking over Father's boyhood, I never realized so plainly before how much he has done for himself. His early life sounded like a pretty old romance. . . . Spindle Hill, Temple School, Fruitlands, Boston, and Concord, would make

fine chapters. The trials and triumphs of the Pathetic Family would make a capital book.

Like her mother's memoir, her father's story remained a ghost. But Louisa's interpretation of his nature in her journals continued to reflect a mingling of pity and impatience, appreciation and irritation. Even her birthday gifts to him indicated her understanding, as when she "gave Father a ream of paper." In 1861 when, as Concord's superintendent of schools, he delivered a report that was "much admired," Louisa noted that "teachers were glad of the hints given, making education a part of religion, not a mere bread-making grind for teacher and an irksome cram for children." She knew whereof she spoke, for she owed much of her own nature to her father's teaching as well as to his failure to make money.

It was partly as a result of her conflicting attitude toward her father — pride in his abstract philosophy and the wish to shield him from mundane responsibilities coupled with exasperation at his inability to support the family — that Louisa became the Alcott paterfamilias. The role was to a great extent self-imposed, and she played it to the end of her life, when her father, stricken with apoplexy, in a sense became her child.

Although Louisa was inordinately proud of her ability to support the "Forlornites," she rebelled often against the role she had assumed. The rebellion crops up in the journals, especially in Louisa's appraisal of her younger sister May. The eldest of the Alcotts, Anna, was Louisa's close companion in spite of the fact that they had few characteristics in common; Louisa dubbed Anna her "conscience." Later on in her life she described their relationship clearly: "A good sister to me all these years in spite of the utter unlikeness of our tastes, temperaments & lives. If we did not love one another so well we never could get on at all." Elizabeth, so early doomed, elicited little in these journals but tender love and pity. In the case of May, however, the relationship was imbued with an ambivalence on Louisa's part that in a way compares with her conflicting emotions toward her father.

As Louisa admired, theoretically at least, her father's philosophical soarings, she admired the artistry of "our 'little Raphael,'" May. In April 1859 the journal records: "May went home after a happy winter at the School of Design, where she did finely, and was pronounced full of promise. . . . we were very proud. No doubt now what she is to be, if we can only keep her along." The "keeping along" and the pride persisted: "Made my first ball dress for May. . . . My tall, blond, graceful girl! I was proud of her." When May went to teach at Syracuse Louisa sewed "like a steam-engine for a week, and get her ready. . . . our youngest . . . on her first little flight alone into the world." The years were punctuated with Louisa's giving and May's receiving: "May began to take anatomical drawing lessons of Rimmer. I was very glad to be able to pay her expenses up & down & clothe her neatly." As late as 1876, when May had made her final journey abroad, Louisa reported: "The money I invest in her pays the sort of interest I like. I am proud to have her show what she can do, and have her depend upon no one but me."

Nonetheless, upon occasion a hint of resentment crept in. In 1864 Louisa remarked of May: "She is a fortunate girl, & always finds some one to help her as she wants to be helped. Wish I could do the same." Later the same year, when most of the family was ill, Louisa wrote with understated pique: "For a week we had a hospital, while May was away in Boston." In 1871, when May decided to return from abroad "as she feels she is needed," Louisa examined her own reaction: "I don't want her to be thwarted in her work more than just enough to make her want it very much."

Louisa's mixed feelings toward her younger sister must have intensified her grief at May's death. May's marriage abroad in 1878 to Ernest Nieriker (her junior by fifteen years) was accepted with common sense if not delirium by the industrious sister at home: "May is old enough to choose for herself, and seems so happy in the new relation that we have nothing to say against it. . . . Send her $1,000 as a gift, and all good wishes for the new life." But Louisa could not help adding: "How different our lives are just now! — I so lonely, sad, and sick; she so happy, well and blest. She always had the cream of things, and deserved it. My time is yet to come somewhere else, when I am ready for it." In 1879, when May was pregnant, Louisa's journal hinted at her self-pity: "She sits happily sewing baby clothes in Paris. Enjoyed fitting out a box of dainty things to send her. Even lonely old spinsters take an interest in babies."

On the last day of 1879 Louisa recorded in her journal the tragedy of May's death following the birth of a daughter. "She wished me to have her baby & her pictures. A very precious legacy! . . . Rich payment for the little I could do for her. I see now why I lived." The next day she gave way more openly to her grief: "Of all the trials in my life I never felt any so keenly as this." A year later it was the same: "My grief meets me when I come home, & the house is full of ghosts."

In her relationship with May's child — the "precious legacy" named Lulu Nieriker — Louisa was seldom ambivalent. From the time she first "held out" her arms to Lulu almost until her own death eight years later, Louisa was aunt, mother, admirer, giver of gifts, comforter, and storyteller. "Miss Alcott's baby" certainly complicated her later life but brightened it, too, and gave to the self-created paterfamilias not only a recipient for bounty but "a new world."

*   *   *

In her journals Louisa Alcott sought to know herself, and there too she revealed the nature of her relationships — ambivalent as they often were — to her family. Thus the journals present the view of the self-analyst, the view from within. To the percipient reader these journals also present the view from without. From their entries her life can be reconstructed, the long road she traveled to become not only the mainstay of a family but a best-selling, almost universally popular author as well as a professional literary experimenter. The story is here: the education that shaped her, the reading that kindled her imagination, the stage mania that influenced her style, her attitude toward work and poverty and toward work and riches. Especially her life as writer is here: her techniques and productivity, her relations with publishers, her financial arrangements. So too are her reactions to her fame, to the world in which she lived, and, at the end, to the illnesses that assailed and consumed her.

In one of her early journal entries Louisa sketched the educational methods that helped mold her into the human being she became. Bronson Alcott, a firm believer in the Socratic approach to pedagogy, introduced to the children's lessons soul-searching questions aimed at "unfoldment" through self-expression. Thus Louisa found herself playing Alcibiades to the Socrates of her father's Fruitlands associate Charles Lane, and at age twelve answering disturbing questions: "What is the difference between faith and hope?" "What are the most valuable kinds of self-denial?" "How shall we learn this self-denial?" Along with the exaltation of self-denial Louisa was early exposed to a type of intellectual acrobatics for which she had little sympathy, especially when she did not "see who is to clothe and feed us all, when we are so poor now."

Louisa profited less from discussions of "What is man?" that sent her to bed "very tired" than from books that gave her "a pleasant time with my mind." John Bunyan's *Pilgrim's Progress*, Sir Walter Scott's novels, later Goethe's *Correspondence* with Bettina and Nathaniel Hawthorne's *Scarlet Letter*, appealed strongly to her and were to influence her writing. Her preference was for thoughtful romances, moral but lively narratives, " 'lurid' things, if true and strong also." By 1852 she determined to read fewer novels, a resolution she never kept, although she did delve deeply into Goethe; Thomas Carlyle, whose "earthquaky style" suited her; Ralph Waldo Emerson, "the god of my idolatry"; "plain" Margaret Fuller; and Mary Wollstonecraft. Biography interested her, and when she read Charlotte Brontë's life she wondered "if I shall ever be famous enough for people to care to read my story."

In March 1859, summing up her activities in her journal, Alcott wrote: "Busy life teaching, writing, sewing, getting all I can from lectures, books, and good people. Life is my college." For a majority of nineteenth-century

American women the lecture hall was the equivalent of a college classroom. Lecturers flocked to Boston, the hub of the universe, and Louisa Alcott heard many of them. When William Thackeray and Charles Dickens joined the lecture circuit in America, she was in the audience. The liberal thinkers of nineteenth-century America planted their ideas in her mind: the essayists George William Curtis and Edwin P. Whipple; the abolitionists Wendell Phillips and William Lloyd Garrison; and the Unitarian ministers Thomas Wentworth Higginson, Cyrus Bartol, and Octavius Brooks Frothingham, who evoked the comment: "Much talk about religion. I'd like to see a little more really *lived*." To the progressive clergyman Theodore Parker she responded with enthusiasm: "He is like a great fire where all can come and be warmed."

As the daughter of Bronson Alcott, Louisa was welcomed to the homes of New England's illustrious. At Parker's Sunday evening receptions she sat "in my corner weekly, staring and enjoying myself." Later, at meetings of the Radical Club, she was one of the "strong-minded ladies out in full force" for inspirational lectures and "aesthetic tea." She soon developed into the keen observer and the amused critic, as when "the talk lasted until two, and then the hungry philosophers remembered they had bodies and rushed away, still talking," or when "the philosophers mount their hobbies and prance away into time and space, while we gaze after them and try to look wise." In her journals Alcott recorded not only the lectures she heard — "Individuality of Character" or "Courage," the "Historical View of Jesus" or "Woman Suffrage" — but her own progress from tyro to wry auditor, an educational process as productive as it was informal.

When she heard Dickens lecture in December 1867, she was "disappointed," finding him "an old dandy." But Louisa Alcott was never disappointed in his novels. The *Pickwick Portfolio* that she and her sisters edited in the early 1850s was the family's version of the *Transactions* of the Pickwick Club created by Dickens. Many of the plays dramatized and performed by the Alcotts were based upon, if not actually transcribed from, *Martin Chuzzlewit*, *Oliver Twist*, *David Copperfield*, and especially *The Old Curiosity Shop*, which provided the source for Alcott's most popular role, that of Mrs. Jarley of the Waxworks.

Alcott's fascination with the stage endured practically all her life and infiltrated most of her writings. When she was seventeen she wrote in her journal: "Anna wants to be an actress, and so do I. We could make plenty of money perhaps, and it is a very gay life. . . . I like tragic plays, and shall be a Siddons if I can. We get up fine ones, and make harps, castles, armor, dresses, water-falls, and thunder, and have great fun." The plays they "got up" — *Norna; or, The Witch's Curse, The Captive of Castile*, and *The Unloved Wife*, Gothic melodramas whose props were daggers, love potions, and death vials —

14

would be published after Louisa's death as *Comic Tragedies*. During the second half of the nineteenth century, when the lecture platform served as college, the stage provided the entertainment of an age. In a barn converted for private theatricals, in a drawing room adapted for charity performances, or at the floodlit proscenium of the Boston Theatre, Louisa Alcott vented her stage fever as actress, dramatist, or member of the audience. The theatre, as she wrote in her journal, was "always my great joy." Whether she delivered a burlesque lecture on "Woman" or acted in *The Jacobite* or *The Rivals*, whether she played *Scenes from Dickens* to raise funds for the Concord Lyceum or portrayed Mrs. Jarley for a church fair, Alcott's mania for greenroom and greasepaint persisted and was incorporated into her books.

In her journals she referred to her own farce, *Nat Bachelor's Pleasure Trip*, as "the everlasting play which is always coming out but never comes." It gained her an interview with Thomas Barry, manager of the Boston Theatre, in 1856, which she recorded with gusto:

> We went all over the great new theater, and I danced a jig on the immense stage. Mr. B. was very kind, and gave me a pass to come whenever I liked. This was such richness I did n't care if the play was burnt on the spot, and went home full of joy. In the eve I saw La Grange as Norma, and felt as if I knew all about that place. Quite stage-struck, and imagined myself in her place, with white robes and oak-leaf crown.

When the farce was finally given a single performance, in 1860, the dramatist "sat in a box" and was offered a bouquet.

Alcott's development from novice to critic in her attendance at lectures was duplicated in her role as spectator of plays. In 1858, when she saw the popular American actress Charlotte Cushman, she "had a stagestruck fit" and actually "had hopes of trying a new life" as an actress. When the hopes were dimmed she determined to "try again by-and-by, and see if I have the gift. Perhaps it is acting, not writing, I'm meant for. Nature must have a vent somehow." The vent she found, of course, in writing: "Worked off my stage fever in writing a story, and felt better."

Alcott missed few of the great performers of the day: Edwin Forrest as Othello, Edwin Booth as Hamlet ("my ideal done at last"), Adelaide Ristori, and Fanny Kemble ("a whole stock company in herself"). Though upon occasion she sat in judgment, she never lost her stage fever. As late as April 1880 she amused herself "dramatizing 'Michael Strogoff.'"

Alcott's fascination with the theatre was part of her education, a source for her writing, and a much-needed antidote to the hardships of her life. The principal hardship seems to have been the early family poverty, which resulted in a state of mind she never discarded. She saw herself as breadwinner, a role made feasible for her by her lifelong work ethic. Carlyle phrased it as a command: "Work today, for the night cometh wherein no man can work," and on this side of the Atlantic it was preached in pulpit, classroom, and lecture hall. Even Bronson Alcott of Spindle Hill had inherited it, although in his case, since it manifested itself orally rather than manually, it proved monetarily unproductive.

At first Louisa Alcott did not realize that the family was poor. In 1843, having heard the story "The Judicious Father," she resolved to "be kind to poor people." By 1850 she was keenly aware that the Alcotts belonged in that category. "Every day is a battle, and I'm so tired I don't want to live; only it's cowardly to die till you have done something." Her year-end notes, summarizing major events and accounts of her earnings, began in 1850. There she wrote: "Poor as poverty but bound to make things go." And so the indoctrination to deny self was coupled with the stricture to work, and Louisa Alcott at age seventeen, teaching at her sister Anna's school in Boston, expressed her feelings in her journal: "School is hard work, and I feel as though I should like to run away from it. But my children get on; so I travel up every day, and do my best. I get very little time to write or think; for my working days have begun."

Those "working days" took varied forms. While Mrs. Alcott opened an employment office in Boston (an outgrowth of her city missionary work), Anna and Louisa taught, Lizzie served as family housekeeper, and May went to school. In May 1853, when her school closed, Louisa went out as "second girl. I needed the change, could do the wash, and was glad to earn my $2 a week. Home in October with $34 for my wages. After two day's rest, began school again with ten children." Besides teaching and washing clothes, Alcott "earned a good deal by sewing in the evening when my day's work was done." She sewed pillowcases and sheets, neckties and handkerchiefs. "I had to work all one night to get them done, . . . Sewing won't make my fortune; but I can plan my stories while I work."

For seven weeks in 1851 Louisa actually went out to service in Dedham, Massachusetts, digging paths through the snow, fetching water from the well, splitting kindling, and sifting ashes. She was certainly aware of her beloved Emerson's pronunciamento: "Let the great soul incarnated in some woman's form . . . go out to service, and sweep chambers and scour floors, and its effulgent daybeams cannot be muffled or hid, but to sweep and scour will instantly appear supreme and beautiful actions."[5] Whether this lofty

5. From Ralph Waldo Emerson, "Spiritual Laws," *Essays* (First Series), ed. Alfred R. Ferguson and Jean Ferguson Carr (Cambridge: Harvard University Press, 1979), pp. 95–96; Madeleine B. Stern, *Louisa May Alcott* (Norman: University of Oklahoma Press, 1950), p. 65.

view made the experience more tolerable Alcott did not indicate. Indeed, the rigors of Dedham were never described in her journals except for the terse mention (in her year-end "Notes" for 1851) of "a month" in Dedham "as a servant . . . starved & frozen . . . $4,00." Decades later she published a story based upon the experience, "How I Went Out to Service."[6]

The rewards of work were for her less philosophical in the Emersonian sense than practical. She exulted in being able to support herself and "help the family." Through the fifties Alcott taught and sewed, swept and dusted — and wrote. In 1858 she "went to Boston on my usual hunt for employment, as I am not needed at home and seem to be the only bread-winner just now." Failing to find work, she underwent a suicidal crisis, which she reported post facto in a breezy letter home[7] but either subsequently erased from her journal or never confided at all. Offers of work soon came, and of thirty dollars earned Alcott sent twenty home. By the end of the decade she could write with satisfaction: "I have done more than I hoped. Supported myself, helped May, and sent something home. Not borrowed a penny, and had only five dollars given me."

The work campaign continued into the sixties with a kindergarten in Warren Street Chapel. The work was distasteful to her, but she "tugged on" and continued to seek employment: "Hate to visit people who ask me to help amuse others, and often longed for a crust in a garret with freedom and a pen. I never knew before what insolent things a hostess can do, nor what false positions poverty can push one into." And later the same year of 1862: "Went to and from C[oncord]. every day that I might be at home. Forty miles a day is dull work; but I have my dear people at night, and am not a beggar." The winter ended for her with "a debt of $40, — to be paid if I sell my hair to do it."[8] Between 1863 and 1868, thanks to the work available for a nineteenth-century woman — teaching, sewing, writing — Louisa Alcott managed to increase her annual income. Her 1863 earnings of about $380 were more than doubled in 1866. She was still "driven by the prospect of bills which must be paid," she still dreaded "debt more than the devil!" but in January 1869 she was able to write in her journal: "Paid up all the debts, thank the Lord! — every penny that money can pay, — and now I feel as if I could die in peace."

Part I of Little Women had appeared in November 1868. Part II would appear in April 1869. That autobiographical novel and its financial success

6. Louisa May Alcott, "How I Went Out to Service. A Story," The Independent (4 June 1874).

7. Louisa May Alcott to the Alcott Family, Boston, [October 1858], SL, pp. 34–36.

8. This was the forty dollars borrowed from James T. Fields for the kindergarten, returned by LMA in 1871. See her letter to Fields, Concord, 3 July 1871, in SL, p. 160.

would divide the author's life in two. But even after the royalties had begun to roll in, snowballing through the years, Louisa Alcott could never forget that her family had once belonged to that class of " 'silent poor' " who were "needy, but respectable, and forgotten because too proud to beg." Periodically she recorded with pride the income that accrued from her writings: in August 1869 she had "$1,200 for a rainy day, and no debts"; in January 1872 her publishers sent her $4,400, and she "paid for the furnace and all the bills. What bliss it is to be able to do that and ask no help!" Despite the increasing prices she was able to command as the years passed, Alcott never lost the compulsion to work and enact the role of family provider. In 1876, when $3,000 was offered her for a serial and publishers were clamoring for her tales, she still was convinced that her "mill must keep grinding even chaff." A decade later, despite weariness and illness, she continued the theme: "I am the only money maker & must turn the mill for others though my grist is ground & in the barn."

Nowhere are the products of the Alcott literary mill more clearly traceable than in the Alcott journals. Through them can be discerned her literary methods and sources, her experimentation and growing professionalism, the details of her earnings. A careful reading of the journals extends our knowledge of the genres she attempted, enlarges the Alcott bibliography, and increases her stature. For all their revelations of her persona, her family, and the ethos of her times, these journals are basically the journals of a writer.

In one of her earliest literary entries Louisa wrote, at age twelve: "I was very dismal, and then went to walk and made a poem." Writing was already a catharsis for her and would continue to be so, especially when she composed her anonymous and pseudonymous thrillers. Only later after much success would it become a burden. In her pre–*Little Women* life she exulted in each small triumph. In 1852, when the *Olive Branch* ran "The Rival Painters. A Tale of Rome," the author wrote: "My first story was printed, and $5 paid for it. It was written in Concord when I was sixteen. Great rubbish! Read it aloud to sisters, and when they praised it, not knowing the author, I proudly announced her name." From the beginning the self-deprecation was coupled with pride of authorship, even when, as in this case, the authorship was indicated only by initials. Three years later the first story was followed by the first book, *Flower Fables*, a compilation of fairy stories imagined for a young neighbor, Emerson's daughter Ellen.

The principal event of the winter is the appearance of my book "Flower Fables." An edition of sixteen hundred. It has sold very well, and people seem to like it. I feel quite proud that the little tales that I wrote

for Ellen E. when I was sixteen should now bring money and fame.
. . . Miss Wealthy Stevens paid for the book, and I received $32.

There was no doubt now that "housemaid, teacher, seamstress" was also "story-teller." Alcott painted a picture of herself and the future Jo March "in the garret with my papers round me, and a pile of apples to eat while I write my journal, plan stories, and enjoy the patter of rain on the roof, in peace and quiet." The planning period when narratives simmered in her mind runs like an unbroken thread through the journals. The planning took place while she worked at various chores and at night, when she slept or should have been sleeping: "I can simmer novels while I do my housework." In 1860, when the first draft of her novel *Moods* was being shaped, "Genius burned so fiercely that for four weeks I wrote all day and planned nearly all night, being quite possessed by my work."

The journals reveal Alcott as a writer seized with the compulsion to write. In 1856 she "wrote a story a month through the summer." In 1859 she "wrote a sequel to 'Mark Field.'⁹ Had a queer time over it, getting up at night to write it, being too full to sleep." She sat for the portrait of writer incarnate as she revised *Moods*:

> From the 2d to the 25th [February 1861] I sat writing, with a run at dusk; could not sleep, and for three days was so full of it I could not stop to get up. Mother made me a green silk cap with a red bow, to match the old green and red party wrap, which I wore as a "glory cloak." Thus arrayed I sat in groves of manuscripts, . . . Mother wandered in and out with cordial cups of tea, worried because I could n't eat. Father thought it fine, and brought his reddest apples and hardest cider for my Pegasus to feed upon. All sorts of fun was going on; but I did n't care if the world returned to chaos if I and my inkstand only "lit" in the same place.

When the stories that had steeped in her mind finally took shape, she became a writing machine. She was early aware that the longer they steeped, the better they would be, writing in 1861: "Stories simmered in my brain, demanding to be writ; but I let them simmer, knowing that the longer the divine afflatus was bottled up the better it would be."

The sources from which she drew her narratives were all about her. From the details of her life and her reading she filled what she dubbed her "idea-box." An early story, "The Cross on the Church Tower," was "suggested by

9. "Mark Field's Success" (sequel to "Mark Field's Mistake") appeared in the *Saturday Evening Gazette* (16 April 1859).

the tower before my window." She found a "hint for a story" when Grandmother Alcott reminisced about the past. In 1872 she wrote: "All is fish that comes to the literary net. . . . I turn my adventures into bread and butter." In the same way she turned the celebration of her mother's birthday or the Centennial Ball in Boston into stories. When May went abroad for the last time, Louisa began "an art novel, with May's romance for its thread." She spun her tales especially from her own character, from the image of herself projected in her journals. Early she sensed the value of such truth, stating in 1858: "I feel as if I could write better now, — more truly of things I have felt and therefore *know*." Aware that the "nearer I keep to nature the better the work is," she transformed life into literature.

From the start she was extraordinarily versatile. She had the temerity to attempt many genres: "Wrote an Indian story"; "Wrote 'A Modern Cinderella,' with Nan for the heroine and John for the hero"; "Wrote a song for the school festival." During the 1860s she was able to spin a host of lurid thrillers. She arranged the letters she had written home from the Union Hotel Hospital into a book, *Hospital Sketches*. Fairy tales and realistic war stories, sentimental romances and Gothics, poured from the inkstand of this "thinking machine in full operation."

Alcott's versatility was no accident. Her development as a professional writer was based in large measure upon her ability to assess the demands of publishers, the tastes of readers. "The weeklies will all take stories," she concluded. But before she offered her contributions she studied the nature of her media. While the Boston *Saturday Evening Gazette* provided a market for sentimental romance, Frank Leslie's gaudy periodicals were emblazoned with serials that featured violence and left subscribers in a state of weekly suspense. Alcott was able to gear most of her tales to weeklies that would accept them. She even submitted a story, "Love and Self-Love," to the *Atlantic Monthly Magazine*, which published it ("my paper boats sailed gaily over the Atlantic"),[10] though it rejected her antislavery tales. Between supplying Frank Leslie with thrillers and cliff-hangers entitled "A Whisper in the Dark" or "The Fate of the Forrests" and supplying publisher James Redpath with fairy tales and war stories, she honed a versatile and indefatigable pen.

Alcott wrote for two principal reasons: writing was a catharsis for her, and writing could be traded for money. In her journals and year-end notes she conscientiously recorded her earnings. Over the winter of 1854–1855 she received $50 for teaching, $50 for sewing, and $20 for stories. The order was soon reversed. The next year a single story, "Genevieve," brought

10. *Atlantic Monthly* published four Alcott stories: "Love and Self-Love" (March 1860), "A Modern Cinderella: or, The Little Old Shoe" (October 1860), "Debby's Début" (August 1863), and "The Brothers" (November 1863), as well as her poem "Thoreau's Flute" (September 1863).

$10, and "prices go up, as people like the tales and ask who wrote them." At twenty-four she wrote of herself: "rather tired of living like a spider, — spinning my brains out for money," but nothing could stop the spinning when $25 for a moral tale "pieced up our . . . gowns and bonnets" and the "inside of my head can at least cover the outside." What she called her " 'head-money' " steadily increased. By the early 1860s her writing was paying much better than the teaching to which James T. Fields had advised her to stick. In 1864 she noted that she had "earned by my writing alone nearly six hundred dollars since last January." By the climactic year of 1868, when Part I of *Little Women* was published, Louisa Alcott was well on her way to becoming a paid professional writer.

Coupled with the desire — the need — for money was the desire for recognition. Alcott's hope and determination to achieve fame as a writer run through the journals. At the beginning it was merely a hope, sometimes a defiant one, as in 1856 after she had written all day. "The boys teased me about being an authoress, and I said I'd be famous yet." When the *Atlantic Monthly* accepted a story in 1859 she wrote: "I've not been pegging away all these years in vain, and may yet have books and publishers and a fortune of my own." In 1863, after *Hospital Sketches* had elicited favorable reactions, she expressed her astonishment, admitting that

things have gone on so swimmingly of late I dont know who I am. A year ago I had no publisher & went begging with my wares; now *three* have asked me for something, several papers are ready to print my contributions. . . . There is a sudden hoist for a meek & lowly scribbler who was told to "stick to her teaching," & never had a literary friend to lend a helping hand! Fifteen years of hard grubbing may be coming to something after all, & I may yet "pay all the debts, fix the house, send May to Italy & keep the old folks cosy," as I've said I would so long yet so hopelessly.

Little Women ended the hopelessness and brought the fame and fortune its author sought. The journals for 1867, 1868, and 1869 recount the sequence of events. In September 1867, "Niles, partner of Roberts [the Boston publishers Roberts Brothers], asked me to write a girls book. Said I'd try. [Horace] Fuller asked me to be the Editor of 'Merry's Museum.' Said I'd try. Began at once on both new jobs, but didn't like either." On the strength of her engagement as editor of the juvenile monthly *Merry's Museum*, she rented a room at 6 Hayward Place, Boston, and set up housekeeping in what she called "Gamp's Garret." Editorship of *Merry's* entailed writing at least one story and an editorial each month and netted her five hundred dollars for the year.

Little Women would not only bring her financial ease for the remainder of her life but change the direction of her literary style, her readership, and her image. The progress of the domestic novel that captured American family life in a net of words and made it part of life and letters in New England can be followed from the author's jottings in her journal. While there is no doubt whatsoever that the story of the March family had been "simmering" — *living* — for years in Alcott's mind, she did not begin to set it down on paper until May 1868, when "Father saw Mr. Niles about a fairy book. Mr. N. wants a *girls' story*, and I begin 'Little Women.' Marmee, Anna, and May all approve my plan. So I plod away, though I don't enjoy this sort of thing. Never liked girls or knew many, except my sisters; but our queer plays and experiences may prove interesting, though I doubt it." A month later she sent "twelve chapters of 'L.W.' to Mr. N. He thought it *dull*; so do I. But work away and mean to try the experiment; for lively, simple books are very much needed for girls, and perhaps I can supply the need." On 15 July she recorded: "Have finished 'Little Women,' and sent it off, — 402 pages. May is designing some pictures for it. Hope it will go." In August the firm of Roberts Brothers "made an offer for the story, but at the same time advised me to keep the copyright; so I shall" — a momentous decision. By the end of August "proof of whole book came. It reads better than I expected. Not a bit sensational, but simple and true, for we really lived most of it; and if it succeeds that will be the reason of it. Mr. N. likes it better now, and says some girls who have read the manuscripts say it is 'splendid!' " On 30 October Niles reported "good news of the book. An order from London for an edition came in. First edition gone and more called for. Expects to sell three or four thousand before the New Year. Mr. N. wants a second volume for spring. Pleasant notices and letters arrive, and much interest in my little women, who seem to find friends by their truth to life, as I hoped."

And so it began. On 1 November Alcott "began the second part of 'Little Women.' " "A little success is so inspiring," she wrote, "that I now find my 'Marches' sober, nice people, and as I can launch into the future, my fancy has more play. Girls write to ask who the little women marry, as if that was the only end and aim of a woman's life. I *won't* marry Jo to Laurie to please any one."[11] Producing almost a chapter a day, Alcott pictured the sisters as young women: Meg marrying, as Anna had done; Amy taking May's place as artist; Jo acting out Louisa's character, writing sensational stories

11. Compare LMA's letter to Elizabeth Powell, Concord, 20 March [1869], *SL*, pp. 124–125: " 'Jo' should have remained a literary spinster but so many enthusiastic young ladies wrote to me clamorously demanding that she should marry Laurie, *or* somebody, that I didnt dare to refuse & out of perversity went & made a funny match for her."

for the *Blarneystone Banner* and the *Weekly Volcano;* Laurie winning not Jo but Amy; and Jo, who should have remained a spinster, finally becoming united with the authoritative, sentimental German Professor Bhaer. On 17 November 1868 Alcott "finished my thirteenth chapter. I am so full of my work, I can't stop to eat or sleep, or for anything but a daily run." On New Year's Day of 1869 Part II was sent to Roberts Brothers. Alcott's technique was still episodic, the technique of the short-story writer; yet the whole coalesced, and soon it developed that, unlatching "the door to one house . . . all find it is their own house which they enter."[12] The local had been transmuted into the universal. *Little Women* was on its way to becoming a book that would not merely lure children from play and old men from the chimney corner but shape characters for generations to come.

In addition it shaped or reshaped the author's life. While her style and subject matter were altered, the sensational smothered, the domestic featured, her work habits persisted. Unprecedented offers ($3,000 for a serial by 1872) kept her at her "mill." Leaving Concord for a room in Boston ("I can't work at home, and need to be alone to spin, like a spider") she "fired up the engine, and plunged into a vortex. . . . Can't work slowly; the thing possesses me, and I must obey till it's done." And so, between 1869 and 1880, she produced six volumes of the so-called Little Women Series (including *An Old-Fashioned Girl, Little Men, Eight Cousins, Rose in Bloom, Under the Lilacs,* and *Jack and Jill),* the autobiographical novel *Work,* the Goethean experiment *A Modern Mephistopheles,* and dozens of short stories. Publishers clamored for the narratives of the writer who was acclaimed America's most successful author of children's books, and so she wrote "three pages at once on impression paper, as Beecher, Roberts, and Low of London all want copy at once." In 1873 she "spent seven months in Boston; wrote a book and ten tales; earned $3,250 by my pen, and am satisfied with my winter's work." She could, if necessary, produce "two [tales] a day, and keep house between times." Her productivity was enormous.

Now that the fame Louisa Alcott had coveted was hers, she found it less a pleasure than a burden. Her early amazement at being treated "like the Queen of Sheba" turned into aversion for being lionized. Requests for autographs, the sudden appearance of inquisitive strangers at her doorstep, made her "porcupiny." When an enthusiastic admirer from the Midwest promised her: " 'If you ever come to Oshkosh, your feet will not be allowed to touch the ground: you will be borne in the arms of the people!' " she determined never to venture to Oshkosh.

12. By Cyrus Bartol. Quoted in Stern, *Louisa May Alcott,* p. [xv].

As a result of unwanted public adulation, Alcott enunciated her principles of authors' rights. "Admire the books," was her injunction, "but let the woman alone if you please, dear public." In 1872 she explained:

People *must* learn that authors have some rights; I can't entertain a dozen a day, and write the tales they demand also. . . .

Reporters sit on the wall and take notes; artists sketch me as I pick pears in the garden; and strange women interview Johnny [her nephew] as he plays in the orchard.

It looks like impertinent curiosity to me; but it is called "fame," and considered a blessing to be grateful for, I find. Let 'em try it.[13]

In the final novel of her Little Women Series, *Jo's Boys,* Alcott inserted a chapter, "Jo's Last Scrape," about lion hunters, autograph fiends, and the rights of authors.

There were of course compensations for such fame. On her journey to New York before she sailed abroad in 1870, the trainboy put a copy of the newly published *Old-Fashioned Girl* into her lap.

When I said I did n't care for it, [he] exclaimed with surprise, —

"Bully book, ma'am! Sell a lot; better have it."

John [Pratt] told him I wrote it; and his chuckle, stare, and astonished "No!" was great fun. On the steamer little girls had it, and came in a party to call on me, very seasick in my berth, done up like a mummy.

And, returning from that journey the following year, she was gratified when "Father and T[homas]. N[iles]. came to meet me with a great red placard of 'Little Men' pinned up in the carriage." Bronson Alcott, lecturing in the west, rode now "in Louisa's chariot, and [was] adored as the grandfather of 'Little Women.' " In 1881 a poor woman in Illinois who had been told to write to Santa Claus for aid wrote instead to Louisa Alcott, who "sent a box & made a story about it. $100." The girl who had struggled so invincibly against poverty had been metamorphosed into the symbol of philanthropic benevolence and had made a story about it that further enriched her! Alcott's life was indeed a drama of contrasts.

The drama is on record in the journals, as well as the world in which it was played out. Invariably it was as a writer that Alcott observed that world.

13. Compare LMA's letter to Viola Price, Boston, 18 December 1885, *SL,* pp. 295–296: "If you can teach your five hundred pupils to love books but to let authors rest in peace, you will give them a useful lesson and earn the gratitude of the long suffering craft, whose lives are made a burden to them by the modern lion hunter and autograph fiend."

As Concord became increasingly dull in her eyes, Boston glittered. In 1860, when the future Edward VII visited America, the future author of *Little Men*

> went to B[oston]. and saw the Prince of Wales trot over the Common with his train at a review. A yellow-haired laddie very like his mother. . . . he openly winked his boyish eye at us; . . . the poor little prince wanted some fun. We laughed, and thought that we had been more distinguished by the saucy wink than by a stately bow. Boys are always jolly, — even princes.

As Bronson's daughter and later as the author of *Little Women*, Alcott was exposed throughout her life to the illustrious. When, in 1864, Hawthorne died, she wrote an intriguing and perplexing account in her journal:

> Hawthorne was found dead while on his trip with Pierce — He was not brought home at all as his family did not wish to see him. We dressed the church on the 23rd [May] for the funeral which was a very peculiar one throughout. The Atlantic Club [Saturday Club] came up & many other persons to do him honor. J[ames]. F[reeman]. Clarke performed the service & all followed to the grave.
>
> On the morning after the news came I sent in some violets from the hill where he used to walk. It pleased Mrs H[awthorne]. very much & she wrote me a note. We did all we could to heal the breach between the families but they held off, so we let things rest.

Nothing further about the Alcott-Hawthorne "breach" appears in the journals. Here there is just enough to whet the biographer's appetite.

Years later, when Alcott's beloved neighbor Emerson died, the journal entry was completely explicit:

> Our best & greatest American gone. The nearest & dearest friend father has ever had, & the man who has helped me most by his life, his books, his society. I can never tell all he has been to me from the time I sang Mignon's song under his window, a little girl, & wrote letters a la Bettine to him, my Goethe, at 15, up through my hard years when his essays on Self Reliance, Character, Compensation, Love & Friendship helped me to understand myself & life & God & Nature.
>
> Illustrious & beloved friend, good bye!

Events as well as people punctuate the journals. The inundation in Rome in 1870 during Alcott's grand tour; the fire in Boston after her return; the Centennial Ball in Concord; the receptions tendered her in New York — all have a place in these pages. But it is especially in her details of the reforms that fermented around her and invited her participation that Alcott's journals reveal the climate of the times.

As early as 1843 she inscribed the vegetarian maxims of Fruitlands in her journal: "Without flesh diet there could be no blood-shedding war" and "Pluck your body from the orchard; do not snatch it from the shamble." Some forty years later Alcott helped start a temperance society in Concord, water being the antidote to spirits as vegetables were to flesh, and both being part of the "newness." In between she joined a gymnastic class that was also an expression of physical reform. Vegetarianism, water cure, calisthenics, each found its way into her journals and into her books.

While Alcott endorsed such crusades against national dyspepsia, the reform movements that enlisted her most ardent support were antislavery and later woman suffrage and the rights of women. Her attitude toward these two major nineteenth-century reform movements is clearly expressed in her journals. In 1851, when she was not yet twenty, she attended an antislavery meeting "and heard splendid speaking from Phillips, Channing, and others. People were much excited, and cheered 'Shadrack and liberty,' groaned for 'Webster and slavery,' and made a great noise. I felt ready to do anything, — fight or work, hoot or cry, — and laid plans to free Simms. I shall be horribly ashamed of my country if this thing happens and the slave is taken back." The fugitive slave Thomas Sims was defended by Alcott's cousin Samuel Sewall but was found guilty of the love of liberty and was returned to slavery. The nation was moving toward Civil War, and the steps in that move were closely observed by the developing writer. In 1859, in Concord, she saw a "Great State Encampment. . . . Town full of soldiers, with military fuss and feathers. I like a camp, and long for a war, to see how it all seems. I can't fight, but I can nurse." In October Captain John Brown of Osawatomie entered Harpers Ferry, freed its slaves, and held the town for thirty hours. Louisa wrote of the event in her journal: "The Harper's Ferry tragedy makes this a memorable month. Glad I have lived to see the Antislavery movement and this last heroic act in it. Wish I could do my part in it." In December John Brown was executed for his deed. According to Alcott: "The execution of Saint John the Just took place on the second. A meeting at the hall, and all Concord was there. Emerson, Thoreau, Father, and [Frank] Sanborn spoke, and all were full of reverence and admiration for the martyr. I made some verses on it, and sent them to the 'Liberator.' "[14]

In April 1861, Alcott recorded the outbreak of war:

14. "With a Rose, That Bloomed on the Day of John Brown's Martyrdom," *The Liberator* (20 January 1860).

26

War declared with the South, and our Concord company went to Washington. A busy time getting them ready, and a sad day seeing them off; for in a little town like this we all seem like one family in times like these. At the station the scene was very dramatic, as the brave boys went away perhaps never to come back again.

I've often longed to see a war, and now I have my wish. I long to be a man; but as I can't fight, I will content myself with working for those who can.

The next month she "took a sail to the forts, and saw our men on guard there. Felt very martial and Joan-of-Arc-y as I stood on the walls with the flag flying over me and cannon all about." By October she was seething with impatience: "Sewing and knitting for 'our boys' all the time. It seems as if a few energetic women could carry on the war better than the men do it so far." Sewing bees, lint picks, and news from the front flash through the journals while the writer "like[s] the stir in the air, and long[s] for battle like a warhorse when he smells powder. The blood of the Mays is up!"

Alcott decided in November 1862 to go to Washington as an army nurse "I want new experiences, and am sure to get 'em if I go. So I've sent in my name, and bide my time writing tales." Her preparations, her departure from home, her journey to Washington, were all recorded in her journals as she "went rushing through the country white with tents, all alive with patriotism, and already red with blood." Her first day at the Union Hotel Hospital, Georgetown, D.C., was spent "seeing a poor man die at dawn, and sitting all day between a boy with pneumonia and a man shot through the lungs."

There are few more poignant, more factual, more stirring accounts of a Civil War hospital than the pages devoted to Nurse Alcott's observations under the date January 1863. Here she has painted the portraits of her patients, with special attention to the unpolished Virginia blacksmith whom she helped to die, and here she has noted the routine and the events of her days. The "stifling ward," the "inevitable fried beef" and "washy coffee," the surgeons (among them Dr. John, who quoted Browning and was given to "confidences in the twilight"), the nurses, the long trains of army wagons, the ambulances outside — all are here in a journal scribbled between duties in the "pestilence-box" that was the Union Hotel Hospital. And here too are graphic accounts of the devastating illness (typhoid pneumonia) that ended her six-week session as army nurse and sent her home to recover.

In the course of that lengthy recuperation Alcott noted that she "recieved $10 for my labors in Washington. Had all my hair . . . cut off & went into caps like a grandma. Felt badly about losing my one beauty. Never mind, it might have been my head & a wig outside is better than a loss of wits inside." Jo March would cut her hair off too, although for a different reason. The events in the writer's life, and the journals that encapsulated those events, were already simmering as sources.

After her recuperation Alcott continued her crusade for the Union cause, attending antislavery meetings and joining antislavery fairs until, in April 1865, she wrote in her journal:

> Richmond taken on the 2ond. Hurrah! Went to Boston & enjoyed the grand jollification. . . .
>
> On the 15th in the midst of the rejoicing came the sad news of the President's assassination & the city went into mourning. I am glad to have seen such a strange & sudden change in a nation's feelings. Saw the great procession, & though colored men were in it one was walking arm in arm with a white gentleman & I exulted thereat.

A few years later she would reiterate: "Glad I have lived in the time of this great movement, and known its heroes so well. War times suit me, as I am a fighting *May*."

During the latter part of Alcott's life another great movement, woman's rights, took the place that antislavery had held earlier. Although she came late to suffrage reform (having generally been too busy living woman's rights to preach them[15]), she came to it with determination. "Was *the first woman to register my name* as a voter," she announced in 1879. "Trying to stir up the women about Suffrage. So timid & slow. . . . Drove about & drummed up women to my Suffrage meeting. So hard to move people out of the old ruts." In 1880 she helped elect a school committee in Concord and "paid my first poll tax. As my head is my most valuable peice of property I thought $2,00 a cheap tax on it. Saw my townswomen about voting &c. Hard work to stir them up. Cake & servants are more interesting." At the 1883 town meeting only "seven women vote. I am one of them & A[nna]. another. A poor show for a town that prides itself on its culture & independence."

Alcott enjoyed poking fun at that town from time to time. The opening of her father's School of Philosophy in Orchard House on 15 July 1879 gave her ample opportunity.

> People laugh but will enjoy some thing new in this dull old town, & the fresh Westerners will show them that all the culture of the world

---

15. See LMA to Lucy Stone, 1 October 1873, *SL*, pp. 178–179: "I am so busy just now proving 'Woman's Right to Labor' that I have no time to help prove 'Woman's Right to Vote.' " See also Madeleine B. Stern, "Louisa Alcott's Feminist Letters," *Studies in the American Renaissance 1978*, ed. Joel Myerson (Boston: Twayne, 1978), pp. 429–452.

is not in Concord. I had a private laugh when Mrs S. asked one of the new comers, with her superior air, "If she had ever looked into Plato?" & the modest lady from Jacksonville answered with a twinkle at me, "We have been reading Plato in *Greek* for the past six years." Mrs S. subsided after that. Oh, wicked L. M. A. who hates sham & loves a joke.

Sham-despising, down-to-earth Louisa Alcott drew an indelible picture of Concord and its summer philosophers:

> The town swarms with budding philosophers, & they roost on our step like hens, waiting for corn. Father revels in it, so we keep the hotel going & try to look as if we like it. If they were philanthropists I *should* enjoy it, but speculation seems a waste of time when there is so much real work crying to be done. Why discuss the Unknowable till our poor are fed & the wicked saved?

And so the "M[argaret]. Fullers in white muslin" and the "Hegels in straw hats" join the parade of characters who illuminate the age in Alcott's journals.

Partly because of the seizure of typhoid pneumonia she suffered during the Civil War, partly because of the medications ministered to her, and partly because of a lifetime of hard work — physical and intellectual — Alcott was prey to a variety of ills. Neither vegetarianism nor water cure, temperance nor gymnastics, homeopathy nor so-called mind cure, seemed to alleviate the aches and anxieties that plagued her. Whether physical or psychosomatic or both, the distress that drove her in December 1886 to a nursing home in Roxbury, Massachusetts, was duly entered in her journals. As the years passed, her preoccupation with her ills intensified until in the end her journal jottings were all but devoted to the clinical indicators of decline.

When she was only thirty-four she noted that she felt "ill most of the time" and with the not uncommon medical ignorance of the day believed she had "magnetized A[nna]'s neuralgia into myself." Neuralgia was only one of the complaints registered frequently in the journals. Others included "headaches, cough, and weariness," "rheumatic fevers and colds," "weariness of nerves." She attributed her indispositions to a few major causes: "the hospital fever and the hard years following," the "picturesque open fires" of the Alcott pre-furnace days, and especially "too hard work." She believed that her twenty-year effort "to make the family independent" had "cost me my health."

It was true enough that her "brain . . . would work instead of rest" and that when she "overdid," she became ill. The medical and pseudomedical treatments she tried — "electricity for my lame arm," the magnetic passes of mind cure, massage, and baths — were merely palliative. The more or less sustained use of morphine or its derivatives for insomnia does not seem to have been perceived as a possible inducer of illness. No, Alcott was convinced that "having overworked the wonderful machine I must pay for it."

Pay for it she did, especially when faced with the long-drawn-out struggle to complete the last of the Little Women Series, *Jo's Boys*. She had written *Little Women* in a matter of months and *Little Men* in less time, but the third book of that trilogy, begun in 1882, was not published until 1886. Its creation was interrupted by family demands (her father's paralytic stroke and the need to care for May's daughter, Lulu), but especially it was interrupted by bouts of indisposition. In December 1884, for example, she "wrote two hours for three days, then had a violent attack of vertigo & was ill for a week." Alcott was not loath to record in her journal the physical ills that slowed the writing of her finale to the saga of the March family. What she did not record was her deep-seated reluctance to bring that saga to an end. Intuitively she must have realized that to bring down the curtain on the Marches was to bring it down on the Alcotts.

After a long battle with bodily ills, both battle and ills appearing and reappearing in the daily entries between 1885 and 1888, Louisa Alcott died on 6 March 1888. The creator of *Little Women*, who had experimented with so many diverse literary genres but was acknowledged as the most popular American writer for the young, was fifty-five years old. Although she probably was suffering from intestinal cancer, the immediate cause of her death was apoplexy. It followed her father's death by only two days, and it occurred in Dr. Rhoda Lawrence's nursing home in Roxbury.

Among the belongings gathered up after her death was her little red leather diary for 1888. Louisa Alcott was not only a faithful diarist throughout her life, but one who reread her diaries. Between 1867 and 1885 she appears to have reread them at least half a dozen times, for during the years 1867, 1873, 1878, 1879, 1880, 1883, and 1885 she inserted interpolations or comments after her original entries throughout her journals. The hardworking author certainly did not spend time rereading her own journals for frivolous reasons. In all likelihood she was searching them, as she searched almost everything in her life, for source material for stories. In addition, her comments indicate that she may have contemplated the future publication of portions of her journals.

The later interpolations reveal Alcott as a woman reaching out to her own childhood, as when, after an 1843 entry about the good resolutions she could not keep, she wrote: "Poor little sinner! *She says the same at fifty.*" Many of the later comments are expository in nature, as if Alcott did indeed have in mind a larger readership. Thus the family trials originally recorded in 1850 were elaborated years later: "We had small-pox in the family this summer, caught from some poor immigrants whom mother took into our garden and fed one day." The latter-day commentator took pride in the contrasts between the meager earnings of 1859 and the munificent rewards of 1876. From the lofty perch of her success she made a few acerbic comments; after her 1856 entry, for example, "C[lapp]. paid $6 for 'A Sister's Trial,' . . . and wants more tales," she wrote: "Should think he would at that price."

By and large, however, the later Alcott interpolations are of interest for their revelations of the author's conversion of life (and the journals that recorded that life) into literature. Her early struggles are likened to those of "Jo in N.Y." while the account of Lizzie's decline is equated with "Jo and Beth." The 1867 description of the aspiring author who "rode to B[oston]. on my load of furniture" was subsequently compared by the author of *An Old-Fashioned Girl* with "Polly & her pie." In 1885, in one of her last amplifications, Alcott commented on her 1868 entry regarding Roberts Brothers' advice to her to keep the copyright of *Little Women*: "An honest publisher and a lucky author, for the copyright made her fortune, and the 'dull book' was the first golden egg of the ugly duckling."

There were times, of course, when Louisa Alcott's journal was neglected for months at a time. However, she habitually tried to restore the narrative of past events and feelings from jottings in what she called a "pocket diary." Smaller in format than the journal, usually leather-bound, these pocket diaries afforded space only for those few lines a day that would capture highlights or — especially in the case of her final years — record the minor events and observations that made up the invalid's world. The pocket diary is recurrently mentioned in the more voluminous journals by Alcott as the source from which she has reconstructed or expanded episodes. Recuperating from the illness she sustained while nursing in an army hospital in Georgetown, D.C., for example, she remarked: "Sat up till nine one night & took no lunch at three A.M. Two facts which I find carefully recorded in my pocket diary in my own shaky hand-writing." During her visit to London in 1865 she mentioned the "pocket diary" in which she wrote "descriptions of all I saw." In her final decade she was either too busy or too ill to keep a sustained journal and could "only jot down a fact now & then." For the last few years of her life the terse entries in Alcott's pocket diary are eloquent, needing no expansion to mirror her decline.

As they are presented here, these journals comprise *all* the extant journals of Louisa May Alcott. They derive from two major sources: the manuscript journals preserved in Harvard University's Houghton Library, and the journals edited after Alcott's death by Ednah Dow Cheney in *Louisa May Alcott: Her Life, Letters, and Journals.*[16] The former — covering the significant pre–*Little Women* years, 1863–1867, and the last years, 1879–1888 — have been subjected to the cancellation lines of a censor who crossed out certain passages without obliterating them. The latter — the published Cheney version — are punctuated with three dots for omission as well as with a plethora of initials in place of names. Now, in this volume, omitted entries have been included wherever possible and full names substituted for initials. The result is richness despite the obvious fact that some of the journals have been destroyed or have vanished.

That knowledge naturally prompts the conjecture as to what has disappeared. References to sexual encounters? Unlikely. Had Alcott formed any close attachments of the kind, she would have woven them into her fiction rather than explicated them in her journals. It is more likely that the discarded sections contained descriptions of emotional family relationships, as well as of monetary or mercenary matters, and details of publishers and publishing, especially of the lurid, sensational stories written anonymously or pseudonymously for gory weekly newspapers. Such conclusions are substantiated by a comparison between a single journal entry as reported by Cheney and as it appears in the unpublished manuscript journal. Dated September 1866, the Cheney version reads:

> Mother sick, did little with my pen. Got a girl, and devoted myself to Mother, writing after she was abed. In this way finished a long tale. But E. would not have it, saying it was too long and too sensational![17]

The manuscript version of the entry for the same date reads:

> Mother sick, did little with my pen.
> Got a girl & devoted myself to mother, writing after she was abed. In this way finished the long tale "A Modern Mephistopheles." But Elliott would not have it, saying it was too long & too sensational! So I put it away & fell to work on other things. . . . Ticknor added to my worries by sending word that the MS. of the fairy tales was lost.
> A nice letter from my Laddie in Poland. He is better & the same dear boy as ever. . . .
> Leslie asked me to write a $50 tale a month for him & I agreed to do it. Hope I may have time.

16. Cheney.
17. Cheney, p. 185.

32

Went to B[oston]. got sheeting, shirting, gowns coal, &c, & paid bills all round.

A shilling copy of "Moods" came from London & a notice saying it was selling fast.

In the Cheney edition, then, we can see that the following omissions were made: the title of a violent sensation story that later became a source for one of Alcott's most atypical books; the reference to a lost manuscript; a comment on the young Polish boy Ladislas Wisniewski, whom Alcott had met in Switzerland and after whom she would partially model Laurie, in *Little Women*; Alcott's continuing commitments to the gaudy Leslie periodicals and the monetary agreements involved; a mention of some errands; and the foreign circulation of her novel *Moods*.

In general, unpleasant or acerbic remarks in the journals were eliminated, as when Louisa Alcott, after having served as traveling companion to Anna Weld, commented: "Had a fuss with Mr W[eld]. but John [Pratt] helped me through & he at last paid me my proper wages. Glad to be done with their service of this sort." Similarly, a suggestive remark about "a little romance" that "couldn't be" was excised, along with references to financial matters, publishers' payments, and any comments regarded by the editor as trivial. Louisa's own occasional use of initials was expanded upon by Cheney, who distrusted the specific. As a result, people, places, periodicals, newspapers, were often not identified. Mention of Alcott's career as a writer of sensation stories was of course truncated if not all but obliterated.

At the outset it must be remembered that Alcott herself and the surviving members of her family (especially her sister Anna) had a hand in such omissions. Indeed, Cheney wrote in the introduction to the *Life, Letters, and Journals*: "Miss Alcott revised her journals at different times during her later life, striking out what was too personal for other eyes than her own, and destroying a great deal which would doubtless have proved very interesting."[18] After the publication of the *Life, Letters, and Journals*, Cheney referred, in a letter to Thomas Niles of Roberts Brothers, to "the many who revised the book."[19] There is no doubt that editor Cheney faced difficulties in producing a volume that would be acceptable to the Alcott family.

In addition to Alcott's own deletions and family pressure, Cheney was influenced in her labors by the editorial practices of the time. Acceptable procedures then included the excising of portions of letters or journals, the blotting out of undesirable lines or paragraphs, the rewriting of passages,

18. Cheney, p. iv.
19. Ednah D. Cheney to Thomas Niles, undated note appended to a letter from N. H. Morison to Ednah D. Cheney, Baltimore, 20 January 1890, Schlesinger Library, Radcliffe College.

the alteration of punctuation, the deleting of personal names, and a disregard for dates.[20] All such omissions or inaccuracies were generally governed by the overall purpose of improving upon the original.

Ednah Cheney was an improver par excellence. Despite her respect for scholarship and her undeniable ability, she was bent upon polishing the rough edges (and there were many) in her subject's life and character. "Duty's Faithful Child," as her father dubbed her, Alcott may well have been, but she was far more. America's best-loved author of juveniles she undoubtedly was, but she was far more. The journals as now presented restore the complexities of her character and the variety of her genius, which the Cheney version wittingly or unwittingly suppressed. It may be productive, therefore, to inquire into the nature of the editor who, when all is said and done, shaped the Alcott image that endured for a century.

Cheney's handwriting, it was noticed, "slanted upward from left to right," and this was construed to indicate "the ascending and aspiring quality of her soul," a "reaching out for higher and better things for herself and for others."[21] She inspired hyperbole. "To see her in the street or at a meeting was as uplifting as to catch a glimpse of Mt. Monadnoc in the distance." When she died, the service was "more like a coronation than a funeral." The dark good looks of her youth improved with age, and through her strong, serious features admirers discerned "the light of a beautiful soul."[22]

Ednah Dow Littlehale,[23] daughter of Ednah Dow and Sargent Littlehale, was born in Boston in 1824 and hence was eight and a half years Louisa Alcott's senior. Their backgrounds had much in common. Ednah's father, like Louisa's, was a staunch supporter of an end to slavery and of woman's rights. In both families there was an "ascending and aspiring" spirit that welcomed all good causes. Like Louisa, Ednah was one of four surviving children, and she too was encouraged to exercise "independent moral judgment." On the other hand, while Bronson Alcott lived almost as long as his

20. For these procedures, see Robert N. Hudspeth and Joel Myerson, "Editing Margaret Fuller's Letters," *Manuscripts* (Summer 1987), pp, 242–247.

21. Horace Bumstead in *1824–1904 Ednah Dow Cheney Memorial Meeting New England Women's Club Boston February 20, 1905* (Boston: Ellis, 1905), p. 33.

22. All quotations are from *Woman's Journal* (26 November 1904), pp. 377, 381.

23. For biographical details about Cheney, see Madelon Bedell, *The Alcotts: Biography of a Family* (New York: Clarkson N. Potter, 1980), pp. 302–309, 319–320; Ednah Dow Cheney, *Reminiscences* (Boston: Lee & Shepard, 1902), passim; "Ednah Dow Littlehale Cheney," *Dictionary of American Biography*, vol. 4 (New York: Charles Scribner's Sons, 1930), pp. 51–52, and *Notable American Women 1607–1950: A Biographical Dictionary*, vol. 1 (Cambridge, Mass.: Belknap Press, 1971), pp. 325–327; Ann Douglas, Introduction to Ednah D. Cheney, *Louisa May Alcott* (New York: Chelsea House, 1980), passim; Granville Hicks, "A Conversation in Boston," in *Critical Essays on Margaret Fuller*, ed. Joel Myerson (Boston: G. K. Hall, 1980), pp. 158–159; Evelyn Shakir, "Ednah Dow Cheney: 'Jack at all trades,'" *American Transcendental Quarterly* (Summer/Fall 1982), pp. 95–115.

daughter and never adequately supported his family, Sargent Littlehale died in 1851 and left his family comfortable.

Ednah Littlehale's education, obtained in private classes and the Mount Vernon School in Boston, came to a climax when she was sixteen and attended Margaret Fuller's "Conversations" on West Street, Boston. Drawn, as so many (including Louisa May Alcott) were to the magnetic and brilliant conversationalist who was almost as much *Ewig-weibliche* as she was feminist, Ednah Cheney responded to Fuller's question: "Is life rich to you?" with the answer: "It is since I have known you." She would later say, comparing Fuller with herself, "She was far greater, richer, more intense. I am diluted."

Some years later, when Ednah was twenty-four, she attended another series of "Conversations," also on West Street, on the subject of man. Those conversations were given by Bronson Alcott. According to Bronson Alcott's biographer Odell Shepard, Bronson "at this time . . . made the first of his several friendships, all of them delightfully naïve and charmingly innocent, with young women. Ednah Dow Littlehale . . . was for several years his devoted and beloved companion."[24] A more recent Alcott family biographer, Madelon Bedell, views the relationship as less naïve than passionate on Bronson's part and describes the friendship as romance.[25] It is definite that on 29 August 1850 Alcott signed a letter to his young companion with the slightly mystifying remark "were I the unforgettable, I should be yours, forever."[26] When she came to write her *Reminiscences*, Ednah would dub Bronson Alcott "the most characteristic of the Transcendentalists . . . a man who could hardly have been what he was anywhere but in New England, but who was no less the heir of Greece and Europe."[27]

It is doubtful that Louisa Alcott was aware of any undue warmth that may have existed in the relationship between her father and Ednah Littlehale. Yet little escaped her watchful eyes. Indeed, when Ednah Littlehale introduced young Frank Sanborn to the Alcotts in 1852, Sanborn would recall that "all through that ceremonious call Louisa sat silent in the background of the family circle, her expressive face and earnest, almost melancholy eyes . . . fixt on the visitors."[28]

On 19 May 1853 the companionship between Bronson Alcott and Ednah Littlehale — whatever its nature had been — was terminated at least tem-

24. Odell Shepard, *Pedlar's Progress: The Life of Bronson Alcott* (Boston: Little, Brown, 1937), p. 442.

25. Bedell, *The Alcotts*, pp. 302–309.

26. Bronson Alcott to Ednah Dow Littlehale, Boston, 29 August 1850, *Letters*, p. 158.

27. Cheney, *Reminiscences*, p. 189.

28. F. B. Sanborn, "Reminiscences of Louisa M. Alcott," *The Independent* (7 March 1912), p. 497, reprinted in *Critical Essays on Louisa May Alcott*, ed. Madeleine B. Stern (Boston: G. K. Hall, 1984), p. 215.

porarily by Ednah's marriage to Seth Cheney. Her senior by fourteen years, Cheney was a "reform-minded" crayon artist "of a South Manchester, Conn., silk manufacturing family."[29] The couple had one child, a daughter, before Seth Cheney died in 1856.

Exposed as she had been throughout her life to high-minded causes and the Transcendental idealists who espoused them, the widow Cheney was well on her way to a life of service. The causes lay all about her; she had but to select those most congenial to her "ascending" nature. Those she advocated were also those Louisa Alcott advocated: antislavery and feminism. Cheney was more of a joiner than Alcott, becoming a founder of the New England Women's Club, a manager of the New England Hospital for Women and Children, an active member of the Massachusetts Woman Suffrage Association. In 1879, when Bronson Alcott opened his Concord School of Philosophy, his erstwhile "beloved companion" was one of the "five chief lecturers" and the only female lecturer, speaking on the history and moral of art.[30] Characteristically, Cheney regarded the invitation to lecture as a duty, acknowledging:

> I had, as I so often have before and since, the painful feeling that I owed this invitation rather to the wish to do honor to women by giving them an equal position than to my own individual merits, for I felt poorly qualified for the task. I believed, however, that it was my duty to appear as a representative woman and do the best I could.[31]

Duty, morality, especially a compulsive sense of service, permeated Cheney's writings as well as her life. Her first book, published in 1860, was a handbook for American citizens, and her output included some hackwork on card games undertaken to support the freedmen's schools, a few books for children's Sunday School reading, one or two family memoirs, and *Gleanings in the Field of Art*. Her most interesting book is *Nora's Return: A Sequel to "The Doll's House" of Henry Ibsen*. There Cheney converts Ibsen's rebellious Nora into a nurse serving the poor and reconciles her to a husband who has learned to recognize the rights of others. "In service for others," Cheney put it, "we secure our own development and happiness."[32] *Nora's Return* is a crystallization of Cheney's philosophy of service, and, most interesting of all, it was written not in the form of a play but in the form of diaries, which become

---

29. *Notable American Women 1607–1950*, vol. 1, p. 326.

30. F. B. Sanborn, *Recollections of Seventy Years* (Boston: Badger, 1909), vol. 2, p. 487.

31. Cheney, *Reminiscences*, p. 121.

32. Ednah D. Cheney, *Nora's Return: A Sequel to "The Doll's House" of Henry Ibsen* (Boston: Lee and Shepard, 1890), Preface. The book is dedicated to the New England Hospital for Women and Children.

the vehicle for self-analysis. By 1890, when *Nora's Return* was published, Ednah Cheney had had considerable experience with diaries and journals.

In 1888, the year of Alcott's death, the Boston firm of L. Prang & Company published a souvenir tribute by Ednah Cheney entitled *Louisa May Alcott, The Children's Friend.* There Cheney wrote of her subject as one "to whom a whole generation looks up with honor and affection as their benefactor and friend. This slight sketch of her life is not intended to take the place of the full biography, which, it is hoped, will be prepared under the auspices of her own family."[33] It may be deduced that negotiations were already under way with the Alcott family and the Alcott publisher, Roberts Brothers, for the work that would appear within a year under the title of *Louisa May Alcott: Her Life, Letters, and Journals.*

The title was an accurate description of the contents. Here indeed was an amalgam of Alcott biography by Cheney, selections from Alcott letters, and selections from Alcott journals. Biography she regarded, as she regarded so much of life, as "another act of service."[34] Her awareness of Alcott's "struggle with the bitter realities of life" merely enforced her belief that Alcott's "religion permeated her whole life." Alcott might "mock at the philosophers of Concord," but Cheney held that "the great [Transcendentalist] doctrine had moulded her thought and was a living principle in her soul."[35] From the pen of an editor with such convictions, Louisa Alcott could emerge only as a glorified benefactor, Duty's Faithful Child, the "children's friend."

The den of Cheney's home in Jamaica Plain was lined with books, including "in a case by itself . . . a full set of Miss Alcott's books, presented by Roberts Brothers."[36] There she sat, editing Alcott's life, letters, and journals, shaping a reputation that would hold for a century. Alcott's "troubled story," though "decipherable," was "never enunciated,"[37] and much that was human in this remarkable human being was sacrificed to improve her image for posterity.

By January 1890, when Cheney wrote to Niles about the published version, she could express her pleasure "that the sale has finally realised your expectations."[38] Reviews of the *Life, Letters, and Journals* were generally favorable. Indeed, *The Critic* went so far as to proclaim that Alcott's "biography is

---

33. Ednah D. Cheney, *Louisa May Alcott, The Children's Friend* (Boston: L. Prang, 1888), p. 3.

34. Douglas, Introduction to Cheney, p. xiii.

35. Cheney, *Reminiscences*, pp. 190–191.

36. Frederick H. Littlehale, *A Complete History and Genealogy of the Littlehale Family in America, From 1633 to 1889* (Boston: Littlehale, 1889), p. 108.

37. Douglas, Introduction to Cheney, *Louisa May Alcott*, p. xxix.

38. Cheney to Niles, undated note appended to a letter from Morison to Cheney, 20 January 1890, Schlesinger Library, Radcliffe College.

her greatest book — the one which will give her most of reputation in the future, by revealing a woman of the noblest character and purest aims."[39] The *Atlantic Monthly* was more perceptive: "What Miss Louisa Alcott would have written had she set about a deliberate sketch of her early life, we cannot say. . . . We wish heartily that Miss Alcott had chosen to tell her own story."[40]

Here in the journals Louisa May Alcott tells that story. Except for passages lost or destroyed, they have been restored as she wrote them, unexcised and unfragmented. After a century of "diluted" journals, they stand as close to the original version as is possible.

In addition, Alcott's journals and year-end notes expand her bibliography. Their perusal reveals a Louisa May Alcott who is the author of numbers of unknown narratives, some of which have been traced while others still await tracing. The author of *Little Women* turns out to be also the author of anonymous thrillers focused upon mesmerism, Hindu thuggism, her stage mania, her intense feminism.[41] Allusions to stories still unearthed provide incentives to Sherlockians who will rescue them from the now-crumbling pages of nineteenth-century story papers and add to an oeuvre that becomes more varied and more interesting as it is explored.

With her letters, these journals now provide as complete a record as can exist of an extraordinary life. Alcott's letters (published for the first time in 1987, as *The Selected Letters of Louisa May Alcott*) were as honest and revealing as her journals. But letters are designed for the single individual to whom they are addressed. Letters answer immediate questions, concern themselves with current problems, sometimes probe the inner self of the writer, often describe the outside scene. Alcott's letters do all this magnificently, for she brought humor, understanding, and skilled reportorial observation to their creation.

All those powers were brought to bear upon her journals. But unlike the letters, the journals (with the exception of some early entries that invited parental perusal) were private records. As such they reflected perhaps more closely than the letters Alcott's emotional life and the recurring problems of her days. Though in later years she destroyed some passages and added elucidating phrases to others, she did not distort her journals for an anticipated readership. If the letters were addressed to individuals, the journals, for the most part, were addressed to herself.

39. *The Critic* (25 October 1890), p. 202.
40. *Atlantic Monthly* (March 1890), p. 420.
41. "A Pair of Eyes; or, Modern Magic," "The Fate of the Forrests," "A Double Tragedy," and "Taming a Tartar." All these have been published in *A Double Life: Newly Discovered Thrillers of Louisa May Alcott*, ed. Madeleine B. Stern (Boston: Little, Brown, 1988).

Therefore these journals (which also yield details of thoughts and events not covered in the letters) are enormously significant. Had Louisa May Alcott been merely the author of one domestic novel that captivated much of the reading world, her journals would have merited publication. Had her reputation been limited to that of America's best-loved author of children's tales, her journals would have taken on importance for critics and historians of the literature of childhood. Now that Alcott is recognized (largely as the result of clues in the journals) as an experimenter who essayed a variety of literary genres and succeeded in many, the need to gather together and publish all the extant journals is even greater. They evoke the writer and her sources, the individual and her development, as well as the life of a nineteenth-century New England family that was transmuted into literature. With *The Selected Letters of Louisa May Alcott*, the journals document her life as it was lived and her work as it was written.

THE JOURNALS,
1843–1888

1843

Friday 4 [August] —

After breakfast I washed the dishes and then had my lessons. Father and Mr Kay and Mr Lane went to the Shakers and did not return till evening.[1] After my lessons I sewed till dinner. When dinner was over I had a bath, and then went to Mrs Williards.[2] When I came home I played till supper time, after which I read a little in Oliver Twist,[3] and when I had thought a little I went to bed. I have spent quite a pleasant day.

Saturday 5 —

I rose early, and after breakfast I did the morning work; I had my lessons. I set the dinner table. After dinner, I had a bath and then went berrying, when I came home. I went to ride with mother and Abba;[4] when I returned I had my supper, and then went to bed.

Tuesday 8 —

After I had bathed and dressed, I came to breakfast. After breakfasting I washed the dishes and then went berrying with Anna and William we did not return untill dinner time.[5] After dinner, I read and made clothes for my doll and had a bath. I sewed till 5 oclock, and went to walk. Lizzy and [I] played out till supper was ready. After supper I washed the dishes, and went to bed.

Thursday 10 —

I rose early. After we had done breakfast I did my morning work. Father Mother Abba and Mr Lane went to Leominster. I ironed a little and read till dinner was ready   after dinner I bathed. Lizzy William and I went black-berring. Mother and Father came home in the evening. Though it was un-pleasant without I was happy within[6]

hay and took care of Abba till supper after which I read a little and then went to bed

Sunday 28 — [7]

After breakfast I read till 9 oclock and Father read a Parable called Nathan.[8] and I liked it very well   he then asked us all what faults we watted [wanted] to get rid of   I said Impatience, and Mr Lane selfwill. We had a dinner of bread and water after which I read thought and walked till supper.

Monday 29th —

I rose at half past 4 and bathed and dressed[9] had my singing lesson   After breakfast I had my lessons after which I helped about dinner. in the afternoon I played and read.

Wednesday 30 —

After breakfast I washed the dishes and then Mother Anna Miss Robie and Harriet[10] and myself went to Leominster to see a house which Father thinks of buying   I liked it pretty well and I enjoyed my ride very much. we did not return till evening.

Thursday 31 —

I had my lessons as usual and played till dinner after which I went to Mrs Dudleys and did not return till supper time[11]

September. — 1843

Friday 1 —

I had my lessons as usual and Mr Lane made a piece of poetry about Pestalossi I will put in[12]

to Pestalossi —

On Pestalossis sacred brow
The modest chesnut wreath
Green yesterday but fadeing now
And pasing as a breath.

————

Mother made up this piece, which I like very much[13]

September 1st. — I rose at five and had my bath. I love cold water! Then we had our singing-lesson with Mr. Lane. After breakfast I washed dishes, and ran on the hill till nine, and had some thoughts, — it was so beautiful up there. Did my lessons, — wrote and spelt and did sums; and Mr. Lane read a story, "The Judicious Father": How a rich girl told a poor girl not to look over the fence at the flowers, and was cross to her because she was unhappy. The father heard her do it, and made the girls change clothes. The poor one was glad to do it, and he told her to keep them. But the rich one was very sad; for she had to wear the old ones a week, and after that she was good to shabby girls. I liked it very much, and I shall be kind to poor people.

Father asked us what was God's noblest work. Anna said *men,* but I said *babies.* Men are often bad; babies never are. We had a long talk, and I felt better after it, and *cleared up.*

We had bread and fruit for dinner. I read and walked and played till supper-time. We sung in the evening. As I went to bed the moon came up very brightly and looked at me. I felt sad because I have been cross today, and did not mind Mother. I cried, and then I felt better, and said that piece from Mrs. Sigourney, "I must not tease my mother."[14] I get to sleep saying poetry, — I know a great deal.

Thursday, 14th. — Mr. Parker Pillsbury came, and we talked about the poor slaves.[15] I had a music lesson with Miss P.[16] I hate her, she is so fussy. I ran in the wind and played be a horse, and had a lovely time in the woods with Anna and Lizzie. We were fairies, and made gowns and paper wings. I "flied" the highest of all. In the evening they talked about travelling. I thought about Father going to England,[17] and said this piece of poetry I found in Byron's poems: — [18]

> "When I left thy shores, O Naxos,
>   Not a tear in sorrow fell;
> Not a sigh or faltered accent
>   Told my bosom's struggling swell."

It rained when I went to bed, and made a pretty noise on the roof.

Sunday, 24th. — Father and Mr. Lane have gone to N[ew]. H[ampshire]. to preach. It was very lovely. . . . Anna and I got supper. In the eve I read "Vicar of Wakefield."[19] I was cross to-day, and I cried when I went to bed. I made good resolutions, and felt better in my heart. If I only *kept* all I make, I should be the best girl in the world. But I don't, and so am very bad.

[Poor little sinner! *She says the same at fifty.* — L. M. A.]

October 8th. — When I woke up, the first thought I got was, "It's Mother's birthday: I must be very good." I ran and wished her a happy birthday, and gave her my kiss. After breakfast we gave her our presents. I had a moss cross and a piece of poetry for her.

We did not have any school, and played in the woods and got red leaves. In the evening we danced and sung, and I read a story about "Contentment." I wish I was rich, I was good, and we were all a happy family this day.

We sang the following song:

Song of May

Hail, all hail, thou merry month of May,
We all hasten to the woods away
Among the flowers so sweet and gay,
Then away to hail the merry merry May —
   The merry merry May —
Then away to hail the merry merry month of May.

Hark, hark, hark, to hail the month of May,
How the songsters warble on the spray,
And we will be as blith[e] as they,
Then away to hail the merry merry May —
Then away to hail the merry merry month of May.

I think this is a very pretty song and we sing it a good deal.

Thursday, 12th. — After lessons I ironed. We all went to the barn and husked corn. It was good fun. We worked till eight o'clock and had lamps. Mr. Russell came.[20] Mother and Lizzie are going to Boston. I shall be very lonely without dear little Betty, and no one will be as good to me as mother. I read in Plutarch.[21] I made a verse about sunset: —

Softly doth the sun descend
   To his couch behind the hill,
Then, oh, then, I love to sit
   On mossy banks beside the rill.

Anna thought it was very fine; but I did n't like it very well.

Friday, Nov. 2nd. — Anna and I did the work. In the evening Mr. Lane asked us, "What is man?" These were our answers: A human being; an animal with a mind; a creature; a body; a soul and a mind. After a long talk we went to bed very tired.

[No wonder, after doing the work and worrying their little wits with such lessons. — L. M. A.]

A sample of the vegetarian wafers we used at Fruitlands: —

Vegetable diet and sweet repose. Animal food and nightmare.	Pluck your body from the orchard; do not snatch it from the shamble.	Without flesh diet there could be no blood-shedding war.

Apollo eats no flesh and has no beard; his voice is melody itself.	Snuff is no less snuff though accepted from a gold box.

Tuesday, 20th. — I rose at five, and after breakfast washed the dishes, and then helped mother work. Miss P[age]. is gone, and Anna in Boston with Cousin Louisa.[22] I took care of Abby (May) in the afternoon. In the evening I made some pretty things for my dolly. Father and Mr. L. had a talk, and father asked us if *we* saw any reason for us to separate. Mother wanted to, she is so tired. I like it, but not the school part or Mr. L.

Eleven years old. *Thursday, 29th.* — It was Father's and my birthday. We had some nice presents. We played in the snow before school. Mother read "Rosamond" when we sewed.[23] Father asked us in the eve what fault troubled us most. I said my bad temper.

I told mother I liked to have her write in my book. She said she would put in more, and she wrote this to help me: —

DEAR LOUY, — Your handwriting improves very fast. Take pains and do not be in a hurry. I like to have you make observations about our conversations and your own thoughts. It helps you to express them and to understand your little self. Remember, dear girl, that a diary should be an epitome of your life. May it be a record of pure thought and good actions, then you will indeed be the precious child of your loving mother.

December 10th. — I did my lessons, and walked in the afternoon. Father read to us in dear Pilgrim's Progress.[24] Mr. L. was in Boston, and we were glad. In the eve father and mother and Anna and I had a long talk. I was very unhappy, and we all cried. Anna and I cried in bed, and I prayed God to keep us all together.[25]

spoken unkindly to the children and been disobedient to mother and father,

Saturday 23 [December] —

In the morning mother went to the Village and I had my lessons and then helped Annie get dinner after which mother came home and Annie went [on] an errand for mother to Mr Lovejoys [26]

we stayed a little while to see their little baby boy   I often wish I had a little brother but as I have not I shall try to be contented with what I have got, (for Mother often says if we are not contented with what we have got it will be taken away from us) and I think it is very true. When we returned from Mr Lovejoys, we played till supper time   in the evening we played cards and when I went to bed I felt happy for I had been obedient and kind to Father and Mother and gentle to my sisters, I wish I could be gentle always.

Sunday 24th —

After breakfast Father started for Boston, When he was gome I read and wrote till dinner after which I washed the dishes and then I made some presents for Christmass   in the evening I read and Mr Palmer came and brought his son T[h]omas [27]   I did not go to bed till 10 oclock

Christmass Day 1843

Monday 25 —

I rose early and sat some looking at the Bon-bons in my stocking   this is the piece of poetry which mother wrote for me

Christmass Rimes

Christmass is here
Louisa my dear
Then happy we'll be
Gladsome and free
God with you abide
With love for your guide
In time you'l go right
With heart and with might,

This is a song which she sang soo[n] after she began to travil to the Bea[u]tiful City.

1

Bless'd be the day that I began
A Pilgrim for to be;

48

And blessed also be that man
 That thereto moved me.
'Tis true 'twas long ere I began
 To seek to live for ever;
But now I run fast as I can,
 'Tis better late than never.
Our tears to joy, our fears to faith,
 Are turned, as we see;
Thus our beginning (as one earth)
 Shews what our end will be. [28]

1

What dange[r] is the Pilgrim is,
 How many are his foes?
How many ways there are to sin,
 No living mortal knows.

2

Some in the ditch are spoiled; yea can
 Lie tumbling in the mire;
Some, though thay shun the frying pan
 Do leap into the fire. [29]

Here is an other

1

Behold ye how these crystal streams do glide
To comfort pilgrims, by the highway side,
The meadows green, besides their fragrant smell
Yield dainties for them! and he who can tell
What pleasant fruit, yea, leaves, these trees do yeild
Will soon sell all, that he may buy this field. [30]

This is the sheepard boys song as he was tending his fathers in the Vall[e]y of Humili[a]tion

 He that is down needs fear no fall;
 He that low no pride;

49

He that is humble ever shall
 Have God to be his guide.

2

I am content with what I have,
 Little be it or much,
And Lord! contentment still I crave
 Becaus[e] thou savest such[31]

[Little Lu began early to feel the family cares and peculiar trials. — L. M. A.][32]
I liked the verses Christian sung and will put them in: —

"This place has been our second stage,
 Here we have heard and seen
Those good things that from age to age
 To others hid have been.

"They move me for to watch and pray,
 To strive to be sincere,
To take my cross up day by day,
 And serve the Lord with fear."[33]

[The appropriateness of the song at this time was much greater than the child saw. She never forgot this experience, and her little cross began to grow heavier from this hour. — L. M. A.]

CONCORD, *Sunday.* — We all went into the woods to get moss for the *arbor* Father is making for *Mr. Emerson.*[34] I miss Anna so much. I made two verses for her: —

TO ANNA.

Sister, dear, when you are lonely,
 Longing for your distant home,
And the images of loved ones
 Warmly to your heart shall come,
Then, mid tender thoughts and fancies
 Let one fond voice say to thee,
"Ever when your heart is heavy,
 Anna, dear, then think of me."
Think how we two have together
 Journeyed onward day by day,
Joys and sorrows ever sharing,
 While the swift years roll away.

50

Then may all the sunny hours
Of our youth rise up to thee,
And when your heart is light and happy,
Anna, dear, then think of me.

[Poetry began to flow about this time in a thin but copious stream. — L. M. A.]

Wednesday. — Read Martin Luther. A long letter from Anna. She sends me a picture of Jenny Lind, the great singer.[35] She must be a happy girl. I should like to be famous as she is. Anna is very happy; and I don't miss her as much as I shall by and by in the winter.

I wrote in my Imagination Book, and enjoyed it very much. Life is pleasanter than it used to be, and I don't care about dying any more. Had a splendid run, and got a box of cones to burn. Sat and heard the pines sing a long time. Read Miss Bremer's "Home" in the eve.[36] Had good dreams, and woke now and then to think, and watch the moon. I had a pleasant time with my mind, for it was happy.

[Moods began early. — L. M. A.]

SOURCES: The diaries kept by LMA at Fruitlands come from three sources. The entries for [3] August through 1 September (with the poem to Pestalozzi) and from [22] through 25 December are from the manuscript at Fruitlands Museums. The entries for 1 September (beginning "I rose at five") through 10 December (excluding "Song of May" in the entry for 8 October) and from [after 25 December] on are from Cheney, pp. 35–40. The entry containing the poem "Song of May" (from "We sang" through "we sing it a good deal.") is from Clara Endicott Sears, *Bronson Alcott's Fruitlands* (Boston: Houghton Mifflin, 1915), pp. 108–109. There is no evidence to indicate why the manuscript's and Cheney's texts have different entries for 1 September, nor why the poem in the 8 October entry is present in Sears but not in Cheney, since Sears's text is obviously based on Cheney's.

Bronson's Fruitlands experiment at Harvard, Massachusetts, fourteen miles from Concord, lasted from June 1843 to January 1844. Bronson's journal for this period is lost, but parts of Mrs. Alcott's journal are at the Houghton Library, Harvard University, and are printed in Bronson's *Journals*, pp. 152–156; fragments from Anna's Fruitlands diary are printed in Sears, *Bronson Alcott's Fruitlands*, pp. 86–104.

The Fruitlands manuscript begins with this fragmentary entry for [3] August: "and he brought his son James with him. When Lizzy and I came home from our walk we played a little. After supper I played some again and then went to bed, having spent a very pleasant day." The references are to LMA's sister Elizabeth Sewall Alcott, born 24 June 1835, and probably the Philadelphia reformer James Kay and his son, James Alfred Kay. Kay was a supporter of the Brook Farm community in West Roxbury, Massachusetts, which he occasionally visited. His son attended the Brook Farm school in 1844.

1. Charles Lane, an English Transcendentalist who returned to America with Bronson in 1842 and provided the financing for Fruitlands. The 4 August entry in the journal of the Shaker community reads: "Two men by the names of Alcott & Lane (Transcendentalest [sic]) and a man from Philadelphia came here took dinner and stayed till towards night[.] They seem to be inquiring into our principles" (*Transcendental Wild Oats and Excerpts from the Fruitlands Diary* [Harvard, Mass.: Harvard Common Press, 1975], p. 31n).

2. Mrs. Willard, a neighbor and frequent visitor to the community, often helped Mrs. Alcott with the chores.

3. Charles Dickens's *Oliver Twist* (1838).

4. LMA's sister Abby May Alcott, born 26 July 1840.

5. LMA's sister Anna Bronson Alcott, born 16 March 1831; Charles Lane's son, William.

6. Manuscript breaks off.

7. LMA has erroneously called Monday the twenty-eighth a Sunday, and Tuesday the twenty-ninth a Monday.

8. In 2 Sam. 12, the prophet Nathan relates a parable to King David, who has sent Bathsheba's husband to die in battle so he may marry her himself. The parable tells of a rich man with many flocks of sheep who kills the only lamb of a neighbor. When David says the rich man should be punished with death for his action, Nathan replies, "Thou art the man."

9. LMA first wrote "dressed," crossed it out and wrote "drest," then crossed out her revision and wrote "dressed" again.

10. Hannah Robie was the sister of the mother of Samuel E. Sewall, whose family was related to the Alcotts by marriage; the identity of Harriet is unknown.

11. Silas, Charlotte, and Ellen Dudley were neighbors.

12. Bronson had incorporated the ideas of the Swiss educator Johann Heinrich Pestalozzi into his own pedagogical program.

13. At this point the Fruitlands manuscript ends and the text taken from Cheney begins. We do not know why the entries for 1 September differ in the two versions.

14. "I Must Not Tease My Mother," by Lydia Sigourney, known as the sweet singer of Hartford.

15. Parker Pillsbury, an antislavery reformer.

16. Ann Page, who taught the girls, was expelled from the community for eating fish. Cheney prints this as "Miss F." in *Louisa May Alcott: Her Life, Letters, and Journals*, which is obviously in error; she does the same in the entry for 20 November.

17. Bronson had visited England in May-October 1842, visiting Alcott House in Ham, Surrey, and meeting Charles Lane. He never went overseas again.

18. These lines, which are not collected in any nineteenth-century edition of Byron's poetical works, were printed as sheet music, headed "an Original Greek Air the words never before published by Lord Byron" (Philadelphia: A. R. Poole, n.d.). This poem will be included in the Oxford University Press edition of Byron's *Complete Poetical Works*, edited by Jerome McGann, to whom we are indebted for this information.

19. Oliver Goldsmith's *Vicar of Wakefield* (1766).

20. Professor William Russell of Andover, an associate of Bronson's in educational reforms.

21. Plutarch's *Morals* (London, 1694) and *Lives*, 8 vols. (London, 1821), were in the library at Fruitlands.

22. LMA's cousin Louisa Willis, the wife of Hamilton Willis, was the daughter of Charles W. Windship (whose first wife was Mrs. Alcott's sister Catherine) and his second wife, Martha Ruggles Windship.

23. Maria Edgeworth's *Rosamond* (1801), a collection of tales for children.

24. John Bunyan's *Pilgrim's Progress* (1678) was a longtime favorite of Bronson's. According to F. B. Sanborn, it was Bronson's "custom for years to borrow and read the Pilgrim's Progress once a year; and this book, more than any other, gave directions to his fancies and visions of life" ("A. Bronson Alcott" in Samuel Orcutt, *History of the Town of Wolcott* [Waterbury, Conn.: American Printing, 1874], p. 243).

25. At this point the text taken from Cheney ends and the Fruitlands manuscript begins again.

26. After Fruitlands failed, the Alcotts stayed with the J. W. Lovejoy family in Still River, Massachusetts, adjacent to Harvard, for five months.

27. Joseph Palmer had been persecuted and jailed for wearing a long, flowing beard. He

and his family stayed on at Fruitlands after the community failed, eventually purchasing the land.

28. From "The Wicket-Gate" (Part Two) in *Pilgrim's Progress.*

29. From "Enchanted Ground" (Part Two) in *Pilgrim's Progress.*

30. From "The River of Life" (Part One) in *Pilgrim's Progress.*

31. From "The Valley of Humiliation" (Part Two) in *Pilgrim's Progress.*

32. At this point, the text taken from Cheney begins again.

33. From "Great-Heart Conducts Them" (Part Two) in *Pilgrim's Progress.*

34. Emboldened by this labor, Bronson, with Henry David Thoreau's help, made a bower for Ralph Waldo Emerson in 1847–1848 (pictured in Milton Meltzer and Walter Harding, *A Thoreau Profile* [New York: Thomas Y. Crowell, 1962], p. 55).

35. The singer Jenny Lind was known as the Swedish nightingale.

36. Fredrika Bremer's *Home* (1843).

1845

January, 1845, Friday. — Did my lessons, and in the P. M. mother read "Kenilworth" to us while we sewed.[1] It is splendid! I got angry and called Anna mean. Father told me to look out the word in the Dic., and it meant "base," "contemptible." I was so ashamed to have called my dear sister that, and I cried over my bad tongue and temper.

We have had a lovely day. All the trees were covered with ice, and it shone like diamonds on fairy palaces. I made a piece of poetry about winter: —

> The stormy winter's come at last,
>   With snow and rain and bitter blast;
> Ponds and brooks are frozen o'er,
>   We cannot sail there any more.
>
> The little birds are flown away
>   To warmer climes than ours;
> They'll come no more till gentle May
>   Calls them back with flowers.
>
> Oh, then the darling birds will sing
>   From their neat nests in the trees.
> All creatures wake to welcome Spring,
>   And flowers dance in the breeze.
>
> With patience wait till winter is o'er,
>   And all lovely things return;
> Of every season try the more
>   Some knowledge or virtue to learn.

[A moral is tacked on even to the early poems. — L. M. A.]

I read "Philothea," by Mrs. Child.[2] I found this that I liked in it. Plato said: —

"When I hear a note of music I can at once strike its chord. Even as surely is there everlasting harmony between the soul of man and the invisible forms of creation. If there were no innocent hearts there would be no white lilies. . . . I often think flowers are the angel's alphabet whereby they write on hills and fields mysterious and beautiful lessons for us to feel and learn."

[Well done, twelve-year-old! Plato, the father's delight,[3] had a charm for the little girl also. — L. M. A.]

Wednesday. — I am so cross I wish I had never been born.

Thursday. — Read the "Heart of Mid-Lothian," and had a very happy day.[4] Miss Ford gave us a botany lesson in the woods.[5] I am always good there. In the evening Miss Ford told us about the bones in our bodies, and how they get out of order. I must be careful of mine, I climb and jump and run so much.

I found this note from dear mother in my journal: —

MY DEAREST LOUY, — I often peep into your diary, hoping to see some record of more happy days. "Hope, and keep busy," dear daughter, and in all perplexity or trouble come freely to your

MOTHER.

DEAR MOTHER, — You *shall* see more happy days, and I *will* come to you with my worries, for you are the best woman in the world.

L. M. A.

A Sample of our Lessons.

"What virtues do you wish more of?" asks Mr. L.

I answer: —

Patience,	Love,	Silence,
Obedience,	Generosity,	Perseverance,
Industry,	Respect,	Self-denial.

"What vices less of?"

Idleness,	Wilfulness,	Vanity,
Impatience,	Impudence,	Pride,
Selfishness,	Activity.	Love of cats.

Mr. L	L.
SOCRATES.	ALCIBIADES.

How can you get what you need? By trying.

How do you try? By resolution and perseverance.

How gain love? By gentleness.

What is gentleness? Kindness, patience, and care for other people's feelings.

Who has it? Father and Anna.

Who means to have it? Louisa, if she can.

[She never got it. — L. M. A.]

Write a sentence about anything. "I hope it will rain; the garden needs it."

What are the elements of *hope*? Expectation, desire, faith.

What are the elements in *wish*? Desire.

What is the difference between faith and hope? "Faith can believe without seeing; hope is not sure, but tries to have faith when it desires."

No. 3.

What are the most valuable kinds of self-denial? Appetite, temper.

How is self-denial of temper known? If I control my temper, I am respectful and gentle, and every one sees it.

What is the result of this self-denial? Every one loves me, and I am happy.

Why use self-denial? For the good of myself and others.

How shall we learn this self-denial? By resolving, and then trying *hard*.

What then do you mean to do? To resolve and try.

[Here the records of these lessons ends, and poor little Alcibiades went to work and tried till fifty, but without any very great success, in spite of all the help Socrates and Plato gave her. — L. M. A.]

Tuesday. — More people coming to live with us; I wish we could be together, and no one else. I don't see who is to clothe and feed us all, when we are so poor now. I was very dismal, and then went to walk and made a poem.

DESPONDENCY.

Silent and sad,
When all are glad,
And the earth is dressed in flowers;
When the gay birds sing
Till the forests ring,
As they rest in woodland bowers.

Oh, why these tears,
And these idle fears
For what may come to-morrow?
The birds find food
From God so good,
And the flowers know no sorrow.

If He clothes these
And the leafy trees,
Will He not cherish thee?
Why doubt His care;
It is everywhere,
Though the way we may not see.

Then why be sad
When all are glad,
And the world is full of flowers?
With the gay birds sing,
Make life all Spring,
And smile through the darkest hours.

CONCORD, *Thursday*. — I had an early run in the woods before the dew was off the grass. The moss was like velvet, and as I ran under the arches of yellow and red leaves I sang for joy, my heart was so bright and the world so beautiful. I stopped at the end of the walk and saw the sunshine out over the wide "Virginia meadows."

It seemed like going through a dark life or grave into heaven beyond. A very strange and solemn feeling came over me as I stood there, with no sound but the rustle of the pines, no one near me, and the sun so glorious, as for me alone. It seemed as if I *felt* God as I never did before, and I prayed in my heart that I might keep that happy sense of nearness in my life.

[I have, for I most sincerely think that the little girl "got religion" that day in the wood when dear mother Nature led her to God. — L. M. A., 1885.]

SOURCE: Cheney, pp. 40–45.
    1. Sir Walter Scott's *Kenilworth* (1821).
    2. *Philothea* (1836), by Lydia Maria Child, an abolitionist and author of numerous works about household management. According to Cheney, " 'Philothea' was the delight of girls. The young Alcotts made a dramatic version of it, which they acted under the trees. Louisa made a magnificent Aspasia, which was a part much to her fancy. Mrs. Child was a very dear friend of Mrs. Alcott, and her daughters knew her well" (Cheney, p. 41).

3. Bronson's interest in Plato dated from his youth, and LMA often called him Plato. Thomas Taylor's five-volume edition of Plato's works (1804) was in the Fruitlands library.

4. Sir Walter Scott's *Heart of Midlothian* (1818).

5. Sophia Foord (or Ford) stayed with the Alcotts in the summer of 1845 and helped with the children's recreation (see Walter Harding, "Thoreau's Feminine Foe," *PMLA* 69 [March 1954]: 110–116). Bronson wrote his brother Junius on 27 July 1845 that "Miss Ford is now with us, and a most useful aid in the house, and care of the children" (*Letters*, p. 122).

1846

Thirteen Years Old.

March, 1846. — I have at last got the little room I have wanted so long, and am very happy about it.[2] It does me good to be alone, and Mother has made it very pretty and neat for me. My work-basket and desk are by the window, and my closet is full of dried herbs that smell very nice. The door that opens into the garden will be very pretty in summer, and I can run off to the woods when I like.

I have made a plan for my life, as I am in my teens, and no more a child. I am old for my age, and don't care much for girl's things. People think I'm wild and queer; but Mother understands and helps me. I have not told any one about my plan; but I'm going to *be* good. I've made so many resolutions, and written sad notes, and cried over my sins, and it does n't seem to do any good! Now I'm going to *work really*, for I feel a true desire to improve, and be a help and comfort, not a care and sorrow, to my dear mother.

SOURCE: Cheney, pp. 47–48.

1. The Alcotts moved into the home they called Hillside on 1 April 1845, after purchasing it with money from the estate of Mrs. Alcott's father, Joseph May. They lived there until 17 November 1848, when they left for Boston. The house still stands in Concord, where it is known as Wayside, the name the Hawthornes gave it during their residence.

2. LMA had written her mother a year earlier that "I have been thinking about my little room which I suppose I never shall have" (*SL*, p. 6).

1847

Fifteen Years Old.

Sunday, Oct. 9, 1847. — I have been reading to-day Bettine's correspondence with Goethe.[1]

She calls herself a child, and writes about the lovely things she saw and heard, and felt and did. I liked it much.

[First taste of Goethe. Three years later R. W. E. gave me "Wilhelm Meister," and from that day Goethe has been my chief idol.[2] — L. M. A., 1885.]

SOURCE: Cheney, p. 48.

1. The letters between Bettina von Arnim and Johann Wolfgang von Goethe, which showed a strong pupil-master relationship, were first published in Germany in 1835 and in America as *Goethe's Correspondence with a Child* in 1841.

2. Goethe's *Wilhelm Meister* (1795–1796). In an updated prose fragment, LMA later recalled that Emerson had given her Goethe's works when she was fifteen and that they "had been my delight ever since" (Cheney, p. 398). *A Modern Mephistopheles* reflects LMA's interest in Goethe.

1850

Journal.

THE SENTIMENTAL PERIOD.

BOSTON, *May*, 1850. — So long a time has passed since I kept a journal that I hardly know how to begin.[1] Since coming to the city I don't seem to have thought much, for the bustle and dirt and change send all lovely images and restful feelings away. Among my hills and woods I had fine free times alone, and though my thoughts were silly, I daresay, they helped to keep me happy and good. I see now what Nature did for me, and my "romantic tastes," as people called that love of solitude and out-of-door life, taught me much.

This summer, like the last, we shall spend in a large house (Uncle May's, Atkinson Street),[2] with many comforts about us which we shall enjoy, and in the autumn I hope I shall have something to show that the time has not been wasted. Seventeen years have I lived, and yet so little do I know, and so much remains to be done before I begin to be what I desire, — a truly good and useful woman.

In looking over our journals, Father says, "Anna's is about other people, Louisa's about herself." That is true, for I don't *talk* about myself; yet must always think of the wilful, moody girl I try to manage, and in my journal I write of her to see how she gets on. Anna is so good she need not take care of herself, and can enjoy other people. If I look in my glass, I try to keep down vanity about my long hair, my well-shaped head, and my good nose. In the street I try not to covet fine things. My quick tongue is always getting me into trouble, and my moodiness makes it hard to be cheerful when I think how poor we are, how much worry it is to live, and how many things I long to do I never can.

So every day is a battle, and I'm so tired I don't want to live; only it's cowardly to die till you have done something.

I can't talk to any one but mother about my troubles, and she has so many now to bear I try not to add any more. I know God is always ready to hear, but heaven's so far away in the city, and I so heavy I can't fly up to find Him.

FAITH

Written in the diary.

Oh, when the heart is full of fears
    And the way seems dim to heaven,
When the sorrow and the care of years
    Peace from the heart has driven, —
Then, through the mist of fallen tears,
    Look up and be forgiven.

Forgiven for the lack of faith
    That made all dark to thee,
Let conscience o'er thy wayward soul
    Have fullest mastery:
Hope on, fight on, and thou shalt win
    A noble victory.

Though thou art weary and forlorn,
    Let not thy heart's peace go;
Though the riches of this world are gone,
    And thy lot is care and woe,
Faint not, but journey hourly on:
    True wealth is not below.

Through all the darkness still look up:
    Let virtue be thy guide;
Take thy draught from sorrow's cup,
    Yet trustfully abide;
Let not temptation vanquish thee,
    And the father will provide.

[We had small-pox in the family this summer, caught from some poor immigrants whom mother took into our garden and fed one day.[3] We girls had it lightly, but Father and Mother were very ill, and we had a curious time of exile, danger, and trouble. No doctors, and all got well. — L. M. A.]

July, 1850. — Anna is gone to L[enox]. after the varioloid [i.e., small-pox]. She is to help Mrs. —— with her baby.[4] I had to take A.'s school of twenty in Canton Street. I like it better than I thought, though it's very hard to be patient with the children sometimes. They seem happy, and learn fast; so I am encouraged, though at first it was very hard, and I missed Anna so much I used to cry over my dinner and be very blue. I guess this is the teaching I need; for as a *school-marm* I must behave myself and guard my tongue and temper carefully, and set an example of sweet manners.

I found one of mother's notes in my journal, so like those she used to write me when she had more time. It always encourages me; and I wish some one would write as helpfully to her, for she needs cheering up with all the care she has. I often think what a hard life she has had since she married, — so full of wandering and all sorts of worry! so different from her early easy days, the youngest and most petted of her family. I think she is a very brave, good woman; and my dream is to have a lovely, quiet home for her, with no debts or troubles to burden her. But I'm afraid she will be in heaven before I can do it. Anna, too, she is feeble and homesick, and I miss her dreadfully; for she is my conscience, always true and just and good. She must have a good time in a nice little home of her own some day, as we often plan. But waiting is so *hard!*

August, 1850. — School is hard work, and I feel as though I should like to run away from it. But my children get on; so I travel up every day, and do my best.

I get very little time to write or think; for my working days have begun, and when school is over Anna wants me; so I have no quiet. I think a little solitude every day is good for me. In the quiet I see my faults, and try to mend them; but, deary me, I don't get on at all.

I used to imagine my mind a room in confusion, and I was to put it in order; so I swept out useless thoughts and dusted foolish fancies away, and furnished it with good resolutions and began again. But cobwebs get in. I'm not a good housekeeper, and never get my room in nice order. I once wrote a poem about it when I was fourteen, and called it "My Little Kingdom."[5] It is still hard to rule it, and always will be I think.

Reading Mrs. Bremer and Hawthorne.[6] The "Scarlet Letter" is my favorite. Mother likes Miss B. better, as more wholesome. I fancy "lurid" things, if true and strong also.

Anna wants to be an actress, and so do I. We could make plenty of money perhaps, and it is a very gay life. Mother says we are too young, and must wait. A. acts often splendidly. I like tragic plays, and shall be a

Siddons if I can.[7] We get up fine ones, and make harps, castles, armor, dresses, water-falls, and thunder, and have great fun.[8]

["Notes and Memoranda"]

1850.

At Uncle May's Atkinson St. Annie goes to Lennox as a nursury girl to Mrs Tappan. L. takes her school in Canton St. with twenty pupils. We all have small pox. Mother is a city missionary, father writes & talks & the girls go to school.[9]

My Earnings

Rival Painters.	$ 5,00
Sewing.	10
School.	50[10]

SOURCES: Text — Cheney, pp. 59–63; "Notes and Memoranda" — manuscript, Houghton Library, Harvard University.

1. Katharine Anthony suggests that LMA left off writing her journal for the previous two years because her mother was too busy working to read it: "Her journal had always been a sort of correspondence with her mother, who read the pages after she had gone to bed at night and left little notes in reply. Without this response, Louisa's confessions ceased to flow" (Louisa May Alcott [New York: Alfred A. Knopf, 1938], p. 77).

2. Mrs. Alcott's brother Samuel Joseph May, a longtime financial supporter of her family, lived at 88 Atkinson Street in Boston.

3. As Bronson wrote his brother Chatfield, the girls had had smallpox "very slightly" and Mrs. Alcott "a little severely," but his case had been so serious that it "kept me in the house a couple of months" (16 September 1850, Letters, p. 159).

4. Caroline Sturgis Tappan and her husband, William, employed Anna in Lenox, Massachusetts, to help with their year-old daughter, Ellen Sturgis Tappan. Mrs. Tappan wrote Mrs. Alcott on 28 May [1850] that if "Anna would like to come & help me take care of my baby, it would be much pleasanter for me, both for her sake & my own, than having a nursery maid, & I think Anna would find much to enjoy in Lenox" (Houghton Library, Harvard University). Anna was paid twelve dollars for two months' work.

5. "My Kingdom," first published in The Sunny Side: A Book of Religious Songs for the Sunday School and the Home (1875), is reprinted in Under the Lilacs (1878) and Cheney, p. 32.

6. Fredrika Bremer's Easter Offering (1850); Nathaniel Hawthorne's Scarlet Letter had been published on 16 March 1850.

7. Sarah Siddons was considered by many the greatest English actress of the day.

8. Some of the plays in which Anna and LMA performed are collected in Comic Tragedies Written by "Jo" and "Meg" and Acted by the "Little Women" (Boston: Roberts Brothers, 1893).

9. At a later date, LMA inserted: "Poor as poverty but bound to make things go."

10. "The Rival Painters. A Tale of Rome" appeared in the 8 May 1852 Olive Branch.

1851

Journal.

1851. — We went to a meeting, and heard splendid speaking from Phillips, Channing, and others.[1] People were much excited, and cheered "Shadrack and liberty," groaned for "Webster and slavery," and made a great noise.[2] I felt ready to do anything, — fight or work, hoot or cry, — and laid plans to free Simms. I shall be horribly ashamed of my country if this thing happens and the slave is taken back.

[He was. — L. M. A.][3]

["Notes and Memoranda"]
1851

At High St.[4]

Father trying to talk. Mother had an Intelligence Office.[5] Annie governess at George Minot's.[6] I at Lovering's as governess.[7] Lizzie housekeeper, Ab at school. Poor as rats & apparently quite forgotten by every one but the Lord.

I go to Dedham as a servant & try it for a month, but get starved & frozen & give it up.[8] $4,00

A Masked Marriage.	10,
Dedham — servant.	4,
Lovering — governess.	40
Sewing & seamstress.	40[9]

SOURCES: Text — Cheney, p. 67; "Notes and Memoranda" — manuscript, Houghton Library, Harvard University.

    1. For the meeting with the reform ministers William Henry Channing and Wendell Phillips, see the entry for 8 April 1851 in Bronson's *Journals*, p. 245.

    2. The politician Daniel Webster's support of the Compromise of 1850 and the resulting

Fugitive Slave Act, which would return slaves who had fled north to their masters in the South, caused Massachusetts to turn against him. Shadrach had the dubious honor of being the first person arrested under the new act, on the morning of 15 February 1851. He was rescued from the Boston Courthouse the same afternoon and spirited to Concord, the first stop on the Underground Railroad for Canada, where he later arrived safely.

3. Thomas Sims was arrested on 3 April 1851 and returned under heavy guard to his master, in Virginia.

4. The Alcotts rented rooms at 50 High Street in Boston.

5. Mrs. Alcott ran an intelligence, or employment, office for people desiring domestic help.

6. Possibly George Minot, a farmer in Concord and friend of both Emerson and Thoreau.

7. LMA tutored the children of Mr. and Mrs. Joseph S. Lovering in Boston.

8. LMA fictionalized her brief stint as a domestic in Dedham in "How I Went Out to Service. A Story" in the 4 June 1874 *Independent*.

9. "A Masked Marriage" appeared in the 18 December 1852 *Dodge's Literary Museum*.

1852

1852. — *High Street, Boston.* — After the small-pox summer, we went to a house in High Street. Mother opened an intelligence office, which grew out of her city missionary work and a desire to find places for good girls. It was not fit work for her, but it paid; and she always did what came to her in the way of duty or charity, and let pride, taste, and comfort suffer for love's sake.

Anna and I taught;[1] Lizzie was our little housekeeper, — our angel in a cellar kitchen; May went to school; father wrote and talked when he could get classes or conversations. Our poor little home had much love and happiness in it, and was a shelter for lost girls, abused wives, friendless children, and weak or wicked men. Father and Mother had no money to give, but gave them time, sympathy, help; and if blessings would make them rich, they would be millionaires. This is practical Christianity.

My first story was printed, and $5 paid for it.[2] It was written in Concord when I was sixteen. Great rubbish! Read it aloud to sisters, and when they praised it, not knowing the author, I proudly announced her name.

Made a resolution to read fewer novels, and those only of the best. List of books I like: —

> Carlyle's French Revolution and Miscellanies.
> Hero and Hero-Worship.
> Goethe's poems, plays, and novels.
> Plutarch's Lives.
> Madame Guion.
> Paradise Lost and Comus.
> Schiller's Plays.
> Madame de Staël.
> Bettine.

67

Louis XIV.
Jane Eyre.
Hypatia.
Philothea.
Uncle Tom's Cabin.
Emerson's Poems. [3]

["Notes and Memoranda"]
1852.

Still at High St.

Father idle, mother at work in the office, Nan & I governessing, Lizzie in the kitchen, Ab doing nothing but grow.

Hard times for all.

School.	75
Rival Prima Donnas.	10
Sewing.	20 [4]

SOURCES: Text — Cheney, pp. 67–68; "Notes and Memoranda" — manuscript, Houghton Library, Harvard University. A two-page account of events during May and November 1852, listing additional works read by LMA, is at the Houghton Library, Harvard University.

1. May's diary for 8 November 1852 notes that "Anna and Louisa have but five scholars but hope to [have] more soon" (Houghton Library, Harvard University). As with most of the other schools kept by the Alcott girls at this period, it was held in the family parlor.

2. "The Rival Painters."

3. Not previously identified are Thomas Carlyle's *French Revolution* (1837), *Critical and Miscellaneous Essays* (1839), and *On Heroes, Hero-Worship, and the Heroic in History* (1841); for LMA's interest in Goethe's works, see Madeleine B. Stern's introduction to *A Modern Mephistopheles and Taming a Tartar* (New York: Praeger, 1987); the French mystic Jean Marie Bouvier de la Motte Guyon; John Milton's *Paradise Lost* (1667) and *Comus* (1634); the works of Johann Christoph Friedrich von Schiller; Anne Louise Germaine, Baronne de Staël-Holstein, author and friend of Goethe's; Louis XIV, the Sun King, ruler of France in the seventeenth century; Charlotte Brontë's *Jane Eyre* (1847); Charles Kingsley's *Hypatia* (1853); Harriet Beecher Stowe's *Uncle Tom's Cabin* (1852); and Emerson's *Poems* (1847).

4. "The Rival Prima Donnas" appeared in the 11 November 1854 *Saturday Evening Gazette*.

1853

1853. — In January I started a little school, — E[ddie]. W[hipple]., W. A., two L's, two H's, — about a dozen in our parlor.[1] In May, when my school closed, I went to L. as second girl.[2] I needed the change, could do the wash, and was glad to earn my $2 a week. Home in October with $34 for my wages. After two day's rest, began school again with ten children. Anna went to Syracuse to teach;[3] Father to the West to try his luck, — so poor, so hopeful, so serene.[4] God be with him! Mother had several boarders, and May got on well at school. Betty was still the home bird, and had a little romance with C.[5]

Pleasant letters from Father and Anna. A hard year. Summer distasteful and lonely; winter tiresome with school and people I did n't like. I miss Anna, my one bosom friend and comforter.

["Notes and Memoranda"]
1853

, Pinckney St.[6] Father had conversations. Mother took boarders. Nan had a school in the house. I went to Mr May's at Leicester as a servant for the summer. Lizzie helped mother & Ab went to the Bowdoin School.[7] Slowly coming out of the Slough of Despond.

My Earnings

Leicester.	32,
School.	100
Sewing.	25

SOURCES: Text — Cheney, p. 69; "Notes and Memoranda" — manuscript, Houghton Library, Harvard University.

1. LMA began the year with "a school of ten children from the ages of 8 to five years" who were "[p]leasant children — not difficult to control — and seem to love her exceedingly — " (n.d., Mrs. Alcott's diary, Houghton Library, Harvard University).

2. Probably at the house of Samuel May, Samuel Joseph May's cousin, who was the Unitarian minister in Leicester, Massachusetts.

3. In the fall of 1853 Anna obtained, with Samuel Joseph May's help, a teaching position at Mrs. Sullivan's school in Syracuse, New York.

4. With the gift of eighteen dollars from Emerson, Bronson left on 25 October for a midwestern tour, from which he returned in February 1854.

5. Katharine Anthony suggests that this was a "slight flurry" with one of LMA's pupils, "the son of a friend of the family who came from Beacon Street for lessons once a week" (*Louisa May Alcott* [New York: Alfred A. Knopf, 1938], p. 85).

6. The Alcotts moved to 21 Pinckney Street in Boston.

7. May entered the Bowdoin Street Grammar School, "her first admission to the Boston Public Schools," on 5 January 1853 (Bronson's "Diary for 1853," p. 19, Houghton Library, Harvard University). Mrs. Alcott hoped she would continue there "untill She is well qualified for teaching in the elementary or primary departments of our Schools. She bears the drill of the formal education better than the other girls would have done" (n.d., diary, Houghton Library, Harvard University). Her parents planned for her to graduate in two and a half years, when she would be fifteen years old.

1854

1854. — *Pinckney Street.* — I have neglected my journal for months, so must write it up. School for me month after month.[1] Mother busy with boarders and sewing. Father doing as well as a philosopher can in a money-loving world. Anna at S[yracuse].

I earned a good deal by sewing in the evening when my day's work was done.

In February Father came home. Paid his way, but no more. A dramatic scene when he arrived in the night. We were waked by hearing the bell. Mother flew down, crying "My husband!" We rushed after, and five white figures embraced the half-frozen wanderer who came in hungry, tired, cold, and disappointed, but smiling bravely and as serene as ever. We fed and warmed and brooded over him, longing to ask if he had made any money, but no one did till little May said, after he had told all the pleasant things, "Well, did people pay you?" Then, with a queer look, he opened his pocket-book and showed one dollar, saying with a smile that made our eyes fill, "Only that! My overcoat was stolen, and I had to buy a shawl. Many promises were not kept, and travelling is costly; but I have opened the way, and another year shall do better."

I shall never forget how beautifully Mother answered him, though the dear, hopeful soul had built much on his success; but with a beaming face she kissed him, saying, "I call that doing *very well.* Since you are safely home, dear, we don't ask anything more."

Anna and I choked down our tears, and took a little lesson in real love which we never forgot, nor the look that the tired man and the tender woman gave one another. It was half tragic and comic, for Father was very dirty and sleepy, and Mother in a big nightcap and funny old jacket.

[I began to see the strong contrasts and the fun and follies in every-day life about this time. — L. M. A.]

Anna came home in March. Kept our school all summer. I got "Flower Fables" ready to print.[2]

["Notes and Memoranda"]
1854.

Pinckney St. Father went West & did well in his line. Mother still took boarders. Nan went to teach Mr Sedgwick's children at Syracuse.[3] I took the home school. Lizzie still little Cinderella & Ab at school getting prizes for drawing. Burns mob.[4] Flower Fables came out Dec 4th & did well, but I only got a very small sum for them owing to Mr Briggs' dishonesty.[5]

School.	100
Sewing.	10
Flower Fables.	35

SOURCES: Text — Cheney, pp. 69–70; "Notes and Memoranda" — manuscript, Houghton Library, Harvard University.

1. Bronson described the school as "a pleasant one of some dozen or fourteen little children, and the profits to all worth naming, they, the teachers, getting good experiences." He estimated that the school brought in eighty dollars a quarter (letter of 13 July 1854 to Mrs. Anna Alcott, *Letters*, p. 183).

2. *Flower Fables* was published in December 1854 by George W. Briggs of Boston.

3. Anna was in Syracuse teaching the children of Charles Sedgwick from June through at least December (see Bronson's "Diary for 1854," p. 306, Houghton Library, Harvard University).

4. After the arrest of Anthony Burns on 24 May 1854, a mob, including Bronson Alcott, tried to gain entry to the Boston courthouse to free him but was repulsed. Burns was returned to his master, in Virginia.

5. No evidence is available to indicate how or if George W. Briggs was unfair to LMA in publishing *Flower Fables*.

1855

Twenty-two Years Old.

PINCKNEY STREET, BOSTON, *Jan.* 1, 1855. — The principal event of the winter is the appearance of my book "Flower Fables." An edition of sixteen hundred. It has sold very well, and people seem to like it. I feel quite proud that the little tales that I wrote for Ellen E. when I was sixteen should now bring money and fame. [1]

I will put in some of the notices as "varieties." Mothers are always foolish over their first-born.

Miss Wealthy Stevens paid for the book, and I received $32. [2]

[A pleasing contrast to the receipts of six months only in 1886, being $8000 for the sale of books, and no new one; but I was prouder over the $32 than the $8000. — L. M. A., 1886.]

April, 1855. — I am in the garret with my papers round me, and a pile of apples to eat while I write my journal, plan stories, and enjoy the patter of rain on the roof, in peace and quiet.

[Jo in the garret. — L. M. A.]

Being behindhand, as usual, I'll make note of the main events up to date, for I don't waste ink in poetry and pages of rubbish now. I've begun to *live,* and have no time for sentimental musing.

In October I began my school; Father talked, Mother looked after her boarders, and tried to help everybody. Anna was in Syracuse teaching Mrs. S[edgwick]'s children.

My book came out; and people began to think that topsey-turvey Louisa would amount to something after all, since she could do so well as house-maid, teacher, seamstress, and story-teller. Perhaps she may.

In February I wrote a story for which C. paid $5, and asked for more. [3]

In March I wrote a farce for W. Warren, and Dr. W. offered it to him; but W. W. was too busy.[4]

Also began another tale, but found little time to work on it, with school, sewing, and house-work. My winter's earnings are, —

School, one quarter	$50
Sewing	$50
Stories	$20

if I am ever paid.

A busy and a pleasant winter, because, though hard at times, I do seem to be getting on a little; and that encourages me.

Have heard Lowell and Hedge lecture,[5] acted in plays, and thanks to our rag-money and good cousin H., have been to the theatre several times, — always my great joy.[6]

Summer plans are yet unsettled. Father wants to go to England: not a wise idea, I think. We shall probably stay here, and A. and I go into the country as governesses. It's a queer way to live, but dramatic, and I rather like it; for we never know what is to come next. We are real "Micawbers," and always "ready for a spring."[7]

I have planned another Christmas book, and hope to be able to write it.[8]

1855. — Cousin L[ouisa]. W[illis]. asks me to pass the summer at Walpole with her.[9] If I can get no teaching, I shall go; for I long for the hills, and can write my fairy tales there.

I delivered my burlesque lecture on "Woman, and Her Position; by Oronthy Bluggage," last evening at Deacon G.'s.[10] Had a merry time, and was asked by Mr. W[arren]. to do it at H. for money.[11] Read "Hamlet" at our club, — my favorite play. Saw Mrs. W. H. Smith about the farce; says she will do it at her benefit.[12]

May. — Father went to C[oncord]. to talk with Mr. Emerson about the England trip.[13] I am to go to Walpole. I have made my own gowns, and had money enough to fit up the girls. So glad to be independent.

[I wonder if $40 fitted up the whole family. Perhaps so, as my wardrobe was made up of old clothes from cousins and friends. — L. M. A.]

WALPOLE, N. H., *June,* 1855. — Pleasant journey and a kind welcome. Lovely place, high among the hills. So glad to run and skip in the woods and up the splendid ravine. Shall write here, I know.

Helped cousin L[ouisa]. in her garden; and the smell of the fresh earth and the touch of green leaves did me good.

Mr. T. came and praised my first book, so I felt much inspired to go and do another.[14] I remember him at Scituate years ago, when he was a young ship-builder and I a curly-haired hoyden of five or six.

Up at five, and had a lovely run in the ravine, seeing the woods wake. Planned a little tale which ought to be fresh and true, as it came at that hour and place, — "King Goldenrod."[15] Have lively days, — writing in A. M., driving in P. M., and fun in eve. My visit is doing me much good.

July, 1855. — Read "Hyperion."[16] On the 16th the family came to live in Mr. W[illis].'s house rent free. No better plan offered, and we were all tired of the city. Here Father can have a garden; Mother can rest and be near her good niece; the children have freedom and fine air; and A[nna]. and I can go from here to our teaching, wherever it may be.

Busy and happy times as we settle in the little house in the lane near by my dear ravine, — plays, picnics, pleasant people, and good neighbors. Fanny Kemble came up, Mrs. Kirkland and others, and Dr. Bellows is the gayest of the gay.[17] We acted the "Jacobite," "Rivals," and "Bonnycastles," to an audience of a hundred, and were noticed in the Boston papers.[18] H. T[icknor]. was our manager, and Dr. B[ellows]., D. D., our dramatic director. Anna was the star, her acting being really very fine. I did "Mrs. Malaprop," "Widow Pottle," and the old ladies.[19]

Finished fairy book in September. Anna had an offer from Dr. Wilbur of Syracuse to teach at the great idiot asylum.[20] She disliked it, but decided to go. Poor dear! so beauty-loving, timid, and tender. It is a hard trial; but she is so self-sacrificing she tries to like it because it is duty.

October. — A. to Syracuse. May illustrated my book, and tales called "Christmas Elves."[21] Better than "Flower Fables." Now I must try to sell it.

[Innocent Louisa, to think that a Christmas book could be sold in October. — L. M. A.]

November. — Decided to seek my fortune; so, with my little trunk of home-made clothes, $20 earned by stories sent to the "Gazette," and my MSS., I set forth with Mother's blessing one rainy day in the dullest month in the year.

[My birth-month; always to be a memorable one. — L. M. A.]

Found it too late to do anything with the book, so put it away and tried for teaching, sewing, or any honest work. Won't go home to sit idle while I have a head and pair of hands.

December. — H[amilton]. and L[ouisa]. W[illis]. very kind, and my dear cousins the Sewalls take me in.[22] I sew for Mollie and others, and write stories.[23] C[lapp]. gave me books to notice. Heard Thackeray.[24] Anxious times; Anna very home-sick. Walpole very cold and dull now the summer butterflies have gone. Got $5 for a tale and $12 for sewing; sent home a Christmas-box to cheer the dear souls in the snow-banks.

["Notes and Memoranda"]
1855

Pinckney St. Nan returns from Syracuse, I pass the summer in Walpole writing a new fairy book. In July we move up to live in Mr. Willis' old house. Nan goes back to teach at the Idiot Asylum in Syracuse. In Nov. I go to Boston to support myself & do it by sewing, teaching & writing.

Lizzie & May study at home & mother rests while Father makes a fine garden & tries the West again.

My Earnings

Lovering, Alice	60
Sewing.	15
"Ruth."	10[25]

SOURCES: Text — Cheney, pp. 79–83; "Notes and Memoranda" — manuscript, Houghton Library, Harvard University.

1. Ellen Tucker Emerson (b. 1839), the second child of Ralph Waldo and Lidian Jackson Emerson. LMA dedicated *Flower Fables* to her because she had been the main audience to whom LMA had read earlier versions of the tales in the book. On 21 December 1854, Ellen had written a friend that when she found a copy of the book, which LMA had inscribed to her, she "fell down in a swoon." Concerning its history, she said that LMA thought it was Ellen "who made her publish them for I showed the written ones to Mother who liked them so much she advised Louisa to print a book" (*The Letters of Ellen Tucker Emerson*, ed. Edith E. W. Gregg, 2 vols. [Kent, Ohio: Kent State University Press, 1982], 1:82). The copy of *Flower Fables* inscribed from LMA to Ellen is at the Houghton Library, Harvard University; her letter accompanying it is printed in *SL*, pp. 10–11.

2. Although LMA lists thirty-two dollars as her profits for *Flower Fables* here, she had given the figure as thirty-five dollars in the "Notes and Memoranda" to 1854.

3. William Warland Clapp, Jr., editor of the *Saturday Evening Gazette.*

4. The farce may be *Nat Bachelor's Pleasure Trip*; William Warren, the actor; Dr. Charles May Windship, the only child of Mrs. Alcott's sister Catherine, who was interested in drama and helped LMA gain access to the Boston theatre scene.

5. Both the poet and essayist James Russell Lowell and the minister Frederic Henry Hedge lectured at the Lowell Institute, in Boston, during this time: Lowell gave a series of twenty-four lectures on English poetry and Hedge a series of six lectures on medieval history.

6. Hamilton Willis, son of Mrs. Alcott's sister Elizabeth May Willis and Benjamin Willis, introduced LMA to Thomas Barry, manager of the Boston Theatre. As LMA reported to Anna, Barry told her that "passes were no longer allowed, but whenever I wished to go to the Theatre

if I would write him a note in the morning or come myself I should always have two seats whenever I liked" (6 November [1856], *SL*, p. 24).

7. Wilkins Micawber, in Charles Dickens's *David Copperfield* (1850), was noted for his "something will turn up" faith.

8. Probably *Christmas Elves*; see journal entry for October 1855.

9. The Alcotts moved to Walpole, New Hampshire, in July 1855, where Benjamin Willis allowed them to live rent-free in one of his houses.

10. LMA often used Oronthy Bluggage, inspired from her readings in Dickens, as a persona for writing monologues (see Alfred Whitman, "Miss Alcott's Letters to Her 'Laurie,' " *Ladies' Home Journal*, 18, no. 10 [September 1901]: 5); Samuel Greele, deacon of the Federal Street Church for almost fifty years, married Louisa May, Mrs. Alcott's sister, in 1823.

11. The Howard Athenaeum, in Boston, a theatre.

12. Mrs. William H. Smith, wife of the stage manager of the Boston Museum, performed LMA's *Nat Bachelor's Pleasure Trip* as an afterpiece to her benefit performance of *The Romance of a Poor Young Man* at the Howard Athenaeum on 4 May 1860.

13. Neither Bronson nor Emerson visited England during this time.

14. Howard Ticknor, eldest son of William D. Ticknor of the publishing firm of Ticknor and Fields.

15. "King Goldenrod" is unlocated.

16. Henry Wadsworth Longfellow's *Hyperion* (1839).

17. The famous British actress Frances Kemble Butler; possibly the novelist Caroline Kirkland; the minister Henry Whitney Bellows of New York.

18. *The Jacobite*, a comic drama by James Robinson Planché; Richard Sheridan's *Rivals*; and *The Two Bonnycastles*, a farce by John Maddison Morton, were often performed by the drama groups in Walpole and Concord in which LMA participated. Playbills for two of these plays, performed in the 1856 season, are reproduced in *SL*, following p. 136. A playbill for the 11 September 1855 performance is at Orchard House.

19. Mrs. Malaprop, a character in *The Rivals*; Widow Pottle, a character in *The Jacobite*.

20. Anna taught for a number of years in Dr. Hervey B. Wilbur's asylum in Syracuse, New York. When Bronson visited him in 1857, Wilbur "spoke tenderly of her, dwelt particularly on her goodness, her devotion, and success in winning the love of every one who knew her" (letter of 16 November to Mrs. Alcott, *Letters*, p. 260).

21. LMA's *Christmas Elves*, which May illustrated "very prettily," was completed in November, and Bronson himself helped "arrange and prepare the MS for the press" (8 November, "Diary for 1855," p. 463, Houghton Library, Harvard University). The book was never published, even though Bronson offered it to Phillips, Sampson of Boston (7 May, "Diary for 1856," p. 358, Houghton Library, Harvard University).

22. Thomas Sewall and his family lived at 98 Chestnut Street in Boston and were LMA's close friends during her stays in that city in the 1850s.

23. Molly Sewall, the wife or daughter of Thomas R. Sewall.

24. The English novelist William Makepeace Thackeray gave a series of lectures entitled "Four Georges of England" on 7, 11, 13, and 21 December and lectured separately on charity and humor on 21 December.

25. "Ruth's Secret" did not appear until the 6 December 1856 *Saturday Evening Gazette*.

1856

January, 1856. — C[lapp]. paid $6 for "A Sister's Trial," gave me more books to notice, and wants more tales. [1]

[Should think he would at that price. — L. M. A.]

Sewed for L. W. Sewall and others. [2] Mr. J. M. Field took my farce to Mobile to bring out; Mr. Barry of the Boston Theatre has the play. [3]

Heard Curtis lecture. [4] Began a book for summer, — "Beach Bubbles." [5] Mr. F. of the "Courier" printed a poem of mine on "Little Nell." [6] Got $10 for "Bertha," and saw great yellow placards stuck up announcing it. [7] Acted at the W[indship].'s.

March. — Got $10 for "Genevieve." [8] Prices go up, as people like the tales and ask who wrote them. Finished "Twelve Bubbles." Sewed a great deal, and got very tired; one job for Mr. G. of a dozen pillow-cases, one dozen sheets, six fine cambric neckties, and two dozen handkerchiefs, at which I had to work all one night to get them done, as they were a gift to him. I got only $4.

Sewing won't make my fortune; but I can plan my stories while I work, and then scribble 'em down on Sundays.

Poem on "Little Paul;" Curtis's lecture on "Dickens" made it go well. [9] Hear Emerson on "England." [10]

May. — Anna came on her way home, sick and worn out; the work was too much for her. We had some happy days visiting about. Could not dispose of B[each]. B[ubbles]. in book form, but C[lapp]. took them for his paper. Mr. Field died, so the farce fell through there. Altered the play for Mrs. Barrow to bring out next winter. [11]

78

June, 1856. — Home, to find dear Betty [i.e., Lizzie] very ill with scarlet-fever caught from some poor children Mother nursed when they fell sick, living over a cellar where pigs had been kept. The landlord (a deacon) would not clean the place till Mother threatened to sue him for allowing a nuisance. Too late to save two of the poor babies or Lizzie and May from the fever.

[L. never recovered, but died of it two years later. — L. M. A.]

An anxious time. I nursed, did house-work, and wrote a story
a month through the summer.

Dr. Bellows and Father had Sunday eve conversations. [12]

October. — Pleasant letters from Father, who went on a tour to N.Y., Philadelphia, and Boston.

Made plans to go to Boston for the winter, as there is nothing to do here, and there I can support myself and help the family. C[lapp]. offers 10 dollars a month, and perhaps more. L[ouisa]. W[illis]., M[olly]. S[ewall]., and others, have plenty of sewing; the play *may* come out, and Mrs. R[eed]. will give me a skyparlor for $3 a week, with fire and board. [13] I sew for her also.

If I can get A[lice]. L[overing]. to governess I shall be all right.

I was born with a boy's spirit under my bib and tucker. I *can't wait* when I *can work*; so I took my little talent in my hand and forced the world again, braver than before and wiser for my failures.

[Jo in N.Y. — L. M. A.]

I don't often pray in words; but when I set out that day with all my worldly goods in the little old trunk, my own earnings ($25) in my pocket, and much hope and resolution in my soul, my heart was very full, and I said to the Lord, "Help us all, and keep us for one another," as I never said it before, while I looked back at the dear faces watching me, so full of love and hope and faith.

BOSTON, *November, 1856. Mrs. David Reed's.* — I find my little room up in the attic very cosey, and a house full of boarders very amusing to study. Mrs. Reed very kind. Fly round and take C[lapp]. his stories. Go to see Mrs. L[overing]. about A[lice]. Don't want me. A blow, but I cheer up and hunt for sewing. Go to hear Parker, and he does me good. [14] Asks me to come Sunday evenings to his house. I did go there, and met Phillips, Garrison, Hedge, [15] and other great men, and sit in my corner weekly, staring and enjoying myself.

When I went Mr. Parker said, "God bless you, Louisa; come again;" and the grasp of his hand gave me courage to face another anxious week.

November 3d. — Wrote all the morning. In the P. M. went to see the Sumner reception as he comes home after the Brooks affair.[16] I saw him pass up Beacon Street, pale and feeble, but smiling and bowing. I rushed to Hancock Street, and was in time to see him bring his proud old mother to the window when the crowd gave three cheers for her. I cheered too, and was very much excited. Mr. Parker met him somewhere before the ceremony began, and the above P. cheered like a boy; and Sumner laughed and nodded as his friend pranced and shouted, bareheaded and beaming.

My kind cousin, L[ouisa]. W[illis]., got tickets for a course of lectures on "Italian Literature,"[17] and seeing my old cloak sent me a new one, with other needful and pretty things such as girls love to have. I shall never forget how kind she has always been to me.

November 5th. — Went with H[amilton]. W[illis]. to see Manager Barry about the everlasting play which is always coming out but never comes. We went all over the great new theater, and I danced a jig on the immense stage. Mr. B. was very kind, and gave me a pass to come whenever I liked. This was such richness I did n't care if the play was burnt on the spot, and went home full of joy. In the eve I saw La Grange as Norma,[18] and felt as if I knew all about that place. Quite stage-struck, and imagined myself in her place, with white robes and oak-leaf crown.

November 6th. — Sewed happily on my job of twelve sheets for H. W., and put lots of good will into the work after his kindness to me.

Walked to Roxbury to see cousin Dr. W[indship]. about the play and tell the fine news. Rode home in the new cars, and found them very nice.

In the eve went to teach at Warren Street Chapel Charity School. I'll help as I am helped, if I can. Mother says no one so poor he can't do a little for some one poorer yet.

Sunday. — Heard Parker on "Individuality of Character," and liked it very much.[19] In the eve I went to his house. Mrs. Howe was there,[20] and Sumner and others. I sat in my usual corner, but Mr. P. came up and said, in that cordial way of his, "Well, child, how goes it?" "Pretty well, sir." "That's brave;" and with his warm hand-shake he went on, leaving me both proud and happy, though I have my trials. He is like a great fire where all can come and be warmed and comforted. Bless him!

Had a talk at tea about him, and fought for him when W. R. said he was not a Christian. He is my *sort;* for though he may lack reverence for other people's God, he works bravely for his own, and turns his back on no one who needs help, as some of the pious do.

Monday, 14th. — May came full of expectation and joy to visit good aunt B.[21] and study drawing. We walked about and had a good home talk, then my girl went off to Auntie's to begin what I hope will be a pleasant and profitable winter. She needs help to develop her talent, and I can't give it to her.

Went to see Forrest as Othello.[22] It is funny to see how attentive all the once cool gentlemen are to Miss Alcott now she has a pass to the new theatre.

November 29th. — My birthday. Felt forlorn so far from home. Wrote all day. Seem to be getting on slowly, so should be contented. To a little party at the B[ond].'s in the eve. May looked very pretty, and seemed to be a favorite. The boys teased me about being an authoress, and I said I'd be famous yet. Will if I can, but something else may be better for me.

Found a pretty pin from Father and a nice letter when I got home. Mr. H. brought them with letters from Mother and Betty, so I went to bed happy.

December. — Busy with Christmas and New Year's tales.[23] Heard a good lecture by E. P. Whipple on "Courage."[24] Thought I needed it, being rather tired of living like a spider, — spinning my brains out for money.

Wrote a story, "The Cross on the Church Tower," suggested by the tower before my window.[25]

Called on Mrs. L[overing]., and she asked me to come and teach A[lice]. for three hours each day. Just what I wanted; and the children's welcome was very pretty and comforting to "Our Olly," as they call me.

Now board is all safe, and something over for home, if stories and sewing fail. I don't do much, but can send little comforts to Mother and Betty, and keep May neat.

December 18th. — Begin with A[lice]. L[overing]., in Beacon Street. I taught C[harly]. when we lived in High Street, A[nna]. in Pinckney Street, and now Al[ice].; so I seem to be an institution and a success, since I can start the boy, teach one girl, and take care of the little invalid.[26] It is hard work, but I can do it; and am glad to sit in a large, fine room part of each day, after my sky-parlor, which has nothing pretty in it, and only the gray tower and blue sky outside as I sit at the window writing. I love luxury, but freedom and independence better.

["Notes and Memoranda"]

1856

Walpole. I pass the winter at Mrs Reed's taking care of myself & sending money home.

Annie left Syracuse sick & in the spring we both went home to find Lizzie very ill. A sad summer. [27]

"Genevieve."	10
"Sister's Trial."	10
Bertha.	10
Mabel's Mayday.	10
Painter's Dream.	10
Woman vs Lady.	10
Sewing.	25
Lovering.	60 [28]

SOURCES: Text — Cheney, pp. 83–88; "Notes and Memoranda" — manuscript, Houghton Library, Harvard University.

1. "The Sisters' Trial" appeared in the 26 January 1856 *Saturday Evening Gazette*.

2. Probably Louisa Winslow Sewall, Samuel E. Sewall's daughter.

3. Joseph M. Field, the prolific dramatist of the Mobile Theatre Company; Barry was considering LMA's adaptation of *The Rival Prima Donnas*, which he eventually declined to produce.

4. During this period, the novelist and essayist George William Curtis was delivering a series of six lectures called "Contemporaneous English Fiction" at the Lowell Institute, in Boston.

5. "Beach Bubbles," a series of poems, appeared in seven weekly installments between 21 June and 23 August 1856 in the *Saturday Evening Gazette*.

6. "Little Nell," a poem based on Charles Dickens's *Old Curiosity Shop*, appeared in the 15 March 1856 *Boston Courier*, which was edited by E. B. Foster.

7. "Bertha" appeared in the 19 and 26 April 1856 issues of the *Saturday Evening Gazette*. A picture of one of the "great yellow placards" appears in the present edition, following p. 164.

8. "Little Genevieve" appeared in the 29 March 1856 *Saturday Evening Gazette*.

9. "Little Paul" appeared in the 19 April 1856 *Saturday Evening Gazette*.

10. Emerson lectured on English civilization at the Freeman Place Chapel in Boston on 27 March 1856.

11. The English actress Mrs. Julia Bennett Barrow.

12. A ticket for Bronson's conversations, dated 20 August 1856, announces five meetings in the series "Private Life; Its Genius, Opportunities, and Influences" (Houghton Library, Harvard University). The conversation for 30 August 1856 is reported in Bronson's *Journals*, pp. 283–284.

13. LMA moved in October 1856 to Mrs. Mary Ann Reed's boardinghouse at 34 Chauncy

Street, which she later depicted as Mrs. Kirke's house in *Little Women*, where "Jo's garret" was located. Her husband, David Reed, published the *Christian Register*.

14. The minister and reformer Theodore Parker, whom LMA considered one of her mentors, as the many references to him in *SL* demonstrate. He was the model for Mr. Power in *Work*.

15. Not previously identified is the reformer William Lloyd Garrison. LMA describes one of these meetings in a letter to Anna Alcott of 6 November [1856], in *SL*, p. 21.

16. Charles Sumner, U.S. senator from Massachusetts, returned to Boston after his caning on the floor of the Senate by Preston S. Brooks of South Carolina. LMA describes his welcome in a letter to Anna Alcott of 6 November [1856], in *SL*, pp. 21–22.

17. Professor Guglielmo Gajani of the University of Bologna began delivering a series of six lectures entitled "The Early Italian Reformers" at the Lowell Institute on 5 November.

18. Anna Caroline de la Grange, whom LMA described as "a fine 'Norma', a classic looking woman, & acted as beautifully as she sang" (letter to Anna Alcott, 6 November [1856], *SL*, p. 24).

19. Theodore Parker lectured at the Music Hall in Boston on 9 November 1856; his topic was the value of individuality in spirit (Parker's "Preaching Record," Boston Public Library).

20. Julia Ward Howe, wife of Parker's friend Samuel Gridley Howe and later author of "The Battle Hymn of the Republic."

21. Louisa Caroline Greenwood May, adopted daughter of Joseph May, became the second wife of George William Bond in 1843.

22. Edwin Forrest, the famous American Shakespearean actor, was engaged for a long run at the Boston Theatre, which included a number of performances of Shakespeare. As LMA described him, "Tho Forrest does not act Shakespere well the beauty of the play shines thro the badly represented parts, & imagining what I should like to see, I can make up a better Macbeth & Hamlet for myself than Forrest with his gaspings & shoutings can give me" (letter to Bronson, 28 November [1855], *SL*, p. 14).

23. Possibly "New Year's Gift," listed in the 1857 "Notes and Memoranda" but unlocated.

24. The critic Edwin Percy Whipple lectured on courage at the Tremont Temple on 10 December.

25. "The Cross on the Old Church Tower" appeared in *On Picket Duty, and Other Tales* (1863).

26. LMA describes the Loverings' children in a letter to Anna Alcott of [28–31] December [1856], in *SL*, p. 30.

27. At a later date, LMA inserted: "Wrote many tales for the Gazette for $10 apiece. Sewed for Miss W. Stevens & L. Willis & taught Alice Lovering again."

28. "Mabel's May Day" appeared in the 24 May 1856 *Saturday Evening Gazette*; "The Lady and the Woman" appeared in the 4 October 1856 *Saturday Evening Gazette*; "Painter's Dream" is unlocated.

1857

Twenty-four Years Old.

January, 1857. — Had my first new silk dress from good little L[ouisa]. W[illis]., — very fine; and I felt as if all the Hancocks and Quincys beheld me as I went to two parties in it on New Year's eve.[1]

A busy, happy month, — taught, wrote, sewed, read aloud to the "little mother," and went often to the theatre; heard good lectures; and enjoyed my Parker evenings very much.

Father came to see me on his way home; little money; had had a good time, and was asked to come again.[2] Why don't rich people who enjoy his talk pay for it? Philosophers are always poor, and too modest to pass round their own hats.

Sent by him a good bundle to the poor Forlornites among the ten-foot drifts in W[alpole].

February. — Ran home as a valentine on the 14th.

March. — Have several irons in the fire now, and try to keep 'em all hot.

April. — May did a crayon head of Mother with Mrs. Murdock; very good likeness.[3] All of us as proud as peacocks of our "little Raphael."
Heard Mrs. Butler read; very fine.[4]

May. — Left the L[overing].'s with my thirty-three dollars; glad to rest. May went home with her picture, happy in her winter's work and success.

Father had three talks at W. F. Channing's.[5] Good company, — Emerson, Mrs. Howe, and the rest.

Saw young Booth in Brutus, and liked him better than his father;[6] went about and rested after my labors; glad to be with Father, who enjoyed Boston and friends.

Home on the 10th, passing Sunday at the Emerson's. I have done what I planned, — supported myself, written eight stories, taught four months, earned a hundred dollars, and sent money home.

June. — All happy together. My dear Nan was with me, and we had good times. Betty was feeble, but seemed to cheer up for a time. The long, cold, lonely winter has been too hard for the frail creature, and we are all anxious about her. I fear she may slip away; for she never seemed to care much for this world beyond home.

Read Charlotte Bronte's life.[7] A very interesting, but sad one. So full of talent; and after working long, just as success, love, and happiness come, she dies.

Wonder if I shall ever be famous enough for people to care to read my story and struggles. I can't be a C. B., but I may do a little something yet.

July. — Grandma Alcott came to visit us.[8] A sweet old lady; and I am glad to know her, and see where Father got his nature. Eighty-four; yet very smart, industrious, and wise. A house needs a grandma in it.

As we sat talking over Father's boyhood, I never realized so plainly before how much he has done for himself. His early life sounded like a pretty old romance, and Mother added the love passages.

I got a hint for a story; and some day will do it, and call it "The Cost of an Idea."[9] Spindle Hill, Temple School, Fruitlands, Boston, and Concord, would make fine chapters.[10] The trials and triumphs of the Pathetic Family would make a capital book; may I live to do it.

August. — A sad, anxious month. Betty worse; Mother takes her to the seashore. Father decides to go back to Concord; he is never happy far from Emerson, the one true friend who loves and understands and helps him.

September. — An old house near R. W. E.'s is bought with Mother's money, and we propose to move.[11] Mother in Boston with poor Betty, who is failing fast. Anna and I have a hard time breaking up.

October. — Move to Concord. Take half a house in town till spring, when the old one is to be ready.[12]

Find dear Betty a shadow, but sweet and patient always. Fit up a nice room for her, and hope home and love and care may keep her.

People kind and friendly, and the old place looks pleasant, though I never want to live in it.

November. — Father goes West, taking Grandma home. We settle down to our winter, whatever it is to be. Lizzie seems better, and we have some plays. Sanborn's school makes things lively, and we act a good deal.[13]

Twenty-five this month. I feel my quarter of a century rather heavy on my shoulders just now. I lead two lives. One seems gay with plays, etc., the other very sad, — in Betty's room; for though she wishes us to act, and loves to see us get ready, the shadow is there, and Mother and I see it. Betty loves to have me with her; and I am with her at night, for Mother needs rest. Betty says she feels "strong" when I am near. So glad to be of use.

December. — Some fine plays for charity.[14]

["Notes and Memoranda"]
1857

Walpole. I pass the winter & Ab at Auntie's taking music & drawing lessons. Father talking in N.Y. Ma Nan & Lizzie freezing in Walpole. Grandma came. Buy a place in Concord & move Sept 2ond. Lizzie ill.[15] a busy sad winter.

Lovering.	60
Sewing.	20
"Agatha's Confession."	10
Our Sunbeam.	10
Cross On The Tower.	10
New Year's Gift.	5
Pea Blossoms.	10[16]

SOURCES: Text — Cheney, pp. 90–92, 95–96; "Notes and Memoranda" — manuscript, Houghton Library, Harvard University.

1. LMA describes her joy at receiving the dress in a letter to Anna Alcott of [28–31] December [1856], in *SL,* pp. 28–29; Mrs. Alcott's great-aunt Dorothy Quincy married John Hancock and was known in family tradition as Madame Hancock.

2. Mrs. Alcott's diary states that Bronson returned home on 1 January and had "realized handsome profits in the sum of $250," but Bronson's journal has him returning home on 30 December with $180 out of the "cash receipts" of $235 "for the tour" (1 January 1857 and 1 January, "Diary for 1857," p. 14, both Houghton Library, Harvard University).

3. Mrs. Murdock, May's art teacher.

4. Frances Kemble Butler gave readings from Shakespeare in Boston on 23, 25, 27, 28, and 30 March, and 1, 3, and 4 April.

5. The reformer William F. Channing. The ticket for Bronson's series of conversations titled "Human Life" lists the dates as 1, 5, and 8 May (Houghton Library, Harvard University). He described these talks in a letter to his wife: "The company is to be select, and limited to some thirty or thirty five persons," including Julia Ward Howe, James Russell Lowell, the poet Henry Wadsworth Longfellow, and May Alcott (29 April 1857, *Letters*, p. 243).

6. The actors Edwin T. Booth and his father, Junius Brutus Booth.

7. Commenting in December 1885, LMA said that her "favorite authors" included Brontë (letter to Viola Price, *SL*, p. 296).

8. Mrs. Joseph Chatfield Alcox, Bronson's mother. The spelling of the family name had been changed in about 1820.

9. "The Cost of an Idea," LMA's attempt at depicting her father's boyhood, was never finished. She again unsuccessfully tried the same idea in "An Old-Fashioned Boy" (see her letter of 29 May [1880] to Mary Mapes Dodge, in *SL*, p. 248).

10. Spindle Hill, Connecticut, where Bronson was born; Bronson's Temple School, in Boston, which flourished in the 1830s.

11. For the purchase from John Moore of what the Alcotts would call Orchard House, see Bronson's letters to Anna, Louisa, and May, 9 and 16 September 1857, *Letters*, pp. 252, 254.

12. The Alcotts lived on Bedford Street, behind Concord Town Hall.

13. Franklin Benjamin Sanborn taught school in Concord from 1855 to 1863. As Ellen Emerson described it, "Mr Alcott and his family have come here to live, and his daughters, perhaps you have heard, have great love and talent for Theatricals. You know how fond of them George Bartlett always was, and how last winter Mr Sanborn became famous in the same way. Well those people have laid their heads together and the result is that a stage has been erected in the Vestry of the Unitarian church, which is to remain there all winter and we are to have a 'Series of Dramatic Entertainments' " (letter of 17 November 1857 to William Emerson, *The Letters of Ellen Tucker Emerson*, ed. Edith E. W. Gregg, 2 vols. [Kent, Ohio: Kent State University Press, 1982], 1:137). For more on LMA's theatrical career, see Madeleine B. Stern, "Louisa Alcott, Trouper," *New England Quarterly*, 16(June 1943): 175–197.

14. On 5 December, Mrs. Alcott wrote her husband that the receipts from the plays totaled twenty-five dollars, which left a net of six dollars for the poor. And on 21 December, Anna wrote her father that "our plays all succeeding finely, & Mr Emerson complimented us highly in all manner of precious words. We shall appear again on Christmas night in 'Scenes from Dickens,' Sanbourne [Sanborn] speaking a fine prologue in the character of 'Yule' old Christmas, & [Ralph Waldo Emerson's daughter] Edith young Christmas, & we're planning to have a good time" (both, Houghton Library, Harvard University).

15. LMA wrote: "Ab dies," then canceled it and wrote: "Lizzie ill."

16. "Agatha's Confession," "Our Sunbeam," and "Pea Blossoms" are unlocated; no appearance of "The Cross on the Old Church Tower" in a periodical has been located.

1858

January, 1858. — Lizzie much worse; Dr. G. says there is no hope.[1] A hard thing to hear; but if she is only to suffer, I pray she may go soon. She was glad to know she was to "get well," as she called it, and we tried to bear it bravely for her sake. We gave up plays; Father came home; and Anna took the housekeeping, so that Mother and I could devote ourselves to her. Sad, quiet days in her room, and strange nights keeping up the fire and watching the dear little shadow try to wile away the long sleepless hours without troubling me. She sews, reads, sings softly, and lies looking at the fire, — so sweet and patient and so worn, my heart is broken to see the change. I wrote some lines one night on "Our Angel in the House."[2]

[Jo and Beth. — L. M. A.]

February. — A mild month; Betty very comfortable, and we hope a little.

Dear Betty is slipping away, and every hour is too precious to waste, so I'll keep my lamentations over Nan's [affairs] till this duty is over.

Lizzie makes little things, and drops them out of windows to the school-children, smiling to see their surprise. In the night she tells me to be Mrs. Gamp, when I give her her lunch, and tries to be gay that I may keep up.[3] Dear little saint! I shall be better all my life for these sad hours with you.

March 14th. — My dear Beth died at three this morning, after two years of patient pain.[4] Last week she put her work away, saying the needle was "too heavy," and having given us her few possessions, made ready for the parting in her own simple, quiet way. For two days she suffered much, begging for ether, though its effect was gone. Tuesday she lay in Father's arms, and called us round her, smiling contentedly as she said, "All here!" I think she bid us good-by then, as she held our hands and kissed us tenderly. Saturday she slept, and at midnight became unconscious, quietly breathing her life away till three; then, with one last look of the beautiful eyes, she was gone.

A curious thing happened, and I will tell it here, for Dr. G. said it was a fact. A few moments after the last breath came, as Mother and I sat silently watching the shadow fall on the dear little face, I saw a light mist rise from the body, and float up and vanish in the air. Mother's eyes followed mine, and when I said, "What did you see?" she described the same light mist. Dr. G. said it was the life departing visibly.

For the last time we dressed her in her usual cap and gown, and laid her on her bed, — at rest at last. What she had suffered was seen in the face; for at twenty-three she looked like a woman of forty, so worn was she, and all her pretty hair gone.

On Monday Dr. Huntington read the Chapel service, and we sang her favorite hymn. Mr. Emerson, Henry Thoreau, Sanborn, and John Pratt, carried her out of the old home to the new one at Sleepy Hollow chosen by herself.[5] So the first break comes, and I know what death means, — a liberator for her, a teacher for us.

April. — Came to occupy one wing of Hawthorne's house (once ours) while the new one was being repaired.[6] Father, Mother, and I kept house together; May being in Boston, Anna at Pratt farm, and, for the first time, Lizzie absent. I don't miss her as I expected to do, for she seems nearer and dearer than before; and I am glad to know she is safe from pain and age in some world where her innocent soul must be happy.

Death never seemed terrible to me, and now is beautiful; so I cannot fear it, but find it friendly and wonderful.

May. — A lonely month with all the girls gone, and Father and Mother absorbed in the old house, which I don't care about, not liking Concord.[7]

On the 7th of April, Anna came walking in to tell us she was engaged to John Pratt; so another sister is gone. J. is a model son and brother, — a true man, — full of fine possibilities, but so modest one does not see it at once. He is handsome, healthy, and happy; just home from the West, and so full of love he is pleasant to look at.

I moaned in private over my great loss, and said I'd never forgive J. for taking Anna from me; but I shall if he makes her happy, and turn to little May for my comfort.

[Now that John is dead, I can truly say we all had cause to bless the day he came into the family; for we gained a son and brother, and Anna the best husband ever known.

For ten years he made her home a little heaven of love and peace; and when he died he left her the legacy of a beautiful life, and an honest name to his little sons. -— L. M. A., 1873.]

June. — The girls came home, and I went to visit L[ouisa]. W[illis]. in Boston. Saw Charlotte Cushman, and had a stagestruck fit.[8] Dr. W[illis]. asked Barry to let me act at his theatre, and he agreed. I was to do Widow Pottle, as the dress was a good disguise and I knew the part well. It was all a secret, and I had hopes of trying a new life; the old one being so changed now, I felt as if I must find interest in something absorbing. But Mr. B. broke his leg, so I had to give it up; and when it was known, the dear, respectable relations were horrified at the idea. I'll try again by-and-by, and see if I have the gift. Perhaps it is acting, not writing, I'm meant for. Nature must have a vent somehow.

July. — Went into the new house and began to settle. Father is happy; Mother glad to be at rest; Anna is in bliss with her gentle John; and May busy over her pictures. I have plans simmering, but must sweep and dust and wash my dish-pans a while longer till I see my way.

Worked off my stage fever in writing a story, and felt better;[9] also a moral tale, and got twenty-five dollars, which pieced up our summer gowns and bonnets all round. The inside of my head can at least cover the outside.

August. — Much company to see the new house. All seem to be glad that the wandering family is anchored at last. We won't move again for twenty years if I can help it. The old people need an abiding place; and now that death and love have taken two of us away, I can, I hope, soon manage to care for the remaining four.

The weeklies will all take stories; and I can simmer novels while I do my housework, so see my way to a little money, and perhaps more by-and-by if I ever make a hit.

October. — Went to Boston on my usual hunt for employment, as I am not needed at home and seem to be the only bread-winner just now.

·　　·　　·　　·　　·　　·　　·　　·

My fit of despair was soon over, for it seemed so cowardly to run away before the battle was over I could n't do it. So I said firmly, "There *is* work for me, and I'll have it," and went home resolved to take Fate by the throat and shake a living out of her.

Sunday Mr. Parker preached a sermon on "Laborious Young Women." Just what I needed; for it said: "Trust your fellow-beings, and let them help you. Don't be too proud to ask, and accept the humblest work till you can find the task you want."

"I will," said I, and went to Mr. P.'s. He was out; but I told Mrs. P. my wants, and she kindly said Theodore and Hannah would be sure to have something for me.[10] As I went home I met Mrs. L[overing]., who had not wanted me, as Alice went to school. She asked if I was engaged, and said A. did not do well, and she thought perhaps they would like me back. I was rejoiced, and went home feeling that the tide had begun to turn. Next day came Miss H. S. to offer me a place at the Girls' Reform School at Lancaster, to sew ten hours a day, make and mend. I said I'd go, as I could do anything with a needle; but added, if Mrs. L. wants me I'd rather do that.

"Of course you had. Take it if it comes, and if not, try my work." I promised and waited. That eve, when my bag was packed and all was ready for Lancaster, came a note from Mrs. L. offering the old salary and the old place. I sang for joy, and next day early posted off to Miss S. She was glad and shook hands, saying "It was a test, my dear, and you stood it. When I told Mr. P. that you would go, he said, 'That is a true girl; Louisa will succeed.' "

I was very proud and happy; for these things are tests of character as well as courage, and I covet the respect of such true people as Mr. P. and Miss S.

So away to my little girl with a bright heart! for with tales and sewing for Mary, which pays my board, there I am fixed for the winter and my cares over. Thank the Lord!

November. — Earned thirty dollars; sent twenty home. Heard Curtis, Parker, Higginson, and Mrs. Dall lecture.[11] See Booth's Hamlet, and my ideal done at last.[12]

My twenty-sixth birthday on the 29th. Some sweet letters from home, and a ring of A[nna].'s and J[ohn].'s hair as a peace-offering. A quiet day, with many thoughts and memories.

The past year has brought us the first death and betrothal, — two events that change my life. I can see that these experiences have taken a deep hold, and changed or developed me. Lizzie helps me spiritually, and a little success makes me more self-reliant. Now that Mother is too tired to be wearied with my moods, I have to manage them alone, and am learning that work of head and hand is my salvation when disappointment or weariness burden and darken my soul.

In my sorrow I think I instinctively came nearer to God, and found comfort in the knowledge that he was sure to help when nothing else could.

A great grief has taught me more than any minister, and when feeling most alone I find refuge in the Almighty Friend. If this is experiencing religion I have done it; but I think it is only the lesson one must learn as it comes, and I am glad to know it.

After my fit of despair I seem to be braver and more cheerful, and grub away with a good heart. Hope it will last, for I need all the courage and comfort I can get.

I feel as if I could write better now, — more truly of things I have felt and therefore *know*. I hope I shall yet do my great book, for that seems to be my work, and I am growing up to it. I even think of trying the "Atlantic." There's ambition for you! I'm sure some of the stories are very flat. If Mr. L. takes the one Father carried to him, I shall think I can do something.[13]

December. — Father started on his tour West full of hope. Dear man! How happy he will be if people will only listen to and *pay* for his wisdom.

May came to B[oston]. and stayed with me while she took drawing lessons.[14] Christmas at home. Write an Indian story.

["Notes and Memoranda"]
1858

Concord. New home preparing. Buy lot at Sleepy Hollow & March 14th Lizzie goes to *her* new home after two years of suffering. We stay at Dr Peabody's till the house is ready.[15] In April Nan is engaged to John Pratt. Pass the summer getting the house in order. In the fall Ab goes to the School of Design. I teach Alice Lovering & stay at Mr Seawall's. The others busy at home & things prospering. No more sewing or going to service for a living, thank the Lord!

My Earnings

Only An Actress.	6
Mark Field.	20
Hope's Treasures.	12
Lovering.	75
Sewing.	10 [16]

SOURCES: Text — Cheney, pp. 96–103; "Notes and Memoranda" — manuscript, Houghton Library, Harvard University.

1. Dr. Christian Geist of Boston attended Lizzie in her last illness. Lizzie had caught scarlet fever in the summer of 1856 while helping a neighbor's sick children and never fully recovered. After a lingering illness, she died on 14 March 1858.

2. "Our Angel in the House" is printed in Cheney, p. 97.

3. In their theatricals, LMA played Sairey Gamp to Anna's Betsey Prig, both characters

from Dickens's *Martin Chuzzlewit* (1844); the two sisters often signed their letters with these names.

4. LMA describes Lizzie's death and burial in a letter to Elizabeth Wells of 19 March [1858], in *SL*, pp. 32–33.

5. The minister Frederic Dan Huntington; John Bridge Pratt, who would become engaged to Anna on 7 April 1858 and marry her on 23 May 1860.

6. The Alcotts moved into a wing of the Wayside while Nathaniel Hawthorne was abroad, serving as U.S. consul at Liverpool, England.

7. Privately, LMA called the house Apple Slump.

8. The actress Charlotte Cushman.

9. "Marion Earle; or, Only an Actress" appeared in *New York Atlas*, 12 September 1858, from the *American Union*; "Only an Actress" appeared also in *Demorest's Monthly Magazine*, April 1876, but is listed in LMA's "Notes and Memoranda" for 1858.

10. Theodore Parker's wife, Lydia Cabot Parker, and his close friend Hannah M. Stevenson. LMA describes this event in a letter to her family of [October 1858] in *SL*, pp. 34–35. LMA's *Hospital Sketches* (1863) is dedicated to Stevenson, who helped get her employment at the Union Hotel Hospital, in Georgetown, during the Civil War.

11. The lectures by George William Curtis and Theodore Parker are unlocated; the minister and reformer Thomas Wentworth Higginson lectured on physical training for Americans on 26 October; the reformer Caroline Healey Dall gave a series of lectures entitled "Woman's Claim to Education" on 1, 8, and 15 November.

12. One attempt at seeing Booth was unsuccessful, and LMA ended up seeing popular comedies instead, which she felt "was better for me than the melancholy Dane, I dare say" (letter to Anna Alcott, November 1858, *SL*, p. 39).

13. James Russell Lowell, editor of the *Atlantic Monthly Magazine*, eventually accepted "Love and Self-Love."

14. LMA was boarding at 98 Chestnut Street in Boston.

15. Nathaniel Peabody, homeopathic physician and brother to the Peabody sisters (Sophia Peabody Hawthorne, Elizabeth Palmer Peabody, Mary Peabody Mann).

16. Probably "Mark Field's Mistake," which appeared in the 12 March 1859 *Saturday Evening Gazette*; "Hope's Treasures" is unlocated.

1859

January, 1859. — Send a parcel home to Marmee and Nan.

Mother very ill. Home to nurse her for a week. Wonder if I ought not to be a nurse, as I seem to have a gift for it. Lizzie, L[ouisa]. W[illis]., and Mother all say so; and I like it. If I could n't write or act I'd try it. May yet. $21 from L[overing].; $15 home.

. . . .

Some day I'll do my best, and get well paid for it.

[$3,000 for a short serial in 1876. True prophet. — L. M. A.]

Wrote a sequel to "Mark Field."[1] Had a queer time over it, getting up at night to write it, being too full to sleep.

March. — "Mark" was a success, and much praised. So I found the divine afflatus did descend. Busy life teaching, writing, sewing, getting all I can from lectures, books, and good people. Life is my college. May I graduate well, and earn some honors!

April. — May went home after a happy winter at the School of Design, where she did finely, and was pronounced full of promise.[2] Mr. T. said good things of her, and we were very proud. No doubt now what she is to be, if we can only keep her along.

I went home also, being done with A[lice]., who went out of town early. Won't teach any more if I can help it; don't like it; and if I can get writing enough can do much better.

I have done more than I hoped. Supported myself, helped May, and sent something home. Not borrowed a penny, and had only five dollars given me. So my third campaign ends well.

May. — Took care of L[ouisa]. W[illis]., who was ill. Walked from C[oncord]. to B[oston]. one day, twenty miles, in five hours, and went to a party in the evening. Not very tired. Well done for a vegetable production!

June. — Took two children to board and teach. A busy month, as Anna was in B[oston].

September. — Great State Encampment here.[3] Town full of soldiers, with military fuss and feathers. I like a camp, and long for a war, to see how it all seems. I can't fight, but I can nurse.

[Prophetic again. — L. M. A.]

October, 1859. — May did a fine copy of Emerson's Endymion for me.[4]
Mother sixty. God bless the dear, brave woman!
Good news of Parker in Florence, — my beloved minister and friend.[5] To him and R. W. E. I owe much of my education. May I be a worthy pupil of such men!

November. — Hurrah! My story was accepted; and Lowell asked if it was not a translation from the German, it was so unlike most tales.[6] I felt much set up, and my fifty dollars will be very happy money. People seem to think it a great thing to get into the "Atlantic;" but I've not been pegging away all these years in vain, and may yet have books and publishers and a fortune of my own. Success has gone to my head, and I wander a little. Twenty-seven years old, and very happy.
The Harper's Ferry tragedy makes this a memorable month.[7] Glad I have lived to see the Antislavery movement and this last heroic act in it. Wish I could do my part in it.

December, 1859. — The execution of Saint John the Just took place on the second. A meeting at the hall, and all Concord was there. Emerson, Thoreau, Father, and Sanborn spoke, and all were full of reverence and admiration for the martyr.[8]
I made some verses on it, and sent them to the "Liberator."[9]

["Notes and Memoranda"]
1859.

Father went West but had bad luck. All at home in the summer with two children to board. Father made superintendent of the schools. John Brown martyred & F. B. S. kidnapped.[10] Nan passed the winter in Boston to be near John. My first tale came out in the Atlantic & my pen began to pay.[11]

Ottilla's Oath.	10
Steel Bracelet.	10
A Phantom Face.	10
Laird of Leigh.	10
Love & Self Love	50
Faith's Tryst.	12 [12]

SOURCES: Text — Cheney, pp. 103–105; "Notes and Memoranda" — manuscript, Houghton Library, Harvard University.

1. "Mark Field's Success" appeared in the 16 April 1859 *Saturday Evening Gazette*.

2. In December 1858, May began studying at the School of Design in Boston under Salisbury Tuckerman, who had been one of Bronson's pupils at the Temple School.

3. Accounts of this encampment of several military units are in "Camp Massachusetts," *Boston Daily Advertiser*, 7 September 1859, p. 1, and in Ellen Emerson's letter of 15 September 1859 to Miss Emma, *The Letters of Ellen Tucker Emerson*, ed. Edith E. W. Gregg, 2 vols. (Kent, Ohio: Kent State University Press, 1982), 1:195.

4. Cheney's note calls this a "fine bas-relief owned by Mr. Emerson" (Cheney, p. 104), although it was probably owned by the Hawthornes. Emerson did own a print of a statue in the Capitoline Museum given him by Samuel Gray Ward.

5. Parker was on a European tour in a last attempt to find relief from the consumption that would cause his death the following year.

6. "Love and Self-Love" appeared in the March 1860 *Atlantic Monthly Magazine*.

7. John Brown attacked the federal arsenal at Harpers Ferry, Virginia, on 16 October and held it for two days before being captured. He was tried and convicted of treason and hanged on 2 December. LMA was "full of admiration for old Brow[n]s courage & pity for his probable end." They were "boiling over with excitement" in Concord "for many of our people (Anti Slavery I mean) are concerned in it. We have a daily stampede for papers, & a nightly indignation meeting over the wickedness of our country, & the cowardice of the human race. I'm afraid mother will die of spontaneous combustion if things are not set right soon" (letter to Alfred Whitman, 8 November [1859], *SL*, p. 49).

8. Bronson called the ceremonies "affecting and impressive; distinguished by modesty, simplicity, and earnestness; worthy alike of the occasion and of the man" (2 December 1859, *Journals*, p. 323). The printed program is reproduced in Milton Meltzer and Walter Harding, *A Thoreau Profile* (New York: Thomas Y. Crowell, 1962), p. 258. Further accounts may be found in the entries for 28 November and 2 December in Bronson's "Diary for 1859," pp. 643–649, 651–658, Houghton Library, Harvard University, and "Services at Concord," in James Redpath, *Echoes of Harper's Ferry* (Boston: Thayer and Eldredge, 1860), pp. 437–454.

9. "With a Rose, That Bloomed on the Day of John Brown's Martyrdom" appeared in the 20 January 1860 *Liberator*.

10. For a description of Sanborn's arrest on 3 April in conjunction with a U.S. Senate hearing about his role in the John Brown affair, see his *Recollections of Seventy Years*, 2 vols. (Boston: Richard G. Badger, 1909), 2:208–212, and "Mr. Sanborn's Account of His Own Arrest," *New York Daily Tribune*, 10 April 1860, p. 6.

11. LMA has written a "+" after "Atlantic," keyed to this comment: "(Atlantic tales marked

with a cross.)" We have not reported her crosses in the "Notes and Memoranda" because the tales appearing in the *Atlantic Monthly Magazine* are identified in the notes.

12. "Ottilla's Oath," "Steel Bracelet," "A Phantom Face," "Laird of Leigh," and "Faith's Tryst" are unlocated.

1860

February, 1860. — Mr. —— won't have "M. L.," as it is antislavery, and the dear South must not be offended.[1] Got a carpet with my $50, and wild Louisa's head kept the feet of the family warm.

March. — Wrote "A Modern Cinderella," with Nan for the heroine and John for the hero.[2]

Made my first ball dress for May, and she was the finest girl at the party. My tall, blond, graceful girl! I was proud of her.

Wrote a song for the school festival, and heard it sung by four hundred happy children.[3] Father got up the affair, and such a pretty affair was never seen in Concord before. He said, "We spend much on our cattle and flower shows; let us each spring have a show of our children, and begrudge nothing for their culture." All liked it but the old fogies who want things as they were in the ark.

April. — Made two riding habits, and May and I had some fine rides. Both needed exercise, and this was good for us. So one of our dreams came true, and we really did "dash away on horseback."[4]

Sanborn was nearly kidnapped for being a friend of John Brown; but his sister and A. W. rescued him when he was handcuffed, and the scamps drove off.[5] Great ferment in town. A meeting and general flurry.

Had a funny lover who met me in the cars, and said he lost his heart at once. Handsome man of forty. A Southerner, and very demonstrative and gushing, called and wished to pay his addresses; and being told I did n't wish to see him, retired, to write letters and haunt the road with his hat off, while the girls laughed and had great fun over Jo's lover. He went at last, and peace reigned. My adorers are all queer.

Sent "Cinderella" to the "Atlantic," and it was accepted. Began "By the River,"[6] and thought that this was certainly to be a lucky year; for after ten years hard climbing I had reached a good perch on the ladder, and could look more hopefully into the future, while my paper boats sailed gaily over the Atlantic.

May. — Meg's [Anna's] wedding.

My farce was acted, and I went to see it.[7] Not very well done; but I sat in a box, and the good Doctor handed up a bouquet to the author, and made as much as he could of a small affair.

Saw Anna's honeymoon home at Chelsea, — a little cottage in a blooming apple-orchard. Pretty place, simple and sweet. God bless it!

The dear girl was married on the 23d, the same day as Mother's wedding.[8] A lovely day; the house full of sunshine, flowers, friends, and happiness. Uncle S. J. May married them, with no fuss, but much love; and we all stood round her. She in her silver-gray silk, with lilies of the valley (John's flower) in her bosom and hair. We in gray thin stuff and roses, — sackcloth, I called it, and ashes of roses; for I mourn the loss of my Nan, and am not comforted. We have had a little feast, sent by good Mrs. Judge Shaw;[9] then the old folks danced round the bridal pair on the lawn in the German fashion, making a pretty picture to remember, under our Revolutionary elm.

Then, with tears and kisses, our dear girl, in her little white bonnet, went happily away with her good John; and we ended our first wedding. Mr. Emerson kissed her; and I thought that honor would make even matrimony endurable, for he is the god of my idolatry, and has been for years.

June. — To Boston to the memorial meeting for Mr. Parker, which was very beautiful, and proved how much he was beloved.[10] Music Hall was full of flowers and sunshine, and hundreds of faces, both sad and proud, as the various speakers told the life of love and labor which makes Theodore Parker's memory so rich a legacy to Boston. I was very glad to have known so good a man, and been called friend by him.

Saw Nan in her nest, where she and her mate live like a pair of turtle doves. Very sweet and pretty, but I'd rather be a free spinster and paddle my own canoe.

August. — "Moods." Genius burned so fiercely that for four weeks I wrote all day and planned nearly all night, being quite possessed by my work.[11] I was perfectly happy, and seemed to have no wants. Finished the book, or a rough draught of it, and put it away to settle. Mr. Emerson offered to read it when Mother told him it was "Moods" and had one of his sayings for motto.[12]

Daresay nothing will ever come of it; but it *had* to be done, and I'm the richer for a new experience.

September. — Received $75 of Ticknor for "Cinderella," and feel very rich. Emerson praised it, and people wrote to me about it and patted me on the head. Paid bills, and began to simmer another.

October. — I went to B[oston]. and saw the Prince of Wales trot over the Common with his train at a review.[13] A yellow-haired laddie very like his mother. Fanny W. and I nodded and waved as he passed, and he openly winked his boyish eye at us; for Fanny, with her yellow curls and wild waving, looked rather rowdy, and the poor little prince wanted some fun. We laughed, and thought that we had been more distinguished by the saucy wink than by a stately bow. Boys are always jolly, — even princes.

Read Richter, and enjoyed him very much.[14]

Mother went to see Uncle S. J. May, and I was housekeeper. Gave my mind to it so energetically that I dreamed dip-toast, talked apple-sauce, thought pies, and wept drop-cakes. Read my book to Nan, who came up to cheer me in my struggles; and she laughed and cried over it and said it was "good." So I felt encouraged, and will touch it up when duty no longer orders me to make a burnt-offering of myself.

November. — Father sixty-one; L. aged twenty-eight. Our birthday. Gave Father a ream of paper, and he gave me Emerson's picture; so both were happy.

Wrote little, being busy with visitors. The John Brown Association asked me for a poem, which I wrote.[15]

Kind Miss R. sent May $30 for lessons, so she went to B[oston]. to take some of Johnstone.[16] She is one of the fortunate ones, and gets what she wants easily. I have to grub for my help, or go without it. Good for me, doubtless, or it would n't be so; so cheer up, Louisa, and grind away!

December. — More luck for May. She wanted to go to Syracuse and teach, and Dr. W[ilbur]. sends for her, thanks to Uncle S. J. May. I sew like a steam-engine for a week, and get her ready. On the 17th go to B[oston]. and see our youngest start on her first little flight alone into the world, full of hope and courage.[17] May all go well with her!

Mr. Emerson invited me to his class when they meet to talk on Genius; a great honor, as all the learned ladies go.

Sent "Debby's Debut" to the "Atlantic," and they took it.[18] Asked to the John Brown meeting, but had no "good gown," so did n't go; but my "pome" did, and came out in the paper. Not good. I'm a better patriot than poet, and could n't say what I felt.

A quiet Christmas; no presents but apples and flowers. No merry-making; for Nan and May were gone, and Betty under the snow. But we are used to hard times, and, as Mother says, "while there is a famine in Kansas we must n't ask for sugar-plums."

All the philosophy in our house is not in the study; a good deal is in the kitchen, where a fine old lady thinks high thoughts and does kind deeds while she cooks and scrubs.

["Notes and Memoranda"]
1860

Father had Conversations in B[oston]. Ab began to mould in clay. Mr Searle boarded with us. School festival & father's fine Report.[19] My Farce played at the Howard in B[oston]. Nan married May 23rd. Settled in Chelsea. Parker dies & Hawthorne returns to C[oncord]. Severance boards.[20] Ab to Syracuse as teacher.

Morning Glories.	15
A Modern Cinderella.	75
Debby's Debut.	50
Monk's Island.	10[21]

SOURCES: Text — Cheney, pp. 120–124; "Notes and Memoranda" — manuscript, Houghton Library, Harvard University.

1. Possibly James Russell Lowell, editor of the *Atlantic Monthly Magazine*, which later raised similar objections to the antislavery aspect of LMA's "My Contraband"; "M. L." appeared in five installments between 24 January and 22 February in the *Boston Commonwealth*.

2. "A Modern Cinderella; or, The Little Old Shoe" appeared in the October 1860 *Atlantic Monthly Magazine*.

3. LMA's "Children's Song" contained descriptions of her Concord neighbors, including Thoreau as "the Hermit of blue Walden" and Emerson as the "Poet of the pines" (see Bronson to his mother, 12 April 1860, *Letters*, p. 311). A copy of the broadside printing of the poem is in Mrs. Alcott's diary, April 1860, Houghton Library, Harvard University; it is also printed in Cheney, pp. 110–111.

4. May wrote Alfred Whitman after one of these outings that "I shall . . . (if my wrist will allow me for it being Fast Day I have spent most of it on horseback, & my hand trembles so I can hardly write,) answer your letter" (5 April [1860], Houghton Library, Harvard University).

5. Sanborn's sister, Sarah, who was presented with a revolver for her actions; Annie Whiting, daughter of Colonel William Whiting of Concord. LMA describes this event in a letter to Alfred Whitman of 5 April [1860] in *SL*, p. 53.

6. "By the River" did not appear until the 10 June 1875 *Independent*.

7. *Nat Bachelor's Pleasure Trip*.

8. Anna Alcott married John Bridge Pratt, son of Brook Farmer Minot Pratt, on 23 May, the same date on which Abigail and Bronson had been married. In attendance were the Alcotts and Pratts, Lidian and Ralph Waldo Emerson, Sanborn, Thoreau, and Elizabeth Palmer Peabody (Boston reformer and longtime acquaintance of the Alcotts and Emersons). The marriage was performed by Samuel Joseph May, assisted by Ephraim Bull, since May was not a licensed minister in Middlesex County (Carrie Pratt to Alfred Whitman, 19 June [1860], Houghton Library, Harvard University). The marriage certificate is at Orchard House.

9. Hope Savage Shaw, wife of Lemuel Shaw, chief justice of the Massachusetts Supreme Court, whose son Lemuel had been a pupil at Bronson's Temple School.

10. Theodore Parker had died in Florence, Italy, on 10 May 1860; for a description of the memorial meeting, see 17 June 1860, Bronson's *Journals*, pp. 327–328.

11. *Moods*, which LMA began in August 1860, was published by A. K. Loring of Boston in December 1864.

12. The motto from Emerson's "Experience" was "Life is a train of moods like a string of beads; and as we pass through them they prove to be many colored lenses, which paint the world their own hue, and each shows us only what lies in its own focus."

13. Edward Albert, Prince of Wales and the future Edward VII, was eighteen years old.

14. Johann Paul Friedrich Richter, the German humorist, who used the pen name Jean Paul.

15. This unlocated poem may have been delivered at the memorial meeting at the Tremont Temple in Boston on 3 December, marking the first anniversary of John Brown's death. An advertisement dated 21 November, announcing the call for the convention by James Redpath, is pasted in Bronson's "Diary for 1860," p. 368, Houghton Library, Harvard University. However, there is no mention of LMA in the accounts of the meeting published in the 8 December *National Anti-Slavery Standard* or the 9 December *Liberator*.

16. The Boston artist David Claypoole Johnston.

17. LMA wrote Alfred Whitman on 25 January [1861] that May "is having great times with six horses in the stables, balls, frozen lakes for skating & no prim sisters to quench her youthful ardor" (Houghton Library, Harvard University).

18. "Debby's Début" appeared in the August 1863 *Atlantic Monthly Magazine*.

19. Bronson's "Superintendent's Report" is in *Reports of the . . . Town of Concord . . . for the Year Ending April 1, 1860* (Concord: Benjamin Tolman, 1860), supplement, pp. 7–35.

20. Seymour Severance, an excellent gymnast, who served as the model for Bopp in "The King of Clubs and the Queen of Hearts."

21. "Monk's Island" is unlocated.

1861

January, 1861. — Twenty-eight; received thirteen New Year's gifts. A most uncommon fit of generosity seemed to seize people on my behalf, and I was blessed with all manner of nice things, from a gold and ivory pen to a mince-pie and a bonnet.

Wrote on a new book — "Success" ["Work"][1] — till Mother fell ill, when I corked up my inkstand and turned nurse. The dear woman was very ill, but rose up like a phoenix from her ashes after what she gayly called "the irrepressible conflict between sickness and the May constitution."

Father had four talks at Emerson's; good people came, and he enjoyed them much; made $30.[2] R. W. E. probably put in $20. He has a sweet way of bestowing gifts on the table under a book or behind a candle-stick, when he thinks Father wants a little money, and no one will help him earn. A true friend is this tender and illustrious man.

Wrote a tale and put it away, — to be sent when "Debby" comes out. "F. T." appeared,[3] and I got a dress, having mended my six-year old silk till it is more patch and tear than gown. Made the claret merino myself, and enjoyed it, as I do anything bought with my "head-money."

February. — Another turn at "Moods," which I remodelled. From the 2d to the 25th I sat writing, with a run at dusk; could not sleep, and for three days was so full of it I could not stop to get up. Mother made me a green silk cap with a red bow, to match the old green and red party wrap, which I wore as a "glory cloak." Thus arrayed I sat in groves of manuscripts, "living for immortality," as May said. Mother wandered in and out with cordial cups of tea, worried because I could n't eat. Father thought it fine, and brought his reddest apples and hardest cider for my Pegasus to feed upon. All sorts of fun was going on; but I did n't care if the world returned to chaos if I and my inkstand only "lit" in the same place.

103

It was very pleasant and queer while it lasted; but after three weeks of it I found that my mind was too rampant for my body, as my head was dizzy, legs shaky, and no sleep would come. So I dropped the pen, and took long walks, cold baths, and had Nan up to frolic with me. Read all I had done to my family; and Father said: "Emerson must see this. Where did you get your metaphysics?" Mother pronounced it wonderful, and Anna laughed and cried, as she always does, over my works, saying, "My dear, I'm proud of you."

So I had a good time, even if it never comes to anything; for it was worth something to have my three dearest sit up till midnight listening with wide-open eyes to Lu's first novel.

I planned it some time ago, and have had it in my mind ever so long; but now it begins to take shape.

Father had his usual school festival, and Emerson asked me to write a song, which I did.[4] On the 16th the schools all met in the hall (four hundred), — a pretty posy bed, with a border of proud parents and friends. Some of the fogies objected to the names Phillips and John Brown. But Emerson said: "Give it up? No, no; I will read it." Which he did, to my great contentment; for when the great man of the town says "Do it," the thing is done. So the choir warbled, and the Alcotts were uplifted in their vain minds.

Father was in glory, like a happy shepherd with a large flock of sportive lambs; for all did something. Each school had its badge, — one pink ribbons, one green shoulder-knots, and one wreaths of pop-corn on the curly pates. One school to whom Father had read Pilgrim's Progress told the story, one child after the other popping up to say his or her part; and at the end a little tot walked forward, saying with a pretty air of wonder, — "And behold it was all a dream."

When all was over, and Father about to dismiss them, F[red]. H[arlow]., a tall, handsome lad came to him, and looking up confidingly to the benign old face, asked "our dear friend Mr. Alcott to accept of Pilgrim's Progress and George Herbert's Poems from the children of Concord, as a token of their love and respect."

Father was much touched and surprised, and blushed and stammered like a boy, hugging the fine books while the children cheered till the roof rung.

His report was much admired, and a thousand copies printed to supply the demand;[5] for it was a new thing to have a report, neither dry nor dull; and teachers were glad of the hints given, making education a part of religion, not a mere bread-making grind for teacher and an irksome cram for children.

April. — War declared with the South, and our Concord company went to Washington.[6] A busy time getting them ready, and a sad day seeing them off; for in a little town like this we all seem like one family in times like these. At the station the scene was very dramatic, as the brave boys went away perhaps never to come back again.

I've often longed to see a war, and now I have my wish. I long to be a man; but as I can't fight, I will content myself with working for those who can.

Sewed a good deal getting May's summer things in order, as she sent for me to make and mend and buy and send her outfit.

Stories simmered in my brain, demanding to be writ; but I let them simmer, knowing that the longer the divine afflatus was bottled up the better it would be.

John Brown's daughters came to board, and upset my plans of rest and writing when the report and the sewing were done.[7] I had my fit of woe up garret on the fat rag-bag, and then put my papers away, and fell to work at housekeeping. I think disappointment must be good for me, I get so much of it; and the constant thumping Fate gives me may be a mellowing process; so I shall be a ripe and sweet old pippin before I die.

May. — Spent our May-day working for our men, — three hundred women all sewing together at the hall for two days.

May will not return to S[yracuse]. after her vacation in July; and being a lucky puss, just as she wants something to do, F. B. S[anborn]. needs a drawing teacher in his school and offers her the place.[8]

Nan found that I was wearing all the old clothes she and May left; so the two dear souls clubbed together and got me some new ones; and the great parcel, with a loving letter, came to me as a beautiful surprise.

Nan and John walked up from Cambridge for a day, and we all walked back. Took a sail to the forts, and saw our men on guard there. Felt very martial and Joan-of-Arc-y as I stood on the walls with the flag flying over me and cannon all about.

June. — Read a good deal; grubbed in my garden, and made the old house pretty for May. Enjoyed Carlyle's French Revolution very much. His earthquaky style suits me.

"Charles Auchester" is charming, — a sort of fairy tale for grown people.[9] Dear old "Evelina," as a change, was pleasant.[10] Emerson recommended Hodson's India, and I got it, and liked it; also read Sir Thomas More's Life.[11] I read Fielding's "Amelia," and thought it coarse and queer.[12] The heroine having "her lovely nose smashed all to bits falling from a post shay" was a new idea. What some one says of Richardson applies to Fielding, "The virtues of his heroes are the vices of decent men."[13]

July. — Spent a month at the White Mountains with L[ouisa]. W[illis]., — a lovely time, and it did me much good.[14] Mountains are restful and uplifting to my mind. Lived in the woods, and revelled in brooks, birds, pines, and peace.

August. — May came home very tired, but satisfied with her first attempt, which has been very successful in every way. She is quite a belle now, and much improved, — a tall blond lass, full of grace and spirit.

September. — Ticknor sent $50.[15] Wrote a story for C[lapp]., as Plato needs new shirts, and Minerva a pair of boots, and Hebe a fall hat.

October. — All together on Marmee's birthday. Sewing and knitting for "our boys" all the time. It seems as if a few energetic women could carry on the war better than the men do it so far.
A week with Nan in the dove-cot. As happy as ever.

November and *December.* — Wrote, read, sewed, and wanted something to do.

["Notes and Memoranda"]
1861.

Father has good talks in B[oston] & reforms our schools. Nan & John happy as turtle doves. Lu writing & grubbing as usual. Mother beginning to feel easy & quiet, Ab busy at the Asylum doing well. John Brown's girls board with us. April 18th war was declared with the South. A month at the White Mts with L[ouisa]. W[illis]. & write letters home that amuse the town.

My Earnings.

A Pair Of Eyes.	40
Whisper In The Dark.	50
M. L.	20
Began Moods.[16]	

SOURCES: Text — Cheney, pp. 124–129; "Notes and Memoranda" — manuscript, Houghton Library, Harvard University.

1. For more about "Success," see the entry for September 1863 and note 35 following it.

2. Bronson wrote in his journal on 10 December 1860 that he had seen F. B. Sanborn to "talk about some conversations which I am proposing to begin perhaps in Jan. I spent the evening with Emerson and talk about his Book *[The Conduct of Life]* and the Conversations which he will attend and promote" ("Diary for 1860," p. 371, Houghton Library, Harvard University). A ticket for the series, dated 27 December 1860, announces that the series will be held at Sanborn's, starting on 5 January, and include meetings entitled "Personal Influence," "Private Life," "Health and Temperance," "Public Spirit," "Education," and "Influence" (Houghton Library, Harvard University). Bronson's account of the 2 February conversation, held at Emerson's, called "Education," is in his *Journals*, p. 334.

3. "Faith's Tryst"; see "Notes and Memoranda" for 1859.

4. "March, march, mothers and grandmamas!" appeared in *Reports of the School Committee . . . of Concord, Mass. . . . Saturday, March 16, 1861* (Concord: Benjamin Tolman, 1861), supplement, pp. 1–2. LMA reports the event in a letter to Anna Alcott Pratt on 8 [i.e. 18? March 1861], in *SL*, pp. 62–64. What is probably a two-page letter fragment by LMA describing the ceremonies is at the Houghton Library, Harvard University (where it is described as a journal fragment).

5. *Superintendent's Report of the Concord Schools . . . for the Year 1860–61* (Concord: Benjamin Tolman, 1861).

6. The Concord Artillery of the State Regiment, Massachusetts Volunteer Militia, was ordered to Washington immediately after the shelling of Fort Sumter on 12 April 1861. They departed Concord on 19 April (see Townsend Scudder, *Concord: American Town* [Boston: Little, Brown, 1947], pp. 227–228, and the Concord town report for 1862).

7. Anne and Sarah Brown. Anne's account of their time in Concord is in Joel Myerson and Daniel Shealy, "Three Contemporary Accounts of Louisa May Alcott, with Glimpses of Other Concord Notables," *New England Quarterly* 59 (March 1986): 116–122.

8. May Alcott succeeded Mary Hammatt as the drawing teacher in Sanborn's school.

9. Elizabeth Sara Sheppard's *Charles Auchester* (1853).

10. Frances Burney's (Madame d'Arblay) *Evelina* (1778).

11. W. S. R. Hodson, *Twelve Years of a Soldier's Life in India* (1860).

12. Henry Fielding's *Amelia* (1751).

13. According to James Boswell, Samuel Johnson "used to quote with approbation a saying of Richardson's, 'that the virtues of Fielding's heroes were the vices of a truly good man' " (Spring 1768, in *Life of Johnson*, new ed., ed. R. W. Chapman with J. D. Fleeman [London: Oxford University Press, 1970], p. 389). We are grateful to Professor Donald Siebert for pointing out this source to us.

14. LMA describes this visit in a letter to Alfred Whitman of 4 August [1861], in *SL*, pp. 67–68, and in a series of letters published in the *Boston Commonwealth* in 1863 (reprinted in Joel Myerson and Daniel Shealy, "Louisa May Alcott on Vacation: Four Uncollected Letters," *Resources for American Literary Study* 14 [Spring-Autumn 1984]: 113–141).

15. Ticknor sent fifty dollars in payment for "Debby's Début."

16. "A Pair of Eyes; or, Modern Magic" appeared in the 24 and 31 October 1863 issues of *Frank Leslie's Illustrated Newspaper* (it was first identified as LMA's and reprinted in *A Double Life: Newly Discovered Thrillers of Louisa May Alcott*, ed. Madeleine B. Stern [Boston: Little, Brown, 1988]); "A Whisper in the Dark" appeared in the 6 and 13 June 1863 issues of *Frank Leslie's Illustrated Newspaper*.

1862

January, 1862. — E. P. Peabody wanted me to open a Kindergarten,[1] and Mr. Barnard gave a room at the Warren Street Chapel.[2] Don't like to teach, but take what comes; so when Mr. F. offered $40 to fit up with, twelve pupils, and his patronage, I began.[3]

Saw many great people, and found them no bigger than the rest of the world, — often not half so good as some humble soul who made no noise. I learned a good deal in my way, and am not half so much impressed by society as before I got a peep at it. Having known Emerson, Parker, Phillips, and that set of really great and good men and women living for the world's work and service of God, the mere show people seem rather small and silly, though they shine well, and feel that they are stars.

February. — Visited about, as my school did not bring enough to pay board and the assistant I was made to have, though I did n't want her.

Went to lectures; saw Booth at the Goulds', — a handsome, shy man, glooming in a corner.

Very tired of this wandering life and distasteful work; but kept my word and tugged on.

Hate to visit people who ask me to help amuse others, and often longed for a crust in a garret with freedom and a pen. I never knew before what insolent things a hostess can do, nor what false positions poverty can push one into.

April. — Went to and from C[oncord]. every day that I might be at home. Forty miles a day is dull work; but I have my dear people at night, and am not a beggar.

Wrote "King of Clubs," — $30.[4] The school having no real foundation (as the people who sent did n't care for Kindergartens, and Miss P[eabody]. wanted me to take pupils for nothing, to try the new system), I gave it up, as I could do much better at something else. May took my place for a month, that I might keep my part of the bargain; and I cleaned house, and wrote a story which made more than all my months of teaching. They ended in a wasted winter and a debt of $40, — to be paid if I sell my hair to do it.

May. — School finished for me, and I paid Miss N. by giving her all the furniture, and leaving her to do as she liked; while I went back to my writing, which pays much better, though Mr. F[ields]. did say, "Stick to your teaching; you can't write." Being wilful, I said, "I won't teach; and I can write, and I'll prove it."

Saw Miss Rebecca Harding, author of "Margret Howth," which has made a stir, and is very good.[5] A handsome, fresh, quiet woman, who says she never had any troubles, though she writes about woes. I told her I had had lots of troubles; so I write jolly tales; and we wondered why we each did so.

June, July, August. — Wrote a tale for B., and he lost it, and would n't pay.[6]

Wrote two tales for L.[7] I enjoy romancing to suit myself; and though my tales are silly, they are not bad; and my sinners always have a good spot somewhere. I hope it is good drill for fancy and language, for I can do it fast; and Mr. L. says my tales are so "dramatic, vivid, and full of plot," they are just what he wants.

September, October. — Sewing Bees and Lint Picks for "our boys" kept us busy, and the prospect of the first grandchild rejoiced the hearts of the family.

Wrote much; for brain was lively, and work paid for readily. Rewrote the last story, and sent it to L[eslie]., who wants more than I can send him. So, between blue flannel jackets for "our boys" and dainty slips for Louisa Caroline or John B., Jr., as the case may be, I reel off my "thrilling" tales, and mess up my work in a queer but interesting way.

War news bad. Anxious faces, beating hearts, and busy minds.

I like the stir in the air, and long for battle like a warhorse when he smells powder. The blood of the Mays is up!

Journal kept at the Hospital, Georgetown, D. C.,
1862.

November. — Thirty years old. Decided to go to Washington as a nurse if I could find a place. Help needed, and I love nursing, and *must* let out my pent-up energy in some new way. Winter is always a hard and a dull time, and if I am away there is one less to feed and warm and worry over.

I want new experiences, and am sure to get 'em if I go. So I've sent in my name, and bide my time writing tales, to leave all snug behind me, and mending up my old clothes, — for nurses don't need nice things, thank Heaven!

December. — On the 11th I received a note from Miss H[annah]. M. Stevenson telling me to start for Georgetown next day to fill a place in the Union Hotel Hospital. Mrs. Ropes of Boston was matron, and Miss Kendall of Plymouth was a nurse there, and though a hard place, help was needed.[8] I was ready, and when my commander said "March!" I marched. Packed my trunk, and reported in B[oston]. that same evening.

We had all been full of courage till the last moment came; then we all broke down. I realized that I had taken my life in my hand, and might never see them all again. I said, "Shall I stay, Mother?" as I hugged her close. "No, go! and the Lord be with you!" answered the Spartan woman; and till I turned the corner she bravely smiled and waved her wet handkerchief on the door-step. Shall I ever see that dear old face again?

So I set forth in the December twilight, with May and Julian Hawthorne as escort, feeling as if I was the son of the house going to war.[9]

Friday, the 12th, was a very memorable day, spent in running all over Boston to get my pass, etc., calling for parcels, getting a tooth filled, and buying a veil, — my only purchase. A. C. gave me some old clothes; the dear Sewalls money for myself and boys, lots of love and help; and at 5 P. M., saying "good-by" to a group of tearful faces at the station, I started on my long journey, full of hope and sorrow, courage and plans.

A most interesting journey into a new world full of stirring sights and sounds, new adventures, and an evergrowing sense of the great task I had undertaken.

I said my prayers as I went rushing through the country white with tents, all alive with patriotism, and already red with blood.

A solemn time, but I'm glad to live in it; and am sure it will do me good whether I come out alive or dead.

All went well, and I got to Georgetown one evening very tired.[10] Was kindly welcomed, slept in my narrow bed with two other room-mates, and on the morrow began my new life by seeing a poor man die at dawn, and sitting all day between a boy with pneumonia and a man shot through the lungs. A strange day, but I did my best; and when I put mother's little black shawl round the boy while he sat up panting for breath, he smiled and said, "You are real motherly, ma'am." I felt as if I was getting on. The man only lay and stared with his big black eyes, and made me very nervous. But all were well behaved; and I sat looking at the twenty strong faces as they looked back at me, — hoping that I looked "motherly" to them; for my thirty years made me feel old, and the suffering round me made me long to comfort every one.

["Notes and Memoranda"]
1862.

I keep a Kinder Garten for six months in Boston. Visit at the Fields & among friends. Make nothing & give up teaching. L. Willis died.[11] Dec. 11th to Washington as an Army nurse. Stay six weeks & fall ill. Am brought home nearly dead & have a fever.[12]

School.	30
Nursing.	10
Pauline's Punishment	100
King Of Clubs.	30[13]

SOURCES: Text — Cheney, pp. 130–132, 140–142; "Notes and Memoranda" — manuscript, Houghton Library, Harvard University.

1. Elizabeth Palmer Peabody's school, based on Johann Heinrich Pestalozzi's educational principles, was at 20 Pinckney Street in Boston. On 22 December 1861, Mrs. Alcott wrote Samuel Joseph May that Peabody's school was so successful, with forty students at ten dollars a quarter, that another one "for a humbler sort of persons" at six dollars a quarter was wanted (SL, p. 72n).

2. Reverend Charles Francis Barnard, minister of the Warren Street Chapel from 1837 to 1866. LMA's kindergarten there failed to bring in sufficient funds for her board. Mrs. Alcott's comment was: "a failure — Swindle of her Time and her money" (26 December 1861, diary, SL, p. 74n).

3. LMA stayed with James T. Fields, publisher of the Atlantic Monthly Magazine, and his wife and her cousin Annie Fields during her teaching stint. She returned the forty dollars lent her by Fields in 1871 (see her letter to Fields, 3 July, SL, p. 160). Later, LMA wrote to Louise Chandler Moulton about this incident that "Fields wanted the school for a little nephew & lent me forty dollars to get books, chairs &c, telling me to give up trying to write & stick to my teaching," and that when Little Women came out, "I returned the money & said I found writing paid so much better than teaching that I thought I'd stick to my pen. He laughed & owned that he made a mistake" ([1883?], in SL, p. 160n).

4. "The King of Clubs and the Queen of Hearts" appeared in seven weekly installments between 19 April and 7 June 1862 in the Monitor, published in Concord by Ripley Bartlett.

5. Margaret Howth (1862), by Rebecca Harding. She married M. L. Clarke Davis in 1863 and was the mother of the author Richard Harding Davis.

6. Probably Ripley Bartlett, editor of the *Monitor*.

7. Frank Leslie, editor of *Frank Leslie's Illustrated Newspaper*.

8. Hannah Ropes, matron of the Union Hotel Hospital in Georgetown, died there from typhoid pneumonia on 20 January 1863; Julia C. Kendall had accompanied Ropes in July 1862 to nurse the soldiers. Information about the Georgetown hospital is from Madeleine B. Stern, "Louisa M. Alcott, Civil War Nurse," *Americana* 37 (April 1943): 296–325; and *Civil War Nurse: The Diary and Letters of Hannah Ropes*, ed. John R. Brumgardt (Knoxville: University of Tennessee Press, 1980).

9. Nathaniel Hawthorne's son, Julian, born in 1846.

10. On 13 December 1862, Hannah Ropes entered in her diary: "We are cheered by the arrival of Miss Alcott from Concord — the prospect of a really good nurse, a gentlewoman who can do more than merely keep the patients from falling out of bed" (*Civil War Nurse*, p. 112).

11. Louisa Willis died on 24 November 1862.

12. At a later date, LMA inserted: "which I enjoy very much, at least the crazy part."

13. "Pauline's Passion and Punishment" appeared in the 3 and 10 June 1863 issues of *Frank Leslie's Illustrated Newspaper*.

1863

January 1863.

Union Hotel Hospital Georgetown D.C.

I never began the year in a stranger place than this; five hundred miles from home, alone among strangers, doing painful duties all day long, & leading a life of constant excitement in this greathouse surrounded by 3 or 4 hundred men in all stages of suffering, disease & death. Though often home sick, heart sick & worn out, I like it — find real pleasure in comforting tending & cheering these poor souls who seem to love me, to feel my sympathy though unspoken, & acknowledge my hearty good will in spite of the ignorance, awkwardness, & bashfulness which I cannot help showing in so new & trying a situation. The men are docile, respectful, & affectionate, with but few exceptions; truly lovable & manly many of them. John Suhre a Virginia blacksmith is the prince of patients, & though what we call a common man, in education & condition, to me is all that I could expect or ask from the first gentleman in the land.[1] Under his plain speech & unpolished manner I seem to see a noble character, a heart as warm & tender as a woman's, a nature fresh & frank as any child's. He is about thirty, I think, tall & handsome, mortally wounded & dying royally, without reproach, repining, or remorse. Mrs Ropes & myself love him & feel indignant that such a man should be so early lost, for though he might never distinguish himself before the world, his influence & example cannot be without effect, for real goodness is never wasted.

Mon 4th — I shall record the events of a day as a sample of the days I spend —

Up at six, dress by gas light, run through my ward & fling up the windows though the men grumble & shiver; but the air is bad enough to breed a pestilence & as no notice is taken of our frequent appeals for better ventilation I must do what I can. Poke up the fire, add blankets, joke, coax, & command; but continue to open doors & windows as if life depended on it; mine does, & doubtless many another, for a more perfect pestilence-box than this house I never saw — cold, damp, dirty, full of vile odors from wounds, kitchens, wash rooms, & stables. No competent head, male or female, to right matters, & a jumble of good, bad, & indifferent nurses, surgeons & attendants to complicate the Chaos still more.

After this unwelcome progress through my stifling ward I go to breakfast with what appetite I may; find the inevitable fried beef, salt butter, husky bread & washy coffee; listen to the clack of eight women & a dozen men; the first silly, stupid or possessed of but one idea, the last absorbed in their breakfast & themselves to a degree that is both ludicrous and provoking, for all the dishes are ordered down the table *full* & returned *empty*; the conversation is entirely among themselves & each announces his opinion with an air of importance that frequently causes me to choke in my cup or bolt my meals with undignified speed lest a laugh betray to these pompous beings that a "child's among them takin notes." Till noon I trot, trot, giving out rations, cutting up food for helpless "boys", washing faces, teaching my attendants how beds are made or floors swept, dressing wounds, taking Dr. Fitz Patrick's orders, (privately wishing all the time that he would be more gentle with my big babies,) dusting tables, sewing bandages, keeping my tray tidy, rushing up & down after pillows, bed linen, sponges, books & directions, till it seems as if I would joyfully pay down all I possess for fifteen minutes rest.

At twelve the big bell rings & up comes dinner for the boys who are always ready for it & never entirely satisfied. Soup, meat, potatoes & bread is the bill of fare. Charley Thayer the attendant travels up & down the room serving out the rations, saving little for himself yet always thoughtful of his mates & patient as a woman with thier helplessness. When dinner is over some sleep, many read, & others want letters written. This I like to do for they put in such odd things & express thier ideas so comically I have great fun interiorly while as grave as possible exteriorly. A few of the men word thier paragraphs well & make excellent letters. John's was the best of all I wrote. The answering of letters from friends after some one has died is the saddest & hardest duty a nurse has to do.

Supper at five sets every one to running that can run & when that flurry is over all settle down for the evening amusements which consist of newspapers, gossip, Drs last round, & for such as need them the final doses for the night. At nine the bell rings, gas is turned down & day nurses go to bed.

Night nurses go on duty, & sleep & death have the house to themselves.

My society consists of Miss Kendal, Miss [Lizzie] Thurber, Mrs Ropes, Mrs Cramer, my room mate, & a few very disagreeable women whom I dont care to know. Drs Otman, Fitz Patrick, Hyde, Smith & Winslow are the gentleman, with Trevor, Gruger & other lesser lords[2] for steward, wardmaster, clerk &c — None at all agreeable (to me) but Otman & Winslow. The former quiet, pious, comely & faithful; the latter plain, odd, sentimental, but kind-hearted as a woman & rather quaint, being bred a Quaker.

He is now surgeon of my ward, succeeding Fitz Patrick whom rather I liked, as he was large, handsome, English, & polite but — he drank & could not perform operations well his hands trembled so, therefore he left to serve as Dr rather than surgeon elsewhere. Dr John, as I call Winslow, goes purring about among the men very friendly, painstaking & fearfully slow. He comes often to our room with books, asks me to his, (where I dont go,) & takes me to walk now & then. Quotes Browning copiously, is given to confidences in the twilight, & altogether is amiably amusing, & exceeding[ly] *young*.

Went with him to hear Channing at the Capitol,[3] & Dr John took me to dine at a German restaurant as we should be too late for the hospital dinner. Had a queer time as no one came to wait upon us for a long while, the dinner was cold & badly served, & when Dr John scolded the landlord he sputtered German, laid the fault to a lame hand & offered us coffee & cigars as an atonement for our uncomfortable meal. The man's airs & the Drs anguish repaid me for my share of the loss.

My work is changed to night watching or half night & half day, from twelve to twelve. I like it as it leaves me time for a morning run which is what I need to keep well, for bad air, food, water, work & watching are getting to be too much for me. I trot up & down the streets in all directions, some times to the Heights, then half way to Washington, again to the hill over which the long trains of army wagons are constantly vanishing & ambulances appearing. That way the fighting lies, & I long to follow.

Ordered to keep [to] my room being threatened with pneumonia. Sharp pain in the side, cough, fever & dizziness. A pleasant prospect for a lonely soul five hundred miles from home! Sit & sew on the boys clothes, write letters, sleep & read; try to talk & keep merry but fail decidedly as day after day goes & I feel no better. Dream awfully, & wake unrefreshed, think of home & wonder if I am to die here as Mrs Ropes the matron is likely to do. Feel too miserable to care much what becomes of me. Dr Smith creaks up twice a day to feel my pulse, give me doses, & ask if I am at all consumptive, or some other cheering question. Dr Otman examines my lungs & looks

sober. Dr John haunts the room coming by day & night with wood, cologne, books & messes like a motherly little man as he is. Nurses fussy &
anxious, matron dying, & every thing very gloomy. They want me to go
home but I *wont* yet.

Jan 16th — Was amazed to see father enter my room that morning, having been telegraphed to by order of Mrs Ropes without asking leave. I was
very angry[4] at first, though glad to see him, because I knew I should have
to go. Mrs Dana, Mrs Boise, Miss Donaldson & Miss Dix came, swarming
in all day long, also Nell Sedgewick & pretty Miss Wansey to take me to
Willard's to be cared for by them.[5] I wouldn't go, prefer[r]ing to keep still,
being pretty ill by that time.

On the 21st I suddenly decided to go home, feeling very strangely &
dreading to be worse.[6] Mrs Ropes died & that frightened the Drs about me
for my trouble was the same typhoid pneumonia. Father, Miss Kendal &
Lizzie Thurber went with me. Miss Dix brought a basket full of bottles of
wine, tea, medicine, & cologne, beside a little blanket & pillow, a fan & a
Testament. She is a kind soul but very queer & arbitrary.[7]
    Was very sorry to go & my "boys" seemed sorry to have me; quite a flock
came to see me off, but I was too sick to have but a dim idea of what was
going on.
    Had a strange excited journey of a day & night, half asleep, half wander-
ing, just conscious that I was going home, & when I got to Boston of being
taken out of the car with people looking on as if I was a sight. I dare say I
was all blauzed crazy & weak. Was too sick to reach Concord that night
though we tried to do so. Spent it at Mr [Thomas] Sewall's, had a sort of
fit; they sent for Dr Hay & I had a a dreadful time of it.[8]
    Next morning felt better & at four went home. Just remember seeing May's
shocked face at the Depot, mother's bewildered one at home, & getting to
bed in the firm belief that the house was roofless & no one wanted to
see me.
    As I never shall forget the strange fancies that haunted me I shall amuse
myself with recording some of them. The most vivid & enduring was a conviction that I had married a stout, handsome Spaniard, dressed in black
velvet with very soft hands & a voice that was continually saying, "Lie still,
my dear." This was mother, I suspect, but with all the comfort I often found
in her presence there was blended an awful fear of the Spanish spouse who
was always coming after me, appearing out of closets, in at windows, or
t[h]reatening me dreadfully all night long. I appealed to the Pope & really

116

got up & made a touching plea in something meant for Latin they tell me. Once I went to heaven & found it a twilight place with people darting thro the air in a queer way. All very busy & dismal & ordinary. Miss Dix, W. H. Channi[n]g & other people were there but I thought it dark & "slow" & wished I hadn't come. A mob at Baltimore breaking down the door to get me; being hung for a witch, burned, stoned & otherwise maltreated were some of my fancies. Also being tempted to join Dr W. & two of the nurses in worshipping the Devil. Also tending millions of sick men who never died or got well.

February.

Recovered my senses after 3 weeks of delirium, & was told I had had a very bad typhoid fever, had nearly died & was still very sick. All of which seemed rather curious for I remembered nothing of it. Found a queer, thin, big-eyed face when I looked in the glass; didn't know myself at all, & when I tried to walk discovered that I couldn't, & cried because "my legs wouldn't go".

Never having been sick before it was all new & very interesting when I got quiet enough to understand matters. Such long long nights — such feeble, idle days, dozing, fretting about nothing, longing to eat & no mouth to do it with, mine being so sore & full of all manner of queer sensations it was nothing but a plague. The old fancies still lingered, seeming so real I believed in them & deluded mother & May with the most absurd stories, so soberly told that they thought them true.

Dr Bartlett came every day & was very kind.[9] Father & mother were with me night & day, & May sung "Birks of Sherfeldie."[10] or read to me to wile away the tiresome hours. People sent letters, money, kind inquiries & goodies for the old "Nuss." Ham [Willis], the Windships, L. Wells & Nan came.[11] Tried to sew; read & write & found I had to begin all over again. Recieved $10 for my labors in Washington. Had all my hair 1 1/2 yard long cut off & went into caps like a grandma. Felt badly about losing my one beauty. Never mind, it might have been my head & a wig outside is better than a loss of wits inside.

March.

Began to get about a little, sitting up nearly all day, eating more regularly & falling back into my old ways. My first job was characteristic, I cleaned out my piece bags & dusted my books, feeling as tired as if I'd cleaned the whole house. Sat up till nine one night & took no lunch at three A.M. Two facts which I find carefully recorded in my pocket diary in my own shaky hand-writing.

117

Father had two courses of Conversations; one at Mr Quincy's very select & fine, the other at a Hall not so good.[12] He was tired out with taking care of me, poor old gentleman, & typhus was not inspiring.

Read a great deal, being too feeble to do much else. No end of rubbish with a few good things as ballast. "Titan" was the one I enjoyed most, though it tired my weak wits to read much at a time.[13] Recalled I wrote some lines on "Thoreau's Flute" which I composed one night on my watch by little Shaw at the Hospital.[14]

On the 28th father came home from Boston bringing word that Nan had a fine boy.[15] We all screamed out when he burst in snowy & beaming; then mother began to cry, May to laugh, & I to say[16] "There, I knew it wouldn't be a girl!" We were all so glad it was safely over & a jolly little lad was added to the feminine family.

Mother went straight down to be sure that "mother & child were doing well," & I fell to cleaning house as good work for an invalid & a vent for a happy *Aunt*.

April.

Had[17] some pleasant walks & drives & felt as if born again everything seemed so beautiful & new. I hope I was, & that the Washington experience may do me lasting good. To go very near to death teaches one to value life, & this winter will always be a very memorable one to me.

Sewed on little shirts & gowns for my blessed nephew, who increased rapidly in s[t]ature & godliness.

Sanborn asked me to do what Conway had suggested & teased about before he left for Europe — viz — to arrange my letters in a printable shape & put them in the Commonwealth.[18] They thought them witty & pathetic, I didn't, but I wanted money so I made three "Hospital Sketches." Much to my surprise they made a great hit, & people bought the papers faster than they could be supplied. The second "A Night" was much liked, & I was glad, for my beautiful "John Sulie" was the hero, & the praise belonged to him.[19] More were wanted & I added a postscript in the form of a letter which finished it up as I then thought.

Received $100 from Frank Leslie for a tale which won the prize last Jan.[20] Paid debts & was glad that my winter bore visible fruit. Sent Leslie another tale. Went to Boston & saw "our baby" — thought him ugly but promising — Got a set of furniture for my room, a long talked of dream of ours.

May.

Spent the first week or two putting the house in order. May painted & papered the parlors. I got a new carpet & rug beside the paper, & put things to rights in a thorough manner. Mother was away with Nan so we had full sweep & she came home to a clean, fresh house.

Nan[21] & the Royal Infanta came as bright as a whole gross of buttons & as good as a hairless, brown angel. Went to Readville & saw the 54th colored Regiments both there & next day in town as they left for the South. Enjoyed it very much, also the Antislavery Meetings.

Had a fresh feather in my cap for Mrs Hawthorne showed Fields "Thoreau's Flute," & he desired it for the Atlantic. Of course I didn't say No. It was printed, copied, praised & glorified — also *paid for*, & being a mercenary creature I liked the $10 nearly as well as the honor of being "a new star" & "a literary celebrity."

June

Began to write on "Moods",[22] feeling encouraged by the commendation bestowed upon "Hospital Sketches" which were noticed, talked & inquired about much to my surprise & delight. Had a fine letter from Henry James, also one from Wasson & a request from Redpath to be allowed to print the Sketches in a book.[23] *Roberts Bros also asked, but I preferred Redpath & said yes, so he fell to work with all his might.*[24]

Went to Class Day for the first time.[25] Had a pleasant day seeing new sights & old friends. Lottie May & her boy made a visit.[26] Gail Hamilton came to the H[oar?]'s, didn't like her as well as Miss Harding.[27]

July.

Sanborn asked for more contributions, & I gave him some of my old Mountain Letters vamped up.[28] They were not good, & though they sold the paper I was heartily ashamed of them, & stopped in the middle, resolving never again to try to be funny lest I should be rowdy & nothing more. I'm glad of the lesson & hope it will do me good.

Had some pleasant letters from Sergeant Bain, one of my boys who has not forgotten me though safely at home far away in Michigan.[29] It gratified me very much & brought back the hospital days again. He was a merry, brave, little fellow & I liked him very much. His right arm was amputated after Fredricksberg & he took it very cheerfully, trying at once to train his left hand to do duty for both, & never complained of his loss.

August.

May went to Clark's Island for a month with some pleasant people.[30] She had a riotously good time boating, singing, dancing, croqueting & captivating. The Island seems to be a most romantic place & she was quite carried away with her admiration of everything about it.

Redpath carried on the publishing of the Sketches vigorously, sending letters, proof & notices daily, & making all manner of offers, suggestions, & prophesies concerning the success of the book & its author.

Wrote a story "My Contraband" & sent it to Fields who accepted & paid $50 for it with much approbation for it & the "Sketches."[31] Leslie sent $40 for "A Whisper In The Dark." & wanted another — Sent "A Pair Of Eyes."

Major Mansfield invited me to Gloucester,[32] but I refused being too busy & too bashful to be made a lion of even in a very small way. Letters from Dr Hyde, Wilkie (home with a wound from Wagner) Chas. Sumner, Mr Hale, & others all about the little "Sketches" which keep on making friends for me, though I dont get used to the thing at all & think it must be all a mistake.[33]

On the 25th my first morning glory bloomed in my room, a hopeful blue, & at night up came my book in its new dress. I had added several chapters to it & it was quite a neat little affair. An edition of 1000, & I to have five cents on each copy.[34]

September.

Redpath anxious for another book. Send him a volume of stories & part of a book to look at. He likes both, but I decide on waiting a little as I'm not satisfied with the stories & the novel needs time.[35] "Sketches" sell well & a new edition is called for.

Dear old Grandma died at Aunt Betsey's in her eighty ninth year, a good woman & much beloved by her children.[36] I sent five dollars to help lay her away, for Aunt B. is poor & it was all I could do for the kind little old lady.

Nan & Freddy made us a long visit & we decided that of all splendid babies he was the king. Such a hearty, happy, funny boy, I could only play with & adore him all the while he stayed, & long for him when he went. Nan & John are very proud of "our son" & well they may be. Grandpa & Grandma think him perfect, & even cold hearted Aunty May condecends to say he is "a very nice thing."[37]

My story in the Atlantic came out & was liked.[38] Recieved $40 from Redpath for "Sketches" — first edition — Wanted me to be editor of a paper, was afraid to try & let it go.[39]

Wrote much on "Moods" over which my family laughed & cried most flatteringly. Long to have it printed but dare not offer it.[40]

October.

Thought much about going to Port Royal to teach contrabands.[41] Fields wanted the letters I should write & asked if I had no book?[42] Father spoke of "Moods" & the great James desired to see it. So I fell to work & finished it off, thinking the world must be coming to an end & all my dreams getting fulfilled in a most amazing way. If ever there was an astonished young woman it is myself, for things have gone on so swimmingly of late I dont know who I am. A year ago I had no publisher & went begging with my wares; now *three* have asked me for something, several papers are ready to print my contributions & F. B. S[anborn]. says "any publisher this side Baltimore would be glad to get a book." There is a sudden hoist for a meek & lowly scribbler who was told to "stick to her teaching," & never had a literary friend to lend a helping hand! Fifteen years of hard grubbing may be coming to something after all, & I may yet "pay all the debts, fix the house, send May to Italy & keep the old folks cosy," as I've said I would so long yet so hopelessly.

May began to take anatomical drawing lessons of Rimmer.[43] I was very glad to be able to pay her expenses up & down & clothe her neatly.[44]

$20 more from Redpath on account.

November.

Sent "Moods" to Redpath as I found that it would be a breach of contract to give it to Fields. R. came up with his wife[45] after reading it & was glad to publish it though he liked "Success" better because he thought it would be more popular. He wanted a Christmas Tale for children & I gave him one that Fields refused years ago.[46] He sent it to the printers at once so there was another little help for this incapable family.[47]

May's Island friend Herbert Pratt came to pass Sunday. He sings well but seems a silly youth though amiable.[48]

Wrote a new story for Fields "On Picket Duty".[49]

Recieved $39 from Leslie for "A Pair Of Eyes," not enough, but I'm glad to get even that & be done with him. Paid debts with it as usual.[50]

A pleasant letter from Col. Higginson praising "The Contraband" which he had just read in Port Royal.[51]

Help make an Afgahn for Wilkie James to be sent him by seven or eight of his Concord friends for he now lies on a sofa & needs a pretty blanket to cover him.[52]

Carpenters shingled the roof & made some other repairs for which I paid.[53]

Was 31 on the 29th, only one or two presents & a dull day as usual.

December.

The principle event of this otherwise quiet month was the Sanitary Fair in Boston & our part in it.[54] At G. B. B's request I dramatised six Scenes from Dickens & went to town on the 14th to play.[55] Things did not go well for want of a good manager & more time. Our night was not at all satisfactory to us owing to the falling through of several Scenes for want of actors.

People seemed to like what there was of it, & after a wearisome week I very gladly came home again. Our six entertainments made two thousand five hundred dollars for the Fair.

Wrote a long tale for Leslie, "Enigma's" but as he objected to paying before hand he did not get it.[56] Also for the Commonwealth "A Hospital Christmas."[57] Also for Redpath rewrote the Fairy Tales one of which he published, but owing to delays it was late for the holidays & badly bound in the hurry, so the poor "Rose Family" fared badly.[58] He paid fifty for that & fifty for "Picket Duty" which Fields refused.

Had a letter from the publisher of a new Magazine called the Civil Service Magazine asking for a long tale.[59] Had no time to write one but will by & by if the thing is good.

While in town recieved ten of T. R. S[ewall]. & twenty of Redpath with which I bought May hat, boots, gloves, ribbons & other little matters, besides furnishing money for her fares up & down to Rimmer.

Christmas a very quiet day, no presents.

["Notes and Memoranda"]
1863

Get well & fall to work. March 28th Nan's boy was born, Fredrick Alcott Pratt. Ab to Clarke's Island. Grandma died. The first colored regiment went to the war.[60] In the Fall Ab went to Rimmer to study moulding.

Hospital Sketches come out & I find I've done a good thing without knowing it.

On Picket Duty.	50
Hospital Sketches.	200
Mountain Letters.	20
My Contraband.	50
Thoreau's Flute.	10

SOURCES: Text and "Notes and Memoranda" — manuscript, Houghton Library, Harvard University.

1. John Suhre, his lung punctured by a rifle ball, died at the age of thirty while LMA nursed him.

2. The physicians Rensselaer Ottman, Lee Smith, and John Winslow; the ward master Richard Trevor; the steward F. R. Gruger.

3. William Henry Channing, chaplain of the House of Representatives. LMA wrote: "a flowery sermon therefore dull to me.," and then canceled it.

4. LMA wrote "mad," then canceled it and wrote "angry."

5. Mrs. M. M. Boyce, a friend of Hannah Ropes's who lived in Georgetown; the well-known nurse Dorothea Dix; Willard's Hotel in Washington.

6. Soon after LMA reported to the Union Hotel Hospital on 13 December 1862, she fell severely ill with fever. Bronson arrived there to tend her on 16 January, found her with a delirious fever (later diagnosed as typhoid), and took her home to Concord on 24 January. Her head was shaved at doctor's orders, and she wore a wig for some time. It was not until 22 March that she was able to leave her room. Bronson describes these events in a series of letters to Anna Alcott Pratt written between 25 January and 4 February 1863 in his *Letters*, pp. 332–335.

7. LMA wrote: "no one likes her & I dont wonder," then canceled it.

8. Dr. Gustavus Hay, 98 Charles Street in Boston.

9. Dr. Josiah Bartlett of Concord. LMA was also treated with the "magnetic power" of a Mrs. Bliss, who "came to Louisa, and did actually find out what was now the difficulty, not by questions, but by holding her hands and reading her with closed eyes." As Sophia Hawthorne described the scene to Annie Fields, after Mrs. Bliss left, "Louisa rose out of bed and walked across the room alone, and even stood up a while for Annie to fit a wrapper which she was making for her! Hitherto she could not stand one moment, and had to be lifted to her easy chair, when she was inclined to sit up. She had also suffered with excruciating backach[e] and limbsach[e]. But Mrs. Bliss took all pain from her back, and yesterday she came down stairs alone! and stayed an hour. She says she intends to hold levees next week" (20 February 1863, in Taylor Stoehr, *Hawthorne's Mad Scientists* [Hamden, Conn.: Archon, 1978], p. 46).

10. In her diary, May calls this song "Birks of Aberfeldy" (10 September 1863, Houghton Library, Harvard University).

11. LMA's cousin Elizabeth Sewall Willis Wells was married to Thomas Goodwin Wells. Their eldest child, Eliza May Wells, was a friend of LMA's.

12. Bronson held the following conversations at the Temperance Hall: "Concord Poets and Authors" (2 March), "The Liberator and the Reformers" (9 March), "The Atlantic Monthly and Its Contributors" (16 March), and "The Transcendental Club and the Dial" (23 March).

13. Jean Paul Friedrich Richter's *Titan* (1800–1803).

14. "Thoreau's Flute" appeared in the September 1863 *Atlantic Monthly Magazine*. For the story of the composition and publication of this poem, see *SL*, pp. 84–85.

15. For the birth of Frederick Alcott Pratt, see LMA's letter to Anna Alcott Pratt of [30 March 1863], in *SL*, p. 83.

16. At a later date, LMA has inserted "like B. Trotwood." Betsey Trotwood was the eccentric great-aunt of the title character in Charles Dickens's *David Copperfield*.

17. Before this sentence, LMA wrote: "Mrs H. began her grand Wed Receptions. No one went." and then canceled it. The reference may be to Caroline Brooks Hoar, wife of Ebenezer Rockwood Hoar, or Elizabeth Prichard Hoar, wife of Edward Sherman Hoar.

18. "Hospital Sketches" appeared in four installments between 22 May and 26 June 1863 in the *Boston Commonwealth* and was published as a book in August 1863 by James Redpath of Boston. Moncure Daniel Conway, reformer and co-editor with Sanborn of the *Boston Commonwealth*, wrote of *Hospital Sketches*: "The series . . . showed every variety of ability, and excited much attention" (*Autobiography, Memories, and Experiences*, 2 vols. [Boston: Houghton Mifflin, 1904], 1:369).

19. The second installment of "Hospital Sketches" — "A Night" — appeared in the 29 May *Boston Commonwealth*.

20. LMA had entered "Pauline's Passion and Punishment" in a contest for a hundred-dollar prize offered by *Frank Leslie's Illustrated Newspaper*.

21. LMA wrote: "The Mays, Uncle & Joe came. Also" and then canceled it. Joseph May was the son of Samuel Joseph and Lucretia Flagge Coffin May.

22. At a later date, LMA inserted "again" after "write."

23. Henry James, Sr., father of the novelist Henry, Jr., and the philosopher William, had written of his pleasure in LMA's "charming pictures of hospital service" (clipping, Alcott Papers, Houghton Library, Harvard University); David Atwood Wasson, a writer of radical religious

works, wrote, "Let me tell you what extreme pleasure I have taken in reading 'Hospital Sketches. Written with such extraordinary wit & felicity of style, & showing such power to portray character! Surely she has a brilliant literary future before her" (copied on the last page of LMA's letter of 29 September [1863] to James Redpath, *SL*, p. 94n).

24. At a later date, LMA inserted an asterisk after "might," keyed to the following: "*(1879) Short-sighted, Louisa! little did you dream that this same Roberts, or rather Bros. (meaning T[homas]. N[iles].) were to help you make your fortune a few years later. Redpath had no skill as a publisher & the Sketches never made much money, but showed me *'my style'*, & taking the hint I went where glory waited me."

25. On 15 June 1863, Bronson wrote in his journal: "Louisa accompanies me to the Schools at Nine Acre Corner and Factory Village" ("Diary for 1863," p. 158, Houghton Library, Harvard University).

26. Charlotte Coffin May, the only daughter of Mrs. Alcott's brother Samuel Joseph May and Lucretia Flagge Coffin May, married Alfred Wilkinson, a Syracuse, New York, banker and merchant, in 1854; the boy may be either Alfred or Marion Wilkinson.

27. LMA wrote: "Too sharp & full of herself. Insisted on talking about religion with Emerson who glided away from the subject so sweetly yet resolutely that the energetic lady gave it up at last. She wore a brown hat all the evening & was very queer." and then canceled it. Gail Hamilton was the pen name of Mary Abigail Dodge; LMA had praised her "Garden" in a letter of 11 May [1862] to Alfred Whitman (see *SL*, p. 77). Miss Harding is probably Rebecca Harding (Davis).

28. "Letters from the Mountains" appeared in four installments between 24 July and 21 August 1863 in the *Boston Commonwealth*.

29. Sergeant Robert Bane, also called Baby B., one of LMA's former hospital patients.

30. LMA wrote: "the Austins, Goodwins, Sanborns & other" and then canceled it. May had gone to Clarks Island, near Plymouth, Massachusetts, with friends on 1 August (Mrs. Alcott's diary, Houghton Library, Harvard University). Mentioned are F. B. Sanborn and his wife Louisa Augusta Leavitt Sanborn; the Concord author Jane Goodwin Austin, her husband, Loring H. Austin, and their daughter Amy; and Hersey and William Goodwin. May's account of this trip is in her diary for 5–23 August (Houghton Library, Harvard University).

31. "The Brothers" appeared in the November 1863 *Atlantic Monthly Magazine*. It was first called "My Contraband; or, the Brothers," but LMA changed the name, at Howard Ticknor's suggestion, because of a recently published story entitled "Our Contraband" (see Ticknor's letter of 4 September 1863 to LMA, Louisa May Alcott Collection, Barrett Library, University of Virginia). LMA used her original title when she reprinted the story in *Hospital Sketches and Camp and Fireside Stories* (Boston: Roberts Brothers, 1869). According to LMA, Fields had "pronounced it 'Capital' " (letter to James Redpath, [early September 1863], *SL*, p. 91).

32. Major James Mansfield and his wife, Frances (Fanny) Hildreth Mansfield.

33. Lieutenant Garth Wilkinson James, a son of Henry James, Sr., had been wounded while serving with Colonel Robert Gould Shaw's all-black regiment at the battle for Fort Wagner in Charleston Harbor; the author and minister Edward Everett Hale.

34. For LMA's negotiations over her royalty on *Hospital Sketches*, see her letter to Redpath of [July? 1863] in *SL*, p. 86.

35. LMA's letter to Redpath of [July? 1863] (*SL*, p. 87) is the first in a series about her autobiographical novel then called *Success*. It was later published as "Work; or Christie's Experiment" in twenty-seven monthly installments between 18 December 1872 and 18 June 1873 in the *Christian Union* and reprinted in book form, in 1873, as *Work: A Story of Experience*, by Roberts Brothers (see *SL*, pp. 87ff).

36. Mrs. Joseph Chatfield Alcox died on 27 August 1863, at the age of ninety, while staying with Bronson's sister Betsey Pardee. Bronson's comments on her influence on his life are in a 5 August entry in his *Journals*, pp. 356–357.

37. At a later date, LMA canceled "cold hearted" and inserted "artistic."

38. For the reception of "Our Contraband," see, for example, LMA's letter to Thomas Wentworth Higginson on 12 November [1863], in *SL*, pp. 96–97.

39. LMA wrote Redpath on 28 August [1863] that the "editorial plan was so like an old dream coming true, that my family shouted over it, as we have had several domestic newspapers conducted" by her, including "The Olive Leaf" (*SL*, pp. 89–90; see Stern, *Louisa May Alcott* (Norman: University of Oklahoma Press, 1950), p. 62, and the several manuscript issues of "The Olive Leaf" at the Houghton Library, Harvard University) and "Pickwick Portfolio" (her childhood newspaper as named and described in *Little Women*; manuscript issues are at the Houghton Library, Harvard University, and the Louisa May Alcott Collection, Barrett Library, University of Virginia; selections are printed in Appendix B, p. 338).

40. At a later date, LMA inserted: "Poor old Moods come out for another touching up."

41. Contrabands were escaped slaves who were regarded as contrabands of war.

42. "Fields spoke of engaging some letters for his Magazine [*Atlantic Monthly Magazine*] if I did go, & I was much disappointed" (letter to Thomas Wentworth Higginson, 12 November [1863], *SL*, p. 96).

43. The artist William Rimmer.

44. LMA wrote: "Had a letter from young Chadwick about the 'Sketches,' which he likes very much." and then canceled it. The reference is probably to the minister John White Chadwick, who would later write Theodore Parker's biography.

45. Caroline Chorpenning Redpath.

46. Possibly *Christmas Elves*.

47. At a later date, LMA canceled "incapable" and inserted "rising."

48. May's diary shows that Herbert Pratt of Plymouth visited her in Concord a number of times in 1863, and she discovered on one visit that he was related to Emerson's wife, Lidian (1 November, Houghton Library, Harvard University). Later, "as brown and jolly and handsome as ever," he visited LMA in Europe in 1870 (see her letter of 10 September 1870 to her family, *SL*, p. 150, and May Alcott's letter to her family, [29? April 1870], copy by Bronson, Houghton Library, Harvard University).

49. At a later date, LMA inserted: "Refused it because it was about slavery." "On Picket Duty" appeared in *On Picket Duty, and Other Tales*, published in December 1863 by James Redpath.

50. LMA wrote: "Cousin Edward Gaylord sent father Grandma's picture in a neat frame." and then canceled it. Edward Gaylord is probably one of the children of Bronson's sister Pamila and her husband, Ransom Gaylord. When he visited Concord, May called him "a nephew of father's from the West" (12 September, diary, Houghton Library, Harvard University).

51. See LMA's letter to Higginson of 12 November [1863], in *SL*, pp. 96–97.

52. At a later date, LMA inserted: "I sent him a little poem with it."; the poem is unlocated. According to May, Ellen Emerson asked her "to choose & decide on the colors" for the afghan (8 November 1863, diary, Houghton Library, Harvard University).

53. At a later date, LMA canceled "for which I paid." and inserted: "for which I proudly paid out of my story money. I call the old house 'the sinking fund' as it swallows up all I can earn."

54. LMA dramatized *Scenes from Dickens* for the Sanitary Commission Fair in Boston on 14 December. She wrote Redpath that "you missed very little in not seeing the Dickens Scenes for so many people seceded that they were very poorly played & the whole thing was a scramble" (23 December [1863], *SL*, p. 100n; she was more positive in her description to Alfred Whitman on 2 January 1864, *SL*, p. 99).

55. George Bartlett, son of the Concord doctor Josiah Bartlett, served as LMA's stage manager.

56. "Enigmas" appeared in the 14 and 21 May 1864 issues of *Frank Leslie's Illustrated Newspaper*.

57. "A Hospital Christmas" appeared in the 8 and 15 January 1864 issues of *Boston Commonwealth*.

58. *The Rose Family. A Fairy Tale* was published in December 1863 by James Redpath.

59. "Love and Loyalty" appeared in six monthly installments between July and December 1864 in the *United States Service Magazine*.

60. Possibly a reference to the First South Carolina Volunteers, a regiment of freed slaves commanded by Thomas Wentworth Higginson from November 1862 to May 1864.

1864

January 1864

New Year's day was a very quiet one. Nan & Freddy were here, & in the evening we went to a dance at the hall. A merry time, for all the town was there as it was for the Soldier's Aid Society, & everyone wanted to help. Nan & I sat in the gallery & watched the young people dance the old year out, the new year in as the clock struck twelve.

On looking over my accounts I find that I have earned by my writing alone nearly six hundred dollars since last January, & spent less than a hundred for myself, which I am glad to know. May has had $70 for herself, & the rest has paid debts or bought necessary things for the family.

Leslie sent $50 after some delay & I sent "Enigmas." Recieved from the Commonwealth $18 for "A Hospital Christmas." Wrote a fairy tale "Fairy Pinafores."[1] "Picket Duty" & other tales came out, first of Redpath's series of "Books for the Camp Fires."[2] Richardson sent again for a long story for the "Civil Service Magazine," tried a war story but couldn't make it go.[3]

Read many books, several of Scotts, Goethe's & Miss Burney's. Story of the Grand. Wayside Inn &c.[4] Mother passed a week with Nan who was poorly. Invited to meet Mrs Howe. Can't bear her so wouldn't go. Mrs Stearns wished me to copy my John Brown poem in her famous Album.[5]

A killer cold snap. Sam Greele's wife died.[6] Wilkie James came up with his Wagner wounds.[7] May began to go to the Bible class, & we read every Sunday eve with mother.

February.

Had a little skirmish with Ripley Bartlett about "King of Clubs & Queen of Hearts" one of the tales in the Camp Fire book.[8] I did not know that it was copyrighted so gave it to Redpath, & his Highness Rip made a great stir about it. Demanded money, threatened law wrote insulting letters & behaved in such a manner that my doubts as to sanity were set at rest forever. He finally gave us the right of publishing our own story & I am done with the dog in the manger. Shall look well after my copyrights in future.

Nan quite sick again. Mother passed most of the month with her so I had to be housekeeper & let my writing go. As well perhaps for my wits are tired & the "divine afflatus" dont descend as readily as it used to do. Must wait & fill up my idea-box before I begin again. There is nothing like work to set fancy agoing.

Redpath came flying up on the 4th to get "Moods" promising to have it out by May. Gave it to him with many fears & he departed content. The next day recieved a telegram to come down at once & see the printers. Went & was told that the story was too long for a single volume & a two volume novel was bad to begin with. Would I cut the book down about half?[9] No, I wouldn't, having already shortened it all it would bear. So I took my "opus" & posted home again promising to try & finish my shorter book in a month. Mother being gone I couldn't do it, but was glad to get "Moods" back because I had rather have Fields or some other publisher get it out. Redpath does not suit me though he does his best I believe.

A dull, busy month, grubbing in the kitchen, sewing, cleaning house & trying to like my duty. Nan so poorly they decide to pass the summer with us. Glad, though it will break up the old quiet. I shall love to have baby here & to know that Nan is happy, for she has not been away from us.

Mrs Stearnes takes a great fancy to May, sends her flowers, offers to pay for her to go to the new Art School, & arranges everything delightfully for her. She is a fortunate girl, & always finds some one to help her as she wants to be helped. Wish I could do the same, but suppose as I never do that it is best for me to work & wait & do all for myself.

Mr Storrs D.D. wrote for a sketch for his little paper "The Drum Beat," to be printed during the Brooklyn Sanitary Fair.[10] A very cordial, pleasant letter which I answered by a little sketch called "A Hospital Lamp." He sent me another friendly letter & all the daily papers as they came out. A very gentlemanly D. D. is Storrs.[11]

Took a turn at my poor "Christie" book [Work] which will never get done I am afraid. Sold the copyright of "H. S's" to Redpath for $25.[12] I am done with it.

March.

Spent a fortnight with Nan who slowly got better. Freddy ill with his teeth. On the nineth Nan went home for the summer. I stayed & moved & packed her things with John. Then home taking Maria to be our girl this summer. Hope the plan will succeed.[13] A busy, month getting settled. Freddy's birthday on the 28th, one year old; he had a dozen little presents laid out in a row when he came down to breakfast & seemed quite overpowered with his riches. On being told to take what he liked best he chose the picture of little Samuel which father gave him, & the old gentleman was much delighted at that.

Was asked for a poem for the great album at the St Louis Fair & sent "Thoreau's Flute" as my best. Also received a letter from the Philadelphia managers asking contributions for the paper to be printed at their Fair.

Wrote nothing this month.

Read Bleak House.[14] Sanitary Papers &c.

April.

At father's request I sent "Moods" to Ticknor & got a very friendly note from Howard T. saying they had so many books on hand that they could do nothing about it now. But his "interest in me as a friend made him anxious to read the book which he had done, & thought it very interesting skil[l]ful & profitable, & hoped a time would come when they could publish it." So I put it back on the shelf & set about my other work feeling pretty sure that if they wouldn't have it there must be something good about it. Dont despair, "Moods," we'll try again by & by![15]

Wrote the first part of a story for Prof. Coppee called "Love & Loyalty," flat, patriotic & done to order. Wrote a new fairy tale "Nellie's Hospital."[16]

Miss Powell had a Gymnastic Class & Nan & I joined.[17] Mrs Sternes sent for me to go & see her, so I went. Found a pleasant house, a sentimental hostess & an odd host, but all very kind & friendly. They asked me to go [to] Niagara with them by & by. Spent the night talked Emerson & every thing else & went to Boston for a week at Molly's to sew for her as Cousin Tom [Sewall] is very poorly.

Hamilton [Willis] was married to Helen Phillips on the 28th — very privately, letting few know of it, & going off to Springfield at once. I pity Mrs W.

Read Oliver Twist, Cecil Dreeme & Scarlet Letter again & like them all better than ever.[18]

May.

Maria had typhoid fever & was off duty for six weeks. I took care of her & Dr B[artlett]. brought her safely through.[19]

Had a letter from a Mrs Gildersleeve asking for my photograph & a sketch of my life for a book called "Heroic Women" which she was getting up. Respectfully refused. Also a letter & flattering notice from "Ruth Hall."[20] & a notice from a Chicago critic with a long extract from "Rose Family." My

Leslie tale "Enigmas" came out & was much liked by readers of sensation rubbish. Having got my $50 I was resigned.

Cousin Henry Bond was killed in the battle of the Wilderness,[21] & Hawthorne was found dead while on his trip with Pierce — He was not brought home at all as his family did not wish to see him.[22] We dressed the church on the 23rd for the funeral which was a very peculiar one throughout. The Atlantic Club[23] came up & many other persons to do him honor. J. F. Clarke performed the service & all followed to the grave.[24]

On the morning after the news came I sent in some violets from the hill where he used to walk. It pleased Mrs H. very much & she wrote me a note.[25] We did all we could to heal the breach between the families but they held off, so we let things rest.

Fields was up & down a good deal, & sent me "Maine Woods" Thoreau's new book.[26] Miss Bartol & Miss Green the artist passed a pleasant day with us.[27]

Read "Campaner Thal," Elective Affinities, & Plato's Dialogues again.[28] Also a curious book on Miscegenation which recalled my story of "M. L."

June.

To town with father on the 3rd to a Fraternity Festival to which we were invited.[29] Had a fine time & was amazed to find my "umble" self made a lion of, set up among the great ones, stared at, waited upon, complimented & made to hold a "laynee" whether I would or no, for Mr Slack kept bringing up people to be introduced till I was tired of shaking hands & hearing the words "Hospital Sketches" uttered in every tone of interest, admiration & respect. Mr Wasson, Whipple, Alger, Clarke, Calthrop, & Chadwick came to speak to me, & many more whose names I forget.[30] It was a very pleasant surprise & a new experience. I liked it, but think a small dose quite as much as is good for me, for after sitting in a corner, & grubbing a la Cinderella it rather turns one's head to be taken out & treated like a Princess all of a sudden.

Herbert Pratt, Willie Swett, Abby & Nellie May came. also many callers, Mrs Hunt the artist's wife, Mrs Furniss Miss Hoar, Mrs Clark & the Jarvises.[31] All praised May's Murcury.

Wrote "The Fate Of The Forrests" for Leslie who sent for a tale.[32]

Also[33] began a tale for the Atlantic,[34] & wrote the third part of "Love & Loyalty" which Coppee accepted at once.

Mrs Mann had a sequel to her Fair & we took part. May had the flower table & made $80, I the refreshments & made $75. The H[awthorne?]'s, P[eabody?]'s & M[ann?]'s very cross & mad.

Father took a talking trip round about & had a fine time.

July

Spent half the month at Mary Sewall's taking care of her father who was slowly dying of paralysis. A busy, quiet time, sewing, nursing & doing errands. The famous Dr Brown-Sequard came to consult with Dr Bowditch & pronounced Mr Sewall past help. [35]

Went home & wrote a story, "An Hour," for the Atlantic, & sent it. [36] As I thought it good was pretty sure they would n't take it. No answer that month Ticknor being away. Also made an article of some letters from Miss Swetts colored pupils at Readville, for the Commonwealth. [37]

August.

Went to Gloucester for a fortnight with May at the Mansfield's. Found a family of six pretty daughters, a pleasant mother, & a father who was an image of one of the Cheeryble Brothers. [38] Had a jolly time boating, driving, charading dancing & picnicing. One mild moonlight night a party of us camped out on Norman's Woe & had a splendid time, lying on the rocks singing, talking, sleeping & rioting up & down. We had a fine time & took coffee at all hours. The moon rose & set beautifully, & the sunrise was a picture I never shall forget. [39]

While at the M's Fanny was engaged, & there being a house full of girls, it made a great stir. The Emersons came down & the Simmons's, also the Newall's who sang finely & were very jolly young men.

Freddy was sick a good deal & we were very anxious about him.

Wrote another fairy tale "Jamie's Wonder Book," [40] & sent the Christmas Stories to Walker & Wise with some lovely illustrations by Miss Greene. [41] They liked the book very much & said they would consult about publishing it though their hands were full.

September

Mrs Dall made a visit & getting hold of my old book of stories liked them & insisted on taking "Moods" home to read. As she had had experience with publishers, was a good business woman & an excellent critic, I let her have it hoping she might be able to give the poor old book the lift it has [been] waiting for all these three years. She took it, read it & admired it heartily, saying that "no American author had showed so much promise; that the plan was admirable, the execution unequal but often magnifecent. That I had a great field before me & my book must be got out." All very agreeable remarks whether true or not. [42]

Mrs Dall sent it to Loring who liked it exceedingly & asked me to shorten it if I could, else it would be too large to sell well. Was much disappointed, said I'd never touch it again & tossed it into the spidery little cupboard where it had so often returned after fruitless trips.

Wrote a blood & thunder story or novelette of several hundred pages to relieve my feelings & called it "V. V."[43]

May sent Murcury to Cattle Show & got a premium. Mr & Mrs Waterston called & admired every thing, were very pleasant & begged us to come & see them.[44]

Walker & Wise like the fairy book & would have got it out if it had not been too late.

October.[45]

October.

Wrote several chapters of Christie [Work] & was getting on finely when as I lay awake one night a way to shorten & arrange "Moods" came into my head. The whole plan laid itself smoothly out before me & I slept no more that night but worked on it as busily as if mind & body had nothing to do with one another. Up early & began to write it all over again. The fit was on strong & for a fortnight I hardly ate slept or stirred but wrote, wrote like a thinking machine in full operation. When it was all rewritten, without copying, I found it much improved though I'd taken out ten chapters & sacrificed many of my favorite things, but being resolved to make it simple, strong & short I let every thing else go & hoped the book would be better for it.[46]

Sent it to Loring & a week after as I sat hammering away at the parlor carpet, dusty, dismal & tired a letter came from Loring praising the story more enthusiastically than ever, thanking me for the improvements, & proposing to bring out the book at once. Of course we all had a rapture & I finished my work "double quick" regardless of weariness, toothache or blue devils.

Next day I went to Boston & saw Loring. A brisk,[47] business-like man who *seemed* in earnest & said many complimentary things about Hospital Sketches & its author. It was agreed to bring out the book immediately & Mrs Dall offered to read the proof with me, Loring to give me ten cents copyright on all copies sold, I forfeiting the copy right on such as are given to newspapers. Settlements to be made once in three months from the time of its publication.

Was glad to have the old thing under way again but didn't quite believe it would ever come out after so many delays & disappointments.

Sewed for Nan & Mary, heard Anna Dickinson & liked her, read "Emily Chester" & thought it an unnatural mess[48] yet just enough like "Moods" in a few things to make me sorry that it came out now.[49]

Nan was poorly so brougth her & Freddy home with me. "Pib" fell ill as soon as he got here. Mother had a very bad turn, John came up sick & I broke down, so for a week we had a hospital.[50]

On Mother's 64th birthday I gave her "Moods" with this inscription — "To Mother, my earliest patron, kindest critic, dearest reader I gratefully & affectionately inscribe my first romance."[51]

A letter from Ticknor asking me to write for the new Magazine "Our Young Folk's,"[52] & saying that "An Hour" was in the hands of the editors.[53]

November.

Proof began to come, & the chapters seemed small, stupid & no more my own in print. I felt very much afraid that I'd ventured too much & should be sorry for it. But Emerson says "that what is true for your own private heart is true for others,"[54] so I wrote from my own life & experience & hope it may suit some one & at least do no harm.

Ticknor accepted a fairy tale I sent him but refused "An Hour," because it was about slavery I suppose. I sent it to the Commonwealth & it was considered *excellent*. Also wrote a Christmas story, "Mrs Podger's Teapot."[55] Ticknor asked to see the other fairy tales & designs & poems as he liked "Nelly's Hospital" so much.

On my 32nd birthday received "Richter's Life" from Nan & enjoyed it so much that I planned a story of two men something like Jean Paul & Goethe, only more every day people. Dont know what will come of it, but if "Moods" goes well "Success" shall follow.

Sewed for Wheeler's colored company & sent them comfort-bags, towels, books, & bed sacks.[56] Mr W. sent me some relics from Point Look Out & a pleasant letter.

December.

On Christmas eve recieved ten copies of "Moods" & a friendly note from Loring. The book was hastily got out, but on the whole suited me, & as the inside was considered good I let the outside go. For a week wherever I went I saw, heard, & talked "Moods;" found people laughing or crying over it, & was continually told how well it was going, how much it was liked, how fine a thing I'd done. I was glad but not proud, I think, for it has always seemed as if "Moods" grew in spite of me, & that I had little to do with it except to put into words the thoughts that would not let me rest until I had.[57]

By Saturday the first edition was gone & the second ready. Several book-sellers ordered a second hundred the first went so fast, & friends could not get it but had to wait till more were ready. I sent one to [Henry] James, [Sr.,] one to mother on Christmas, & several to friends here & there.

Spent a fortnight in town at Mary's shopping, helping Nan & having plays. Heard Emerson once.[58] Sold my Novelle to Elliot for $50.[59] He offered 25 more if I'd let him put my *name to it*, but I wouldn't. Gave Clapp "Mrs Podger's Teapot" which was much liked. Sent Leslie the rest of his story & got $50. Slack paid $35 for "An Hour". Richardson promised a $100 for "Love & Loyalty", so my year closes with a novel well launched & about $300 to pay debts & make the family happy & comfortable till spring. Thank God for the "success of the old year, the promise of the new! — ["]

["Notes and Memoranda"]

1864

Nan & family spent the summer at home. May at Rimmer's. Father busy with garden & schools & writing for the Commonwealth. H. Willis married again. S. Greeley's wife died. H. Bond killed. Hawthorne died May 20th. Visit Gloucester. Ab moulds a fine Murcury. Moods published Dec 25th goes well & makes a little stir. T. R. S[ewall]. died in Sept.

Earnings[60]

A Hospital Christmas.	18
A Golden Wedding.	20
An Hour.	45
Love & Loyalty.	105
Mrs Podgers.	25
Enigmas.	50
Fate of the Forrests.	50
The Rose Family	50[61]

SOURCES: Text and "Notes and Memoranda" — manuscript, Houghton Library, Harvard University.

1. "Fairy Pinafores" appeared in *Cupid and Chow-Chow* (Boston: Roberts Brothers, 1874), vol. 3 of *Aunt Joe's Scrap-Bag*.

2. Redpath made *On Picket Duty, and Other Tales* the first number of his *Books for Camp Fire* series, also called *Books for Camp and Home*.

3. Charles B. Richardson of the *United States Service Magazine*.

4. Henry Wadsworth Longfellow's *Tales of a Wayside Inn* (1863).

5. Mary E. Stearns, wife of the antislavery reformer George Luther Stearns, was a financial angel to all the Alcotts, underwriting the publication of Bronson's *Emerson* (1865) and helping May attend art school. Her album also included a poem on Brown by Bronson (see his letter of 7 February 1864 to Mrs. Stearns in *Letters*, p. 351).

6. Annie Greele, wife of Samuel Sewall Greele (the son of LMA's uncle Samuel Greele), died on 2 January 1864.

7. May noted that "he looks well though not able to use his foot yet" (3 January 1864, diary, Houghton Library, Harvard University).

8. Samuel Ripley Bartlett had protested LMA's reprinting the story, claiming that he owned the copyright. But, as LMA wrote James Redpath, the story "was never wholly paid for," the *Monitor* "died in a little while & was not much known nor read while it lasted," and, finally, it "seems neither neighborly nor necessary to make objections now, & it does not appear to me that we have either of us done anything unlawful or unjust" (29 January [1864], *SL,* pp. 101–102).

9. LMA actually cut *Moods* later at A. K. Loring's suggestion, trimming ten chapters from the manuscript. In her preface to the revised edition published by Roberts Brothers in 1882, LMA wrote that "several chapters have been omitted, several of the original ones restored; and those that remain have been pruned of as much fine writing as could be done without destroying the youthful spirit of the little romance."

10. "The Hospital Lamp" appeared in the 24 and 25 February 1864 issues of the *Daily Morning Drum-Beat,* edited by Richard Salter Storrs.

11. LMA wrote two paragraphs: "Mrs Mann got up a Fair for Colored Orphans at Georgetown. We helped & the thing made $500." and "Had a letter from C. B. Richardson of New York & Professor H Coppee of Philadelphia asking me to write a war story for the new United States Civil Service Magazine which the[y] propose." and then canceled them.

Mary Peabody Mann, widow of the educator Horace Mann, got up fairs in Concord to raise money for her sister Elizabeth Palmer Peabody's drive to build an orphanage for black children in Washington, D.C.; Henry Coppée edited the *United States Service Magazine.*

12. Redpath wrote LMA on 1 December 1863 that because his Camp Fire series made such small profits, he could not grant a copyright or royalty; the "very best" he could do was give her fifty dollars "in addition to what I have paid" (Louisa May Alcott Collection, Barrett Library, University of Virginia). LMA replied on 2 February [1864] that she was still unsure about the copyright, and she asked him to "make me an offer" (*SL,* p. 104).

13. Apparently the plan did not succeed, for May noted in her diary on 5 June that "Marie still ailing" (Houghton Library, Harvard University).

14. Charles Dickens's *Bleak House* (1853).

15. At a later date, LMA inserted: "(Alas, we did try again!)"

16. "Nelly's Hospital" appeared in the April 1865 *Our Young Folks* and was published as a pamphlet the same year by the United States Sanitary Commission.

17. According to Ellen Emerson, Elizabeth Powell had come to Concord in the spring of 1865 "to lead the Gymnasium" (*The Letters of Ellen Tucker Emerson,* ed. Edith E. W. Gregg, 2 vols. [Kent, Ohio: Kent State University Press, 1982], 1:320). She later became dean of Swarthmore College.

18. Theodore Winthrop's *Cecil Dreeme* (1861).

19. At a later date, LMA inserted: "Good little Portugese girl."

20. LMA wrote James Redpath: "I don't know who she is" (18 May [1864], New Hampshire Historical Society).

21. Henry May Bond, the son of George William and Sophia Augusta May Bond, died on 14 May 1864.

22. Hawthorne had died on 19 May while on a walking trip to New Hampshire with Franklin Pierce. His funeral services at Sleepy Hollow cemetery on 23 May were attended by Emerson, Oliver Wendell Holmes, Henry Wadsworth Longfellow, James Russell Lowell, and John Greenleaf Whittier.

23. That is, the Saturday Club of Boston, which included Hawthorne and Emerson as members.

24. The minister James Freeman Clarke, who had also performed the wedding ceremony

of Nathaniel and Sophia Peabody Hawthorne. LMA's poem to Hawthorne, written in November 1862, nicely describes her feelings about him; see Rita K. Gollin, "Louisa May Alcott's 'Hawthorne,' " *Essex Institute Historical Collections* 118 (January 1982): 42–48.

25. No letters between LMA and Sophia Hawthorne have been found; see Edwin Haviland Miller, "A Calendar of the Letters of Sophia Peabody Hawthorne," *Studies in the American Renaissance 1986*, ed. Joel Myerson (Charlottesville: University Press of Virginia, 1986), pp. 199–281.

26. In reading *The Maine Woods*, published on 28 May 1864, LMA felt as if "Thoreau were walking with me again" (see her letter of 28 May [1864] to James T. Fields, in *SL*, pp. 105–106).

27. Elizabeth Bartol, daughter of the Unitarian minister Cyrus A. Bartol; Elizabeth B. Greene illustrated LMA's *Morning-Glories, and Other Stories* (1868).

28. Jean Paul Friedrich Richter's *Campaner Thal and Other Writings* (1864); Goethe's *Elective Affinities* (1809).

29. Bronson briefly describes this event, at which "Louisa receives much attention," in his journal, and pastes in an unidentified newspaper clipping about the meeting (3 June, "Diary for 1864," pp. 187ff, Houghton Library, Harvard University).

30. Not previously identified are the ministers Charles W. Slack, William Rounseville Alger, and S. R. Calthrop.

31. Willie Swett, a friend from the Clarks Island excursion; Abigail Williams May, youngest daughter of Samuel May and Mary Goddard May, was Mrs. Alcott's first cousin; Louisa Perkins Hunt, wife of the artist William Morris Hunt; probably Annis Jenks Furness, wife of William Henry Furness, Unitarian minister in Philadelphia; Caroline Hoar.

32. At a later date, LMA inserted: "Rubbish keeps the pot boiling." "The Fate of the Forrests" appeared in three installments between 11 and 25 February 1865 in *Frank Leslie's Illustrated Newspaper*. It was first identified as LMA's and reprinted in *A Double Life: Newly Discovered Thrillers of Louisa May Alcott*, ed. Madeleine B. Stern (Boston: Little, Brown, 1988).

33. Before this paragraph, LMA wrote: "Also made an article of some letters from Willie Swett's colored soldiers for the Commonwealth." and then canceled it. "Colored Soldiers' Letters" appeared in the 1 July 1864 *Boston Commonwealth*.

34. No more works by LMA appeared in the *Atlantic Monthly Magazine*.

35. The physicians C. E. Brown-Séquard and Henry I. Bowditch.

36. "An Hour" appeared in the 26 November and 3 December 1864 issues of the *Boston Commonwealth*.

37. "Colored Soldiers' Letters."

38. The Cheeryble brothers were two kind and generous merchants in Charles Dickens's *Nicholas Nickleby* (1838–1839).

39. May's account is equally enthusiastic: "Yesterday we came from Gloucester after a most delightful fortnight of parties, seeing the forts, rowing, camping out, charades &c till Lu & I are quite reconciled to being quiet again at home. . . . spending the night [at Norman's Woe] without tents, being merely wrapped in our shawls was without exception the most perfect bliss I shall ever know" (14 August, diary, Houghton Library, Harvard University).

40. For the story of "Jamie's Wonder Book," see *Louisa's Wonder Book: An Unknown Alcott Juvenile*, ed. Madeleine B. Stern (Mount Pleasant: Central Michigan University, 1975).

41. Walker, Wise and Company was succeeded by Horace B. Fuller, who would later publish *Morning-Glories* and *Merry's Museum*; Elizabeth Greene illustrated *The Rose Family*, as well as *Merry's Museum*.

42. At a later date, LMA inserted: "(Proved to be quite *untrue* in the end. 1878)."

43. "V. V.: or, Plots and Counterplots" (by "A. M. Barnard") appeared in four installments between 4 and 25 February 1865 in *Flag of Our Union*.

44. Bronson knew Mr. Waterston "as a youth when I came to Boston in 1828, and I knew him as a teacher of the Sailors in Salem House" (21 September 1864, "Diary for 1864," p. 326, Houghton Library, Harvard University).

LMA wrote: "Also Mrs W. R. Johnson from Washington." and then canceled it. Mrs. Walter R. Johnson was a friend of Bronson's from Washington, whom he had visited when he went to bring Louisa home from the Union Hotel Hospital in 1863.

45. LMA wrote: "Dusty, dismal & tired I was hammering away at the parlor carpet which I'd taken up & put down again all alone when May came in with" and then canceled it. This cancellation accounts for the blank space after the first October listing in our text; after canceling the first October entry, LMA began a second one by writing "October" again.

46. At a later date, LMA inserted: "(It was n't — 1867)."

47. LMA wrote "pleasant" after "brisk" and then canceled it.

48. At a later date, LMA canceled "mess," inserted and canceled "thing," and finally inserted "story"; Anna E. Dickinson lectured on 25 October on "Chicago — The Last Ditch"; *Emily Chester* (1864), published anonymously by Mrs. Anne Seemüller.

49. LMA wrote: "Went to the theatre & found the 'Marble Heart' rather flat." and then canceled it.

50. LMA wrote: "while May went visiting in Boston." and then canceled "went visiting" and inserted "was away," then canceled the entire passage.

51. For the copy of *Moods* inscribed to Mrs. Alcott, see LMA's letter to her mother of [25 December 1864], in *SL*, p. 106.

52. Ticknor and Fields began publishing *Our Young Folks* in January 1865.

53. At a later date, LMA inserted: "(Didn't take it owing to the fact of its being antislavery.) 1877."

54. Paraphrased from Emerson's "Self-Reliance."

55. "Mrs. Podger's Teapot. A Christmas Story" appeared in the 24 December 1864 *Saturday Evening Gazette*.

56. Possibly Lieutenant Charles P. Wheeler of the Fifth Massachusetts Cavalry.

57. At a later date, LMA inserted: "Dont know why."

58. Emerson gave four lectures in Boston during December: "Social Aims" on the fourth, "Resources" on the eleventh, "Table Talk" on the eighteenth, and "Books" on the twenty-fifth.

59. James R. Elliott, editor of *Flag of Our Union*, in which "V. V.: or, Plots and Counterplots" appeared.

60. As the first entry in the list, LMA wrote: "Moods 1st payment [—] 236" and then canceled it.

61. "A Golden Wedding: and What Came of It" appeared in the 29 April and 6 May issues of the *Boston Commonwealth*.

1865

January. 1865.

The month began with some plays at the town hall to raise funds for the Lyceum. We did very well, & some "Scenes from Dickens" were excellent. Father lectured & preached a good deal, being asked like a regular minister & paid like one. He enjoyed it very much & said good things on the new religion which we ought & shall have. May had orders from Canada & England for her paper knives[1] & did well in that line.

Notices of "Moods" came from all directions, & though people didn't understand my ideas owing to my shortening the book so much, the notices were mostly favorable & gave quite as much praise as was good for me. I had letters from Mrs Parker, Chadwick, Sanborn, Greene the artist, T. Higginson & some others, all friendly & flattering.

Went to Boston to A. S. Anniversary & had a lively time for all the dear "brothers & sisters" pecked at one another violently & acted like a set of naughty children.[2] Father made an excellent speech, & told them they ought to be ashamed of themselves. They *were*, & behaved better after the old man had mildly scolded em.

Mrs Sargent had a party & we went & played games with Phillips, Thomson & other amiable parties.[3]

I wrote little this month but sewed & visited. Clapp paid $25 for "Podgers" & wanted more.

February.

Curtis & Higginson lectured, one like an actor the other like a man who forgot himself in his subject which was the Freedmen.[4]

By F. B. S[anborn]'s advice I sent a copy of "Moods" to Conway in England.[5]

Went to Boston to help Mary break up; Heard Murdock read & James lecture on Carlyle.[6] Saw more notices of "Moods" & received more letters, several from strangers, & some very funny. People seem to think the book finely written, very promising, wise & interesting, but some fear it is n't moral because it speaks freely of marriage.

Wrote a new Novelette for Elliott "A Marble Woman" & got $75 for it[7] with which I made things comfortable at home with wood, coal, flour, clothes &c. Mr Elliott wants tales, poems, sketches & novelletes, so I can spin away ad libitum.

Wrote a little on poor old "Success" but being tired of novels I soon dropped it & fell back on rubbishy tales, for they pay best & I cant afford to starve on praise, when sensation stories are written in half the time & keep the family cosy.

May had German parties & there were several public dances which she adorned. Carrie P[ratt]. was very sick & I went to nurse her.[8] Annie & Freddy came up for a few days to see "Gammer."[9]

Earned $75 this month.

March

Recieved $105 for "Love & Loyalty" & a request for more, but the "U. S. Civil Service Magazine" is not in my line so I'm done with it. Paid debts of course, & went to work to earn more.

Ticknor printed "Nelly's Hospital" & paid $25 for it. Not enough, but he thinks he'll bring out the book for me, so I said nothing.

Annie & Freddy made a visit which we enjoyed very much. He is growing & fine boy & shows the effect of all the love that has surrounded him ever since he was born.

I went to Boston & heard father lecture before the Fraternity.[10] Met [Henry] James [Sr.] there & he asked me to come & dine, also called upon me with Mrs James.[11] I went & was treated like the Queen of Sheba. Henry [Jr.] wrote a notice of "Moods" for the North American[12] & was very friendly, being a literary youth.[13]

Acted in some public plays for the N. E. Female Hospital & had a pleasant time.[14]

Leslie asked me to be a regular contributor to his new paper "The Chimney Corner," & I agreed if he'd pay before hand, he said he would & bespoke two tales at once $50 each.[15] Longer ones as often as I could & whatever else I liked to send. So here's another source of income & Alcott brains seem in demand.[16]

Recieved $105 of Coppée — 25 of Ticknor — 5 of Elliott for a little poem. [17]

April

Richmond taken on the 2ond. [18] Hurrah! Went to Boston & enjoyed the grand jollification. Saw Booth again in Hamlet & thought him finer than ever. [19] Had a pleasant walk & talk with Phillips.

On the 15th in the midst of the rejoicing came the sad news of the President's assassination & the city went into mourning. I am glad to have seen such a strange & sudden change in a nation's feelings. Saw the great procession, & though colored men were in it one was walking arm in arm with a white gentleman & I exulted thereat.

Sewed, cleaned house & wrote a story for Leslie, "A Double Tragedy." [20]

Nan went to housekeeping in a pleasant house at Jamaica Plain, & I went to help her move. Gave Mary a last lift & every thing was done up after six months of fuss. She gave as many useful things & lent Nan others so that her little home looked very neat & pretty. It was beautiful to see how Freddy enjoyed the freedom after being cooped up all winter, & how every morning, whether it rained or shone, he looked out & said with a smile of perfect satisfaction, "Oh, pretty day," for all days *were* pretty to him.

Loring paid $236 on Moods — Leslie $50 for one tale —

May

Mother went on a visit to Nan & May turned housekeeper when I offered to pay her $25 if she would fall to until July when a party to the Adirondac Mts. is to come off. She did capitally, & after I'd done the scrubbing up I went to my pen & wrote Leslie's second tale "Ariel, A Legend Of The Lighthouse." [21]

Had a fine letter from Conway & a notice in the "Reader," an English paper. [22] He advised sending copies to several of the best London papers & Loring did so. English people dont understand "Transcendental Literature" as they call "Moods." My next book shall have no *ideas* in it, only facts, & the people shall be as ordinary as possible, then critics will say its all right. [23]

June. [24]

On the 24th Anna's second boy was born at half past three in the morning, [25] Lizzie's birthday. A fine little lad who took to life kindly & seemed to find the world all right. Freddy couldn't seem to understand it at first & told his mother that "the babee" had got his place. But he soon loved the "tunning sing," [26] & would stand watching it with a grave face, till some funny little idea found vent in still funnier words or caresses.

Nan[27] was very happy with her two boys, so was John, though both had wished for a daughter.[28]

July

While at Nan's Mrs Bond Jr. asked if I would go abroad with her sister, I said "Yes," but as I spoke neither French nor German she didn't think I'd do. I was sorry, but being used to disappointment went to work for Nan & bided my time, which came very soon.

Mr Wm F. Weld hearing that I was something of a nurse & wanted to travel proposed my going with his invalid daughter.[29] I agreed though I had my doubts, but every one said "Go", so after a week of work & worry I did go. On the 19th we sailed in the China, Anna & Geo Weld & myself. John, Lucy [Sewall], & Mrs May went to see me off. I could not realize that my long desired dream was coming true, & fears that I might not see all the dear home faces when I came back made my heart very full as we steamed down the harbor & Boston vanished.

Was not very sick but uncomfortable all the way & found the Ladies Saloon my only refuge till we were nearly across. Anna was not ill at all & Geo scorned the idea. Enjoyed intervals of quiet & had many fine glimpses of the sea in its various moods. Sunsets & sun rises, fogs, icebergs, rain storms & summer calms. No pleasant people on board so I read & whiled away the long days as I best could.

We had a very quiet & quick passage of nine days & on Sat. the 29th steamed up the Mersey at dawn & got to Liverpool at nine. I was heartily glad to set my feet on the solid earth again & thought I'd never go to sea again. Rested & looked about a little & took a drive about the dirty city. I never saw so many beggars nor such desperate looking ones.

Monday went up to London. There we stayed four dull, drizzly days for Anna was ill & Geo sight seeing. I amused myself in my usual way, looking well about me & writing descriptions of all I saw in letters or my pocket diary. Went to the Parks, Westminster Abbey & some of the famous streets.[30]

August

Went up to London & there spent four dull, drizzly days, for Anna was ill & Geo. sight-seeing. I amused myself in my usual quiet way looking well about me & writing down all I saw in my pocket diary or letters. Went to Parks, Westminster Abbey & some of the famous streets. I felt as if I'd got into a novel while going about in the places I'd read so much of. Saw no one I knew & thought English weather abominable.

On the 5th to Dover through a lovely green country; took steamer there to Ostende, but was ill all the way & saw nothing but a basin. Spent two days at a queer hotel near the fine Promenade which was a very foreign & brilliant scene. To Brussels on the 7th. Here I enjoyed much for the quaint old city was full of interesting things. The ancient Square where the statues of Egmont & Horn stand was my delight, for the old Dutch houses were still standing & every thing was so new & strange I wanted to stay a month.

To Cologne on the 9th & the country we passed through was like a big picture book. The city was very hot, dirty & evil-smelling — We saw the Cathedral got Eau d'Cologne, & very gladly left after three days spent by me in nursing both my companions who gave out here.

On the 12th began a lovely voyage up the Rhine. It was too beautiful to describe so I shall not try, but I feel richer & better for that memorable day. We reached Coblentz at sunset & I was up half the night enjoying the splendid view of the fortress opposite the town, the moonlight river with its bridge of boats & troops crossing at midnight.

A second day still more charming took us through the famous parts of the Rhine & filled my head with pictures that will last all my life. Anna was ill before we reached Biebrich so we stopped at a little town & had a queer time, for no one spoke English & we only a little bad French. night there & next day reached Schwalbach after many trials & tribulations.

The place is a narrow valley shut in between high hills; the town being divided into two parts; the lowest is the original town, queer old houses, churches & narrow streets, the upper part near the springs is full of fine hotels, pleasant grounds & bath houses.

We took lodgings with Madame Genth wife of the Forst-meister (forest master). Two rooms, & began the water under Dr Genth's care.[31] He thought Anna improved, & her quiet life seemed to do her good. I tried my best to suit & serve her but dont think I did so very well, yet many would have done still worse I fancy, for hers is a very hard case to manage & needs the patience & wisdom of an angel.

We walked a little, talked a little, bathed & rode a little, worried a good deal, & I grubbed away at French with no master & small success.

We had two pleasant neighbors Martha Aschmann & Marie Barow. Prussians, but they soon left.

September.

Still at Schwalbach, Anna doing her best to get well & I doing mine to help her. No letters yet from home & I begin to be very anxious. Rather dull days bathing, walking, & quiddling about.

A letter from home on the 20th. All well & happy, thank God! It touched & pleased me very much to see how they missed me, thought of me, & longed to have me back. Every little thing I ever did for them is now so tenderly & gratefully remembered, & my absence seems to have left so large a gap that I begin to realize how much I am to them in spite of all my faults. The letters made me very happy, & every thing brightened immensely. Anna got stronger & when Geo. came on the 28th was able to start off next day on the way to Vevay where we are to pass some weeks before we go to Nice.

Went to Wiesbaden first, a pleasant gay place full of people. Saw the gambling hall & people playing, the fine grounds & drives, & then went on to Frankfort. Here I saw & enjoyed a good deal. The statues of Goethe, Schiller, Faust, Gutenburg & Schaeffer in the Squares. Goethe's house, a tall plain building with each story projecting over the lower & a Dutch roof. A marble slab over the front door recording the date of Goethe's birth. I took a look at it & wanted to go in as it was empty, but there was no time.[32]

Got some pictures of the great statues, Geo Sand & the house. Frankfort is a pleasant old city on the river & I'm glad to have been there.

October.

Went to Heidelburg, a charming place surrounded by Mts. We went to the Castle & had a fine time roving about the ruins, looking at the view from the great terrace, admiring the quaint stone images of knights, saints, monsters & angels, & visiting the big tun in the cellar by torchlight.[33] The moon rose while we were there & completed the enchantment of the scene. The drive home was like looking at a picture book for the street was narrow, the carriage high & we looked in at the windows seeing pretty scenes. Here men drinking beer in a Dutch looking room, then little children going to bed, a pair of lovers with a pot. of flowers between them, an old woman brooding over the fire like a witch, & in one room some one lay dead surrounded by candles.

From H. we went to Baden Baden, a very fashionable place. The old chateau was my delight & we passed a morning going up & down to visit it. Next to Freilburg where the Cathedral delighted me extremely, being full of old carved images & grotesque designs. The market place with the fountains, statues, water running beside the streets & queer costumes.

Basle came next & a fireman's fête made the city very gay. The hotel was on the river & moonlight made a Venetian scene for me with the lighted bridge, covered gondola-like boats & music from both shores.[34]

On our way to Berne I caught my first glimpse of the Alps Oct 8th, mother's birthday. Tall, white, spectral looking shapes they were, towering above the green hills & valleys that lay between. Clouds half hid them & the sun glittered on the everlasting snow that lay upon their tops. Sharp, strange outlines against the sky they became as night came on, & in the morning I had a fine view of the Jung Frau, the Blumlis, the Wetter horn & Monck from the terrace at Berne. B. was a queer old city but I saw little of it. [35]

Freiburg No. 2 was the most romantic place we have been in. The town is built in a wide crevice or valley between two steep hills so that suspension bridges are hung from height to height over a winding river & the streets of the town. Watch towers stand all about on the hills, & give a very romantic air to the place. The hotel overhung this valley, & from our rooms we went out along a balcony to a wide paved platform with a fountain in the middle, an aviary, & flowers all about. The view down the valley was charming, the airy bridges, green or rocky slopes, busy squares below, cows & goats feeding on the hills, the towers, the old church & a lovely blue sky overhead. I longed to sketch it.

At Lausanne we stopped at the Hotel Gibbon & saw the garden where the great historian wrote his history. [36] The view of the lake was lovely with rocky Mts opposite, little towns at their feet, vineyards along the hillsides & pretty boats on the lake the water of which was the loveliest blue.

To Vevay at last, a pleasant hour's sail to a very pleasant place. [37] We took rooms at the Pension Victoria & Geo. left us to go on to Paris &c.

Our landlady was an Englishwoman who had married a French courier. Very kind sort of people, rooms comfortable, meals good & surroundings agreeable. Our fellow boarders varied from time to time. An English Dr & wife, a fine old lady with them who looked like Marie Antoinette. Two Scotch ladies named Glennie, very pleasant well bred ladies who told me about Beattie who was their grandfather & Walter Scott whom they knew. A young Englishman & his wife, Mr Josephs a fat American, Mrs Thacker & daughter, English & jolly. Col Polk & family, rebels, & very bitter & rude to us. Had queer times with them. [38]

I did not enjoy the life nor the society after the first novelty wore off for I missed my freedom & grew very tired of the daily worry which I had to go through with. Anna improved & that was a great satisfaction to me. [39]

November.

Took some French lessons with Mademoiselle Germain & learned a little, but found it much harder than I thought & often got discouraged I was so stupid. Anna got much better & some new people came. The Dr & his set left, & in their place came a Russian family, an Irish lady & daughter, & a young Pole with whom we struck up a friendship. [40] *Ladislas Weisneiwsky* was very gay & agreeable, & being ill & much younger than us we petted him. He played beautifully, & was very anxious to learn English, so we taught him that & he taught us French.

The Thackers were very friendly, & Miss Ann's lover was also kind &

agreeable. On my birthday Anna gave me a pretty painting of Chillon. Ladislas promised me the notes of the beautiful Polish National Hymn & played me his sweetest airs as a present after wishing me "All good & happiness on earth & a high place in Heaven as my reward." It was a wild, windy day, very like me in its fitful changes of sunshine & shade. Usually I am sad on my birthday, but not this time, for though nothing very pleasant happened I was happy & hopeful & enjoyed everything with unusual relish. I feel rather old with my 33 years but have much to keep me young, & hope I shall not grow older in heart as the time goes on. I thought much of dear father on this 66th birthday, & missed the little ceremony that always takes place on these occasions. Hope I shall be safely at home before another Nov. comes.

December.

A little romance with L[adislas]. W[isniewski]. [undeciphered].[41] L. very interesting & good. Pleasant walks & talks with him in the chateau garden & about Vevey. A lovely sail on the lake, & much fun giving English & receiving French lessons. Every one very kind & the house quite home like. Much indecision about going to Nice owing to the cholera. At last we decided to go, & started on the 6th to meet Geo. at Geneva. L. went with us to Lausanne kissed our hands at parting & went back to V[evey]. disconsolate. Sad times for A. & I but we journeyed away to Nice & tried to forget our troubles. A flat uninteresting country till we approached the sea.

Nice very pleasant, climate lovely & sea beautiful. Geo. fixed us at Pension Milliet No 3 Rue St Etienne & then hurried home to America.

Anna very poorly for a week or two, Dr Pantaleoni, the famous Roman exile & Dr tended her & thought he could help her. We lived in our own rooms & saw no one but the Dr & Consul & a few American callers. A pleasant drive every day on the Promenade, a wide curving mall along the bay with Hotels & Pensions on one side & a flowery walk on the other. Gay carriages & people always to be seen. Shops full of fine & curious things, picturesque castles, towers & walls on one hill, a light house on each point of the moon shaped bay, boats & our fleet on the water, gardens, olive & orange trees, queer cactuses & palms all about on the land. Monks, priests, soldiers, peasants &c.

Dull days here, often homesick & very tired of doing nothing pleasant or interesting. Try to study French, but with little time, less talent & no teacher I did not get on very fast. Anna troubled about Laddie who was in a despairing state of mind. I could not advise them to be happy as they desired, so everything went wrong & both worried.[42] Dr Pantaleoni was very kind & fatherly also the Consul.[43]

A gay party in the eve at the Hotel.

Earnings for 1865 $745

["Notes and Memoranda"]
1865

Father lectured & preached. Not chosen for Supt. again.[44] Paid up the debts with my first "Moods" money, & made all things easy. Began to feel rich for stories were asked for faster than I could write them & my dream of supporting the family seemed to be coming true at last. Notices of my book in all directions & much talk about it. It was spoilt by shortening. I shall know better another time & criticism will do me good. M. K. S. breaks up housekeeping & goes to St Paul.[45]

Earnings

V. V.	50
A Marble Woman.	75
A Double Tragedy.	50
Nelly's Hospital.	25
Moods — 1st payment.	236
Ariel.	50
Moods	14[46]

SOURCES: Text and "Notes and Memoranda" — manuscript, Houghton Library, Harvard University.

1. At a later date, LMA canceled "paper knives" and wrote: "pretty pen & ink work."

2. The meeting of the Massachusetts Anti-Slavery Society on 26–27 January at the Melodeon, with Wendell Phillips as the featured speaker, was reported in the *Boston Commonwealth*.

3. Mary E. Fiske Sargent, who, with her husband, John T. Sargent, would later found the Radical Club, meetings of which LMA attended.

4. Thomas Wentworth Higginson spoke on the freedmen of South Carolina on 8 February, and George William Curtis on political infidelity on 15 February, both at the Concord Lyceum.

5. The copy of *Moods* was included with LMA's letter of 18 February 1865 to Moncure Daniel Conway (*SL*, pp. 107–108).

6. On 29 January, James E. Murdoch finished a series of dramatic readings; on 19 February, Henry James, Sr., gave a talk entitled "English and American Ideals." The latter was possibly similar to the lecture about which Ellen Emerson wrote her father, which was "a long comparison between you and Mr. Carlyle" and during which "he fixed his eyes on me . . . it was very doubtful which [of us] would give way but I didn't, and at last he turned his eyes away at the last sentence" (24 January 1865, in *The Letters of Ellen Tucker Emerson*, ed. Edith E. W. Gregg, 2 vols. [Kent, Ohio: Kent State University Press, 1982], 1:329).

7. "A Marble Woman: or, The Mysterious Model" appeared in four installments between 20 May and 10 June 1865 in *Flag of Our Union.*

8. Carrie Pratt, LMA's sister-in-law, died in 1866 at the age of twenty-nine.

9. That is, "Grandma" in baby talk.

10. Bronson gave the following lectures: "Our Time and Its Teachers" on 3 February, "American Religion" on 5 February, "Race and Complexion" on 3 March, and "Religious Views and Issues of Our Time" on 5 March.

11. Mary Walsh James.

12. Henry James, Jr., writing in the September 1865 *North American Review*, said that the "two most striking facts" of the book were "the author's ignorance of human nature, and her self-confidence in spite of this ignorance" (101:280).

13. LMA inserted: "he gave me advice as if he had been so as a girl. My curly crop made me look young tho 31 — " at a later date.

14. On 14 March, LMA's troupe performed *The Jacobite* and *The Cricket on the Hearth,* adapted from Dickens. The *Boston Commonwealth* commended "two daughters and a son-in-law of Mr. A. Bronson Alcott" for their "superior histrionic ability" (18 March 1865, p. 2).

15. The first issue of *Frank Leslie's Chimney Corner* was published on 3 June 1865.

16. At a later date, LMA inserted: "whereat I sing 'Hallyluyer!' & fill up my inkstand."

17. "In the Garret" appeared in the 18 March 1865 *Flag of Our Union.*

18. The Union army entered Richmond on 3 April.

19. Edwin Booth performed in *Hamlet* at the Boston Theatre on 1 April.

20. "A Double Tragedy. An Actor's Story" appeared in the 3 June 1865 *Frank Leslie's Chimney Corner.* It was first identified as LMA's and reprinted in *A Double Life: Newly Discovered Thrillers of Louisa May Alcott,* ed. Madeleine B. Stern (Boston: Little, Brown, 1988).

21. "Ariel. A Legend of the Lighthouse" appeared in the 8 and 15 July 1865 *Frank Leslie's Chimney Corner.* It was first identified as LMA's and reprinted in *A Double Life.*

22. "Transcendental Fiction," *Reader* 5 (15 April 1865): 422–423 (reprinted in *Critical Essays on Louisa May Alcott,* ed. Madeleine B. Stern [Boston: G. K. Hall, 1984], pp. 66–69).

23. At a later date, LMA inserted: "I seem to have been playing with edge tools without knowing it. The relations between Warwick Moor & Silvia are pronounced impossible, yet a case of the sort exists in Concord & the woman came & asked me how I knew it. I did *not* know or guess, but perhaps felt it without any other guide, & unconsciously put the thing into my book, for I changed the ending about that time. It was meant to show a life affected by *moods,* not a discussion of marriage which I knew little about, except observing that very few were happy ones."

24. At a later date, LMA inserted two paragraphs: "Busy writing, keeping house & sewing. Company often, & strangers begin to come demanding to see the authoress who does not like it & is porcupiny." and "Admire the books but let the woman alone if you please, dear public."

25. John Sewall Pratt, Anna's second and last child.

26. "Tiny thing" in baby talk.

27. After "Nan," LMA wrote: "got up finely &" and then canceled it.

28. LMA wrote: "Lucy Sewall was her Dr & did capitally. I was housekeeper & old Miss Adams 'nurse'." and then canceled it. Lucy Sewall was Samuel E. Sewall's daughter and a Boston physician.

29. LMA accompanied Anna Weld and her half brother George on a European trip that lasted from 19 July 1865 to 19 July 1866. Their father, William Fletcher Weld, was a Boston shipping merchant.

30. Much of this material is repeated in the entry for August.

31. Adolph Genth, author of *The Iron Waters of Schwalbach* (1856).

32. At a later date, LMA inserted: "The W[eld].s said, 'Who was Goethe to fuss about?' "

33. The Heidelberg tun, a wine cask with the capacity of forty-nine thousand gallons, is described by Herman Melville in Chapter 77 of *Moby-Dick.*

34. At a later date, LMA inserted: "I walk while A. rests, & enjoy sights from my window when she is asleep as I cannot leave her at night."

35. At a later date, LMA inserted: "except the bears & shops. No time."

36. Edward Gibbon's *History of the Decline and Fall of the Roman Empire* (1776–1788).

37. Vevey, Switzerland, is on the shores of Lake Geneva, across from the Alps of Savoy.

38. LMA describes these people in "Life in a Pension" as "Wiggy Dr [B.] and his faded wife", Margaret and Ellen Glennie, who knew the Scottish poet James Beattie and novelist Sir Walter Scott; Mr. Wood, the "agent for a hardware concern in Birmingham," and his wife, who tried to pass themselves off as well-connected aristocracy; Mr. Joseph, "the fat Frenchman"; Colonel Polk and his family from South Carolina; and Ann Chatterly, aged thirty-five, and beau, "a Teutonic admirer [who] smoked cigarettes at the shrine of Ann, and proved the depth of his passion by teaching her Italian in German" (*Independent* 19 [7 November 1867]: 2).

39. At a later date, LMA inserted: "1885   Now, having been a nervous invalid myself, I understand what seemed whims, selfishness & folly at the time I was with A."

40. The character of Laurie in *Little Women* was partially based on Ladislas Wisniewski. As LMA wrote Alfred Whitman in 1869, " 'Laurie' is you & my Polish boy 'jintly'. You are the sober half & my Ladislas (whom I met abroad) is the gay whirligig half, he was a perfect dear" (6 January, *SL*, p. 120). See also LMA's "My Polish Boy" in the 26 November and 3 December 1868 issues of *Youth's Companion*.

41. LMA scratched out whatever word or words were originally written here, destroying the paper (the only instance in her journals of such a cancellation), then inserted at a later date: "Couldn't be."

42. At a later date, LMA canceled "them" and inserted "him," then canceled the entire passage.

43. At a later date, LMA inserted: "A dull Christmas within doors though a lovely day without. Windows open, roses blooming, air mild & city gay. With friends, health & a little money how jolly one might be in this perpetual summer."

44. Bronson had been appointed superintendent of schools for Concord in April 1859 at a salary of one hundred dollars per year. Despite doing an excellent job, he was not reappointed in 1865, due to what Odell Shepard described as "a political 'deal' rather than to any well-founded dissatisfaction with his work" (Bronson's *Journals*, p. 371n).

45. At a later date, LMA inserted: "In July went to Europe with Anna Weld. Spent the summer in Schwalbach, the autumn at Vevey, the winter at Nice. Hard work with a fretful invalid, but I enjoyed much."

46. At a later date, LMA inserted: "Mr Weld for 6 months [—] 200."

1866

January 1866.
Nice.

Rained all New Year's day & I spent it sewing, writing & reading an American newspaper which came in the morning, my only present. I hoped for letters but got none & was much disappointed. Anna was ill so I had to receive in American style. Mr Perkins, Cooper & the Consul called. At dinner we drank the healths of all at home, & also Laddie's, in our bottle of champagne.

A quiet dull time generally, driving sometimes, walking a little, writing letters & tending Anna who was not much better for Dr P[antaleoni]'s dosing. Now & then I got a pleasant walk by myself away among the vineyards & olive trees or down into the queer old city. I soon tired of the fashionable Promenade for every one was on exhibition. Sometimes before or after the fashionable hour I walked there & enjoyed the sea & sky.

A ball was given at our Pension & we went. A queer set, Russians, Spaniards, French English Americans Italians Jews & Sandwich Islanders. They danced wildly, dressed gaily & sounded as if the "confusion of tongues" was come again. A few pleasant Americans called on us but we were very lonely & uncomfortable.

Decided to take an Appartement No 10 Rue Geoffredo, paying 600 fs for ten weeks, 6 rooms, all large & handsome. Dr P got us a good maid & on the 17th we went to our new quarters. Madame Rolande was French governess for 6 years to Victoria's children & was a funny old party.[1]

Couldn't sleep at all for some nights & felt very poorly for my life didn't suit me & the air was too exciting.

February

Got on excellently with our housekeeping for Julie proved a treasure & we were very comfortable. Had many lovely drives & saw something of Nice &

its beauties. To Cimies, an old Franciscan monastary near the ruins of a Roman Ampitheatre. The convent stands where a temple of Diana once stood, & is surrounded by ancient ilex trees. A monk in his cowl, brown robe, sandals & rope girdle did the honors of the church, which was dark & full of bad pictures. San André with its chateau & grotto, Villa Franco in a lovely little bay, the Wood of Var, where the daisies grew, Valrosa, a villa in a rose garden, & the Porte were all interesting. Also Castle-hill which over looks the town.

Anna sent away Dr P. & got much better. I decided to go home in May though A. wants me to stay. I'm tired of it & as she is not going to travel my time is too valuable to be spent in fussing over cushions & carrying shawls. I'm rather fond of her but she wears upon me & we are best apart. With her sister & a servant she will be as cosy as *she* can be any where.[2]

The Carnival occurred. Funny but not so fine a sight as I expected. Also went to the Theatre to see Lady Tartuffe. Had a pleasant time though I could not understand much. The acting was so natural & good that I caught the plot & with a little telling from Hosmer knew what was going on.

Saw Madame Blüm & her daughter Camilla, Danish, who knew Miss Bremer whose death they told me about.[3]

Wrote a little on three stories which would come into my head & worry me till I gave them a "went."

Good letters from home. All well & busy & longing for me in the spring.

March.

A tedious month which might have been quite the reverse had I been free to enjoy it in my own way. Anna poorly & fidgety, nothing right in heaven or on earth. Read French, walked to my favorite places & wrote letters when I found time.

Went often to Valrosa a lovely villa buried in roses. Got a wheeled chair & a man to draw it, then with books, lunch & work I tempted Anna out into the woods & we had some pleasant hours. She seemed better at times & I hoped; but nothing lasted long.

Burr Hosmer came a good deal, full of German philosophy & poetry. Conceited but better than no one.[4]

April.

Went to the Cathedral to see the Easter ceremonies. Fine music, the Gloria was sung, a Franciscan monk preached, the Bishop blessed everyone, I was fussed over like a great doll. A very splendid scene.

Saw Ristori twice, once in Medea & once in Elizabeth.[5] Never saw such acting; especially in Queen Bess, it was splendid, & the changes from the young, violent, coquettish woman to the peevish old crone dying with her crown on, vain, ambitious & remorseful.

Young Washburn & his sister came to Nice, very pleasant Boston people with whom we had some agreeable times. Both of us needed society & enjoyed it.

May.

On the first day of the month left Anna & Nice & started alone for Paris feeling as happy as a freed bird. Anna cried & seemed to feel badly, but it was best to part, & having come to that conclusion long ago I never changed my mind, but made her as comfortable as I could with a maid & companion & then turned my face toward home rejoicing.

Julie & B. G. H[osmer]. went to the Station & saw me off, poor Teresa fell upon my neck & moaned, & Madame gave some letters & her blessing.

A pleasant journey. Laddie waiting for me in Paris to take me to my room at Madame Dyne's. A very charming fortnight here; the days spent in seeing sights with Laddie, the evenings in reading, writing, hearing "my boy" play, or resting. Saw me only all that I wished to see in a very pleasant way & on the 17th reluctantly went to London.

Passed a fortnight at a lovely old place on Wimbledon Common with the Conways, [6] going to town with them to see the lions. Royal Exhibition, Hampton Court, Kensington & British Museums, Crystal Palace, & many other pleasant places.

But none were lovelier to me than the old farm house with the thatched roof, the common of yellow gorse, larks going up in the morning, nighten gales at night, hawthorne every where, & Richmond Park full of deer close by. Also Robin Hood's barn.

June.

Passed the first ten days of the month at Aubury House with the Peter Taylors. [7] A lovely English house with kind, pure & friendly people. Saw many interesting persons. Miss Cobbe, Jean Ingelow, Miss Garret, Madame Bodichon, Matilda Blind; Mill, Bright, Gladstone, Hughs & the rest at the House of Commons where Mr T. took me. [8]

Went to a dinner party or two, theatres, to hear Dickens read, [9] a Concert, Conversazione & Receptions, seeing English society, or rather one class of it, & liking what I saw.

On the 11th went to board with Mrs Travers in Westbourne Grove Terrace. A pleasant little room, plain living & for society Mrs T. & daughter, two sisters from Dublin, & ten young men, barristers, clerks ministers & students. A guinea a week.

Very free & jolly, roaming about London all day, dining late & resting, chatting, music or fun in the eve.

Saw the Tower, Windsor, Parks, Gardens, & all manner of haunts of famous men & women. Milton's house, Johnson's in Ball-Court Lamb's, Sairy Gamp's, Saracen's Head. The Charter House where Thackary was when a lad. Furnival's Inn where Dickens wrote Pickwick, Bacon's Walk, & endless memorable sights. St Paul's I liked better than Notre Dame.

Rutledge gave me $25 for Moods.[10]

July

At Mrs Travers till the 7th. Saw Routledge about "Moods". He took it & gave £5. $25 for it. Would like another book & was very friendly.[11] Said good bye all round & at 6 A.M. on the 7th left for Liverpool with Mr Williams who saw to my luggage & went part way. Reached the Africa safely & saw little Cooper the first thing.

A trip of fourteen stormy, dull, long, sick days; but at last at 11 at night we sailed up the harbor in the moonlight & I saw dear John waiting for me on the wharf. Slept on board, & next day reached home at noon to find father at the station, Nan & babies at the gate, May flying wildly round the lawn & Marmee crying at the door. Into her arms I went & was at home at last! Happy days, talking & enjoying one another. Many people come to see me & all said I was much improved, of which I was glad as there was, is, & always will be room for it. Had a fuss with Mr W[eld]. but John helped me through & he at last paid me my proper wages. Glad to be done with them.[12]

Found Mother looking old, sick & tired. Father as placid as ever. Nan poorly but blest in her babies. May full of plans as usual. Freddie very stout & loving, & my Jack the dearest, prettiest merriest boy that ever kissed & loved every body.[13]

Aug.

Soon fell to work on some stories for things were, as I expected, behind hand when the money-maker was away. Found plenty to do as orders from Elliott, Leslie, Independent, U.S.C.S. Magazine & several other offers waited for me. Wrote two long tales for Leslie & got $200 for them. One for Elliott for which he paid $75, also a bit of poetry for $5,00.[14] He wanted a long one in 24 Chapters & I wrote it in a fortnight 185 pages, beside work, sewing nursing & company.

Sent S. E. S. the first $100 on my account,[15] could have sent $300 but it was needed so I gave it up unwillingly & must work away for the rest. Mother lent the money that I might stay longer & see England, as I had missed

much while condemned to "hard work & solitary confinement for nine months,"
as she expressed it. [16]

September.

Mother sick, did little with my pen.

Got a girl & devoted myself to mother, writing after she was abed. In this
way finished the long tale "A Modern Mephistopheles." [17] But Elliott would
not have it, saying it was too long & too sensational! So I put it away & fell
to work on other things. [18]

E Wells married S. Greele, a foolish match. [19] Went to the wedding &
had a dull time. Ticknor added to my worries by sending word that the MS.
of the fairy tales was lost. [20]

A nice letter from my Laddie in Poland. He is better & the same dear boy
as ever. [21]

Leslie asked me to write a $50 tale a month for him & I agreed to do it.
Hope I may have time.

Went to B[oston]. got sheeting, shirting, gowns coal, &c, & paid bills all
round.

A shilling copy of "Moods" came from London & a notice saying it was
selling fast.

October.

Wrote a sketch for Independent of Cobbe, Ingelow &c. for which he paid
$25. [22]

Mother still very poorly. Nan & babies a great care, very hard times all
round. [23]

November.

Mother slowly mending. A sensible Western woman, Mrs Konshner, came
& bathed & rubbed her & did her a deal of good. [24] She left her room &
seemed more like herself; I never expect to see the strong, energetic "marmee" of old times, but, thank the Lord, she is still here though, pale & weak,
quiet & sad. All her fine hair gone & face full of wrinkles, bowed back &
every sign of age. [25]

Nan & babies went on the 8th to board with John at East Boston for the
winter in a cosy pair of rooms with young Ricketson. [26] Sorry yet glad to
have them go, shall miss the dear babies but must have quiet for mother &
writing.

Father prepared to go West & started on the 23 for St Louis to talk to the
young philosophers. [27] Hope they will remember to pay the old one. [28]

Wrote two tales for Leslie $100 & one for Elliott $60. [29]

December.

A *dull* month, feeling ill most of the time & driven by the prospect of bills which must be paid. Wrote all I could, took care of mother & went to Boston once.

Found Nan very neat & cosy in her new rooms & the boys well & happy.[30]

Sent a Christmas box to the laddies & got one in return with Longfellow's new book for me,[31] & something pretty for us all. No one else thought of us. Se[l]dom do.[32]

Father returned on the 20th thin, tired, hungry & dirty, very glad to get home to his cider & berries & be cuddled by his old lady. He brought $200 & had a pleasant time.[33]

Got more leisure to write after he came, & had a fire in my room & fell to work; but the climate is so different from that where I was last year that I had heavy colds all the time which made me dull & poorly & I seem to have magnetized A's neuralgia into myself.

Sick in my bed several days & the house rather "hospitally", all being ill.

Paid bills, but never expect to see the end of em.

Wrote a Sketch for Gilmore. "The Baron's Gloves," a long one for Elliott, a sketch of Dickens & Spurgeon for the Independent & a wild Russian story "Taming a Tartar."[34]

Hope next year will be happier & easier.

["Notes and Memoranda"]
1866

At Nice till May when I left A. W. to go to back to Germany & I went alone to Paris. "Laddie" there, & we had a fine time for a fortnight. To London, & spent 6 weeks with the Conways, Taylors, & at Mrs Travers. Enjoyed it very much. Saw many people. Jean Ingelow, Miss Cobbe, Miss Garrett, Mill, Bright, Gladstone & D'Isreali.[35] Home in July & fell to work with a will, finding every thing behind hind [hand]. Wrote 12 tales in less than three months besides much care & company.

1866

My Malady.	100
Freaks of a Genius.	100
Hope's Debut.	50
Thrice Tempted.	50
Baron's Gloves.	100
Behind A Mask.	80
Abbot's Ghost.	60

Taming a Tartar.	100
Sketches for Ind.	55
Ticknor — lost Ms.	180
Loring on "Moods".	25
Poems.	10
Routledge on "Moods"	25
Mr Weld — expences &c.	168 [36]

SOURCES: Text and "Notes and Memoranda" — manuscript, Houghton Library, Harvard University.

1. Madame Rolande and her daughter Julie are described in LMA's "Royal Governess," which appeared in the 9 July 1868 *Independent*.

2. LMA wrote: "Hosmer, a young Germanized American came much to see us." and then canceled it.

3. The Swedish novelist Fredrika Bremer had died on 31 December 1865.

4. At a later date, LMA inserted: "Queer times with him."

5. LMA also heard Adelaide Ristori sing at the opera in November 1867 and April 1870.

6. LMA stayed with Moncure Daniel Conway and his wife, Ellen, during part of her stay in London.

7. Peter Alfred Taylor and his wife, Clementia, of Aubrey House in Notting Hill.

8. Frances Power Cobbe, who edited Theodore Parker's works in England; the poet Jean Ingelow; Elizabeth Garrett, who had been refused admission to medical school because of her sex but obtained her medical degree by attending lectures on her own; Madame Bodichon, a friend of the poets Elizabeth Barrett and Robert Browning; Mathilde Blind, a woman suffrage reformer; the philosopher John Stuart Mill; the author and minister Henry Arthur Bright; the politician William E. Gladstone; and possibly the Irish judge Henry George Hughes.

9. In an untitled note in the 21 September 1867 *Boston Commonwealth*, LMA wrote of Dickens that "youth and comeliness were gone, but the foppishness remained; and the red-faced man, with false teeth, and the voice of a worn-out actor, had his scanty grey hair curled" (p. 1).

10. *Moods* was published in England in August 1866 by George Routledge of London. Upon receiving her twenty-five dollars, LMA wrote Mrs. Conway that "as Paradise Lost went for £10 I ought to be satisfied with £5 for my *great* work. Oh, the vanity of authors!" ([early July 1866], *SL*, p. 113n).

11. LMA wrote: "To the Princess Theatre & saw 'Fast Family' & 'Helen'. Very flat." and then canceled it. F. C. Burnard's *Fast Family* was playing at the Royal Adelphi Theatre with *Helen; or Taken from the Greek*, a burlesque opera based on Jacques Offenbach's *La Belle Hélène*.

12. At a later date, LMA changed "them" to "their" and inserted "service of this sort."

13. John Bridge Pratt wrote Alfred Whitman that "Louisa has got back; didn't have a very good time, so confined that she had very little time to see until after she left her companion, & then looking with all the eyes she had, & all the feet she had, & all the hands she had & *all* the faculty she had till she contrived to see considerable for a lone woman, without funds, in a short space of time" (11 November 1866, Houghton Library, Harvard University).

14. "Behind a Mask: or, A Woman's Power" appeared in four installments between 13 October and 3 November 1866 in *Flag of Our Union*, which also printed LMA's poem "Our Little Ghost" on 15 September 1866.

15. LMA's cousin Samuel E. Sewall, lawyer, antislavery and woman's rights activist, and trusted financial adviser to the Alcotts.

16. LMA wrote: "May to the [Clarks] Island for a fortnight." and then canceled it.

17. The manuscript of this early version of *A Modern Mephistopheles* is at the Houghton Library, Harvard University. The differences between it and the version published in 1877 are described in Madeleine B. Stern's introduction to *A Modern Mephistopheles and Taming a Tartar*, ed. Stern (New York: Praeger, 1987), pp. xi–xvi.

18. At a later date, LMA inserted: "(No Name long afterward.)"

19. Eliza May Wells married Samuel Greele on 5 September 1866.

20. Howard Ticknor wrote LMA on 7 September 1866 that her manuscript had been "lost in the hurly-burly" (Louisa May Alcott Collection, Barrett Library, University of Virginia). For more on this book, see *Louisa's Wonder Book: An Unknown Alcott Juvenile*, ed. Madeleine B. Stern (Mount Pleasant: Central Michigan University, 1975).

21. LMA wrote: "May did a crayon of L. Wells." and then canceled it.

22. "Glimpses of Eminent Persons" appeared in the 1 November 1866 *Independent*.

23. LMA wrote: "Read Clarissa Harlowe & Pamela." and then canceled it (Samuel Richardson's *Clarissa* [1748], with its main character Clarissa Harlowe, and *Pamela* [1741–1742]).

24. This may be the same as the Dr. Karsner Mrs. Alcott mentions as attending her in January and February of 1867 (27 and 28 January, 10 February, diary, Houghton Library, Harvard University).

25. At a later date, LMA inserted: "Life has been so hard for her & she so brave, so glad to spend herself for others. Now we must live for her."

26. Probably Walton Ricketson, son of Daniel Ricketson of New Bedford, a friend of Thoreau's and the Alcotts'.

27. Bronson had been in St. Louis earlier in the year to meet with the St. Louis Philosophical Society and with William Torrey Harris, who asked him to contribute to the new *Journal of Speculative Philosophy*.

28. LMA wrote two paragraphs: "Abby May called. Kitty Sargent made a visit. Also M. D. M. on a visit." and "Nan & boys spend Thanksgiving with us." and then canceled them. Kitty Sargent was John T. and Mary Fiske Sargent's daughter.

29. "The Abbot's Ghost; or, Maurice Treherne's Temptation" appeared in four installments between 5 and 26 January 1867 in *Flag of Our Union*.

30. LMA wrote: "Saw Aunt May, E Wells, Auntie, M. D. M. & Lucy [Sewall?]. Got some things for mother & trotted home again." and then canceled it.

31. Henry Wadsworth Longfellow's *Flower-de-Luce* (1867), published in December 1866.

32. At a later date, LMA inserted: "Out of sight &c."

33. According to F. B. Sanborn, Bronson "is the worse for his western tour and feels the weight of old age" (letter of 23 February 1867 to Benjamin Lyman, in *Young Reporter of Concord*, ed. Kenneth Walter Cameron [Hartford, Conn.: Transcendental Books, 1978], p. 45).

34. "The Baron's Gloves" appeared in four installments between 20 June and 4 July 1868 in *Frank Leslie's Chimney Corner*; the work for Elliott may have been *The Mysterious Key, and What It Opened*, published in December 1867 by Elliott, Thomes & Talbot of Boston; "A Dickens Day" appeared in the 26 December 1867 *Independent*; "Taming a Tartar" appeared in four installments between 30 November and 21 December 1867 in *Frank Leslie's Illustrated Newspaper* (it was first identified as LMA's and reprinted in *A Modern Mephistopheles and Taming a Tartar*, ed. Stern).

35. The author and politician Benjamin Disraeli.

36. "The Freak of a Genius" appeared in five weekly installments between 20 October and 17 November 1866 in *Frank Leslie's Illustrated Newspaper*; "Hope's Debut" appeared in the 6 April 1867 *Frank Leslie's Chimney Corner*; "Thrice Tempted" appeared in the 20 July 1867 *Frank Leslie's Chimney Corner*. "My Malady" (which LMA later wrote "F Leslie" by) is unlocated.

LMA's account book shows thirteen dollars for "Poems" (Houghton Library, Harvard University).

1867

January 1867.

Sick from too hard work. Did nothing all the month but sit in a dark room & ache.[1] Head & eyes full of neuralgia.[2]

Feb.

Ditto ditto. Mother rheumatic fever had bad time with her eyes.

Mar

Ditto ditto., Got a little better at one time but tried to work & down I went again worse than ever.

April.

Slowly mending. Nan came to pass the summer at the Pratts.

May.

Still gaining, but all feeble. Mother half blind, Father lame & I weak, nervous & used up generally. Cold, wet weather & dull times for every one.

June.

Better, & began to write. Ticknor paid $150 for the lost Ms.[3] Loring $25 on "Moods" & Fuller wanted a fairy book.[4]

Went to Class Day. Had plays.[5] Company M. R. S. Ade M[ay]. [Elizabeth?] Greene & Co.[6] Nan. Johnny 2 years old.[7]

July.

Wrote Fairy tales for a Christmas book.[8]

Uncle May came. Gave May & me each $50 for a summer trip. Took $25 of mine & gave Mother the rest for bills.

Aug.

Went[9] to Clarke's Island with May & a Concord party.[10]

Spent a harem scarem fortnight & came to Plymouth in a gale of wind. Candor Club &c.[11]

Got to work again after my long vacation, for bills accumulate & worry me. I dread debt more than the devil!

Finished fairy book for Fuller — 12 stories prose & verse.

September

Niles, partner of Roberts, asked me to write a girls book. Said I'd try.

Fuller asked me to be the Editor of "Merry's Museum."[12] Said I'd try.

Began at once on both new jobs, but didn't like either.

The Radical Club met at Sargent's.[13] Fine time, Bartol inspired, Emerson chairman, Alcott on his legs, strong-minded ladies out in full force, aesthetic tea for res freshment.

Uncle Chatfield Alcott & his daughter Abby came.[14] Lotty May & the Sewalls. Nan & family made a visit.

Elliott for a tale   50

October

Agreed with Fuller to be editor for $500 a year. Read MSS. write 1 story each month & an editorial. On the strength of this engagement went to Boston, took a room No 6 Hayward Place, furnished it & set up house-keeping for myself. Cannot keep well in C[oncord]. so must try Boston, & not work too hard.

On the 28th rode to B[oston]. on my load of furniture with Fred, feeling as if I was going to camp out in a new country. Hoped it would prove a hospitable & healthy land.[15]

Proof of "Morning Glories," came to me & I worked away at my editorials but didn't enjoy it.

Gov. Andrews died.[16]

Loring paid for "Moods"   27
Leslie for one tale   40

November.

May got up a drawing class, coming from C[oncord]. every day to my room, so making it doubly useful.

Played several times for charity.[17]

A happy birthday though no presents for I was well & busy & had sent $140 home this month to make things comfortable.

Lord & Lady Amberly made a stir in B[oston].[18] Saw them at the Club. Saw Ristori & admired her even more than I did at Nice.

Bonner paid for an article	100
Fuller	20
Loring for "Kitty"	50
Independent for Sketch	15
Ford	20[19]

December.

"Morning Glories" came out. People liked it but Fuller did not make it go well for want of money.[20]

Ford of "The Youth's Companion" wants two stories a month. Redpath is to be thanked for that.

Heard Dickens & was disappointed.[21]

Fuller	55
Ford	20
M. R. S.	15

["Notes and Memoranda"]
1867

Mother sick in Sept. feeble all winter. In Feb had eyes operated on for Irites at L. Ws. Brookline.[22] May taught & did pen & ink work. Father went West but didn't make much.[23] Nan & boys at home in the summer. In Dec I fell sick having worked too hard. Shut up from Dec. to May. Wrote a fairy Book for Fuller. In Sept. became Editor of Merry's Museum. In Oct. took a room in B. & wrote all winter for Ford Fuller, Leslie &c.

1867

La Jeune.	40
Dr Donn.	22
Turtle's Ball	40
Fuller	75
Bonner 1 column.	100
Loring "Moods".	27
Ford	40
Countess Irma	25
A Look & a Laugh.	25
Kitty's Class Day.	50
Morning Glories.[24]	

SOURCES: Text and "Notes and Memoranda" — manuscript, Houghton Library, Harvard University.

1. LMA wrote "Dr K[arsner]. here quiddling." and then canceled it.

2. F. B. Sanborn wrote a friend that "Louisa Alcott has been alarmingly ill — not that her life was in danger but her writing organs — her head being overworked and taking revenge by neuralgia. She is now forbidden to either read or write — which is to her a great deprivation" (letter of 23 February 1867 to Benjamin Lyman, in Young Reporter of Concord, ed. Kenneth Walter Cameron [Hartford, Conn.: Transcendental Books, 1978], p. 45).

3. Howard Ticknor had written LMA on 5 June 1867 that he planned to "effect some sort of settlement" for losing her manuscript, and a week later he wrote her that he would be sending thirty dollars for the loss of illustrations and an additional sum to cover what he estimated was the loss of sales on twenty-five hundred copies (Houghton Library, Harvard University; Louisa May Alcott Collection, Barrett Library, University of Virginia). On 28 January [1874?], LMA wrote James R. Osgood that she had received $150 from Ticknor and Fields "for my loss of time & trouble" (SL, p. 181). For more on this episode, see Louisa's Wonder Book: An Unknown Alcott Juvenile, ed. Madeleine B. Stern (Mount Pleasant: Central Michigan University, 1975).

4. Morning-Glories, and Other Stories was published in January 1868 by Horace B. Fuller of Boston.

5. About this adaptation of John Townsend Trowbridge's Coupon Bonds, which took place on 8 July, Sanborn wrote, "Geo. Bartlett, Miss Alcott etc. are to give a dramatic entertainment after the old fashion" (letter of 7 July 1867 to Benjamin Lyman, in Young Reporter of Concord, ed. Cameron, p. 45). A playbill is at Orchard House.

6. Adeline May, daughter of Samuel Joseph May's cousin Samuel May and Sarah Russell May.

7. At a later date, LMA inserted: "Leslie [—] 75," "Ticknor for lost Ms & plates [—] 150," and "Paid bills." She also wrote: "Read H. Walpole's Letters." and then canceled it; the reference may be to the nine-volume edition of The Letters of Horace Walpole, Peter Cunningham (1861–1866).

8. That is, Morning-Glories. LMA wrote: "To Gloucester with Martha Bartlett & friends. A quiet time." and then canceled it.

9. Before this paragraph, LMA wrote: "Made a visit at Belmont." and then canceled it.

10. Sanborn, who was visiting friends in nearby Plymouth, "went over to the Island where were the Alcotts, Mrs. Austen, Fanny Lombard and other ladies — all in a houseful" (letter of 8 September 1867 to Benjamin Lyman, in Young Reporter of Concord, ed. Cameron, p. 45).

11. According to May, the Candor Club was founded to play the game Candor, which was "the greatest fun as all had to answer with perfect truth all kind of trying questions" (11 August 1863, diary, Houghton Library, Harvard University).

12. Horace B. Fuller, publisher of Merry's Museum, which LMA edited from 1868 to 1870.

13. Bronson thought the "attendance was large, the talk free and broad. Emerson read a paper of Counsel, very subtle and acceptable" (letter of 17 September 1867 to William Torrey Harris, Letters, p. 412). As John Weiss described the meeting, "Mr. Emerson read a paper filled with good hints for preachers, for instance — to mind his Truth, and not his audience — to be undisturbed at the absence in many minds of rapport with your Truth, — to value the Sunday opportunity of delivering a discourse — to say always the best and highest thing attainable — to have two thirds of an eye open to Nature and only one third to the style, speech, &c." (journal entry, 16 September 1867, Massachusetts Historical Society). Emerson's lecture was called "The Preacher" (see The Preacher [Boston: G. E. Ellis, 1880]).

14. Chatfield Alcott, Bronson's younger brother.

15. At a later date, LMA inserted: "("Polly" & her pie.)" The poem "What Polly Found in Her Stocking" appeared in the January 1868 Merry's Museum.

16. John Albion Andrew, former governor of Massachusetts, died on 30 October 1867.

17. LMA appeared in *Mrs. Jarley's Waxworks*, based on Dickens's works.

18. At a later date, LMA inserted: "Lady A. called." For the visit of John Russell, Viscount Amberley, and his wife, Katherine Stanley Russell, to the Radical Club on 14 November, see Bronson's *Letters*, pp. 414–415; *The Letters and Journals of Thomas Wentworth Higginson*, ed. Mary Thacher Higginson (Boston: Houghton Mifflin, 1921), p. 227; and Mary E. Sargent, *Sketches and Reminiscences of the Radical Club* (Boston: Roberts Brothers, 1880), pp. 21–25.

19. Robert Bonner, editor of the *New York Ledger*; *Kitty's Class Day* was published in mid-April 1868 by A. K. Loring of Boston; Daniel Sharp Ford, editor of the *Youth's Companion*.

20. At a later date, LMA inserted: "& tact."

21. At a later date, LMA inserted: "An old dandy."

22. Mrs. Alcott had her eyes operated on at Lizzie Wells's house. Iritis is an inflammation of the iris.

23. Probably a reference to Bronson's trip to St. Louis in March (see his "Autobiographical Collections," 7:246–247, Houghton Library, Harvard University).

24. "La Jeune; or Actress and Woman" appeared in the 18 April 1868 *Frank Leslie's Chimney Corner*; "A Look and a Laugh" appeared in the 4 July 1868 *Frank Leslie's Chimney Corner*. "Dr Donn," "Turtle's Ball," and "Countess Irma" are unlocated.

1868

January, 1868. Gamp's Garret, Hayward Place, Boston. — The year begins well and cheerfully for us all. Father and Mother comfortable at home; Anna and family settled in Chelsea; May busy with her drawing classes, of which she has five or six, and the prospect of earning $150 a quarter; also she is well and in good spirits.

I am in my little room, spending busy, happy days, because I have quiet, freedom, work enough, and strength to do it. F[uller]. pays me $500 a year for my name and some editorial work on Merry's Museum; "The Youth's Companion" pays $20 for two short tales each month; L[eslie]. $50 and $100 for all I will send him; and others take anything I have. My way seems clear for the year if I can only keep well. I want to realize my dream of supporting the family and being perfectly independent. Heavenly hope!

I have written twenty-five stories the past year, besides the fairy book containing twelve.[1] Have earned $1,000, paid my own way, sent home some, paid up debts, and helped May.

For many years we have not been so comfortable: May and I both earning, Annie with her good John to lean on, and the old people in a cosey home of our own.

After last winter's hard experience, we cannot be too grateful.

To-day my first hyacinth bloomed, white and sweet, — a good omen, — a little flag of truce, perhaps, from the enemies whom we have been fighting all these years. Perhaps we are to win after all, and conquer poverty, neglect, pain, and debt, and march on with flags flying into the new world with the new year.

Thursday, 7th. — A queer day. Up early, and had my bread and milk and baked apples. Fed my doves. Made May a bonnet, and cut out a flannel wrapper for Marmee, who feels the cold in the Concord snowbanks. Did my editorial work in the P. M., and fixed my dresses for the plays. L[eslie]. sent $50, and F[ord]. $40, for tales. A[nna]. and boys came.

To Dorchester in evening, and acted Mrs. Pontifex, in "Naval Engagements," to a good house.[2] A gay time, had flowers, etc. Talked half the night with H. A. about the fast ways of young people nowadays, and gave the child much older-sisterly advice, as no one seems to see how much she needs help at this time of her young life.

Dreamed that I was an opera dancer, and waked up prancing.

Wednesday, 15th. — Wrote all day. Did two short tales for F[ord?]. In the evening with A[deline]. M[ay]. to hear Fanny Kemble read "The Merchant of Venice."[3] She was a whole stock company in herself. Looked younger and handsomer than ever before, and happy, as she is to be with her daughters now. We went to supper afterwards at Mrs. Parkman's,[4] and saw the lioness feed. It was a study to watch her face, so full of varying expression was it, — always strong, always sweet, then proud and fierce as she sniffed at nobodies who passed about her. Being one, I kept away, and enjoyed the great creature afar off, wondering how a short, stout, red woman *could* look so like a queen in her purple velvet and point lace.

Slipped behind a door, but Dr. Holmes[5] found me out, and affably asked, "How many of you children are there?" As I was looking down on the top of his illustrious head, the question was funny. But I answered the little man with deep respect, "Four, sir." He seemed to catch my naughty thought, and asked, with a twinkle in his eye, looking up as if I were a steeple. "And all as tall as you?" Ha! ha!

18th. — Played again at D[orchester?]., and had a jolly time. Home early, and putting off my fine feathers, fell to work on my stories. F[uller]. seems to expect me to write the whole magazine, which I did not bargain for.

To Nan's in P. M., to take care of her while the Papa and Freddie went to C[oncord]. The dear little man, so happy and important with his bit of a bag, six pennies, and a cake for refreshment during the long journey of an hour.

We brooded over Johnny as if he were a heavenly sort of fire to warm and comfort us with his sunny little face and loving ways. She is a happy woman! I sell *my* children; and though they feed me, they don't love me as hers do.

Little Tranquility played alone all day, and made a pretty picture sitting in "marmar's" lap in his night-gown, talking through the trumpet to her. She never heard his sweet little voice in any other way. Poor Nan!

Wednesday, 22d. — To the club with Father. A good paper on the "Historical View of Jesus."[6] Father spoke finely. It amuses me to see how people listen and applaud *now* what was hooted at twenty years ago.

The talk lasted until two, and then the hungry philosophers remembered they had bodies and rushed away, still talking.

[Hard to feed. — L. M. A.]

Got a snow-slide on my bonnet, so made another in the P. M., and in the evening to the Antislavery Festival.[7] All the old faces and many new ones. Glad I have lived in the time of this great movement, and known its heroes so well. War times suit me, as I am a fighting *May*.

24th. — My second hyacinth bloomed pale blue, like a timid hope, and I took the omen for a good one, as I *am* getting on, and have more than I can do of the work that I once went begging for. Enjoyed the little spring my little flower made for me, and Buzzy, my pet fly, moved into the sweet mansion from his hanging garden in the ivy pot.

Acted in Cambridge, Lucretia Buzzard and Mrs. Jarley.[8]

Sunday, 31st. — Last day of the month, but I'm not satisfied with my four weeks' work. Acting for charity upsets my work. The change is good for me, and so I do it, and because I have no money to give.

Four tales this month. Received $70; sent $30 home. No debts.

February 1st. — Arranged "Hospital Sketches and War Stories" for a book.[9] By taking out all Biblical allusions, and softening all allusions to rebs., the book may be made "quite perfect," I am told. Anything to suit customers.

Friday, 14th. — My third hyacinth bloomed this A. M., a lovely pink. So I found things snug, and had a busy day chasing — — who dodged. Then I wrote my tales. Made some shirts for my boys, and went out to buy a squash pie for my lonely supper. It snowed; was very cold. No one paid, and I wanted to send some money home. Felt cross and tired as I trudged back at dusk. My pie turned a somersault, a boy laughed, so did I, and felt better. On my doorstep I found a gentleman who asked if Miss A. lived here. I took him up my winding stair and found him a very delightful fly, for he handed me a letter out of which fell a $100 bill. With this bait Mr. B[onner]. lured me to write "one column of Advice to Young Women," as Mrs. Shaw and others were doing. If he had asked me for a Greek oration I would have said "yes." So I gave a receipt, and the very elegant agent bowed himself away, leaving my " 'umble" bower full of perfume, and my soul of peace.

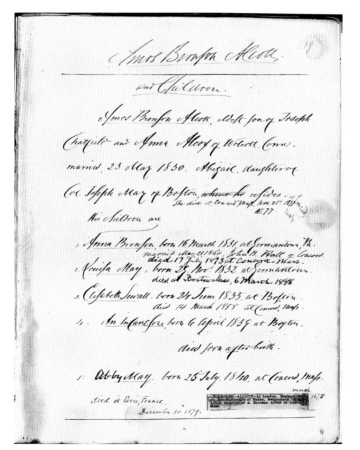

Miss Alcott's wishes as to her journals —

These journals are kept only for my own reference, & I particularly desire that if I did die before I destroy them that they may all be burned unread or copied by any one.

Dec. 1875 — S. M. A.

Louisa May Alcott's instructions for the destruction of her journals

Page from Bronson Alcott's journal describing his family

Bronson Alcott's Spindle Hill Homestead

Abigail May Alcott

Advertising poster for "Bertha" (1856)

1861.	My Earnings.	
Father has good talks in B & reforms our schools. Nan & John happy as turtle doves. Lu writing & grubbing as usual. Mother beginning to feel easy & quiet. Ab busy at the Asylum doing well. John Brown's girls board with us. April 19th war was declared with the South. A month at the White Mts with L. W. & write letters home that amuse the town.	A Pair Of Eyes.	40
	Whisper In The Dark.	50
	M. L.	20
	Began Moods.	
		110

1862.		
I keep a Kinder Gar- ten for six months in Boston. Visit at the Fields & among friends. Make nothing & give up teaching. L. Willis died. Dec 11th to Washing- ton as an Army nurse. Stay six weeks & fall ill. Am brought home nearly dead & have a fever which I enjoy very much, at least the crazy part.	School.	30
	Nursing.	10
	Pauline's Punishment	100
	King Of Clubs.	30
		170

1862		
Get well & fall to work. March 29th Nan's boy was born, Fredrick Alcott Pratt. Ab to Clarke's Island. Grandma died. The first colored regiment went to the war. In the Fall Ab went to Rimmer to study moulding. Hospital Sketches come out & I find I've done a good thing without knowing it.	On Picket Duty.	50
	Hospital Sketches.	200
	Mountain Letters.	20
	†My Contraband.	50
	†Thoreau's Flute.	10
		330

Page from Louisa May Alcott's "Notes and Memoranda"

a dreadful time of it.

Next morning felt better & at four went home. Just remember seeing May's shocked face at the depot, mother's bewildered one at home, & getting to bed in the firm belief that the house was roofless & no one wanted to see me.

As I never shall forget the strange fancies that haunted me I shall amuse myself with recording some of them. The most vivid & enduring was a conviction that I had married a stout, handsome Spaniard, dressed in black velvet with very soft hands & a voice that was continually saying, "die still, my dear." This was mother, I suspect, but with all the comfort I often found in her presence there was blended an awful fear of the Spanish spouse who was always coming after me, appearing out of closets, in at windows, or threatening me dreadfully all night long. I appealed to the Pope & really got up & made a touching plea in something meant for Latin they tell me. Once I went to heaven & found it a twilight place with people darting thro the air in a queer way. All very busy & dismal & ordinary. Mrs Dix, W. H. Channing & other people were there but I thought it dark & "slow" & wished I hadn't come. A mob at Baltimore breaking down the door to get me; being hung for a witch, burned, stoned & otherwise maltreated were some of my fancies. Also being tempted to join Dr W. & two of the nurses in worshipping the Devil. Also tending millions of rich men who never died or got well.

Front wrapper of The Rose Family (1864)

Louisa May Alcott

Louisa May Alcott

John Bridge Pratt in theatrical costume

John Bridge Pratt

Front wrapper from Merry's Museum *(1869)*

May Alcott's frontispiece illustration to the first
part of Little Women (1868)

Alice Bartlett

May Alcott Nieriker's drawing of her sister Louisa
as "The Golden Goose"

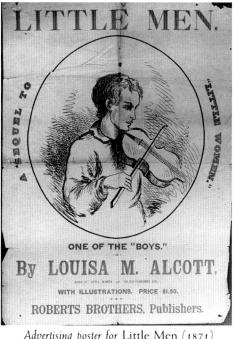

Advertising poster for Little Men (1871)

Advertising poster for Work (1873)

Title page of Work (1873)

May Alcott Nieriker's drawing of her father
in his study

Ernest Nieriker

May Alcott Nieriker's painting of her husband in their Paris salon

Louisa May Nieriker ("Lulu")

Drawing of a session at the Concord School of Philosophy from Frank Leslie's Illustrated Newspaper *(14 August 1880)*

Emerson's death — Thursday 27th

Mr Emerson died at 9 p.m. suddenly. Our best & greatest American gone. The nearest & dearest friend father has ever had, & the man who has helped me most by his life, his books, his society. I can never tell all he has been to me from the time I sung Mignon's song under his window, a little girl, & wrote letters a la Bettine to him, my Goethe, at 15, up through my hard years when his essays on Self Reliance, Character, Compensation, Love & Friendship helped me to understand myself & life & God & Nature. Illustrious & beloved friend, good bye!

Sunday 30th Emerson's funeral. I made a golden lyre of jonquils for the church & helped trim it up. Private services at the house & a great crowd at the church. I alten read his sonnet & Judge Hoar & others spoke. Now he lies in Sleepy Hollow among his brothers under the pines he loved.

I sat up till midnight to write an article on R. W. E. for the Youth's Companion, that the children may know something of him. A labor of love.

Page from Louisa May Alcott's journal describing the death of Ralph Waldo Emerson

Louisa May Alcott's cottage at
Nonquitt, Massachusetts

Anna Alcott
'Meg'

Anna Alcott Pratt

Louisa May Alcott sitting on a porch

Page from Louisa May Alcott's journal describing her father's last days

Fred Pratt

Jessica Cate Pratt

Thriftily taking advantage of the enthusiastic moment, I planned my article while I ate my dilapidated pie, and then proceeded to write it with the bill before me. It was about old maids. "Happy Women" was the title,[10] and I put in my list all the busy, useful, independent spinsters I know, for liberty is a better husband than love to many of us. This was a nice little episode in my trials of an authoress, so I record it.

So the pink hyacinth was a true prophet, and I went to bed a happy millionaire, to dream of flannel petticoats for my blessed Mother, paper for Father, a new dress for May, and sleds for my boys.

Monday, 17th. — Father came full of plans about his book.[11] Went with him to the Club. P. read a paper, and the Rabbi Nathan talked.[12] A curious jumble of fools and philosophers. The Club should be kept more select, and not be run by one person.

Tuesday, 25th. — Note from Lady Amberly as I sat sewing on my ninepenny dress. She wanted to come and see me, and I told her to do so, and I'd show her how I lived in my sky-parlor, — spinning yarns like a spider. Met her at the Club, and liked her, so simple and natural.

Acted for Mr. Clarke's Church Fair in the evening.[13] Did Mrs. Jarley three times. Very hoarse with a cold, but kept my promise.

"Proverb Stories" suggested, and "Kitty's Class-Day" written.[14]

Friday, 28th. — Packed for home, as I am needed there, and acted Jarley for the third evening. Have done it nine times this week, and my voice is gone.

I am sorry to leave my quiet room, for I've enjoyed it very much.

Written eight long tales, ten short ones, read stacks of manuscripts, and done editorial work. Acted for charity twelve times.

Not a bad two months' work. I can imagine an easier life, but with love, health, and work I can be happy; for these three help one to do, to be, and to endure all things.

March, April, and May. — Had the pleasure of providing Marmee with many comforts, and keeping the hounds of care and debt from worrying her. She sits at rest in her sunny room, and that is better than any amount of fame to me.

May, 1868. — Father saw Mr. Niles about a fairy book. Mr. N. wants a *girls' story,* and I begin "Little Women." Marmee, Anna, and May all approve my plan. So I plod away, though I don't enjoy this sort of thing. Never liked girls or knew many, except my sisters; but our queer plays and experiences may prove interesting, though I doubt it.

[Good joke. — L. M. A.]

June. — Sent twelve chapters of "L. W." to Mr. N. He thought it *dull,* so do I. But work away and mean to try the experiment; for lively, simple books are very much needed for girls, and perhaps I can supply the need.

Wrote two tales for Ford, and one for F[uller]. L[eslie]. clamors for more, but must wait.

July 15th. — Have finished "Little Women," and sent it off, — 402 pages. May is designing some pictures for it.[15] Hope it will go, for I shall probably get nothing for "Morning Glories."

Very tired, head full of pain from overwork, and heart heavy about Marmee, who is growing feeble.

[Too much work for one young woman. No wonder she broke down. 1876. — L. M. A.]

August. — Roberts Bros. made an offer for the story, but at the same time advised me to keep the copyright; so I shall.

[An honest publisher and a lucky author, for the copyright made her fortune, and the "dull book" was the first golden egg of the ugly duckling. 1885. — L. M. A.]

August 26th. — Proof of whole book came. It reads better than I expected. Not a bit sensational, but simple and true, for we really lived most of it; and if it succeeds that will be the reason of it. Mr. N. likes it better now, and says some girls who have read the manuscripts say it is "splendid!" As it is for them, they are the best critics, so I should be satisfied.

September. — Father's book came out. Very simple outside, wise and beautiful within. Hope it will bring him praise and profit, for he has waited long.

No girl, Mother poorly, May busy with pupils, Nan with her boys, and much work to be done. We don't like the kitchen department, and our tastes and gifts lie in other directions, so it is hard to make the various Pegasuses pull the plan steadily.

October 8th. — Marmee's birthday; sixty-eight. After breakfast she found her gifts on a table in the study. Father escorted her to the big red chair, the boys prancing before blowing their trumpets, while we "girls" marched behind, glad to see the dear old Mother better and able to enjoy our little fête. The boys proudly handed her the little parcels, and she laughed and cried over our gifts and verses.

I feel as if the decline had begun for her; and each year will add to the change which is going on, as time alters the energetic, enthusiastic home-mother into a gentle, feeble old woman, to be cherished and helped tenderly down the long hill she has climbed so bravely with her many burdens.

October 26th. — Came to Boston, and took a quiet room in Brookline Street. Heard Emerson in the evening. Sent a report of it to A. P. for the "Standard" at his desire. [16]

Anna is nicely settled in her new house, and Marmee is with her. Helped put down carpets and settle things.

30th. — Saw Mr. N[iles]. of Roberts Brothers, and he gave me good news of the book. An order from London for an edition came in. [17] First edition gone and more called for. Expects to sell three or four thousand before the New Year. [18]

Mr. N. wants a second volume for spring. Pleasant notices and letters arrive, and much interest in my little women, who seem to find friends by their truth to life, as I hoped.

November 1st. — Began the second part of "Little Women." I can do a chapter a day, and in a month I mean to be done. A little success is so inspiring that I now find my "Marches" sober, nice people, and as I can launch into the future, my fancy has more play. Girls write to ask who the little women marry, as if that was the only end and aim of a woman's life. I *won't* marry Jo to Laurie to please any one.

Monday, 16th. — To the Club for a change, as I have written like a steam engine since the 1st. Weiss read a fine paper on "Woman Suffrage." [19] Good talk afterward. Lunched with Kate Field, Celia Thaxter, and Mr. Linton. [20] Woman's Club in P. M.

17th. — Finished my thirteenth chapter. I am so full of my work, I can't stop to eat or sleep, or for anything but a daily run.

29th. — My birthday; thirty-six. Spent alone, writing hard. No presents but Father's "Tablets."

I never seem to have many presents, as some do, though I give a good many. That is best perhaps, and makes a gift very precious when it does come.

December. — Home to shut up the house, as Father goes West[21] and Mother to Anna's. A cold, hard, dirty time; but was so glad to be off out of C[oncord]. that I worked like a beaver, and turned the key on Apple Slump with joy.

May and I went to the new Bellevue Hotel in Beacon Street. She does n't enjoy quiet corners as I do, so we took a sky-parlor, and had a queer time whisking up and down in the elevator, eating in a marble café, and sleeping on a sofa bed, that we might be genteel. It did not suit me at all. A great gale nearly blew the roof off. Steam pipes exploded, and we were hungry. I was very tired with my hard summer, with no rest for the brains that earn the money.

["Notes and Memoranda"]
1868

Busy in my little room at Hayward Place from Oct to Mar. Wrote a good deal, saw many people, acted nine times for charitable fairs.

Fuller paid $500 a year for being Editor. Ford $20 a month for two little tales, & the other people took all I would write. May got up a drawing class in B[oston]. Had 36 pupils & got on well.

Nan took rooms in Chelsea. Father & mother quiet at home. Radical Club started. Lord & Lady Amberly came. Wrote 3 Proverb tales for Loring. In the summer to Leicester & Glosater. In the Fall Roberts asked me to write a girls book. Scribbled "Little Women." Came out in Oct. Sold finely. R. delighted & wanted another. paid me $300 on account Christmas day.

Father's book "Tablets" came out & sold well. Much admired.

Second part of "L. W." came out New Year.[22] I went in Oct to a room in Brookline St to write & there did Vol II. In Nov. Nan took a house in Malden, Pa & Ma boarded with her & May & I took rooms 17 Beacon St.

1868

Romance of a Bouquet	25
Fatal Follies	25
Blue & Grey	
Aunt Kipp	100
Psyche's Art.	100
Perilous Play	25
Fate In A Fan	25
Morning Glories	33
One year of M. M.	500
Ford	180
A Royal Governess	10
Little Women 1st	300[23]

SOURCES: Text — Cheney, pp. 193–202; "Notes and Memoranda" — manuscript, Houghton Library, Harvard University.

1. Probably a reference to *Morning-Glories*, though it contained fourteen stories.

2. Mrs. Pontifex, a character in Charles Dance's farce *Naval Engagements*.

3. Frances Kemble Butler read from Shakespeare's *Merchant of Venice* at the Music Hall on 15 February.

4. Probably Caroline Hall Parkman, widow of the minister Francis Parkman and mother of the historian of the same name.

5. The poet and novelist Oliver Wendell Holmes, Sr.

6. After Octavius Brooks Frothingham's paper entitled "The Historical Position of Jesus," John Weiss noted, "Alcott was better than usual" (diary entry, 20 January 1868, Massachusetts Historical Society).

7. The annual meeting of the Massachusetts Anti-Slavery Society was held on 23 January at Mercantile Hall, with Wendell Phillips and Octavius Brooks Frothingham as featured speakers.

8. LMA had played the part of Lucretia Buzzard in John Maddison Morton's farce *The Two Buzzards* as early as 1856.

9. *Hospital Sketches and Camp and Fireside Stories* was published on 16 August 1869 by Roberts Brothers of Boston.

10. "Happy Women" appeared in the 11 April 1868 *New York Ledger*.

11. Bronson's *Tablets*, also published by Roberts Brothers, was issued in September 1868. At his meeting with Roberts Brothers, Bronson wrote LMA, "I spoke of '*The Story for the Girls*' which R. & B.'s asked you to write. And find that they expect it and would like to have it ready by September at longest. They want a book of 200 pages or more just as you choose" (19 February 1868, *Letters*, p. 427).

12. According to Bronson, at this meeting of the Radical Club on 12 February, a Mr. Parker read "a good paper on Parkerism and this is ably discussed by Bartol and others" ("Diary for 1868," p. 43, Houghton Library, Harvard University).

13. This is probably the fair for the New England Hospital for Women and Children held at the Warren Street Chapel on 24–28 February.

14. *Proverb Stories* was not published until 1882 (Boston: Roberts Brothers).

15. May Alcott was unhappy with the four pictures she drew for the first volume of *Little Women*. The critics agreed: the *Nation* called them "indifferently executed," with a "want of anatomical knowledge" and an "indifference to or non-recognition of the subtle beauty of the lines of the female figure," and even claimed that the artist "has not closely studied the text which she illustrates" (review of *Little Women*, 7 [22 October 1868]: 335).

16. Aaron Powell, editor of the *National Anti-Slavery Standard*, in which "Mr. Emerson's Third Lecture" appeared in the 31 October 1868 issue. Emerson's talk was titled "Historical Notes of American Life and Letters" and dealt mainly with Brook Farm (see Daniel Shealy, "Ralph Waldo Emerson's Lecture on Brook Farm," *Concord Saunterer* 18, no. 2 [December 1985], 28–29, which reprints LMA's report).

17. The first volume of the English edition of *Little Women* was published in early December 1868 by Sampson Low of London.

18. All 2,000 copies of the first printing of *Little Women* were sold in September. Another 4,500 were printed by the end of the year (this and other information about the printings of LMA's books are from the Roberts Brothers account books owned by Little, Brown and Company, now deposited at the Houghton Library, Harvard University).

19. The minister John Weiss; his paper "Woman," and an account of the subsequent discussion, are in Mary E. Sargent, *Sketches and Reminiscences of the Radical Club* (Boston: Roberts Brothers, 1880), pp. 41–46.

20. The authors Kate Field and Celia Thaxter; William James Linton, English author and reformer who had immigrated to America.

21. Bronson began another western trip on 11 December.

22. The second volume of *Little Women* was published in April 1869 by Roberts Brothers.

23. "The Romance of a Bouquet" appeared in the 27 June 1868 *Frank Leslie's Illustrated Newspaper;* "The Blue and the Gray. A Hospital Sketch" appeared in the June 1868 *Putnam's Magazine;* both *Aunt Kipp* and *Psyche's Art* were published in mid-May 1868 by A. K. Loring of Boston, both separately and collected with *Kitty's Class Day* as *Louisa M. Alcott's Proverb Stories;* "Perilous Play" appeared in the 13 February 1869 *Frank Leslie's Chimney Corner;* "A Royal Governess" appeared in the 9 June 1868 *Independent.* "Fatal Follies" and "Fate in a Fan" are unlocated.

LMA's account book lists "A Mummy's Curse" and "Which Wins" for both 1868 and 1869, but the stories are listed in her journals in the "Notes and Memoranda" for 1869 only; $60, rather than $50 (inserted at a later date), for "Blue & Grey"; $500.96, rather than $500, for "One year of M. M."; and LMA states the money from "Ford" was for "Four little stories" (Houghton Library, Harvard University).

1869

January, 1869. — Left our lofty room at Bellevue and went to Chauncey street.[1] Sent the sequel of "L. W." to Robert's on New Year's Day. Hope it will do as well as the first, which is selling finely, and receives good notices. F[ord]. and F[uller]. both want me to continue working for them, and I shall do so if I am able; but my headaches, cough, and weariness keep me from working as I once could, fourteen hours a day.

In March we went home, as Mother was restless at Nan's, and Father wanted his library. Cold and dull; not able to write; so took care of Marmee and tried to rest.

Paid up all the debts, thank the Lord! — every penny that money can pay, — and now I feel as if I could die in peace. My dream is beginning to come true; and if my head holds out I'll do all I once hoped to do.

April. — Very poorly. Feel quite used up. Don't care much for myself, as rest is heavenly even with pain; but the family seem so panic-stricken and helpless when I break down, that I try to keep the mill going. Two short tales for L[eslie]., $50; two for Ford, $20; and did my editorial work, though two months are unpaid for. Roberts wants a new book, but am afraid to get into a vortex lest I fall ill.[2]

People begin to come and stare at the Alcotts. Reporters haunt the place to look at the authoress, who dodges into the woods à la Hawthorne, and won't be even a very small lion.

Refreshed my soul with Goethe, ever strong and fine and alive. Gave S. E. S[ewall]. $200 to invest. What richness to have a little not needed!

July. — . . . Spent in Canada with my cousins, the Frothinghams, at their house at Revière du Loup, — a little village on the St. Lawrence, full of queer people.[3] Drove, read, and walked with the little ones. A pleasant, quiet time.

August. — . . . A month with May at Mt. Desert.[4] A gay time, and a little rest and pleasure before the old pain and worry began again.

Made up $1,000 for S. E. S. to invest. Now I have $1,200 for a rainy day, and no debts. With that thought I can bear neuralgia gayly.

["Notes and Memoranda"]
1869

Jan 1st

May & I left Beacon St. for quieter rooms in Chauncey St.

Sick all winter & wrote nothing but little tales for Ford Fuller & Leslie.

Paid Pa & Ma's board as well as my own. Clubs, free church lectures, Conversations & plays. Pa had fine talks. May taught.

In Mar. Pa Ma & self came home. Do little all summer, Poorly. May returns in May. In July I pass a month in Canada. Home & then off for a short visit to Mt. Desert. Write nothing but a tale for Fuller "An Old Fashioned Girl."[5]

A good of money of "L. W." 12 hundred of which I give S. E. S. to invest for me. Pay all the debts & make every one as comfortable as I can.

In Aug. Hospital Sketches was republished with 8 stories — 2000 copies sold the first week.[6]

In Oct. May & I went to board in Pinckney St.[7] Pa & Ma to Nan. I was very poorly. No voice, went to Dr Bowditch every day to have my windpipe burnt with a caustic.[8] May gave lessons.

Made a book of Old Fashioned Girl & Roberts hurried it through the press in order to have it out early.

Recieved

Little Women Vol I	Mar.	228
" " " " II	May	250
Which Wins		25
Mummy		25
Mademoiselle		25
Mrs Vane's Charade		25
Through the Fire		25
Honor's Fortune		25[9]
Fuller. 12 months		500
Ford.		
"O. F. Girl" Fuller		

172

Little Women	June	250
" " " "	Aug.	926
	Nov.	500
Putnam "Scarlet Hose".		
H. & H.. Fairy Pinafores.		50
H. & H. Poem		10 [10]

SOURCES: Text — Cheney, pp. 202, 207–208; "Notes and Memoranda" — manuscript, Houghton Library, Harvard University.

1. From the Bellevue Hotel, LMA moved to a boardinghouse at 53 Chauncy Street, Boston.

2. Bronson wrote a friend that "Louisa is not so much sick as worn by winter's cold and damp, which still persist in lingering out into genial June. Presently, she hopes to take to the mountains and snuff health and spirits, instead of this present capricious catarrh, now of six months visitation, cheating her out of temper and time, coveted for thought and creation" (letter of 6 June 1869 to Ellen Chandler, *Letters*, pp. 477–478).

3. The Unitarian minister Octavius Brooks Frothingham would become a leader in the Free Religious Association. A distant cousin of LMA's, he offered her the hospitality of the family's summer place at Rivière du Loup, Quebec.

4. LMA liked to vacation at Mount Desert, Maine, an island about seventy miles east of Augusta.

5. "An Old-Fashioned Girl" appeared in monthly installments between July and December 1869 in *Merry's Museum* and was published as a book in April 1870 by Roberts Brothers.

6. The first printing of *Hospital Sketches and Camp and Fireside Stories* was 3,000 copies.

7. LMA and May boarded at 43 Pinckney Street in Boston.

8. On 7 December 1869, LMA declined an invitation from a Miss Batchelder to visit her at Mount Desert because "I am forbidden to talk & therefore am obliged to play the part of a dumb waiter" (Houghton Library, Harvard University).

9. LMA wrote: "Leslie" vertically by these last four stories.

10. In 1869, Roberts Brothers printed 15,000 copies of Part 1 of *Little Women* and 18,000 of Part 2.

"Lost in a Pyramid; or, the Mummy's Curse" appeared in the 16 January 1869 *New World*; "Mrs Vane's Charade" appeared in the 21 August 1869 *Frank Leslie's Chimney Corner*; "Scarlet Stockings" appeared in the July 1869 *Putnam's Magazine*. "Which Wins," "Mademoiselle," "Through the Fire," and "Honor's Fortune" are unlocated.

LMA's account book lists $300, rather than $228, for the March payment on the first part of *Little Women*; the $500 from "Fuller. 12 months" as being for twelve stories in *Merry's Museum*, all but one ("John" in September) identified as hers; $240, rather than $100 (inserted at a later date), from "Ford" for twenty-four contributions to the *Youth's Companion*, of which she gives the titles for sixteen: "The Lace-Makers" (15 April 1869), "Foolish Fashions" (17, 24 April 1869), "Lafayette's Visits" (13 May 1869), "Our Owl" (24 June 1869), "Uncle Tom's Shipwreck" (1 July 1869), "Who Did It?" (15 July 1869), "Playing Lady" (21 October 1869), "Bunny's Revenge" (18 November 1869), "Kitty's Cattle Show" (18 November 1869), "In the Tower" (23 December 1869), "Jimmy's Joke" (30 December 1869), "Uncle Smiley's Boys" (3, 10 February 1870), "Betsey's Bandbox" (unlocated), "A Good Daughter" (unlocated), "Harriet Tubman" (unlocated), and "Matty Kilburn" (unlocated). The account book also gives $180 as the sum for " 'O. F. Girl' Fuller"; $65, rather than $100 (entered at a later date), for "Scarlet Hose"; two stories for "Leslie," "Betrayed" and "La Belle Bayadine," for which she received $25 each, which are unlocated; and lists one story for *Hearth and Home*, "More People," for which she received $50 and which is unlocated.

1870

Second Trip to Europe.

April. — . . . On the first day of the month (fit day for *my* undertaking I thought) May and I went to N.Y. to meet A. B., with John for escort.[1] Every one very kind. Thirty gifts, a parting ball among our house-mates, and a great cake. Half-a-dozen devoted beings at the station to see us off. But I remember only Father and Mother as they went away the day before, leaving the two ambitious daughters to sail away, perhaps forever.

Marmee kept up bravely, and nodded and smiled; but at the corner I saw the white handkerchief go up to the eyes, after being gayly waved to us. May and I broke down, and said, "We won't go;" but next day we set forth, as young birds will, and left the nest empty for a year.

Sailed on the 2d in a gale of wind in the French steamer "Lafayette" for Brest. Our adventures are told in "Shawl Straps."[2]

"O. F. G." came out in March, and sold well.[3] Trainboy going to N.Y. put it into my lap; and when I said I did n't care for it, exclaimed with surprise, —

"Bully book, ma'am! Sell a lot; better have it."

John told him I wrote it; and his chuckle, stare, and astonished "No!" was great fun. On the steamer little girls had it, and came in a party to call on me, very seasick in my berth, done up like a mummy.

Spent some charming weeks in Brittany.

June and July. — "O. F. G." was published in London by Sampson Low & Co.[4] We left Dinan on the 15th, and had a lovely trip through France to Vevay and Bex.

Talk of war between France and Prussia.[5]

Much excitement at Vevay. Refugees from Lyons come in. Isabella and Don Carlos were there, with queer followers.

September. — . . . On the 3d came news of the Emperor's surrender.[6] Great wailing among the French here. All well at home. Books going finely; no debts.

We decide to go to Rome for the winter, as May pines for the artist's Paradise; and war will not trouble us I hope.

October, 1870. — A memorable month . . . Off for Italy on the 2d. A splendid journey over the Alps and Maggiore by moonlight.

Heavenly days at the lakes, and so to Milan, Parma, Pisa, Bologna, and Florence. Disappointed in some things, but found Nature always lovely and wonderful; so did n't mind faded pictures, damp rooms, and the cold winds of "sunny Italy." Bought furs at Florence, and arrived in Rome one rainy night.

November 10*th.* — In Rome, and felt as if I had been there before and knew all about it. Always oppressed with a sense of sin, dirt, and general decay of all things. Not well; so saw things through blue glasses. May in bliss with lessons, sketching, and her dreams. A[lice]. had society, her house, and old friends. The artists were the best company; counts and princes very dull, what we saw of them. May and I went off on the Campagna, and criticised all the world like two audacious Yankees.

Our apartment in Piazza Barbarini was warm and cosey; and I thanked Heaven for it, as it rained for two months, and my first view most of the time was the poor Triton with an icicle on his nose.

We pay $60 a month for six good rooms, and $6 a month for a girl, who cooks and takes care of us.

29*th.* — My thirty-eighth birthday. May gave me a pretty sketch, and A[lice]. a fine nosegay.

["Notes and Memoranda"]
1870

At Pinckney St till April.

On New Year's day Roberts sent me $2,500 with a nice note.[7]

May had 30 pupils & got on well. Pa out West having a fine time.[8] Ma at Nan's.

Alice Bartlett invites May to go abroad with her for a year, & I decide to go as duenna, hoping to get better. April 2ond. We three sail from N.Y. in a French steamer for Brest.

Arrive in 12 days, go to Dinan in Brittany & board with Madame Coste.

"Old Fashioned Girl" came out the day we left & was a success. Came out in England in June, Sampson Low & Son.

Left Dinan in June & went to Vevey, Bex, & Geneva for three months.

In Oct to Italy. Saw the lakes, Alps Florence Milan, Parma Bolongna Pisa. To Rome in Nov. Took apartments in Piazza Barberini & were very cosy. Much company, artists &c.

Galleries, Campangna Carnival &c.

I was very poorly & enjoyed little.

Dec. 23rd saw John's death in a paper & soon learned it was a fact.[9]
Sad time.[10]

Received

Roberts on L. W.   2,500[11]

SOURCES: Text — Cheney, pp. 210–211, 254–255; "Notes and Memoranda" — manuscript, Houghton Library, Harvard University.

1. LMA, May Alcott, and Alice Bartlett left New York aboard the French steamer *Lafayette* on 2 April 1870, arriving at Brest, France, on 14 April. May had agreed to accompany twenty-four-year-old Alice only if LMA could go also.

2. "Shawl Straps" appeared in four installments between 13 March and 3 April 1872 in the *Christian Union* and was published as *Shawl Straps*, vol. 2 of *Aunt Jo's Scrap-Bag*, in November 1872 by Roberts Brothers.

3. Roberts Brothers printed 27,500 copies of *An Old-Fashioned Girl* in March.

4. *An Old-Fashioned Girl* was published in April by Sampson Low of London.

5. France declared war on Germany on 19 July.

6. Napoleon III surrendered to Germany on 2 September.

7. LMA is a little off on her dates: her letter to Roberts Brothers, thanking them for the $2,500 "which made my Christmas an unusually merry one," is dated 28 December 1869 (see *SL*, p. 129).

8. Bronson wrote LMA in August 1870: "My prospects are fair as to my Western tour. I ought not to return home without my $2000 at least, since I go advertised . . . and I may get as far as San Francisco" (*Letters*, p. 521).

9. John Bridge Pratt died on 27 November 1870. For LMA's reactions, see her letters to Anna Alcott Pratt of [December? 1870?], *SL*, p. 153, and to Mrs. Edward Henry Barton of 9 January [1871], *SL*, p. 153n.

10. At a later date, LMA inserted: "Wrote Little Men." *Little Men* was published in June 1871 by Roberts Brothers.

11. In 1869, Roberts Brothers printed 13,000 copies of the first part of *Little Women*, 11,000 of the second part, 37,000 of *An Old-Fashioned Girl*, and 1,000 of *Hospital Sketches and Camp and Fireside Stories*.

1871

1871. — *Rome.* — Great inundation. Streets flooded, churches with four feet of water in them, and queer times for those who were in the overflowed quarters. Meals hoisted up at the window; people carried across the river-like streets to make calls; and all manner of funny doings. We were high and dry at the Piazza Barbarini, and enjoyed the flurry.[1]

To the Capitol often, to spend the A.M. with the Roman emperors and other great men. M. Aurelius as a boy was fine; Cicero looked very like W. Phillips; Agrippina in her chair was charming; but the other ladies, with hair *à la sponge*, were ugly; Nero & Co. a set of brutes and bad men. But a better sight to me was the crowd of poor people going to get the bread and money sent by the king; and the splendid snow-covered hills were finer than the marble beauty inside. Art tires; Nature never.

Professor Pierce and his party just from Sicily,[2] where they had been to see the eclipse, — all beaming with delight, and well repaid for the long journey by a *two minutes'* squint at the sun when darkest.

Began to write a new book, "Little Men," that John's death may not leave A. and the dear little boys in want. John took care that they should have enough while the boys are young, and worked very hard to have a little sum to leave, without a debt anywhere.

In writing and thinking of the little lads, to whom I must be a father now, I found comfort for my sorrow. May went on with her lessons, "learning," as she wisely said, how little she knew and how to go on.

February. — A gay month in Rome, with the carnival, artists' fancy ball, many parties, and much calling.

Decided to leave May for another year, as L[oring]. sends $700 on "Moods,"[3] and the new book will provide $1000 for the dear girl; so she may be happy and free to follow her talent.

March. — Spent at Albano. A lovely place. Walk, write, and rest. A troop of handsome officers from Turin, who clatter by, casting soft glances at my two blond signorinas, who enjoy it very much.[4] Baron and Baroness Rothschild were there, and the W.'s from Philadelphia, Dr. O. W. and wife, and S. B.[5] Mrs. W. and A[lice]. B[artlett]. talk *all day*, May sketches, I write, and so we go on. Went to look at rooms at the Bonapartes.

April. — Venice. Floated about for two weeks seeing sights. A lovely city for a short visit. Not enough going on to suit brisk Americans. May painted, A[lice]. hunted up old jewelry and friends, and I dawdled after them.

A very interesting trip to London, — over the Brenner Pass to Munich, Cologne, Antwerp, and by boat to London.

May. — A busy month. Settled in lodgings, Brompton Road, and went sight-seeing. Mrs. P. Taylor, Conway, and others very kind. Enjoyed showing May my favorite places and people.

A[lice]. B[artlett]. went home on the 11th, after a pleasant year with us. I am glad to know her, for she is true and very interesting. May took lessons of Rowbotham and was happy.[6] "Little Men" came out in London.[7]

I decided to go home on the 25th, as I am needed. A very pleasant year in spite of constant pain, John's death, and home anxieties. Very glad I came, for May's sake. It has been a very useful year for her.

June. — After an anxious passage of twelve days, got safely home. Smallpox on board, and my room-mate, Miss D., very ill. I escaped, but had a sober time lying next door to her, waiting to see if my turn was to come. She was left at the island, and I went up the harbor with Judge Russell, who took some of us off in his tug.[8]

Father and T[homas]. N[iles]. came to meet me with a great red placard of "Little Men" pinned up in the carriage. After due precautions, hurried home and found all well. My room refurnished and much adorned by Father's earnings.

Nan well and calm, but under her sweet serenity is a very sad soul, and she mourns for her mate like a tender turtle-dove.

The boys were tall, bright lads, devoted to Marmee, and the life of the house.

Mother feeble and much aged by this year of trouble. I shall never go far away from her again. Much company, and loads of letters, all full of good wishes and welcome.

"Little Men" was out the day I arrived. Fifty thousand sold before it was out.[9]

A happy month, for I felt well for the first time in two years. I knew it would n't last, but enjoyed it heartily while it did, and was grateful for rest from pain and a touch of the old cheerfulness. It was much needed at home.

July, August, September. — Sick. Holiday soon over. Too much company and care and change of climate upset the poor nerves again. Dear Uncle S. J. May died; our best friend for years.[10] Peace to his ashes. He leaves a sweeter memory behind him than any man I know. Poor Marmee is the last of her family now.

October. — Decided to go to B[oston].; Concord is so hard for me, with its dampness and worry. Get two girls to do the work, and leave plenty of money and go to Beacon Street to rest and try to get well that I may work.[11] A lazy life, but it seemed to suit; and anything is better than the invalidism I hate worse than death.

Bones ached less, and I gave up morphine, as sunshine, air, and quiet made sleep possible without it. Saw people, pictures, plays, and read all I could, but did not enjoy much, for the dreadful weariness of nerves makes even pleasure hard.

November. — May sent pleasant letters and some fine copies of Turner.[12] She decides to come home, as she feels she is needed as I give out. Marmee is feeble, Nan has her boys and her sorrow, and one strong head and hand is wanted at home. A year and a half of holiday is a good deal, and duty comes first always. Sorry to call her back, but her eyes are troublesome, and housework will rest them and set her up. Then she can go again when I am better, for I don't want her to be thwarted in her work more than just enough to make her want it very much.

On the 19th she came.[13] Well, happy, and full of sensible plans. A lively time enjoying the cheerful element she always brings into the house. Piles of pictures, merry adventures, and interesting tales of the fine London lovers.

Kept my thirty-ninth and Father's seventy-second birthday in the old way. Thanksgiving dinner at Pratt farm. All well and all together. Much to give thanks for.

December. — Enjoyed my quiet, sunny room very much; and this lazy life seems to suit me, for I am better, mind and body. All goes well at home, with May to run the machine in her cheery, energetic style, and amuse Marmee and Nan with gay histories. Had a furnace put in, and all enjoyed the new climate. No more rheumatic fevers and colds, with picturesque open fires. Mother is to be cosey if money can do it. She seems to be now, and my long-cherished dream has come true; for she sits in a pleasant room, with no work, no care, no poverty to worry, but peace and comfort all about her, and children glad and able to stand between trouble and her. Thank the Lord! I like to stop and "remember my mercies." Working and waiting for them makes them very welcome.

Went to the ball for the Grand Duke Alexis.[14] A fine sight, and the big blonde boy the best of all. Would dance with the pretty girls, and leave the Boston dowagers and their diamonds in the lurch.

To the Radical Club, where the philosophers mount their hobbies and prance away into time and space, while we gaze after them and try to look wise.[15]

A merry Christmas at home. Tree for the boys, family dinner, and frolic in the evening.

A varied, but on the whole a good year, in spite of pain. Last Christmas we were in Rome, mourning for John. What will next Christmas bring forth? I have no ambition now but to keep the family comfortable and not ache any more. Pain has taught me patience, I hope, if nothing more.

["Notes and Memoranda"]
1871

In Rome till Mar. 15th when we went to Albano. April to Venice. May in London. Here Alice left us for home after a happy year.

I stayed till June & then returned to America leaving May to study & paint.

Small pox aboard the Malta. An anxious time, but I escaped & found all well at home.

July so ill I could [do] nothing & felt as if my year of travel was all lost. Dr R. did his best all summer in vain.[16]

In August dear Uncle S. J. May died. In Oct. went to Boston to board at Mrs Rand's Beacon St. To rest, & try to get well.

Wrote a few tales. Great fire at Chicago.[17] Pa did not go West. May came home in Nov.

Got slowly better. Went to the Grand Duke's Ball.

Christmas tree & all at home.

Recieved

Roberts — July	7,654
Low —	330
Scrap Bag No 1	
Loring — Moods —	248
H. & H.	100
Christian Register	20[18]

SOURCES: Text — Cheney, pp. 257–261; "Notes and Memoranda" — manuscript, Houghton Library, Harvard University.

1. LMA also describes these events in "Recent Exciting Scenes in Rome," in the 3 February 1871 *Boston Daily Evening Transcript* (reprinted in *SL*, pp. 153–158).

2. Benjamin P. Pierce, professor of mathematics at Harvard.

3. George W. Carleton, who would publish his own edition of *Morning-Glories* in 1871, wrote a fellow publisher on 28 December 1870 about "Loring's selling last summer over 10,000 of 'Moods' (an apparently dead & buried book) on the strength of Miss Alcott's sudden popularity as the author of 'Little Women' etc." (letter to James R. Osgood, in Ellen B. Ballou, *The Building of the House: Houghton Mifflin's Formative Years* [Boston: Houghton Mifflin, 1970], pp. 186–187.

4. This incident is described in *Shawl-Straps*, pp. 183–190.

5. Alice Bartlett's cousins, the Warrens (see *SL*, pp. 139, 143n); Sophia Elizabeth Bond, daughter of George William and Sophia Augusta May Bond.

6. Thomas Leeson Rowbotham.

7. The English edition of *Little Men* was published on 15 May by Sampson Low of London.

8. Thomas Russell, collector of the Boston Custom House.

9. Roberts Brothers printed 38,000 copies of *Little Men* by the end of June.

10. Samuel Joseph May died on 1 July 1871.

11. LMA boarded at 23 Beacon Street.

12. May was best known for her copies of J. M. W. Turner's paintings, which the famous British art critic John Ruskin called "the best reproductions of Turner's works that had ever been done" (quoted by Daniel Chester French in Caroline Ticknor, *May Alcott: A Memoir* [Boston: Little, Brown, 1928], p. xxi). The next year, when Ellen Emerson saw May, she "learned from her that she had . . . a hundred dollars for one of her copies" (letter of 27 January 1872 to Edward Waldo Emerson, *The Letters of Ellen Tucker Emerson*, ed. Edith E. W. Gregg, 2 vols. [Kent, Ohio: Kent State University Press, 1982], 1:364).

13. May had stayed on in London after LMA had returned in June. Her visit to Concord lasted until 26 April 1873.

14. This event at the Boston Theatre was reported in "The Grand Duke in Boston," *New York Tribune*, 9 December 1871, p. 1. For an account of a similar ball held shortly afterward in New York, see Mary Clemmer Ames, *Outlines of Men, Women, and Things* (New York: Hurd and Houghton, 1873), pp. 56–65.

15. The Radical Club meeting on 19 December featured C. C. Everett's paper "The Relations of Christ to the Present Age." Among those present were Calvin and Harriet Beecher Stowe (*Boston Daily Advertiser*, 19 December 1871, p. 1).

16. Dr. William Rimmer. LMA wrote a jocular poem to Rimmer to show her appreciation; it begins, "Faithful as a leech, / Helpful as a blister, / Soothing as morphine / To a nervous sister" (February 1872, Houghton Library, Harvard University).

17. The famous Chicago fire, which began on 8 October, found its way into "Through the Fire. Romance of Chicago, the Ruined City," which appeared in the 13 January 1872 *Frank Leslie's Chimney Corner*.

18. "Kate's Choice" appeared in the 13 and 20 January 1872 issues of *Hearth and Home*; "Women in Brittany" appeared in the 6 January 1872 *Christian Register*.

In 1871, Roberts Brothers printed 44,000 copies of *Little Men*, 15,000 of *My Boys*, and 36,000 of LMA's other books.

1872

January, 1872. — Roberts Brothers paid $4,400 as six months' receipts for the books. A fine New Year's gift. S. E. S[ewall]. invested $3,000, and the rest I put in the bank for family needs. Paid for the furnace and all the bills. What bliss it is to be able to do that and ask no help!

· · · · · · · ·

Mysterious bouquets came from some unknown admirer or friend. Enjoyed them very much, and felt quite grateful and romantic as day after day the lovely great nosegays were handed in by the servant of the unknown.

February and March. — At Mrs. Stowe's desire,[1] wrote for the "Christmas Union" an account of our journey through France, and called it "Shawl Straps." . . . Many calls and letters and invitations, but I kept quiet, health being too precious to risk, and sleep still hard to get for the brain that would work instead of rest.

Heard lectures, — Higginson, Bartol, Frothingham, and Rabbi Lilienthal.[2] Much talk about religion. I'd like to see a little more really *lived.*

April and May. — Wrote another sketch for the "Independent," — "A French Wedding;"[3] and the events of my travels paid my winter's expenses. All is fish that comes to the literary net. Goethe puts his joys and sorrows into poems; I turn my adventures into bread and butter.

· · · · · · · ·

June, 1872. — Home, and begin a new task. Twenty years ago I resolved to make the family independent if I could. At forty that is done. Debts all paid, even the outlawed ones, and we have enough to be comfortable. It has cost me my health, perhaps; but as I still live, there is more for me to do, I suppose.

July, 1872. — May makes a lovely hostess, and I fly round behind the scenes, or skip out of the back window when ordered out for inspection by the inquisitive public. Hard work to keep things running smoothly, for this sight-seeing fiend is a new torment to us.

August. — May goes to Clark's Island for rest, having kept hotel long enough. I say "No," and shut the door. People *must* learn that authors have some rights; I can't entertain a dozen a day, and write the tales they demand also. I'm but a human worm, and when walked on must turn in self-defence.

Reporters sit on the wall and take notes; artists sketch me as I pick pears in the garden; and strange women interview Johnny as he plays in the orchard.

It looks like impertinent curiosity to me; but it is called "fame," and considered a blessing to be grateful for, I find. Let 'em try it.

September. — To Wolcott, with Father and Fred.[4] A quaint, lovely old place is the little house on Spindle Hill, where the boy Amos dreamed the dreams that have come true at last.

Got hints for my novel, "The Cost of an Idea," if I ever find time to write it.

Don't wonder the boy longed to climb those hills, and see what lay beyond.

October. — Went to a room in Allston Street, in a quiet, old-fashioned house.[5] I can't work at home, and need to be alone to spin, like a spider.

Rested; walked; to the theatre now and then. Home once a week with books, etc., for Marmee and Nan. Prepared "Shawl Straps" for Roberts.

November. — Forty on the 29th. Got Father off for the West, all neat and comfortable.[6] I enjoyed every penny spent, and had a happy time packing his new trunk with warm flannels, neat shirts, gloves, etc., and seeing the dear man go off in a new suit, overcoat, hat, and all, like a gentleman. We both laughed over the pathetic old times with tears in our eyes, and I reminded him of the "poor as poverty, but serene as heaven" saying.

Something to do came just as I was trying to see what to take up, for work is my salvation. H. W. Beecher sent one of the editors of the "Christian Union" to ask for a serial story. They have asked before, and offered $2,000, which I refused; now they offered $3,000, and I accepted.

Got out the old manuscript of "Success," and called it "Work." Fired up

183

the engine, and plunged into a vortex, with many doubts about getting out. Can't work slowly; the thing possesses me, and I must obey till it's done. One thousand dollars was sent as a seal on the bargain, so I was bound, and sat at the oar like a galley-slave.

F[ord]. wanted eight little tales, and offered $35 apiece; used to pay $10.[7] Such is fame! At odd minutes I wrote the short ones, and so paid my own expenses. "Shawl Straps," Scrap-Bag, No. 2, came out, and went well.

Great Boston fire; up all night.[8] Very splendid and terrible sight.

December. — Busy with "Work." Write three pages at once on impression paper, as Beecher, Roberts, and Low of London all want copy at once.

[This was the cause of the paralysis of my thumb, which disabled me for the rest of my life. — L. M. A.]

Nan and the boys came to visit me, and break up the winter. Rested a little, and played with them.

Father very busy and happy. On his birthday had a gold-headed cane given him. He is appreciated out there.

["Notes and Memoranda"]
1872

January Roberts paid $4,403 on the books. S. E. S[ewall]. invested $3000 & the rest I paid debts with & made things comfortable. $231 for the furnace &c.

Lionized a good deal & did not like it. Radical Club Free Religion Meeting. Saw people & had an idle time, but got better steadily. In June went home. Much company. Mother poorly, Nan sad, May tired, & L. M. A. tried to make things go. May rests from her housekeeping & I take her place. In Sept. to Wolcott with Pa & Fred.

Oct. went to B[oston]. as usual. Took a room in Allston St. & tried to dawdle but was so much better I longed to work.

Beecher sent to ask me to write a serial for the Christian Union. Offered $3000 & I accepted it.

Took it up & re wrote my half done story of "Christie." Called it "Work".

Great Boston fire in Nov.

May kept house & painted.

Pa went West & had a fine time. Small pox panic in B[oston]. & horse disease.

A busy time.

July 24th Mr Emerson's house burned.[9]

Recieved

Roberts Bros.	4,403
C. U. story	100
C. U. Shawl Strap	200
H. H. Cupid & Chow-chow.	100
Independent	100
Roberts Bros. July	95
Christian Union "Work"	3000
D. Ford —	200
Scrap Bag No 2.	
Loring Moods	52
Low on books	340
Carleton	702 [10]

SOURCES: Text — Cheney, pp. 261–262, 266–268; "Notes and Memoranda" — manuscript, Houghton Library, Harvard University.

1. Harriet Beecher Stowe had written LMA on 2 January 1872 that the editors of the *Christian Union* "are desirous of securing you in their corps of contributors & at their request I write to know if you could furnish us with one or two short stories, similar to those in Aunt Joe's [sic] scrap bag — & on what terms?" (Houghton Library, Harvard University).

2. Thomas Wentworth Higginson gave a lecture entitled "The Character of Buddha" on 3 March as part of the Free Religious Association series at Horticultural Hall (printed in the *Boston Commonwealth*, 9 March 1872, p. 2); Cyrus Bartol talked at the Radical Club on 3 March ("Quite a brilliant evening," wrote John Weiss in his diary [Massachusetts Historical Society]); Octavius Brooks Frothingham spoke on Borromeo the saint at the Radical Club in February (printed in the *Boston Commonwealth*, 24 February 1872, p. 4); Rabbi Max Lilienthal delivered a talk called "The Religious Idea in History" on 18 February as part of the Free Religious Association series (printed in the *Boston Commonwealth*, 24 February 1872, p. 2).

3. "Pelagie's Wedding" appeared in the 6 June 1872 *Independent*.

4. Bronson wrote a friend: "Louisa and I leave early tomorrow morning for Connecticut, taking little Freddy with us. We make but a flying visit to the old homesteads in Wolcott . . . intending to return on Saturday following. Louisa has not seen the spot, since she was a mere child, and has, I suspect, designs on the place and people for a future story. You will be pleased to learn that she has recovered some thing of her former fire and freshness and is at her pen again at intervals" (letter of 3 September 1872 to Ellen Chandler, *Letters*, p. 562).

5. LMA was staying with Mrs. Pamelia May at 7 Allston Street in Boston.

6. Bronson had left on 8 November on another one of his midwestern lecture tours.

7. LMA published the following stories in the *Youth's Companion* over the next few months: "Grandma's Team" (28 November 1872), "The Mystery of Morlaix" (19 December 1872), "Bonfires" (9 January 1873), "Huckleberry" (16 January 1873), and "Mama's Plot" (6 February 1873).

8. LMA provides a graphic description of this fire in her letter of [10? November 1872] to Anna Alcott Pratt, in *SL*, pp. 169–171.

9. For descriptions of the fire at Emerson's house on 24 July 1872, what LMA called "a topsy turvy day," see LMA's letter of [27? July 1872] to Louisa Wells, in *SL*, pp. 166–167; *The Letters of Ralph Waldo Emerson*, ed. Ralph L. Rusk, 6 vols. (New York: Columbia University Press, 1939), 6:214, for the account in the 24 July *Boston Daily Advertiser*; *The Letters of Ellen Tucker Emerson*, ed. Edith E. W. Gregg, 2 vols. (Kent, Ohio: Kent State University Press, 1982), 1:676–682;

and Madeleine B. Stern, "The Alcotts and the Emerson Fire," *American Transcendental Quarterly* 36 (Fall 1977), pt. 1, 7–9, which prints Anna Alcott Pratt's account of the fire and its aftermath.

10. In 1872, Roberts Brothers printed 27,500 copies of LMA's works.

"Cupid and Chow-Chow" appeared in the 18 and 25 May 1872 issues of *Hearth and Home*; the story in the *Independent* was "Pelagie's Wedding"; "Work; or Christie's Experiment" appeared in the *Christian Union* and was published as *Work: A Story of Experience* in June 1873 by Roberts Brothers; the second "Scrap Bag" is *Aunt Jo's Scrap-Bag: Shawl-Straps*.

1873

January, 1873. — Getting on well with "Work;" have to go slowly now for fear of a break-down. All well at home.

A week at Newport with Miss Jane Stewart. Dinners, balls, calls, etc. Saw Higginson and "H. H."[1] Soon tired of gayety, and glad to get home to my quiet den and pen.

Roberts Brothers paid me $2,022 for books. S. E. S[ewall]. invested most of it, with the $1,000 F. sent. Gave C. M. $100, — a thank-offering for my success. I like to help the class of "silent poor" to which we belonged for so many years, — needy, but respectable, and forgotten because too proud to beg. Work difficult to find for such people, and life made very hard for want of a little money to ease the necessary needs.

February and March. — Anna very ill with pneumonia; home to nurse her. Father telegraphed to come home, as we thought her dying. She gave me her boys; but the dear saint got well, and kept the lads for herself. Thank God!

Back to my work with what wits nursing left me.

Had Johnny for a week, to keep all quiet at home. Enjoyed the sweet little soul very much, and sent him back much better.

Finished "Work," — twenty chapters. Not what it should be, — too many interruptions. Should like to do one book in peace, and see if it wouldn't be good.

April. — The job being done I went home to take May's place. Gave her $1,000, and sent her to London for a year of study. She sailed on the 26th, brave and happy and hopeful. I felt that she needed it, and was glad to be able to help her.

I spent seven months in Boston; wrote a book and ten tales; earned $3,250 by my pen, and am satisfied with my winter's work.

May. — D[aniel]. F[ord]. wanted a dozen little tales, and agreed to pay $50 apiece, if I give up other things for this. Said I would, as I can do two a day, and keep house between times. Cleaned and grubbed, and did n't mind the change. Let head rest, and heels and feet do the work.

Cold and dull; but the thought of May free and happy was my comfort as I messed about.

June and July. — Settled the servant question by getting a neat American woman to cook and help me with the housework.

Peace fell upon our troubled souls, and all went well. Good meals, tidy house, cheerful service, and in the P.M. an intelligent young person to read and sew with us.

It was curious how she came to us. She had taught and sewed, and was tired, and wanted something else; decided to try for a housekeeper's place, but happened to read "Work," and thought she'd do as Christie did — take anything that came.

I was the first who answered her advertisement, and when she found I wrote the book, she said, "I'll go and see if Miss A. practises as she preaches."

She found I did, and we had a good time together. My new helper did so well I took pale Johnny to the seaside for a week; but was sent for in haste, as poor Marmee was very ill. Mental bewilderment came after one of her heart troubles (the dropsy affected the brain), and for three weeks we had a sad time. Father and I took care of her, and my good A. S. kept house nicely and faithfully for me.

Marmee slowly came back to herself, but sadly feeble, — never to be our brave, energetic leader any more. She felt it, and it was hard to convince her that there was no need of her doing anything but rest.

August, September, October. — Mother improved steadily. Father went to the Alcott festival in Wolcott, A. and boys to Conway for a month; and it did them all much good.[2]

I had quiet days with Marmee; drove with her, and had the great pleasure of supplying all her needs and fancies.

May busy and happy in London. A merry time on Mother's birthday, October 8. All so glad to have her still here; for it seemed as if we were to lose her.

Made a little story of it for F[ord]., — "A Happy Birthday," — and spent the $50 in carriages for her.[3]

November and December. — Decided that it was best not to try a cold, lonely winter in C[oncord]., but go to B[oston]. with Mother, Nan, and boys, and leave Father free for the West.

Took sunny rooms at the South End, near the Park, so the lads could play out and Marmee walk.[4] She enjoyed the change, and sat at her window watching people, horse-cars, and sparrows with great interest. Old friends came to see her, and she was happy. Found a nice school for the boys; and Nan enjoyed her quiet days.

["Notes and Memoranda"]

1873

New Years day recieved of Roberts 2,022. S. E. S[ewall]. invested 1,622. Sent Aunt C. M. $100

Went to Newport for ten days in Feb. with Jane Stuart. Made a lion of with dinners &c & fled to my den used up.

Annie dangerously ill. Sent for Pa. I went home & we had a sad time. She got well & I hurried to finish up "Work" after many interruptions. Completed it in March. 20 chapters.

Worries at home. May tired out, so April 26th we sent her off to paint all summer in London.

Home May 1st to keep house. A dull hard time. No girl, no help, Mother poorly, Nan at P[ratt]. Farm & Concord more like a tomb than ever.

May very happy copying Turner at the National Gallery, so that cheered me up & I grubbed on till I found a nice girl to help me.[5]

D. Ford offered $50 for short tales. Wrote several.

Mother very ill.

Recieved

Roberts Bros. Jan.			2,022
" " Work.	July		5,000
Moods			35
Ford			170
Independent			100
Co:[6]			

Invested.

Mortgage for A[nna].	2,000
Mortgage for L.	3,000

SOURCES: Text — Cheney, pp. 269–272; "Notes and Memoranda" — manuscript, Houghton Library, Harvard University.

1. The novelist Helen Hunt Jackson.

2. The Wolcott Centennial Celebration on 10–11 September is detailed by Bronson in his own words and in clippings in his "Diary for 1873," pp. 721–752, Houghton Library, Harvard University.

3. "A Happy Birthday" appeared in the 5 February 1874 *Youth's Companion*.

4. LMA stayed at 26 East Brookline Street.

5. At a later date, LMA inserted: "Miss Tsalter."

6. In 1873, Roberts Brothers printed 20,000 copies of *Work* and 17,916 copies of LMA's other works.

The stories in the *Independent* may be "Annie's Whim" (28 August 1873) and "Transcendental Wild Oats" (18 December 1873).

1874

January, 1874. — Mother quite ill this month. Dr. Wesselhoeft does his best for the poor old body, now such a burden to her.[1] The slow decline has begun, and she knows it, having nursed her mother to the same end.

Father disappointed and rather sad, to be left out of so much that he would enjoy and should be asked to help and adorn. A little more money, a pleasant house and time to attend to it, and I'd bring all the best people to see and entertain *him*. When I see so much twaddle going on I wonder those who can don't get up something better, and have really good things.

When I had the youth I had no money; now I have the money I have no time; and when I get the time, if I ever do, I shall have no health to enjoy life. I suppose it's the discipline I need; but it's rather hard to love the things I do and see them go by because duty chains me to my galley. If I come into port at last with all sail set that will be reward perhaps.

Life always was a puzzle to me, and gets more mysterious as I go on. I shall find it out by and by and see that it's all right, if I can only keep brave and patient to the end.

May still in London painting Turners, and doing pretty panels as "potboilers." They sell well, and she is a thrifty child. Good luck to our midsummer girl.

February. — Father has several conversations at the Clubs and Societies and Divinity School.[2] No one pays anything; but they seem glad to listen. There ought to be a place for him.

Nan busy with her boys, and they doing well at school, — good, gay, and intelligent; a happy mother and most loving little sons.

I wrote two tales, and got $200.[3] Saw Charles Kingsley, — a pleasant man.[4] His wife has Alcott relations, and likes my books. Asked us to come and see him in England; is to bring his daughters to Concord by and by.

March. — May came home with a portfolio full of fine work.[5] Must have worked like a busy bee to have done so much.

Very happy in her success; for she has proved her talent, having copied Turner so well that Ruskin (meeting her in the National Gallery at work) told her that she had "caught Turner's spirit wonderfully." She has begun to copy Nature, and done well. Lovely sketches of the cloisters in Westminster Abbey, and other charming things.

I write a story for all my men, and make up the $1,000 I planned to earn by my "pot-boilers" before we go back to C[oncord].

A tablet to Grandfather May is put in Stone Chapel, and one Sunday A.M. we take Mother to see it.[6] A pathetic sight to see Father walk up the broad aisle with the feeble old wife on his arm as they went to be married nearly fifty years ago. Mother sat alone in the old pew a little while and sung softly the old hymns; for it was early, and only the sexton there. He asked who she was, and said his father was sexton in Grandfather's time.

Several old ladies came in and knew Mother. She broke down thinking of the time when she and her mother and sisters and father and brothers all went to church together, and we took her home saying, "This is n't my Boston; all my friends are gone; I never want to see it any more."

[She never did. — L. M. A.]

April and May. — Back to Concord, after May and I had put all in fine order and made the old house lovely with her pictures. When all were settled, with May to keep house, I went to B[oston]. for rest, and took a room in Joy Street.

The Elgin Watch Company offered me a gold watch or $100 for a tale.[7] Chose the money, and wrote the story "My Rococo Watch" for them.

October. — Took two nice rooms at the Hotel Bellevue for the winter;[8] May to use one for her classes. Tried to work on my book, but was in such pain could not do much. Got no sleep without morphine. Tried old Dr. Hewett, who was sure he could cure the woe. . . .[9]

November. — Funny time with the publishers about the tale; for all wanted it at once, and each tried to outbid the other for an unwritten story.[10] I rather enjoyed it, and felt important with Roberts, Low, and Scribner all clamoring for my " 'umble" works. No peddling poor little manuscripts now, and feeling rich with $10. The golden goose can sell her eggs for a good price,[11] if she is n't killed by too much driving.

December. — Better and busier than last month.

All well at home, and Father happy among his kind Westerners.[12] Finish "Eight Cousins," and get ready to do the temperance tale, for F[ord]. offers $700 for six chapters, — "Silver Pitchers."[13]

["Notes and Memoranda"]

1874

In Boston this winter with Mother still feeble after her summer's illness. Board at Mrs Fernald's on Franklin Sq.[14] Father started to go West but hard times sent him home & he stayed with us. Talked, lectured & sat about. Good letters from May in London. Nan & boys boarded next door to us.

I wrote for St Nick Graphic, Independent & Ford as expenses were heavy mother being ill & comforts needed.[15]

Go to Radical Club. Centennial Tea party & a few lectures. Kingsley lectures & we call on him.[16]

Tablet to Grandpa May put up by the family in Kings Chapel. Mother & Father go to see it one sunday & walk up the aisle as they did when married.

Sumner died.[17] A grand funeral.

In March May came with a grand year's work. Fine copies of Turner & many lovely sketches of her own.

Went home & all spent the summer in C[oncord]. A[lice]. Bartlett visited us. Ill a good deal, tired with a hard winter.

In Oct. took rooms at the Bellevue. Girls at home. Pa at the West. May giving lessons & selling pictures.

I write a little & go to Dr Hewett to be cured.

Received	$
Tale for Graphic.	100
Hearth & Home.	100
Independent.	200
St Nicholas.	200
Elgin Watch Co.	100
Ford.	500
R. Bros. on Books.	2,814
Carlton on "M.G."	136
Loring on Moods.	14
Of Sampson Low.	894
Scrap Bag No. 3.[18]	

S. E. S[ewall]. Invested for me.

Water Bonds for Anna.	2,000[19]

SOURCES: Text — Cheney, pp. 272–274; "Notes and Memoranda" — manuscript, Houghton Library, Harvard University.

1. Dr. Conrad Wesselhoeft, longtime homeopathic physician to the Alcotts, to whom LMA dedicated *Jo's Boys*.

2. According to Bronson, "I have met a pleasant circle of students at Cambridge and expect to meet them again. Then I am to open the next Radical Club at Dr. Bartols', and speak at the Sunday series at Horticultural Hall. I have thoughts of trying for subjects, *The Ages*, at the Club, and *Modern Reformatory Ideas and Methods'* in my Sunday Lecture. In this last I can speak of Western life and thought by way of illustration" (letter of 7 February 1874 to William Torrey Harris, *Letters*, p. 625).

Contemporary newspapers list lectures entitled "Concord Authors," at the New-England Historic Genealogical Society (4 February; reported in the *Boston Commonwealth*, 7 February 1874, p. 3), and "Modern Reformatory Ideas and Methods," at the Horticultural Hall (reported in the *Boston Commonwealth*, 21 February 1874, p. 2). Bronson's "Diary for 1874" mentions these, as well as opening discussions at the Radical Club meetings of 2 and 16 February, and speaking before the Ladies of the Physiological Society on health and temperance on 5 February (Houghton Library, Harvard University).

3. According to LMA's account book, she received, for tales, $100 from the *New York Weekly Graphic*, $100 from Ford (for two tales), and $100 from *Hearth and Home* (Houghton Library, Harvard University).

4. The minister and novelist Charles Kingsley and his wife, Fanny Grenfell Kingsley; Bronson describes his conversation on 24 February 1874 with Kingsley about their "family relations" in his *Journals*, p. 447.

5. The artist William Merritt Chase had bought two of May's pictures for $100 the previous month (see LMA's letter of 17 February [1874] to Chase, Louisa May Alcott Collection, Barrett Library, University of Virginia).

6. Bronson's copy of the inscription on the tablet, his recollections of his marriage, and his description of this visit to King's Chapel are in the entry for 1 March in his "Diary for 1874," pp. 250–254, Houghton Library, Harvard University.

7. "My Rococo Watch" appeared in *The National Elgin Watch Company Illustrated Almanac for 1875* (New York: Elgin National Watch Co., 1874), pp. 22–26.

8. The Hotel Bellevue was at 17 Beacon Street in Boston.

9. Dr. Simon C. Hewett, a bonesetter who had treated both Bronson and Emerson. LMA's account book shows a payment of $98.75 to Hewett in January 1875 (Houghton Library, Harvard University).

10. For the bidding among Roberts Brothers, Sampson Low of London, and *St. Nicholas* for the rights to serialize *Eight Cousins*, see SL, pp. 186–188. *Eight Cousins* appeared in twenty-five installments between 5 December 1874 and 27 November 1875 in *Good Things* and in ten monthly installments between January and October 1875 in *St. Nicholas* and was published as a book on 25 September 1875 by Roberts Brothers and Sampson Low.

11. When LMA was abroad in 1870, Thomas Niles continually inquired about the progress of her next work. Her answer to these incessant queries was a poem, "The Lay of a Golden Goose" (printed in Cheney, pp. 204–207), which suggests that more work will prevent her from regaining her health and thus kill off the goose that lays the golden eggs.

12. Bronson's latest western trip lasted from October 1874 to April 1875.

13. "Silver Pitchers. A Temperance Tale" appeared in six weekly installments between 6 May and 10 June 1875 in the *Youth's Companion* and was published as a book in June 1876 by Roberts Brothers.

14. Possibly Mrs. Oliver Fernald's, at 6 Hayward Place in Boston.

15. "Rose and Forget-Me-Nots" appeared in the March 1874 *St. Nicholas*; "The Autobiography of an Omnibus" appeared in the October 1874 *St. Nicholas*; "How I Went Out to Service. A Story" appeared in the 4 June 1874 *Independent*.

LMA published seven stories in the *Youth's Companion* during this period: "A Happy Birthday" (5 February 1874), "Lost in a London Fog" (9 April 1874), "Dolly's Bedstead" (30 April 1874), "What the Girls Did" (14 May 1874), "A Little Cinderella" (25 June 1874), "London Bridges" (23 July 1874), and "Tribulation's Travels" (21 January 1875).

16. Charles Kingsley lectured on Westminster Abbey (with an introduction by Mark Twain) on 17 February and on the first discoverers of America on 23 February.

17. Charles Sumner died on 11 March 1874.

18. In 1874, Roberts Brothers printed 9,610 copies of LMA's works. Her account book shows her profits for the year as $5,158.46 (which she has incorrectly added as $6,111), rather than the $5,058 in the "Notes and Memoranda" (Houghton Library, Harvard University).

"Little Neighbors" appeared in the 11 and 18 April 1874 *Hearth and Home*; the third "Scrap Bag" was *Aunt Jo's Scrap-Bag: Cupid and Chow-Chow*, published in December 1873 by Roberts Brothers.

LMA's account book shows $100, rather than $200, for both "Independent" and "St Nicholas"; $300, rather than $500, for "Ford"; $2,814.06, rather than $2,814, for "R. Bros. on Books"; $14.40, rather than $14, for "Loring on Moods"; and $500 for "Scribner payment," not listed in the "Notes and Memoranda."

19. LMA wrote: "Mortgage for Anna. [—] 2,000," "Provedent Saving Bank. [—] 500," and "Five Cents Bank. [—] 500," then canceled them, probably because these entries are repeated in the next year's "Notes and Memoranda."

1875

January, 1875 — . . . Father flourishing about the Western cities, "riding in Louisa's chariot, and adored as the grandfather of 'Little Women,' " he says. [1]

February. — Finish my little tale and go to Vassar College on a visit. [2] See M. M., [3] talk with four hundred girls, write in stacks of albums and school-books, and kiss every one who asks me. Go to New York; am rather lion-ized, and run away; but things look rather jolly, and I may try a winter there some time, as I need a change and new ideas.

March. — Home again, getting ready for the centennial fuss. [4]

April. — On the 19th a grand celebration. General *break-down*, owing to an unwise desire to outdo all the other towns; too many people. . . .

June, July, August, 1875. — Kept house at home, with two Irish incapables to trot after, [5] and ninety-two guests in one month to entertain. [6] Fame is an expensive luxury. I can do without it. This is my worst scrape, I think. I asked for bread, and got a stone, — in the shape of a pedestal.

September and October, 1875. — I go to Woman's Congress in Syracuse, [7] and see Niagara. Funny time with the girls.

Write loads of autographs, dodge at the theatre, and am kissed to death by gushing damsels. One energetic lady grasped my hand in the crowd, exclaiming, "If you ever come to Oshkosh, your feet will not be allowed to touch the ground: you will be borne in the arms of the people! Will you come?" "Never," responded Miss A., trying to look affable, and dying to

196

laugh as the good soul worked my arm like a pump-handle, and from the gallery generations of girls were looking on. "This, this, is fame!"

November, December. — Take a room at Bath Hotel, New York, and look about me.[8] Miss Sally Holly is here, and we go about together.[9] She tells me much of her life among the freedmen, and Mother is soon deep in barrels of clothes, food, books, etc., for Miss A. to take back with her.

See many people, and am very gay for a country-mouse. Society unlike either London or Boston.

Go to Sorosis, and to Mrs. Botta's, O. B. Frothingham's, Miss Booth's, and Mrs. Croly's receptions.[10]

Visit the Tombs, Newsboys' Home, and Randall's Island on Christmas Day with Mrs. Gibbons.[11] A memorable day. Make a story of it. Enjoy these things more than the parties and dinners.

["Notes and Memoranda"]
1875

Write 8 Cousins for St Nick, also a serial for Ford.[12]

Keep house in the summer while the girls go to Walpole.

Much company.

In Oct. go to Syracuse, Niagara & New York where I settle for the winter. See much of N.Y. people. Go to Clubs, dinners receptions, galleries & theatres. Write a few tales for Ford to pay my way.

Saw many notable folks. Beecher, Joachim Miller, Stedman, Stoddard the Bottas, Bret Hearte, Dr Holland, Sally Holly, Conway, Phillips & many others.[13]

Went much to the theatre & enjoyed it more than anything else.

Received.	
Serial for St N.	2,000
Serial for Ford	700
Tales for Ind.	200
Graphic	100
Four tales for Ford.	200
St Nicholas	200
R. Bros. on Act.	775
Carlton.	32
Low on Act.	500
Low for 8 Cousins	560
" on Act	590[14]

197

Invested.

Provident Bank.	1,000
Five Cent Bank.	500
Mortgage for A.	2,000

SOURCES: Text — Cheney, pp. 275–277; "Notes and Memoranda" — manuscript, Houghton Library, Harvard University.

1. As Bronson wrote LMA from Milwaukee, "You would esteem sufficiently dramatic for a new play of the Alcott type. — 150 girls all rising and raising hands at the Master's question. 'How many have read Miss Alcotts Little Women,' and then I need not tell what followed. After my little story of the famous lady was told in plain terms as the subject allowed scores of hands were stretched, arm over arm, by the gathered group, to take that of the 'papa.' And then as many autographs were inscribe[d] in Albums and little slips extemporized at the moment. What shall poor papa do but bear it gracefully and be himself" (4 February 1875, Letters, p. 646). An 1875 poster, announcing a "Conversation" by "Dr. Brunson [sic] Alcott, the Concord Sage and Gifted Sire of Louisa M. Alcott! Authoress of 'Little Women,' Etc.," is reproduced in SL, following p. 264.

2. LMA later reported on her visit to Vassar at a meeting of the Sorosis Club: "She said at Vassar College the girls, as usual, asked for a speech, and when she also, as usual, told them that she never had and never intended to make one, they requested that she would place herself in a prominent position and turn around slowly. This she consented to do" ("Personalities," New York Graphic, 18 December 1875, p. 374).

3. Professor Maria Nora Mitchell of Vassar College later attended the Concord School of Philosophy, in 1879, and was elected the second president of the Association for the Advancement of Women.

4. LMA is referring to the grand celebration of the centennial of the Revolutionary War battle at Concord; see her accounts of it in a letter of 20 [i.e., 13] April 1875 to Frederick W. G. May in SL, pp. 191–192, and a letter entitled "Woman's Part in the Concord Celebration" in the 1 May 1875 Woman's Journal (reprinted in Madeleine B. Stern, "Louisa Alcott's Feminist Letters," Studies in the American Renaissance 1978, ed. Joel Myerson [Boston: Twayne, 1978], pp. 438–441); Proceedings of the Centennial Celebration of Concord Fight (Concord: The Town, 1876); and Stern, Louisa May Alcott (Norman: University of Oklahoma Press, 1950), pp. 241–243.

5. LMA's account book shows payments during the summer to Mary, Hatch, Messer, and Holden, some or all of whom were probably these servants (Houghton Library, Harvard University).

6. As LMA wrote a Mrs. Woods on 20 July [1875], "I dont believe any one knows how bored we are by company, over a hundred a month, most of them strangers. A whole school came without warning last week & Concord people bring all their company to see us. This may seem pleasant, but when kept up a whole season is a great affliction. . . . So I have resolved to defend Marmee's health & home at the point of the bayonet, & be called a cross patch for my pains" (SL, p. 193).

7. LMA's description of this meeting, after which "the stage filled in a minute (it seemed to me,) with beaming girls all armed with Albums and cards and begging to speak to Miss A. . . . and I finally had to run for my life with more girls all along the way, and Ma's clawing me as I went," is in her letter of [18 October 1875] to Bronson, in SL, p. 198.

8. Dr. Eli Peck Miller's Bath Hotel at 39 West Twenty-sixth Street was known more formally as the New York Hygienic Institute and Turkish Bath.

9. For LMA's involvement with the antislavery reformer Sallie Holley, see her letter of 26 November [1876] to her, in SL, pp. 218–219.

10. LMA's description of her reception in New York is in her letter of 12[–13] December [1875] to Bronson, in *SL,* pp. 205–207. Anne Charlotte Lynch Botta ran a famous literary salon in New York for many years; Mary L. Booth edited *Harper's Bazaar;* Jane Cunningham Croly edited *Demorest's Monthly Magazine.*

The Sorosis Club was founded by Jane Croly in 1868 to promote women's interests in art, science, and literature. According to the *New York Graphic,* LMA was "formally presented to the club by the President as the 'most successful woman author in America' " ("Personalities," 18 December 1875, p. 374).

11. The Tombs was a notorious New York prison; LMA describes her visit to the News-boys' Lodging House in New York in a letter of 4 December 1875 to Frederick and John Pratt, in *SL,* pp. 202–204; Abby Hopper Gibbons ministered to the orphans on Randall's Island; LMA's visit to Randall's Island is described in her letters of 25 December 1875 to her family, in *SL,* pp. 210–213, and of the same date to Anna Rice Powell, in Aaron M. Powell, *Personal Reminiscences of the Anti-Slavery and Other Reforms* (New York: Caulon Press, 1899), pp. 240–241, and an anonymous account, "Charity's Open Hand," *New York Daily Tribune,* 27 December 1875, p. 5.

12. *Silver Pitchers.*

13. Not previously identified are Henry Ward Beecher of Brooklyn, one of America's most popular preachers; Cincinnatus Hiner Miller, who wrote as Joachin Miller, a western poet noted as much for his flamboyant behavior as for his verses; the poet and anthologist Edmund Clarence Stedman; Richard Henry Stoddard, a popular author and lecturer; Anne Botta's husband Vincenzo, who taught at the University of the City of New York; the author Bret Harte; and Dr. Josiah Gilbert Holland, editor of *Scribner's Monthly Magazine.*

14. In 1875, Roberts Brothers printed 16,000 copies of *Eight Cousins* and 11,000 copies of LMA's other works. Her account book lists her profits for the year as $7,264, rather than $5,857 in the "Notes and Memoranda" (Houghton Library, Harvard University).

"Eight Cousins" was reprinted in *St. Nicholas;* "By the River" appeared in the 10 June 1875 *Independent;* "Letty's Tramp" appeared in the 23 December 1875 *Independent;* "The Boy's Joke, and Who Got the Best of It" appeared in the 25 December 1875 *New York Christmas Graphic;* LMA published five stories in the *Youth's Companion* during 1875: "Tribulation's Travels" (21 January), "Red Tulips" (25 February), "What a Shovel Did" (15 April), "Old Major" (5 August), and "My Little School-Girl" (4 November); "Marjorie's Birthday Gifts" appeared in the January 1876 *St. Nicholas;* "Helping Along" appeared in the March 1876 *St. Nicholas.*

LMA's account book also lists $500 from the previous year for "Serial for St N."; $100 for two tales from Ford, rather than $200 for four tales; and $1,311 from "R. Bros. on Act.," rather than $775 (LMA canceled this at a later date and inserted "1456").

1876

January, 1876. — Helped Mrs. Croly receive two hundred gentlemen.[1]

A letter from Baron Tauchnitz asking leave to put my book in his foreign library, and sending 600 marks to pay for it.[2] Said, "Yes, thank you, Baron."

Went to Philadelphia to see Cousin J. May installed in Dr. Furness's pulpit.[3] Dull place is Philadelphia. Heard Beecher preach; did not like him. . . .

Went home on the 21st, finding I could not work here. Soon tire of being a fine lady.

February and March. — Took a room in B[oston]., and fell to work on short tales for F[ord]. T. N[iles]. wanted a centennial story; but my frivolous New York life left me no ideas. Went to Centennial Ball at Music Hall, and got an idea.

Wrote a tale of " '76," which with others will make a catchpenny book.[4] Mother poorly, so I go home to nurse her.

April, May, and June. — Mother better. Nan and boys go to P[ratt]. farm. May and I clean the old house. It seems as if the dust of two centuries haunted the ancient mansion, and came out spring and fall in a ghostly way for us to clear up.

Great freshets and trouble.

Exposition in Philadelphia; don't care to go.[5] America ought to pay her debts before she gives parties. "Silver Pitchers," etc., comes out, and goes well. Poor stuff; but the mill must keep grinding even chaff.

June. — Lovely month! Keep hotel and wait on Marmee.

Try to get up steam for a new serial, as Mrs. Dodge wants one, and Scribner offers $3,000 for it.[6] Roberts Brothers want a novel; and the various newspapers and magazines clamor for tales. My brain is squeezed dry, and I can only wait for help.

July, August. — Get an idea and start "Rose in Bloom," though I hate sequels.[7]

September. — On the 9th my dear girl sails in the "China" for a year in London or Paris. God be with her! She has done her distasteful duty faithfully, and deserved a reward. She cannot find the help she needs here, and is happy and busy in her own world over there.

[She never came home. — L. M. A.]
Finish "Rose."[8]

.   .   .   .

November. — "Rose" comes out; sells well.
. . . Forty-four years old. My new task gets on slowly; but I keep at it, and can be a prop, if not an angel, in the house, as Nan is.

December. — Miss P.[9] sends us a pretty oil sketch of May, — so like the dear soul in her violet wrapper, with yellow curls piled up, and the long hand at work. Mother delights in it.

She (M.) is doing finely, and says, "I am getting on, and I feel as if it was not all a mistake; for I have some talent, and will prove it." Modesty is a sign of genius, and I think our girl has both. The money I invest in her pays the sort of interest I like. I am proud to have her show what she can do, and have her depend upon no one but me. Success to little Raphael! My dull winter is much cheered by her happiness and success.

["Notes and Memoranda"]
1876.

Left New York the middle of Jan as mother was feeble & I tired of a gay life.

Went to the Bellevue & tried to write, but could not so home to nurse mother who seemed to need more care.

Nan at P[ratt]. Farm. May housekeeper. Pa lecturing about & getting old.

A dull summer. Nan & boys to Walpole. May & I by turns to York Me. Nice old place.

In Sept. write Sequel to 8 Cousins, in less than four weeks. Published Dec. 2ond 10,00[0] copies.[10] Dull times but went well.

May went abroad in Sept for a year or two of study in London & Paris.

201

Nan housekeeper, I nurse, chambermaid & money maker.
Dull times.

Recieved.	$
Roberts Bros on Act. Jan.	3,348
Carlton on Act.	16
Ford	100
Scribner a tale.	100
Ford a tale.	50
Canada on 8. Cousins	102
Low on Act.	260
Roberts Bos. — July	1080[11]

Reinvested	
In Trust Co.	3,013
Mortgage.	3,500
" " "	4,500
St Louis City Bond.	1,039

SOURCES: Text — Cheney, pp. 294–296; "Notes and Memoranda" — manuscript, Houghton Library, Harvard University.

1. LMA's account of this party is in her letter of 1[–2] January 1876 to her mother, in SL, pp. 214–215.

2. Bernhard Tauchnitz of Leipzig published a two-volume German edition of Little Women in 1876.

3. Joseph May.

4. "Independence" was included in Silver Pitchers.

5. The Philadelphia Centennial Exposition, with 249 buildings spread over 465 acres, was held from 10 May to 10 November 1876.

6. Mary Mapes Dodge, editor of St. Nicholas, conducted a lengthy correspondence with LMA; "Under the Lilacs" appeared in monthly installments between December 1877 and October 1878 in St. Nicholas and was published as a book in October 1878 by Roberts Brothers.

7. Rose in Bloom, a sequel to Eight Cousins, was published in November 1876 by Roberts Brothers.

8. LMA sent the final chapters to Mrs. Dodge in her letter of 26 September 1876 (Princeton University Library).

9. Rose Peckham, an artist friend of May's.

10. Roberts Brothers sold out the first printing of 10,000 copies of Rose in Bloom in November.

11. In 1876, Roberts Brothers printed 16,828 copies of Rose in Bloom and 16,500 copies of LMA's other works. According to LMA's account book, her earnings in 1876 were $6,554, rather than the $5,056 listed in the "Notes and Memoranda" (Houghton Library, Harvard University).

"A New Way to Spend Christmas" appeared in the 9 March 1876 Youth's Companion; "An

Evening Call" appeared in the 13 April 1876 *Youth's Companion;* "A Visit to the Tombs" appeared in the 25 May 1876 *Youth's Companion.*

LMA's account book also lists $3,348.15, rather than $3,348, from "Roberts Bros. on Act. Jan." and $160 from Tauchnitz and $100 from Ford for two tales not listed in the "Notes and Memoranda."

1877

January, February, 1877. — The year begins well. Nan keeps house; boys fine, tall lads, good and gay; Father busy with his new book;[1] Mother cosey with her sewing, letters, Johnson,[2] and success of her "girls."

Went for some weeks to the Bellevue, and wrote "A Modern Mephistopheles" for the No Name Series.[3] It has been simmering ever since I read Faust last year. Enjoyed doing it, being tired of providing moral pap for the young. Long to write a novel, but cannot get time enough.

May's letters our delight. She is so in earnest she will not stop for pleasure, rest, or society, but works away like a Trojan. Her work admired by masters and mates for its vigor and character.

March. — Begin to think of buying the Thoreau place for Nan.[4] The $4,000 received from the Vt. and Eastern R. Rs. must be invested, and she wants a home of her own, now the lads are growing up.

Mother can be with her in the winter for a change, and leave me free to write in B[oston]. Concord has no inspiration for me.

April. — May, at the request of her teacher, M. Muller, sends a study of still life to the Salon.[5] The little picture is accepted, well hung, and praised by the judges. No friend at court, and the modest work stood on its own merits. She is very proud to see her six months' hard work bear fruit. A happy girl, and all say she deserves the honor.

"M. M." appears and causes much guessing. It is praised and criticised, and I enjoy the fun, especially when friends say, "I know you did n't write it, for you can't hide your peculiar style."

Help to buy the house for Nan, — $4,500. So she has her wish, and is happy. When shall I have mine? Ought to be contented with knowing I help both sisters by my brains. But I'm selfish, and want to go away and rest in Europe. Never shall.

May, June. — Quiet days keeping house and attending to Marmee, who grows more and more feeble. Helped Nan get ready for her new home.

Felt very well, and began to hope I had outlived the neuralgic worries and nervous woes born of the hospital fever and the hard years following.

May living alone in Paris, while her mates go jaunting, — a solitary life; but she is so busy she is happy and safe. A good angel watches over her. Take pleasant drives early in the A.M. with Marmee. She takes her comfort in a basket wagon, and we drive to the woods, picking flowers and stopping where we like. It keeps her young, and rests her weary nerves.

July. — Got too tired, and was laid up for some weeks. A curious time, lying quite happily at rest, wondering what was to come next.

August. — As soon as able began "Under the Lilacs," but could not do much.

September. — On the 7th Marmee had a very ill turn, and the doctor told me it was the beginning of the end. (Water on the chest.) She was so ill we sent for Father from Walcott; and I forgot myself in taking care of poor Marmee, who suffered much and longed to go.

As I watched with her I wrote "My Girls," to go with other tales in a new "Scrap Bag,"[6] and finished "Under the Lilacs." I foresaw a busy or a sick winter, and wanted to finish while I could, so keeping my promise and earning my $3,000.

Brain very lively and pen flew. It always takes an exigency to spur me up and wring out a book. Never have time to go slowly and do my best.

October. — Fearing I might give out, got a nurse and rested a little, so that when the last hard days come I might not fail Marmee, who says, "Stay by, Louy, and help me if I suffer too much." I promised, and watched her sit panting life away day after day. We thought she would not outlive her seventy-seventh birthday, but, thanks to Dr. W[esselhoeft]. and homœopathy, she got relief, and we had a sad little celebration, well knowing it would be the last. Aunt B[ond]. and L. W[ells]. came up, and with fruit, flowers, smiling faces, and full hearts, we sat round the brave soul who faced death so calmly and was ready to go.

I overdid and was very ill, — in danger of my life for a week, — and feared to go before Marmee. But pulled through, and got up slowly to help her die. A strange month.

November. — Still feeble, and Mother failing fast. On the 14th we were both moved to Anna's at Mother's earnest wish.

A week in the new home, and then she ceased to care for anything. Kept her bed for three days, lying down after weeks in a chair, and on the 25th, at dusk, that rainy Sunday, fell quietly asleep in my arms.

She was very happy all day, thinking herself a girl again, with parents and sisters round her. Said her Sunday hymn to me, whom she called "Mother," and smiled at us, saying "A smile is as good as a prayer." Looked often at the little picture of May and waved her hand to it, "Good-by, little May, good-by!"

Her last words to Father were, "You are laying a very soft pillow for me to go to sleep on."

We feared great suffering, but she was spared that, and slipped peacefully away. I was so glad when the last weary breath was drawn, and silence came, with its rest and peace.[7]

On the 27th it was necessary to bury her, and we took her quietly away to Sleepy Hollow. A hard day, but the last duty we could do for her; and there we left her at sunset beside dear Lizzie's dust, — alone so long.

On the 28th a memorial service, and all the friends at Anna's, — Dr. Bartol and Mr. Foote of Stone Chapel.[8] A simple, cheerful service, as she would have liked it.

Quiet days afterward resting in her rest.

My duty is done, and now I shall be glad to follow her.

December. — Many kind letters from all who best knew and loved the noble woman.

I never wish her back, but a great warmth seems gone out of life, and there is no motive to go on now.

My only comfort is that I *could* make her last years comfortable, and lift off the burden she had carried so bravely all these years. She was so loyal, tender, and true; life was hard for her, and no one understood all she had to bear but we, her children. I think I shall soon follow her, and am quite ready to go now she no longer needs me.

["Notes and Memoranda"]
1877

An eventful year. May in Paris. Has a picture accepted in the May Salon. Gets on finely with her art.

Spent a month at Bellevue in Jan. writing M[odern]. M[ephistopheles].

Buy the Thoreau house for Anna, & pay 2500 & she $2000. She moves in July.

Wrote "Under the Lilacs" at odd times.

Ill in Aug. Mother ill in September, & the end began. Three months of suffering patiently borne & on the 25th of Nov. she died peacefully.

Shut up the old house & go to live with Anna. Father goes about & talks. I am ill all winter with little hope of recovery, but pull through with care & kindness & in March begin to hope I may do something more in the world.

Recieved	$
For M. M.	600.00
Roberts Bros. Jan.	4268.00
For R. in B.	500.00
Carleton.	20.00[9]
Roberts on Act.	500.00
" " "	200.00
Loring.	53.00
Roberts on Act.	400.00
Ford.	100.00[10]

Invested

House for A[nna].	2500.00

SOURCES: Text — Cheney, pp. 296–301; "Notes and Memoranda" — manuscript, Houghton Library, Harvard University.

1. Bronson's *Table-Talk* was published in April 1877 by Roberts Brothers.

2. Samuel Johnson, the British poet and essayist.

3. *A Modern Mephistopheles* was published anonymously in April 1877 by Roberts Brothers in its No Name series. Part of the series' success came from the way it allowed readers to guess the author of each work. For more information, see *A Modern Mephistopheles and Taming a Tartar*, ed. Madeleine B. Stern (New York: Praeger, 1987).

4. Anna Pratt purchased the Thoreau House at 26 Main Street in Concord from Sophia Thoreau's estate in April or May 1877 for $4,500, of which $2,500 came from LMA; see also LMA's letter of 6 March [1877] to George A. Thatcher, in *SL*, p. 221.

5. The artist Charles Louise Müller; May's painting of *Nature Morte*, now at Orchard House, is reproduced in *American Transcendental Quarterly* 47–48 (Summer-Fall 1980): 140.

6. *My Girls*, vol. 4 of *Aunt Jo's Scrap-Bag*, was published in December 1877 by Roberts Brothers.

7. Abigail May Alcott died on 25 November 1877. LMA's letter of that date to May Alcott, describing her mother's last moments, is in *SL*, pp. 225–226.

8. LMA also describes her mother's funeral in a letter of 16 December [1877] to Mrs. A. D. Moshier, in *SL*, pp. 226–227. H. W. Foote, minister of King's Chapel (where the Alcotts had been married), read scriptures; the Unitarian minister Cyrus Bartol gave a eulogy; and

William Lloyd Garrison gave his recollections of Mrs. Alcott's role in the antislavery conflict (*Concord Freeman*, 6 December 1877, p. 1).

9. LMA wrote: "M[odern]. M[ephistopheles].   600.00" and then canceled it.

10. In 1877, Roberts Brothers printed 5,500 copies of *My Girls* and 12,786 copies of LMA's other works. According to LMA's account book, her earnings this year were $7,988, rather than the $6,641 listed in the "Notes and Memoranda" (Houghton Library, Harvard University).

"Clams, A Ghost Story" appeared in the 3 May 1877 *Youth's Companion;* "Clara's Idea" appeared in the 13 September 1877 *Youth's Companion.*

LMA's account book lists $4,642, rather than $4,268, from "Roberts Bros. Jan."; $250, rather than $200, from "Roberts on Act."; and the $100 from Ford under 1876.

After "Ford," LMA wrote: "Trust Fund" and then canceled it.

1878

January, 1878. — An idle month at Nan's, for I can only suffer.

Father goes about, being restless with his anchor gone. Dear Nan is house-mother now, — so patient, so thoughtful and tender; I need nothing but that cherishing which only mothers can give.

May busy in London. Very sad about Marmee; but it was best not to send for her, and Marmee forbade it, and she has some very *tender friends* near her.

February. — . . . Wrote some lines on Marmee.[1]

March, 1878. — A happy event, — May's marriage to Ernest Nieriker,[2] the "tender friend" who has consoled her for Marmee's loss, as John consoled Nan for Beth's. He is a Swiss, handsome, cultivated, and good; an excellent family living in Baden, and E. has a good business. May is old enough to choose for herself, and seems so happy in the new relation that we have nothing to say against it.

They were privately married on the 22nd, and went to Havre for the honeymoon, as E. had business in France; so they hurried the wedding. Send her $1,000 as a gift, and all good wishes for the new life.

April. — Happy letters from May, who is enjoying life as one can but once. E. writes finely to Father, and is a son to welcome I am sure. May sketches and E. attends to his business by day, and both revel in music in the evening, as E. is a fine violin player.

How different our lives are just now! — I so lonely, sad, and sick; she so happy, well and blest. She always had the cream of things, and deserved it. My time is yet to come somewhere else, when I am ready for it.

Anna clears out the old house; for we shall never go back to it; it ceased to be "home" when Marmee left it.

I dawdle about, and wait to see if I am to live or die. If I live, it is for some new work. I wonder what?

May. — Begin to drive a little, and enjoy the spring. Nature is always good to me.

May settles in her own house at Meudon, — a pretty apartment, with balcony, garden, etc. . . . I plan and hope to go to them, if I am ever well enough, and find new inspiration in a new life. May and E. urge it, and I long to go, but cannot risk the voyage yet. I doubt if I ever find time to lead my own life, or health to try it.

June and July. — Improving fast, in spite of dark predictions and forebodings. The Lord has more work for me, so I am spared.

Tried to write a memoir of Marmee; but it is too soon, and I am not well enough.

    •   •   •   •   •   •   •   •

May has had the new mother and brother-in-law with her, and finds them most interesting and lovable. They seem very proud of her, and happy in her happiness. Bright times for our youngest! May they last!

[They did. — L. M. A.]

    •   •   •   •   •   •   •   •

Got nicely ready to go to May in September; but at the last moment gave it up, fearing to undo all the good this weary year of ease has done for me, and be a burden on her. A great disappointment; but I've learned to wait. I long to see her happy in her own home.

Nan breaks her leg; so it is well I stayed, as there was no one to take her place but me. Always a little chore to be done.

October, November. — Nan improved. Rode, nursed, kept house, and tried to be contented, but was not. Make no plans for myself now; do what I can, and should be glad not to have to sit idle any longer.

On the 8th, Marmee's birthday, Father and I went to Sleepy Hollow with red leaves and flowers for her. A cold, dull day, and I was glad there was no winter for her any more.

November 25th. — A year since our beloved Marmee died. A very eventful year. May marries, I live instead of dying, Father comes to honor in his old age, and Nan makes her home our refuge when we need one.

December. — A busy time. Nan gets about again. I am so well I wonder at myself, and ask no more.

Write a tale for the "Independent," and begin on an art novel, with May's romance for its thread.[3] Went to B[oston]. for some weeks, and looked about to see what I could venture to do. . . .

So ends 1878, — a great contrast to last December. Then I thought I was done with life; now I can enjoy a good deal, and wait to see what I am spared to do. Thank God for both the sorrow and the joy.

["Notes and Memoranda"]
1878

March 22ond May was married in London to E. Nieriker. Honeymoon at Havre, first home at Meudon. Very happy.

Begin a memoir of mother but have to give it up. Cannot work.

A queer wild season with eclipses, tornadoes, great heat, rain & tempest.

Guests from the West. Talk of a School of Philosophy.[4] Father very happy.

In Nov. Hamilton Willis died.[5]

Spent a month in Boston writing a story about May's artist life.[6]

1878 ends more happily than last year. Then I was ill, sad & with little hope. Now all looks brighter & all are well. So we can thank God for the sunshine after the rain.

Recieved.

Jan. Scribner	3,000
Roberts Bros.	1,336
" " " "	200
Tale to Independent.	100
Ford	50
St Nicholas	100

Wrote

Tale for Ford[7]
Tale for W.s Journal[8]

Invested.

Furnace for A.	300
1 Old Colony Bond	1,000
B. M. & C. R. R.	1,000[9]
Sent May	1,000

211

SOURCES: Text — Cheney, pp. 301, 315–317; "Notes and Memoranda" — manuscript, Houghton Library, Harvard University.

1. "Transfiguration" appeared in *A Masque of Poets* (Boston: Roberts Brothers, 1878), pp. 164–166.

2. May had become engaged to twenty-two-year-old Ernest Nieriker, a Swiss business-man, in February and married him in London on 22 March 1878.

3. "John Marlow's Victory" appeared in the 19 December 1878 *Independent*; LMA's *Diana and Persis*, left unfinished at her death, has been edited by Sarah Elbert (New York: Arno, 1978).

4. The Concord School of Philosophy began unofficially with a lecture series in 1878 and officially ran from 1879 to 1888.

5. Hamilton Willis died on 16 November 1878.

6. LMA wrote: "The Carnival spoilt my work so I gave it up & went home." and then canceled it.

7. By this entry, LMA wrote "50" and then canceled it.

8. In 1878, Roberts Brothers printed 9,068 copies of *Under the Lilacs* and 7,286 copies of LMA's other works. According to LMA's account book, her income for the year was $6,669, rather than the $4,786 listed in the "Notes and Memoranda" (Houghton Library, Harvard University).

"Mrs. Gay's Prescription" appeared in the 24 August 1878 *Woman's Journal*.

LMA's account book lists $1,746.20, rather than $1,336, from "Roberts Bros."; and $27.27 from Canadian sales not present in the "Notes and Memoranda."

9. The Boston, Concord, and Montreal Railroad.

1879

Concord.

1879.

Jan.

At the Bellevue in my little room writing.

Got two books well started but had too many interruptions to do much, & dared not get into a vortex for fear of a break down.[1]

Went about & saw people & tried to be jolly.

Did Jarley for Mr Clarks Fair.[2] Also for Author's Carnival at Music Hall.[3] A queer time. Too old for such pranks. A sad heart & a used up body make play hard work I find.

Read Mary Wollstoncraft, Dosia, Danieli Helène &c. I like Grèville's books.[4]

Invest $1000 for Fred's schooling &c. Johnny has his $1000 also safely in the bank for his education & any emergency.

Roberts Bros. for six months $2500.00
Independent for tale   100.00[5]

Feb.

Home to Concord rather used up. Find a very quiet life is best, for in B[oston]. people beset me to do things & I try & get so tired I cannot work. Dr C[onrad]. [Wesselhoeft] says, "Rest is your salvation," so I rest. Hope for Paris in the spring as May begs me to come.

She is leading what she calls "an ideal life" painting, music, love & the world shut out. People wonder & gossip, but M. & E[rnest]. laugh & are happy. Wise people to enjoy this lovely time as long as they can for it never lasts.

Went to dinner at the Revere House of the Papyrus Club.[6] Mrs Burnett & Miss A. were guests of honor. Dr Holmes took me in, & to my surprise I found myself at the Presidents right hand with Mrs B. Holmes Stedman & the great ones of the land. Had a gay time. Dr H. very gallant. "Little Women" often toasted with more praise than was good for me.

Saw Mrs Burnett at a lunch & took her & Mrs. M. M. Dodge to Concord for a lunch.[7] Most agreeable women.

A visit at H. W. s. Mission time at Church of the Advent. Father Knox Little preached & waked up the sinners.[8] H. hoped to convert me, & took me to see Father K. L. A very interesting man, & we had a pleasant talk, but I found that we meant the same thing tho called by different names, & his religion had too much ceremony about it to suit me. So he gave me his blessing & promised to send me some books. (Never did.)

Pleasant times with my "rainy day friend" as I call Dr. H.[9] She is a great comfort to me with her healthy, common sense & tender patience, aside from skill as a doctor, & beauty as a woman. I love her much & she does me good.

Poor S. P. very ill.[10] Go often to see her & feel great sympathy with her.

March.

At home. Sew, read & write a little. Nan's birthday on the 16th (48). The best woman I know, always reasonable, just, kind, & forgiving. A heavenly temper & a tender heart. A good sister to me all these years in spite of the utter unlikeness of our tastes, temperaments & lives. If we did not love one another so well we never could get on at all. As it is I am a trial to her & she to me sometimes, our views are so different. Dear, loving soul, God bless & keep her long to be our comfort.

Rather poorly. Had to lie & read much. Read "Deronda" & found it dull except "Gwen" & "Grandcourt."[11] G. E. is wise but heavy. Wrote "Little Travelers" for St N. $100.[12]

Happy letters from May. Her hopes of a little son or daughter in the autumn give us new plans to talk over. I *must* be well enough to go to her then.

April.

Very poorly & cross. So tired of being a prisoner to pain. Long for the old strength when I could do what I liked & never know I had a body. Life not worth living in this way. But having overworked the wonderful machine I must pay for it, & should not growl I suppose as it is just.

To B[oston]. to see Dr. L[awrence].[13] Told me I was better than she ever dreamed I could be, & need not worry. So took heart & tried to be cheerful in spite of aches & nerves. Warm weather comforted me, & green grass did me good.

Poor S. P. failing fast. Not my fate yet.

Put a new fence round A[nna]'s garden. Bought a phaeton so I might drive as I cannot walk much, & father loves to take his guests about.

May. & June.

Go to B[oston]. for a week but dont enjoy seeing people. Do errands & go home again. Saw "Pinafore" a pretty play.[14]

Much company.

Emorys looked at the Orchard House & liked it. Will hire it probably.[15] Hope so as it is forlorn standing empty. I never go by without looking up at Marmee's window where the dear face used to be, & May's with the picturesque vines round it. No golden haired, blue gowned Diana ever appears now. She sits happily sewing baby clothes in Paris.

Enjoyed fitting out a box of dainty things to send her.[16] Even lonely old spinsters take an interest in babies.

June.

A poorly month. Try to forget my own worries & enjoy the fine weather, my little carriage, & good friends. Souls are such slaves to bodies it is hard to keep up out the slough of despond when nerves jangle & flesh aches.

Emory's took the old house. Pleasant people.

Went with father one Sunday to the Prison & told the men a story.[17] Thought I could not face 400 at first, but after looking at them during the sermon I felt that I could at least *amuse* them, & they evidently needed something new. So I told a hospital story with a little moral to it, & was so interested in watching the faces of some young men near me who drank in every word that I forgot myself & talked away "like a mother." One put his head down, & another winked hard, so I felt that I had caught them, for even one tear in that dry, hard place would do them good. Miss M. C. & father said it was well done, & I felt quite proud of my first speech.[18] (Sequel later.)

July.

Wrote a little tale called "Jimmy's Cruise in the Pinafore," for St. N. $100.[19]

A short visit to Leicester.[20]

S. P. very low; eager to be gone. Got a nurse for her. Watched with her now & then.

On the 15th the School of Philosophy began in the study at Orchard House.[21] Thirty students, Father the Dean. He has *his* dream realized at last, & is in glory with plenty of talk to swim in. People laugh but will enjoy some thing new in this dull old town, & the fresh Westerners will show them that all the culture of the world is not in Concord. I had a private laugh when Mrs S. asked one of the new comers, with her superior air, "If she had ever looked into Plato?" & the modest lady from Jacksonville answered with a twinkle at me, "We have been reading Plato in *Greek* for the past six years." Mrs S. subsided after that.[22] Oh, wicked L. M. A. who hates sham & loves a joke.

Was *the first woman to register my name* as a voter.[23]

Aug.

To B[oston]. with a new "Scrap Bag".[24] "Jimmy" to the fore. Wrote a little tale.

The town swarms with budding philosophers, & they roost on our step like hens, waiting for corn. Father revels in it, so we keep the hotel going & try to look as if we like it. If they were philanthropists I *should* enjoy it, but speculation seems a waste of time when there is so much real work crying to be done. Why discuss the Unknowable till our poor are fed & the wicked saved?

A young poet from N.Y. came. Nice boy. Sixteen callers to day. Trying to stir up the women about Suffrage. So timid & slow.

Get Nan & boys off to Nonquitt.[25]

Happy letters from May. Sophy N. is with her now.[26] All well in the Paris nest.

Wrote a story "Victoria" for Jenny June. $200[27]

Elly D. died.[28] Lovely boy.

Passed a week in Magnolia with Dr H[osmer].[29]

School ended for this year. Hallylujah!

September.

Home from the seaside refreshed, & go to work on a new serial for St N. "Jack & Jill".[30] Have no plan yet but a boy, a girl & a sled, with an upset to start with. Vague idea of working in Concord young folks & thier doings. After two years of rest I am going to try again. It is so easy to make money now & so pleasant to have it to give. A chapter a day is my task, & not that if I feel tired. No more 14 hours a day. Make haste slowly now.

Drove about & drummed up women to my Suffrage meeting. So hard to move people out of the old ruts. I haven't patience enough. If they wont see & work I let em alone & steam along my own way.

May sent some nice little letters of an "Artist's Holyday;" & I had them printed. Also a book for artists abroad.[31] Very useful & well done.

Eight chapters done. Too much company for work. Scribner sent $500 on act for J. & J.

October.

8th Dear Marmee's birthday. Never forgotten. Lovely day. Go to Sleepy Hollow with flowers. Her grave is green, black berry vines with red leaves trail over it. A little white stone with her initials is at the head, & among the tall grass over her breast a little bird had made a nest. Empty now, but a pretty symbol of the refuge that tender bosom always was for all feeble & sweet things. Her favorite asters bloomed all about, & the pines sang overhead. So she & dear Beth lie quietly asleep in God's Acre, & we remember them more tenderly with each year that brings us nearer them & home.

Went with Dr H[osmer]. to the Woman's Prison at Sherburne.[32] A lovely drive & very memorable day & night. Read a story to the 400 women & heard many interesting tales. A much better place than Concord Prison with its armed wardens & "knock down & drag out" methods. Only women here & they work wonders by patience, love, common sense & to the belief in salvation for all.

First proofs from Scribner. Mrs D[odge]. likes the story, so I peg away very slowly. Put in "Elly D." as one of my boys. The nearer I keep to nature the better the work is. Young folks much interested in the story & all want to "go in". I shall have a hornet's nest about me if all are not *angels*.

Father goes West.[33]

I mourn much because all say I must not go to May. Not safe & I cannot add to Mamma Nieriker's cares at this time by another invalid, as the voyage would upset me I am so sea sick.

Give up my hope & long cherished plan with grief. May sadly disappointed. I know I shall wish I had gone. It is my luck!

November.

Went to Boston for a month as some solace for my great disappointment. Take my room at the Bellevue & go about a little. Write on "J. & J."

Anxious about May.

8th Little *Louisa May* Nieriker arrived in Paris at 9 p.m. after a short journey.[34] All doing well. Much rejoicing. Nice little lass & May very happy. Ah, if I had only been there! Too much happiness for me.

25th Two years since Marmee went. How she would have enjoyed the little grand-daughter & all May's romance. Perhaps she does?

Went home on my birthday (47). Tried to have a little frolic for Nan & the boys, but it was rather hard work.

Not well enough to write much so give up my room. Can lie round at home & its cheaper.

December.

May not doing well. The weight on my heart is not all imagination. She was too happy to have it last, & I fear the end is coming. Hope it is my nerves, but this peculiar feeling has never mis led me before.

Invited to the breakfast to O. W. H[olmes]. No heart to go.

First chapter of "J. & J." came out in St N. Write very little.

8th Little Lu one month old. Small but lively. Dont like her nurse. May too nervous to nurse her. Oh, if I could only be there to see, to help! This is a penance for all my sins. Such a tugging at my heart to be by poor May alone so far away. The N.s are devoted & all is done that can be, but not one of her "very own" is there.

Father came home.

Mr Williams drowned under the ice Xmas eve.[35]

29th May died at 8 a.m. after three weeks of fever & stupor. Happy & painless most of the time. At Mr W.s funeral on the 30th I *felt* the truth before the news came.

Wed. 31st

A dark day for us. A telegram from Ernst to Mr Emerson tells us "May is dead."[36] Anna was gone to B[oston]. Father to the P.O. anxious for letters, the last being overdue, I was alone when Mr E[merson]. came. E. sent to him knowing I was feeble & hoping Mr E. would soften the blow. I found him looking at May's portrait, pale & tearful with the paper in his hand. "My child, I *wish* I could prepare you, but alas, alas!" there his voice failed & he gave me the telegram.

I was not surprised & read the hard words as if I knew it all before. "I *am* prepared," I said & thanked him. He was much moved & very tender. I shall remember gratefully the look, the grasp, the tears he gave me, & I am sure that hard moment was made bearable by the presence of this our best & tenderest friend. He went to find father but missed him, & I had to tell both him & Anna when they came. A very bitter sorrow for all.

I never shall forgive myself for not going even if it put me back. If I had lived to see her & help her die, or save her, I should have been content.

The dear baby may comfort E. but what can comfort us?

It is the distance that is so hard, & the thought of so much happiness ended so soon. "Two years of perfect happiness" May called those married years, & said, "If I die when baby comes dont mourn for I have had as much happiness in this short time as many in twenty years."

She wished me to have her baby & her pictures. A very precious legacy! All she had to leave. Rich payment for the little I could do for her.

I see now why I lived. To care for May's child & not leave Annie all alone.

["Notes and Memoranda"]
1879

In Boston part of Jan. Author's Carnival. Wrote & went about.

Father had Conversations at Mr Cook's & went round preaching.[37] All well & busy.

In Feb. dined with the Papyrus Club at the Revere House with the younger set of literary folk. Dr Holmes, & all the sisters invited for the first time. Very pleasant.

Nov. 8th May's little girl was born. Named Louisa May Nieriker. May very ill for seven weeks, & on Dec. 29th she died. Buried at Mont Rouge.[38] E[rnest]. broke up his house & went to Baden with the baby who was given to me for my own by May. Longed to go for it but dared not being still too feeble.

Recieved.

Trust Fund	60
W[ilmington]. R.R.	40
N.Y. Bank	35
Roberts Bros.	2,500
Tale for St Nick	40
U.S. Bond	30
O.C. Bond	35
Mortgages	271
Tauchnitz	95.
	150[39]
Interest	100
R. Bros.	550
Int.	165
Int.	407
Int.	100[40]

Invested.

Provident Bank for J[ohn].	1,000
Concord Bank.	1,000

Wrote

Tale for St Nick   J & J. Serial   3,000
Tale for Demorest   200
Scrap Bag.

SOURCES: Text and "Notes and Memoranda" — manuscript, Houghton Library, Harvard University.

1. Probably *Jimmy's Cruise in the Pinafore* and *Jack and Jill.*

2. *Mrs. Jarley's Waxworks* was included in a partial repeat performance of the dramatic productions from the Authors' Carnival (see note 3) on 7–8 February.

3. Bronson called this performance on 22 January "a brilliant affair," noting that LMA's part "is extemporized, much to the entertainment of the vast audience, by its wit, sentiment, and drollery" ("Diary for 1879," p. 44, Houghton Library, Harvard University). The *Boston Daily Advertiser* reported the event in detail, noting that the *Waxworks* (which contained excerpts from *The Pickwick Papers, Oliver Twist,* and *The Cricket on the Hearth*) was placed on the program between the Dickens reception and the Mother Goose tableaux, and described LMA's costume as follows: "In dress and appearance she was the typical show-woman. She wore a short, green-stuff gown with a narrow, ruffle around it, pink stockings, laced slippers, a red shawl worn mantlewise, a collar almost wide enough to be a cape, and a bonnet which was enough to throw a modern milliner into convulsions. It was of green silk lined with pink, a feather stood assertively upright, and nodding emphasis to all her words. Her hair was arranged in puffs on the side of her face, and she wore silver-bowed spectacles" ("The Carnival of Authors," 20, 22, 23 January, pp. 4, 4, 1).

4. Mary Wollstonecraft, the English feminist and mother of Mary Shelley; Henry Gréville was the pseudonym of Alice Marie Céleste Durand, author of *Dosia* (1877). LMA heard Durand lecture in 1885, "a stout, rosy little woman, not young nor pretty but simple bright & intelligent" (letter of 29 November [1885] to Laura Hosmer, Louisa May Alcott Collection, Barrett Library, University of Virginia).

5. According to LMA's account book, this is "J. M's S. Sermon" ("John Marlow's Victory").

6. Frances Hodgson Burnett, author of *Little Lord Fauntleroy* (1886), and LMA were honored at a meeting of the Papyrus Club in Boston in the spring of 1879. LMA reviewed her book in the December 1886 *Book Buyer.*

7. Along with Mrs. Burnett, LMA invited her son Vivian (who served as the model for Little Lord Fauntleroy) and Mary Mapes Dodge, editor of *St. Nicholas* (Marjorie Worthington, *Miss Alcott of Concord* [Garden City, N.Y.: Doubleday, 1958], pp. 269–270).

8. The Episcopal Church of the Advent, nearby at Bowdoin and Mount Vernon streets, had Charles C. Grafton as its minister, assisted by Canon Knox-Little.

9. Laura Whiting Hosmer practiced medicine in Concord after her marriage to Henry Joseph Hosmer in December 1874.

10. LMA's account book shows that she paid a nurse for "S. P." and gave her other monies during this time (Houghton Library, Harvard University).

11. George Eliot's *Daniel Deronda* (1876) featured Gwendolen Harleth as a poor girl who marries a wealthy man, Henleigh Mallinger Grandcourt, to escape from poverty, but he breaks her spirit. This plot is similar to those used by LMA in her thrillers, but in them the woman is victorious.

12. "Two Little Travellers" appeared in the June 1879 *St. Nicholas.*

13. Dr. Rhoda Ashley Joy Lawrence attended the Female Seminary in Charlestown, Massachusetts, took charge of the Western Union Telegraph Office in Jamaica Plain, Massachu-

setts, and studied at the Boston University School of Medicine. She established a nursing home at Dunreath Place, Roxbury, where LMA spent her last years.

14. *H. M. S. Pinafore*, by William Gilbert and Arthur Sullivan, had first been produced in London the previous year.

15. Samuel H. Emery of Quincy, Illinois, and his wife did take Orchard House for the summer.

16. On 28 June 1879, May noted in her diary that she had received a box from home with "mother's own fruit knife, which is most precious to me & some little things for the newcomer in October as my sisters take great delight in the prospect & enjoy making tiny garments already, to save me the trouble" (Houghton Library, Harvard University).

17. A state prison had opened in 1878 in West Concord.

18. Bronson's account of this trip with Miss McClure is in the entry for 8 June in his "Diary for 1879," pp. 351–353, Houghton Library, Harvard University.

19. "Jimmy's Cruise in a 'Pinafore' " appeared in the October 1879 *St. Nicholas*.

20. LMA's cousin Adeline May lived in Leicester, Massachusetts.

21. The first session of the Concord School of Philosophy lasted from 15 July to 16 August 1879. Reflecting on the summer's events, LMA wrote Mary Mapes Dodge that "I have had a very busy summer but have been pretty well & able to do my part in entertaining the 400 philosophers" (21 August [1879], *SL*, p. 235).

22. The participants are probably Frank Sanborn's wife, Louisa, and a Mrs. Wolcott (see Bronson's "Diary for 1879," pp. 476, 492, Houghton Library, Harvard University).

23. LMA's report of her efforts to register women to vote in Concord at this time is in a letter of [ca. 11 October 1879] to the *Woman's Journal*, in *SL*, pp. 237–238.

24. *Jimmy's Cruise in the Pinafore*, vol. 5 of *Aunt Jo's Scrap-Bag*, was published in October 1879 by Roberts Brothers.

25. LMA frequently vacationed at Nonquitt, near New Bedford, Massachusetts, eventually buying a cottage there (pictured in *SL*, following p. 264).

26. Sophie Nieriker, Ernest's sister.

27. Jane Cunningham Croly; "Victoria. A Woman's Statue" appeared in monthly installments between March and May 1881 in *Demorest's Monthly Magazine*.

28. Ellsworth Devens died at the age of seventeen on 8 August 1879. LMA used her recollections of him, with his mother's permission, in *Jack and Jill*, which is dedicated to "the schoolmates of Ellsworth Devens" (see LMA's letter of 15 November [1879] to Ann E. Devens, in *SL*, p. 239).

29. Magnolia, Massachusetts, is southwest of Gloucester. Bronson noted in his journal on 1 September that LMA "has been at the seaside during the week past" and pasted in a clipping about her staying at Willow Cottage while there ("Diary for 1879," p. 563, Houghton Library, Harvard University).

30. "Jack and Jill" appeared in monthly installments between December 1879 and October 1880 in *St. Nicholas* and was published as *Jack and Jill: A Village Story* in October 1880 by Roberts Brothers.

31. These "letters of an 'Artist's Holyday' " are unlocated. When LMA had earlier approached Daniel Ford of the *Youth's Companion* with her sister's letters, he replied that "your name is before the public — whatever you write is read, and an article of your sister[']s, with *your name over it*, would be more eagerly read." Because of this, he said, he would pay LMA half her normal rate if he could use her name but only twenty dollars — his rate "to my very best unknown writers" — per letter without her name (14 August 1873, Louisa May Alcott Collection, Barrett Library, University of Virginia). May's book is *Studying Art Abroad* (Boston: Roberts Brothers, 1879), the manuscript of which (partially in LMA's hand) is at the Houghton Library, Harvard University.

32. Sherborn is located sixteen miles south of Concord.

33. Bronson's latest trip lasted for two months.

34. Louisa May Nieriker (nicknamed Lulu) was born on 8 November 1879.

35. Charles H. S. Williams was forty-one years old.

36. May Alcott Nieriker died on 29 December 1879 and left Lulu to LMA to raise.

37. Joseph Cook, a well-known lecturer on theological subjects, allowed Bronson the opportunity to follow his own lecture, "Socialism and Universal Suffrage," on 13 January with a conversation entitled "The Transcendental Club and the Dial," which about fifty people attended (see Bronson's "Diary for 1879," pp. 31–34, including a clipping from an unidentified newspaper about the conversation, and "Mr. Alcott's 'Conversation,' " *Boston Daily Advertiser*, 15 January 1879, p. 4).

38. LMA relates an account of May's funeral at Montrouge Cemetery in a letter of 14 January 1880 to Elizabeth Wells, in *SL*, p. 243.

39. In the space before this figure, LMA wrote "Banks" and then canceled it.

40. In 1879, Roberts Brothers printed 18,280 copies of LMA's works. According to LMA's account book, her literary earnings for the year were $4,395, rather than the $6,385 listed in the "Notes and Memoranda" (Houghton Library, Harvard University).

Tauchnitz paid LMA 400 marks for *Little Men*, a German edition of which he published in 1879.

LMA's account book also lists $250 from Roberts Brothers, $10 from George Carleton, and $500 from Scribner's not present in the "Notes and Memoranda."

1880

1880.

Jan. 1st.

A sad day mourning for May. Of all the trials in my life I never felt any so keenly as this, perhaps because I am so feeble in health that I cannot bear it well. It seems so hard to break up that happy little home & take May just when life was richest, & to leave me who have done my task & could well be spared. Shall I ever know why such things happen?

Letters came telling us all the sad story. May was unconscious during the last weeks & seemed not to suffer. Spoke now & then of "getting ready for Louy" & asked if she had come. All was done that love & skill could do but in vain. E[rnest]. is broken hearted & good Madame N[ieriker]. & Sophie find their only solace in the poor baby.

May felt a foreboding & left all ready in case she died. Some trunks packed for us, some for the N. sisters. Her diary written up, all in order. Even chose the grave yard where she wished to be out of the city. E. obeys all her wishes sacredly.

Tried to write on "J[ack]. & J[ill]." to distract my mind, but the wave of sorrow kept rolling over me & I could only weep & wait till the tide ebbed again.

Of Roberts Bros.   1692.65

1880

Feb.

More letters from E[rnest]. & Madame N[ieriker]. Like us they find comfort in writing of the dear soul gone now there is nothing more to do for her. I cannot make it true that our May is dead, lying far away in a strange grave, leaving a husband & child whom we have never seen. It all reads like a pretty romance, now death has set its seal on these two happy years & we shall never know all that she alone could tell us.

Many letters from friends in France, England & America full of sympathy for us & love & pride & gratitude for May, who was always glad to help, forgive & love every one. It is our only consolation now.

Father & I cannot sleep but he & I make verses as we did when Marmee died. Our grief seems to flow into words. He writes "Love's Morrow," & [I] "Our Madonna."[1]

Lulu has gone to Baden with Grandmamma & E. means to break up his little home. "Cannot bear its loneliness" he says. His letters prove him to be all that May told us. A most excellent & noble man, full of the deepest love for her & a desire to be & do all that she & we desire. I hope to know him & thank him for the happiness he gave her.

Finish "J. & J." The world goes on in spite of sorrow & I must do my work. Both these last serials were written with a heavy heart. "Under the Lilacs" when Marmee was failing, & "Jack & Jill" while May was dying. Hope the grief did not get into them.

Hear R. W. E. lecture for his 100th time.[2]

Mary Clemmer writes for a sketch of my life for a book of "Famous Women."[3] Dont belong there.

Read Memoirs of Madame de Remusat.[4] Not very interesting. Beauties seldom amount to much. Plain Margaret Fuller was worth a dozen of them.[5] "Kings In Exile", a most interesting book; a very vivid & terrible picture of Parisian life & royal weakness & sorrow.[6]

Put papers &c. in order. Feel as if one should be ready to go at any moment.

Slept all I could, life is so heavy I try to forget it in blessed unconsciousness when I can.

March.

A box came from May with pictures, clothes, vases, her ornaments, little work basket, & in one of her own sepia boxes her pretty hair tied with blue ribbon. All that is now left us of this bright soul, but the baby soon to come. Treasures all.

A sad day & many tears dropped on the dear dress, the blue slippers she last wore, the bit of work she laid down when the call came the evening Lulu was born. The fur lined sack feels like May's arms round me, & I shall wear it with pleasure. The pictures show us her great progress these last years.

To Boston for a few days on business & to try to forget. Got gifts for Annie's birthday on the 16th 49 years old. My only sister now, & the best God ever made. Repaired her house for her.

Lulu is not to come till Autumn. Great disappointment, but it is wiser to wait as summer is bad for a young baby to begin here.

29th   Town Meeting.[7] 20 women there & voted first thanks to father. Polls closed, in joke we thought as Judge Hoar proposed it. Proved to be in earnest & *we* elected a good school committee. Quiet time, no fuss.

April.

So sad & poorly went to B[oston]. for a change. Old room at Bellevue.

Amused myself dramatizing "Michael Strogoff".[8] Read, walked, & rested. Reporters called for story of my life. Did not get much. Made my will, dividing all I have between Nan & the boys with father as a legacy to Nan, & Lulu her mother's pictures & small fortune of $500.[9]

May.

Thirty girls from Boston University called.[10] Told stories, showed pictures, wrote autographs, pleasant to see so much innocent enthusiasm even about so poor a thing as a used up old woman. Bright girls, simple in dress, sensible ideas of life, & love of education. I wish them all good luck.

Ordered a stone for May's grave like Marmees & Beth's, for some day I hope to bring her dust home.[11]

23rd is the anniversary of Mother's wedding, if she had lived it would have been the Golden Wedding.

Went to see St Botolph's Club rooms.[12] Very prim & neat, with easy chairs every where, stained glass, & a pious little *bar* with nothing but a moral ice pitcher & a butler like a bishop. The reverend gentlemen will be comfortable & merry & fancy, as there is a smoking room & card tables as well as library & picture gallery. Divines now a days are not as godly as in old times it seems.

Went to the Unitarian Dinner at Music Hall. Very dull. Better eaters than speakers most of them. Too much money & too fine churches, more hard work & real christianity would suit me better.

Mrs Dodge wants a new serial, but I doubt if I can do it.[13] Boys, babies, illness & business of all sorts leave no time for story telling. Reality makes romance seem pale & flat now.

Low $348.00[14]

June.

Annie ill.

We all enjoy the new rooms very much & father finds his study delightful.

Prepare the Orchard House for W. T. Harris who is to rent it.[15]

North End Mission children at Walden Pond. Help give them a happy day. 1100 of them.

Get Annie & John off to Walpole.

Cleaned house.

Madame N[ieriker]. sends a picture of Lulu. A funny, fat, little thing in her carriage. Dont realize that it is May's child, & that she is far away in a French cemetary never to come home to us again.

It is decided that Baby is to come to us in Sept. Take passage for Mrs G[iles] in the Somania to sail Aug 21st & return Sept. 8th. I cannot go.

24th Lizzie's birthday & Johnny's. He is 15. A lovely, good boy whom every one loves. Got the Dean a new suit of clothes as he must be nice for his duties at the School [of Philosophy]. Plato's toga was not so costly but even he did not look better than my handsome old philosofer.

July. & Aug.

To York with boys. Rest & enjoy the fine air.[16] Home in Aug. & let Annie go down. 400 callers since the School began. Philosophy is a bore to outsiders.

Got things ready for my baby. Warm wrapper & all the dear can need on her long journey. On the 21st saw Mrs Giles off. The last time I went it was to see May go. She was sober & sad, not gay as before. Seemed to feel it might be a longer voyage than we knew. The last view I had of her was standing alone in the long blue cloak waving her hand to us, smiling with wet eyes till out of sight. How little we dreamed what an experience of love, joy, pain & death she was going to!

A lonely time with all away. My grief meets me when I come home, & the house is full of ghosts.

September.

Put papers in order, & arrang[e] things generally to be in order when our Lulu comes. Make a cosy nursery for the darling, & say my prayers over the little white crib that waits for her if she ever comes. God watch over her!

Paid my first poll tax. As my head is my most valuable peice of property I thought $2,00 a cheap tax on it. Saw my townswomen about voting &c. Hard work to stir them up. Cake & servants are more interesting.

18th in Boston waiting for the steamer that brings my treasure. The ocean seems very wide & terrible when I think of the motherless little creature coming so far to us.

19th Lulu & Sophie N[ieriker]. arrived with poor G[iles]. worn out by anxiety. A stormy passage, & much care, being turned out of the state room

I had engaged for them & paid for by a rude N.Y. dress maker. No help for it so poor G went to a rat hole below & did her best.

Xmas tale for Graphic. $100
    "   "   " Harpers Young People $100 [17]

As I waited on the wharf while the people came off the ship I saw several babies & wondered each time if that was mine. At last the Captain appeared, & in his arms a little yellow haired thing in white, with its hat off as it looked about with lively blue eyes & hobbled prettily. Mrs G. came close by it, & I knew it was Lulu. Behind walked a lovely brown eyed girl with an anxious face, all being new & strange to Sophie.

I held out my arms to Lulu only being able to say her name. She looked at me for a moment, then came to me saying "Marmar?" in a wistful way & nestling close as if she had found her own people & home at last, as she had, thank Heaven!

I could only listen while I held her & the others told thier tale. Then we got home as soon as we could, & dear Baby behaved very well though hungry & tired.

The little Princess was received with tears & smiles, & being washed & fed went quietly to sleep in her new bed, while we brooded over her & were never tired of looking at the little face of "May's baby".

She is a very active, bright child, not pretty yet, being browned by sea air & having only a yellow down on her head & pug nose. Her little body is beautifully formed, broad shoulders, fine chest, & lovely arms. A happy thing, laughing & waving her hands, confiding & bold, with a keen look in the eyes so like May, who hated shams & saw through them at once. She always comes to me, & seems to have decided that I am really "Marmar." My heart is full of pride & joy, & the touch of the dear little hands seems to take away the bitterness of grief. I often go at night to see if she is *really* here, & the sight of the little yellow head is like sunshine to me.

Father adores her, & she loves to sit in his strong arms. They make a pretty picture as he walks in the garden with her to "see birdies". Anna tends her as she did May, who was her baby once, being ten years younger, & we all find life easier to like now the Baby has come. Sophie is a sweet girl, with much character & beauty. A charming sister in love or in law.

October.

Happy days with Lulu & So[p]hie. Getting acquainted with them. Lulu is rosy & fair now, & grows pretty in her native air. A merry little lass who seems to feel at home & blooms in an atmosphere of adoration. People come to see "Miss Alcott's baby", & strangers way-lay her little carriage in the street to look at her, but she does not allow herself to be kissed.

As Father wants to go West I decide to hire Cousin L. W.s house furnished for the winter, [18] so that Sophie & the boys can have & a pleasant time. S. misses the gayety of her home life in stupid Concord where the gossip & want of manners strikes her very disagreeably. Impertinent questions are asked her & she is amazed at the queer, rude things people do & say.

Get settled, & find things in a bad state, though told that "all would be in order." A hard mixed up family to run, but if Lulu is well we wont mind rats & drains, & dirt & cold & broken promises.

November. (48 on the 29th.)

Lively times with plumbers, gas men, ratcatchers & Health officers. Get fixed at last. Hire piano for Sophie, read French & English with her. A bright well-educated girl far ahead of ours.

8th   Lulu's birthday. One year old. Her gifts were set out on a table for her to see when she came down in the a.m. A little cake with *one* candle, a rose crown for the queen, a silver mug, dolly, picture books, gay ball, toys, flowers & many kisses.

She sat smiling at her treasures just under her mother's picture. Suddenly, attracted by the sunshine on the face of the portrait which she knows is "Marmar" she held up a white rose to it calling "Mum! Mum!" & smiling at it in a way that made us all cry.

A happy day for her, a sad one to us.

Thanksgiving — family dinner.

Father at Syracuse having Conversations at Bishop Huntington's & a fine time everywhere. [19]

December.

Too busy to keep much of a journal. My life is absorbed in my baby. On the 23rd she got up & walked alone. Had never crept at all, but when ready ran across the room & plumped down, laughing triumphantly at her feat.

Xmas — tried to make it gay for the young folks, but a heavy day for Nan & me. Sixty gifts were set out on different tables, & all were much pleased. Sophie had many pretty things, & gave to all generously.

29th   A year since May died. Earnst is in Brazil, being so broken in health & spirits a change was necessary. He writes us tender, beautiful letters every month full of love for his baby & sorrow for May. Madame N[ieriker]. also writes often, & Lulu & S[ophie]. are ties that hold the two families close in spite of the wide sea & never having seen one another.

A hard year for all, but when I hold my Lulu I feel as if even death had its compensations. A new world for me.

Called down one day to see a young man. Found it one of those to whom I spoke at the prison in Concord last June. Came to thank me for the good my little story did him since it kept him straight & reminded him that it is never too late to mend. Told me about himself & how he was now going to begin anew & wipe out the past. He had been a miner & coming East met some fellows who made him drink. While tipsy he stole some thing in a Drs office & having no friends here was sentenced to 3 year[s] in prison. Did well & was now out. Had a prospect of going on an expedition to S. America with a geological surveying party. An interesting young man. Fond of books, anxious to do well, intelligent & seemed eager to atone for his one fault.

Gave him a letter to S. G. at Chicago.[20] Wrote to the Warden who confirmed *Donald's* story & spoke well of him. Miss Willard wrote me later of him & he seemed doing well. Asked if he might write to me & did so several times, then went to S. A. & I hear no more. Glad to have said a word to help the poor boy.

["Notes and Memoranda"]
1880

Year opens sadly as we mourn for our poor May.

Hoped to get Lulu in the spring but had to wait till Sept. Mrs Giles goes for her, & on the 20th the dear little creature arrives.

Devote myself to her & find life much brighter though I am still very poorly.

Recieved.

Dividends	Jan.

Wrote.

Jack & Jill	St. N.[21]

Invested.

For A[nna]. Jan	1600.

SOURCES: Text and "Notes and Memoranda" — manuscript, Houghton Library, Harvard University.

1. LMA's "Our Madonna" is printed in Caroline Ticknor, *May Alcott: A Memoir* (Boston:

Little, Brown, 1928), pp. 308–309; for Bronson's "Love's Morrow," first published as a pamphlet in 1880, see his *Journals*, pp. 515–516, and *Letters*, pp. 798–799.

2. Emerson's lecture on 4 February 1880, his one hundredth at the Concord Lyceum, was called "Historic Notes, Life and Letters in Massachusetts." According to the records of the Lyceum, "A very large audience was present and . . . rose en masse to receive him. Mr. Emerson read his lecture with a clearness and vigor remarkable, considering his advanced age" (Kenneth Walter Cameron, *The Massachusetts Lyceum During the American Renaissance* [Hartford, Conn.: Transcendental Books, 1969], p. 189).

3. Mary Clemmer Ames may have been assigned the chapter on LMA for *Our Famous Women* (1884), eventually done by Louise Chandler Moulton (see *SL*, pp. 267–268), or a never-published volume on LMA in the Famous Women Series begun by Roberts Brothers in 1883.

4. Claire de Rémusat's *Memoirs of Madame de Rémusat*, trans. Paul de Rémusat (1879).

5. Margaret Fuller, Transcendentalist author best known for her feminist work, *Woman in the Nineteenth Century* (1845).

6. Alphonse Daudet's *Kings in Exile* (1879).

7. The reports of this meeting by LMA in a letter of 30 March 1880 to the *Woman's Journal* and in the 1 April 1880 *Concord Freeman* are both printed in *SL*, pp. 245–247.

8. Jules Verne's *Michel Strogoff* (1876). LMA's manuscript of this is at the Houghton Library, Harvard University.

9. LMA's will, signed 10 July 1887, left all her copyrights to John Pratt, who was to divide the income among his mother, brother, Lulu, and himself.

10. Bronson describes this visit on 8 May in his "Diary for 1880," p. 153, Houghton Library, Harvard University.

11. Although May's "dust" was never brought home, there is a marker for her, similar to those for the other Alcotts, in the family plot at Sleepy Hollow Cemetery.

12. St. Botolph's Club was founded in 1880 along the lines of the Century Club of New York.

13. LMA did not publish another serial in *St. Nicholas*.

14. Sampson Low wrote LMA on 24 February 1880 that it was sending £70.18.3 on her account (Houghton Library, Harvard University).

15. William Torrey Harris rented Orchard House in 1880 and bought it four years later.

16. LMA liked to vacation in York, Maine, on the coast between Kittery and Wells.

17. "How It All Happened" appeared in the 21 December 1880 *Harper's Young People*.

18. LMA rented Elizabeth Sewall Willis Wells's house at 81 Pinckney Street in Boston for the winter.

19. Bishop Frederic Dan Huntington had been installed at the Calvary Church in Syracuse in May 1880.

20. Samuel Sewall Greeley, LMA's cousin.

21. In 1880, Roberts Brothers printed 7,858 copies of *Jack and Jill* and 21,560 copies of LMA's other works.

1881

March. [1]

Voted for School Committee. [2]

October. [3]
October.

Had the house painted.

Tried to get up a Suffrage Club, but the women need so much coaxing it is hard work. Got Miss Cobbe's "Duties of Women" & Mrs Robinson's History of Suffrage in Mass. for them to read. [4] Novels suit them better.

Wrote a Preface for Parker's Prayers just got out by F. B. Sanborn. [5]

November.   (49 on 29th.)

Wrote a Preface to the new edition of "Moods." [6]

7th   Lulu vaccinated.

8th   Gave my baby *two* kisses when she woke, & escorted her down to find a new chair decked with ribbons & a doll's carriage lined with pink, toys, pictures, flowers & a cake with a red & a blue candle burning gaily.

Wrote a tale for The Soldier's Home "My Red Cap," & one for the Woman's Hospital Fair "A Baby's Birthday." [7] Also a tale for Ford.

December.

Rather poorly.

A poor woman in Ill. writes me to send her children some Xmas gifts, being too poor & ill to get any. They asked her to write to Santa Claus & she wrote to *me*. Sent a box & made a story about it. $100.

Lulu much interested, & kept bringing all her best toys & clothes "for poor little boys." A generous baby. [8]

231

SOURCE: Manuscript, Houghton Library, Harvard University.

1. There are no entries for January and February, even though LMA has written the names of the months as headings.

2. The *Concord Freeman* reported that only "a score of ladies are posted as qualified to vote" and that at the town meeting, of the twenty ladies present, just fourteen voted (17 March, p. 1; 31 March, p. 4).

3. There are no entries for April through September, even though LMA has written the names of the months as headings.

4. Frances Power Cobbe's *Duties of Women* (1881); LMA was helpful in persuading Roberts Brothers to publish Harriet H. Robinson's *Massachusetts in the Woman's Suffrage Movement* in 1881 (see her letter of 12 February 1881 to Thomas Niles, in *SL*, p. 252).

5. LMA's preface appeared in the second edition of Parker's *Prayers*, published by Roberts Brothers in January 1882.

6. LMA's preface to the new edition, published by Roberts Brothers in January 1882, briefly stated the book's history: "When 'Moods' was first published . . . it was so altered, to suit the taste and convenience of the publisher, that the original purpose of the story was lost sight of, and marriage appeared to be the theme instead of an attempt to show the mistakes of a moody nature, guided by impulse, not principle" (p. v).

7. "My Red Cap" appeared in the 7–10 December 1881 *Sword and the Pen*, published by the Soldiers' Home Bazaar; "A Baby's Birthday" is unlocated but had Joe Collins as the hero (see LMA's letter of 19 November [1881] to Horace P. Chandler, Dalhousie University).

8. In 1881, Roberts Brothers printed 34,580 copies of LMA's works.

1882

January. 1882.

Of Roberts Bros.   3757.08

February.

[blank]

March.

Helped start a Temperance Society. Much needed in C[oncord]. a great deal of drinking, not among the Irish but young Americans, gentlemen as well as farmers & mill hands. Women anxious to do something but find no interest beyond a few. Have meetings & try to learn how to work. I was secretary & wrote records, letters, & sent pledges &c. Also articles in C. Freeman & Woman's Journal about the Union & Town Meeting.[1]

Pretty well. Played & walked with Lulu who grows bravely & is a bonny lass, full of promise, health & lovely ways. A strong will & quick temper, but very tender, generous & noble instincts.

April.

Read over & destroyed Mother's Diaries as she wished me to do. A wonderfully interesting record of her life from her delicate, cherished girlhood through her long, hard, romantic married years, old age & death. Some time I will write a story or a Memoir of it.

Lulu's teeth trouble her, but in my arms she seems to find comfort, for I tell stories by the dozen, & lambs, piggies & "tats" soothe her little woes. Wish I were stronger so that I might take all the care of her. We seem to understand one another but my nerves make me impatient, & noise wears upon me.

Mr Emerson ill.[2] Father goes to see him. E. held his hand looking up at the tall, rosy old man, & saying with that smile of love that has been father's sunshine for so many years, *"you* are very well, Keep so, keep so." After father left he called him back & grasped his hand again as if he knew it was for the last time, & the kind eyes said "Good by, my friend."

Thursday 27th

Mr Emerson died at 9 p.m. suddenly. Our best & greatest American gone. The nearest & dearest friend father has ever had, & the man who has helped me most by his life, his books, his society. I can never tell all he has been to me from the time I sang Mignon's song under his window,[3] a little girl, & wrote letters a la Bettine to him, my Goethe, at 15, up through my hard years when his essays on Self Reliance, Character, Compensation, Love & Friendship helped me to understand myself & life & God & Nature.[4]

Illustrious & beloved friend, good bye!

Sunday 30th   Emerson's funeral.

I made a golden lyre of jonquils for the church & helped trim it up. Private services at the house & a great crowd at the church. Father read his sonnet & Judge Hoar & others spoke.[5] Now he lies in Sleepy Hollow among his brothers under the pines he loved.[6]

I sat up till midnight to write an article on R. W. E. for the Youth's Companion, that the children may know something of him.[7] A labor of love.

May. (27 boys signed pledge.)

Temperance work. Meetings. I give books to schools. Wrote an article for Mrs Croly on R. W. E.[8]

Lulu had a croupy turn. Shut myself up with her & sung & told stories for a week. Soon all right again. Seldom ill.

Sophie came to visit us. Much changed for the better. A fine girl. Wilful but has high ideals of love & duty, independence & life. Will not marry for money. Many lovers, but she says "I wish to live my own life before I marry. When I truly love it will be well. Seeing May & Ernst I know what *real* love is, & I will have no other." A wise girl.

June.

Lulu gives up her bottle bravely.

I visited A[lice]. B[artlett]. in Mattapoiset for a week. A queer time, driving about or talking over our year in Europe. School children called on me with flowers &c.

24th   John's 17th birthday. A dear boy, good & gay, full of love, man-

234

liness & all honest & lovely traits like his father & mother. Long life to my boy!

July.

School of P[hilosophy]. opens on the 17th in full force. I arrange flowers, oak branches &c & then fly before the reporters come. Father very happy. Westerners arrive, & the town is blue with ideal speculators. Penny has a new barge, we call it the "Blue Plato," (not the Black Maria)[9] & watch it rumble by with M. Fullers in white muslin & Hegel's in straw hats,[10] while stout Penny grins at the joke as he puts money in his purse. The first year C[oncord]. people stood aloof & the strangers found it hard to get rooms. Now everyone is eager to take them, & the School is pronounced a success because it brings money to the town. Even philosophers cant do without food, beds & washing, so all rejoice & the new craze flourishes. If all our guests *paid* we should be well off. Several hundred a month is rather wearing. Father asked why we never went, & Annie showed him a long list of 400 names of callers, & he said no more.

Aug & Sept.

[blank]

October.

To Hotel Bellevue[11] with John who goes to Chauncey Hall school. Fred to Conservatory of Music for flute teaching.[12] Both busy & happy.

Missed my dear baby, but need quiet. Brain began to work & plans for tales to simmer. Began Jo's Boys, as Mrs Dodge wants a serial.[13]

Get some good clothes. Very snappy.

Sophie came with new & romantic adventures after her summer in Newport & N.Y.

24th Telegram that father had had a paralytic stroke.[14] Home at once & found him stricken down. Anxious days. Little hope.

Got H. W. into the Hospital & went to see him often. A little help needed *now* to set the boy up.

Harpers Young Folks.	$100
St N. tale	125[15]

November.

Gave up our rooms & I went home to help with the new care. My Lulu ran to meet me, rosy & gay, & I felt as if I could bear anything with this little sunbeam to light up the world for me.

Poor father, dumb & helpless! feeble mind slowly coming back. He knows us, but lies asleep most of the time. Get a nurse & wait to see if he will rally. It is sad to see the change one moment made, turning the hale handsome old man into this pathetic wreck. The 40 sonnets last winter & the 50 lectures at the School last summer were too much for a man of 83.[16] He was warned by Dr W[esselhoeft]. but F. B. S[anborn].[17] thought it folly to stop, & now poor father pays the penalty of breaking the laws of health. I have done the same, may I be spared this end!

Lulu's 3rd birthday. A. M. C. gave her a great dolly & many pretty things came from friends who never forget "May's baby."

December.

Father much better than any one dared to hope. Tries to talk, but soon gets excited & cries or shouts. Sits up a little, & eats more. Sometimes speaks in his sleep & seems to be lecturing. "I am taking a prediciment." "True godliness & the ideal." "The devil is never real, only truth." &c.[18]

SOURCE: Manuscript, Houghton Library, Harvard University.

1. "W.C.T.U. of Concord" appeared in the 30 June 1882 *Concord Freeman;* "Letter from Louisa M. Alcott" appeared in the 11 February 1882 *Woman's Journal.* According to the first article, four hundred names appeared on the society's roll.

2. Emerson, already in feeble health, had caught pneumonia.

3. Mignon's song, sung by an enigmatic character in Goethe's *Wilhelm Meister.*

4. Three years later, LMA recommended to a friend Emerson's "Compensation," "Love," "Friendship," "Heroism," "Self-Reliance," and "Manners" (because of a reference to Bronson). In addition, she mailed copies of both series of *Essays* (1841, 1844), *The Conduct of Life* (1860), and "the poems" (letters of 16 February, 15 March, to Maggie Lukens, in *SL,* pp. 285–288).

5. Bronson's sonnet, which he later incorporated into "Ion, a Monody," is in Oliver Wendell Holmes, *Ralph Waldo Emerson* (Boston: Houghton Mifflin, 1884), p. 355; "The Funeral of Emerson" is described (along with an engraving) in *Harper's Weekly Magazine,* 26 (13 May 1882): 292.

6. Charles Chauncy, Edward Bliss, and William Emerson were all buried in the Emerson family plot at Sleepy Hollow Cemetery.

7. "Reminiscences of Ralph Waldo Emerson" appeared in the 25 May 1882 *Youth's Companion.*

8. "R. W. Emerson" appeared in the July 1882 *Demorest's Monthly Magazine.*

9. A Black Maria is a police vehicle used for transporting prisoners.

10. The German philosopher Georg Wilhelm Friedrich Hegel.

11. The Hotel Bellevue had recently been converted to an apartment hotel.

12. Anna wrote to Alfred Whitman on 15 May 1881 that "Fred has just entered the Conservatory of Music to perfect his flute & piano playing as he has a decided talent & loves it more than any thing else" (Houghton Library, Harvard University). Fred's flute is at Orchard House.

13. *Jo's Boys and How They Turned Out* was published in October 1886 by Roberts Brothers. Mrs. Dodge wrote LMA on 18 October 1882: "Pray never let anything for children go 'elsewhere' without letting me see it" (Louisa May Alcott Collection, Barrett Library, University of Virginia).

14. Bronson suffered a paralytic stroke on 24 October, causing both physical and mental impairments. LMA's first reaction, she wrote Maria S. Porter, was that "it is so pathetic to see my handsome, hale, active old father changed at one fell blow into this helpless wreck" ([after 24 October 1882], *SL*, p. 260). He never wrote again; both his journals and letters cease in October 1882.

15. "A Christmas Dream" appeared in the 5 and 12 December 1882 issues of *Harper's Young People*; "Grandmamma's Pearls" appeared in the December 1882 *St. Nicholas*.

16. LMA complained to Maria S. Porter that "he wrote those forty remarkable sonnets last winter, and these, with his cares as Dean of the School of Philosophy and his many lectures there, were enough to break down a man of eighty-three years. I continually protested and warned him against overwork and taxation of the brain, but 'twas of no avail" ([after 24 October 1882], *SL*, pp. 260–261). The sonnets were published as *Sonnets and Canzonets* by Roberts Brothers in April 1882.

17. At a later date, LMA canceled Sanborn's name.

18. In 1882, Roberts Brothers printed 46,186 copies of LMA's works.

1883

January.

Too busy to keep a diary. Can only jot down a fact now & then.

Father improving. Much trouble with nurses. Incapable, lazy or nervous with too much tea. Have no idea of health. Wont walk, sit over the fire & drink tea three times a day. Ought to be an intelligent, hearty set of women. Could do better myself. Have to fill up all the dificiences, & do double duty.

People come to see father but it excites him & we have to deny him.

Tauchnitz for book 400 marks. $94.[1]

Feb.

To B[oston]. for a week of rest having got Mrs H.[2] settled with father & all comfortable for Nan.

Slept, read, walked & saw people.

Began a book called "Genius".[3] Shall never finish it I dare say, but must keep a vent for my fancies to escape at. This double life is trying & my head will work as well as my hands.

March.

To give A[nna]. rest I took Lulu & maid to the Bellevue for a month. Lulu very happy with her new world. Enjoys her walks, the canary I get her, & the petting *she* gets from all. Showed her to friends. Want them to know May's child. Had her picture taken by Notman.[4] Very good.

16th   Anna's birthday. Spent the day with her.

28th   Fred's birthday. Gave him $100 for a bicycle.[5] Fine boy, true, intelligent, industrious & loving. God bless & keep him!

April.

2ond   Town meeting. Seven women vote. I am one of them & A. an-other. A poor show for a town that prides itself on its culture & independence.

6th   Go home to stay. Father needs me. New nurse, many callers, Lulu fretful, Annie tired, Father feeble. Hard times for all.

Wrote a story for St. N. at odd moments.[6] Nurses & doctors take a deal of money.

May.

Take care of Lulu, as we can find no good woman to walk & dress & play with her. The ladies are incapable or proud, the girls vulgar or rough, so my poor baby has a bad time with her little tempers & active mind & body. Could do it myself if I had the nerves & strength, but am needed else where & must leave the child to some one. Long to go away with her & do as I like. Shall never lead my own life.

June.

Get J. H. a nice little person for Lulu, & we get on very well.

Mrs F. the nurse got tipsey & had to go.[7] A sad pity as she is a good nurse & does very well with father who is hard to take care of being unreasonable, fretful & weak.

July.

Go to Nonquitt with Miss H. & Lulu for the summer. A quiet, healthy place with pleasant people & fine air. Turn Lulu loose with H. to run after her, & try to rest.

Lulu takes her first bath in the sea. Very bold, walks off toward Europe up to her neck & is much afflicted that I wont let her go to the bottom & see the "little trabs". Makes a Cupid of herself & is very pretty & gay.

The boys revel in the simple pleasures of N. A fine place for them to be in.

Wrote a tale for St N. "Sophie's Secret" 100.[8]

August.

Home to C[oncord]. & let A[nna]. come for her holyday.

Much company.

The Bramin Chunder Mozoomdar preached & had a Conversation at Mrs Emerson's.[9] A most interesting man. Curious to hear a Hindoo tell how the life of Christ impressed him.

Write another tale for St N. "Onawandah." $100.[10]

September.

Anna Lulu & boys come home well & brown, especially my girl who is a fine specimen of a hearty, happy, natural child.

Miss H. left & we tried a pretty Dane. Too lofty & soon proved she knew nothing about children. Sent her off. Love & patience are needed with a child like L. Force & indifference make her naughty. I can always manage her.

October.

Tried Miss M. for Lulu.[11] No idea of government, sick & sad. Sent her off & took care of L. myself.

Drove with father who enjoys his outings very much.

November.

8th Lulu's birthday. A. McC. with a fine dolly. A gay time for our baby.

27th Decide to lessen care & worry at home so take rooms in Boylston St. & with Lulu set forth to make a home of our own. The whole parlor floor gives my lady room to run in doors & the Public Garden opposite is the out door play ground.

Miss C. comes as governess & we settle down.[12] Fred boards with us.

Heard Mat[t]hew Arnold.[13]

29th Birthday — 51. Home with gifts to poor father, 84. Found a table full for myself.

December.

25th Home with gifts for all. Sad day.

See H. Martineau's statue.[14] Very fine.

See Irving & Ellen Terry.[15] Enjoy it very much.

Harper for a tale $50.[16]

St N. "Eli's Education" — $100.[17]

["Notes and Memoranda"]
1883.
Nov 29
Age 51.

Father improved. Very busy with him & Lulu all winter.

In March to B[oston]. for a week of rest.

Took Lulu & nurse to board for a month at the Bellevue to relieve A[nna]. Father so much care. All worn out. Took care of L. Had some good pictures of her taken by Notman.

April 2. 7 women vote at Concord Town Meeting. A & I are there. Wrote a little.

E[rnest]. N[ieriker]. sent in May $160 to L. Troubles with nurses. Go to Nonquitt in July for two months with Lulu & Miss H. A hard summer but L. was well.

In Oct. Sophie N[ieriker]. made a visit.

Nov. 24 to B[oston]. for the winter with L. at 101 Boylston St. Family at home too large with Pa & his nurses.

A busy winter. L. improves in temper.

See Irving & Terry.

Rec'd.

Roberts Bros.	July.	1950.00
" " "	Jan.	
Mark		400 [18]
Tauchnitz.		$94.00
Harper		50.00 [19]
Dividends in Mar.		120.00
Dividends in Nov.		102.00
" " " in Dec.		598.00

Wrote

July.	Sophie's Secret	St Nick
Dec.	Xmas tale	Harper.

Invested.

Feb.	At[chison]. & Topeka	3000.

Taxes	197.

SOURCES: Text and "Notes and Memoranda" — manuscript, Houghton Library, Harvard University.

1. Tauchnitz published a German edition of An Old-Fashioned Girl in 1883.

2. LMA's account book shows that a Miss H. came on 16 February (Houghton Library, Harvard University).

3. "Genius" was never completed.

4. James Notman, son of the famous Canadian photographer William Notman, had a studio in Boston; one of his pictures of LMA is in SL, following p. 264.

5. This may possibly be the bicycle pictured with John Pratt in SL, following p. 264.

6. "Little Pyramus and Thisbe" appeared in the September and October 1883 issues of St. Nicholas.

7. LMA's account book shows that a Mrs. F. was paid from 2 April through 25 June (Houghton Library, Harvard University).

8. "Sophie's Secret" appeared in the November and December 1883 issues of *St. Nicholas*.

9. Pratap Chunder Mozoomder lectured at the Unitarian Church in Concord on 2 September, discussing religious reform in India (an account of his lecture is in the 7 September 1883 *Concord Freeman*, p. 1); see also the description in *The Letters of Ellen Tucker Emerson*, ed. Edith E. W. Gregg (Kent, Ohio: Kent State University Press, 1982), 2:515.

10. "Onawandah" appeared in the April 1884 *St. Nicholas*.

11. LMA's account book shows that a Miss M. started work on 12 October (Houghton Library, Harvard University).

12. LMA's account book shows that a Miss Cassall was employed during this period (Houghton Library, Harvard University).

13. In his lectures in Boston in 1883, Matthew Arnold told his audiences that Emerson was neither a first-rate philosopher, poet, nor prose writer and that his real value lay in the inspirational quality of his work. Boston did not take this very well.

14. Harriet Martineau, an English reformer and author.

15. The English actor and manager Henry Irving, the actress Ellen Terry, and their Lyceum Theatre Company of London were engaged from 10 to 24 December at the Boston Theatre. LMA and Terry had met at a Papyrus Club dinner on 15 December.

16. "Bertie's Box. A Christmas Story" appeared in the 1 January 1884 *Harper's Young People*.

17. "Eli's Education" appeared in the March 1884 *St. Nicholas*.

18. This refers to the next entry and the 400 marks paid by Tauchnitz.

19. In 1883, Roberts Brothers printed 39,050 copies of LMA's works.

1884

1884.

January

New Year's day is made memorable by my solemnly *spanking* my child. Miss C[assall]. & others assure me it is the only way to cure her wilfulness. I doubt it, but proving that mothers are usually too tender & blind I correct my dear in the old fashioned way.

She proudly says, "Do it, do it!" & when it is done is heart broken at the idea of Aunt Wee wee's giving her pain.[1] Her bewilderment was pathetic, & the effect, as I expected, a failure. Love is better, but also endless patience.

Roberts Bros.   4857.00

Story for St N.[2]

Mr B. invests $2120 for A & boys.

February

2ond — Wendell Phillips died.[3] I shall mourn for him next to R. W. E. & Parker.

6th   Funeral at Hollis St church. Sat between Fred. Douglass & his wife.[4] A goodly gathering of all left of the old workers. Glad & proud to be among them.

Lulu begins going to a Kindergarten for two hours each day. Does her good to be with other children. Miss C[assall]. can teach from books, but has no idea of amusing or training a child. Heart not in her work.

Tale for St N. "Abby." $100.[5]

March.

16th   Annie's birthday 53. Home with gifts for the good sister.

28th   Fred 21. A dress suit my gift & $1000 in the bank.

Tale for St N. "The Banner of Beaumanior" $100.[6]

H. H. invests $4000 for Nan, boys, & self.[7]

April.

Miss C[assall]. goes. No love in her. Cold & tired & careless. Get old Maria for a time & Lu & I are happy. We understand one another, & with her I can be as much of a child as she. Dr D. found me on the floor playing lion, hair down, roaring & romping to L's great delight. C. thought it undignified to play as children play.

Home to C[oncord]. after a queer winter. Annie had a quiet one, but was glad to get us back.

Try electricity for my lame arm.

Tale for St N. "Daisy's Jewel Box" $100.[8]

May.

Busy cleaning house & sewing for Lulu. Get a flag for the Juvinile Temperance Society.

11th   tale for St N. $100.[9]

June.

Sell the Orchard House to W. T. Harris for $3500.[10] Glad to be done with it, though after living in it for 25 years it is full of memories. But places have not much hold on me when the persons who made them dear are gone. Mr H. will not beautify it as father did but will keep it neat & father is willing he should have it.

Bought a cottage at N[onquitt]. $2000 for two lots house & furniture. All like it & it is a good investment I'm told.

24th   To Nonquitt with Lulu & K. & John.[11] Fixed my house & enjoyed the rest & quiet immensely. Lulu wild with joy at the freedom. Food at Mrs M's.[12]

Didn't work well. Her idea of economy was one potatato all round & tea at 5 for 30 people. Satin gowns for the girls & not enough to eat.

July. & Aug.

Restful days in my little house which is cool & quiet, & without the curse of a kitchen to spoil it.

Lulu happy & well.[13] & everyone full of summer fun.

On the 7th of Aug. I went home & let A[nna]. go for her holyday.

Took care of father & house & idled away the hot days with books & letters. Drove with father as he enjoyed it very much.

Changed nurses. A great trouble, these strangers coming into the family so often. We have no home life.

Aug. Sept.

All at home. Great fuss with girls. A[nna]. & I tired out with our large & mixed family.

S. & Low £84.[14]

October.

To Boston with John & take rooms at the Bellevue. Very tired of home worry & fly for rest to my old refuge with J[ohn]. & F[red]. to look after & make a home for.

Repairs on house. Always something to do.

Saw Irving. Always enjoy him though he is very queer. Terry always the same though charming in her way.[15]

November.

Find Bellevue uncomfortable & expensive so take rooms in Chestnut St. for self & boys.[16] John at Chase's Art Rooms,[17] F[red]. a reporter while waiting for something permanent. Both very happy to be in B.

8th   My Lulu's birthday. Go home with flowers, gifts & a grateful heart that the dear little girl is so well & happy & good. A merry day with the little queen of the house.

17th   Home for a week & A[nna]. took my place for a change & a little fun with the lads.

29th   Our birthdays, Father 85 L. M. A. 52. Quiet day. Always sad for thinking of Mother & John & May who all left us this month.

December.

Began again on "Jo's Boys" as T. N[iles]. wants a new book very much & I am tired of being idle. Wrote two hours for three days, then had a violent attack of vertigo & was ill for a week. Head wont bear work yet. Put away papers & tried to dawdle & go about as other people do.

Pleasant Xmas with Lulu & Nan & poor father who loves to see us about him. A narrow world now but a happy one for him.

Last day of the year. All well at home except myself. Body feeble but soul improving.[18]

SOURCE: Manuscript, Houghton Library, Harvard University.
   1. "Aunt Wee Wee" was Lulu's name for LMA.

2. "Grandma's Story" appeared in the January 1884 *St. Nicholas.*

3. Wendell Phillips died on 2 February 1884.

4. The abolitionist Frederick Douglass and his wife, Helen Pitts Douglass.

5. "Tabby's Table-Cloth" appeared in the February 1884 *St. Nicholas.*

6. "The Banner of Beaumanoir" appeared in the June 1884 *St. Nicholas.*

7. Laura Hosmer's husband, Henry Joseph Hosmer.

8. "Daisy's Jewel-Box, and How She Filled It" appeared in the September 1884 *St. Nicholas.*

9. "Jerseys, or, The Girl's Ghost" appeared in the July 1884 *St. Nicholas.*

10. William Torrey Harris, a founder of the St. Louis Hegelian movement, edited the *Journal of Speculative Philosophy,* helped to organize the Concord School of Philosophy, and coauthored with F. B. Sanborn *A. Bronson Alcott: His Life and Philosophy* (1893).

11. LMA's account book shows that Kate began work on 18 June (Houghton Library, Harvard University).

12. LMA's account book shows that she paid twenty dollars a week on 21 and 28 July to a Mrs. M (Houghton Library, Harvard University).

13. LMA wrote "H. enjoying her lover" and then canceled it.

14. Sampson Low wrote LMA on 3 September 1884 that it was sending her £84.10.8 on her account through 30 June of that year (Houghton Library, Harvard University).

15. Henry Irving, Ellen Terry, and their Lyceum Theatre Company were in Boston for a three-week run beginning 20 October, performing mainly Shakespeare's plays.

16. LMA had taken rooms at 31 Chestnut Street with John and Fred.

17. Chase's Gallery at 7 Hamilton Place.

18. In 1884, Roberts Brothers printed 54,000 copies of LMA's works.

1885

January 1885.

1st   Pleasant greeting from brother Ernst [Nieriker] by telegram. Never forgets us. Opera in the eve. Emma Nevada.[1] Not much. Sent box home. Very cold.

John had his first dress suit. Happy boy!

Several pleasant Sunday evenings at E. P. Whipples. See Mrs Burnett & like her.

Visit Blind Asylum & North End Mission.

Lulu passed a week with me for a change.

Tried the Mind Cure with Mrs Newman.[2] Agreeable at first. Blue clouds & sunshine in my head. Mesmerism, though Mrs N. said it was *not*. Breath short, heart fluttered, seemed to float away. Could not move. Very quiet after it. Queer times. Will try the experiment & gratefully accept any miracle that can be wrought for me.

Roberts Bros. pay	$5948.00
St N.	300.00
Invest for A[nna].	2120.00

January 1

Sent parcel home. Sewed & read. Dull day. Feel better. Nice box from A[nna]. Opera in eve. Nevada. Telegram from Ernst.

January 2

Cold. Made up accounts. Sewed, & read. Poorly & lazy. Call on Mrs Bigelow.

January 3

Sewed, read. Pay Dr W[esselhoeft]. $19. Run in p.m.[3] Saw A. R. & E. W.[4] All sick. Read in eve. New stove. J[ohn]. went home. I dared not go.

January 4

Read, rested. Wrote to A[nna]. & Miss Hubbard.[5] Called on A[nna]. R[icketson]. & E[lizabeth]. W[ells]. Better. J[ohn]. brought books & letters from C[oncord].

January 5

Went to see the W.s, R. & E.[6] Talked with L[ulu].

January 6

Errands in a.m. Read in p.m. Took care of E. G. Great fuss. Miss B. ill.

January 7

Sewed in a.m. Errands in p.m. M. G. with tickets in eve. F[red]. to W.

January 8

Shopping in a.m. Met Mrs C. Read. With A[nna]. R[icketson]. to walk in p.m. To concert in eve. Feel better. O out all day.

January 9

[blank]

January 10

Sewed in a.m. To Museum with Mrs C. in p.m. Colleen Bawn.[7] Read in eve. J. M. called. F[red]. $5,00.

January 11

Rested & read. Fanny came. Gave J[ohn]. $5,00 of his 15 for lunch. To Whipple's in eve with F[red?]. Pleasant time.

January 12

Wrote for Lulu, & to A. Walk, sew & read. Feel better. Confusion in eve.

January 13

To Blind School & North End mission with Mrs C. Very interesting day. Story of Charlie Davis.

January 14

Sewed till lunch. Errands. In p.m. Mrs. C. R[uth]. W[ells]. A[deline]. May & girls. Read in eve. Carlyle last vol.

January 15

Write to A[nna]. & M[ilbrey]. G[reen].[8] Shop $6,16. Make a bonnet. Call on E[lizabeth]. W[ells]. Mrs Porter came.[9]

January 16

Snow. Out in a.m. Called on E[lizabeth]. W[ells]. & R[uth]. In p.m. to see Mrs F. H. Burnett & Mrs Newman. Wrote in eve. Feel better.

January 17–21

[blank]

January 22

K. came at 10.[10] O out a.m. & p.m. To see N. D. in eve. with F[red]. Mrs N[ewman]. can come next week. L[ulu]. very good.

January 23

Errands. Saw E[lizabeth]. W[ells]. & A[nna]. R[icketson]. Sent basket to A[nna].

January 24

At 10 a.m. to W. H. Channing's memorial service at B. Hereford's church.[11] Jarley in p.m. To bed at 9, very tired.

January 25

K[ate?]. to church. L[ulu]. & C. play. I write.

January 26

Cold. Out shopping. T. N[iles]. $5948. for 6 months.

January 27

Out with S.

January 28

Shopping in a.m. To play with L[ulu]. in p.m. Mrs N[ewman]. in eve. Quiet warm hands.

January 29

L[ulu]. went home. Mrs N[ewman]. Queer feeling in head. Blue light, no breath, heart beat. Slept all p.m. Read in eve.

January 30

Mrs N[ewman]. A better time. Slept all p.m. & night. Am better. Eve at A[nna]. R[icketson]'s. Mrs Nowell & A. R. called.

January 31

Out shopping. Mrs N[ewman]. Nothing new. Home at 3. All well.

February.

Home for a day or two. Father walks better & seemed better.

My mind-cure not a success. First I am told to be "passive". So I do, say & think nothing. No effect. Then I am not "positive" enough, must exert my mind. Do so & try to grasp the mystery. Then I am *"too positive"* & must not try to *understand* anything. Inconsistency & too much hurry. God & Nature cant be hustled about every ten minutes to cure a dozen different ails. Too much money made & too much delusion all round.

Mrs Burnett is trying it. Says it quiets her mind but does n't help her body. Too much is claimed for it.

Read Geo. Eliot's Life.[12] Glad it is not gossipy. No one's business what she thought & did. Dr Munroe with good plain Massage does me more good than Mrs N[ewman]. & "letting divine strength flow in."[13]

Dickens Carnival, Fine.[14] A memorable moment. Irving in "E. Aram".[15]

February 1

With A[nna]. & Lulu. Pa well. Walked alone. Saw S. H. A[nna]. $100 for house. Good nap & slept well.

February 2

Home at 10. Mrs N[ewman]. No light. Sewed & rested. Saw house with A[nna]. R[icketson]. Liked it. Saw L. W. & Mrs G.[16]

February 3

Errands. Mrs N[ewman]. Box home. L. L., S. R. Mrs Whipple & Mrs Smith called. Read in eve.

February 4

Miss Hubbard. Errands. Mrs N[ewman].

February 5

Mrs N[ewman]. Shopping in a.m. people in p.m. Box home.

February 6

Snow. Nothing to do. Rather blue.

February 7

Shopping & Fortune. Mc Giheneys in p.m. & eve. [17]

February 8

Quiet day. Read & rested. To Whipples in the eve. Mrs F. H. Burnett &c. pleasant eve.

February 9

Sewed. Errands. Read Geo. Eliot's Life in p.m. Very interesting. J[ames]. M[urdoch?]. in eve. A[deline]. May.

February 10

N[ewman]. Wrote letters in a.m. Sent C. M.'s story to H. Y. P. [18] Bundle home. Wrote to Slack & Mrs W.

February 11

Went to N[ewman]. Had a good time. Felt light. Couldnt move hands. Quiet & light all the eve. Read G[eorge]. E[liot].

February 12

Errands in a.m. To Dr M[unroe]. Pay $2,00 & Dr A. $8,00 for L[ulu]. [19] J[ames]. M[urdoch?]. in eve.

February 13

N[ewman]. To Dr M. in a.m. Good time. H[enry]. H[osmer]. comes. Give him $2000 to invest. A[nna]. sends $60. Shop.

February 14

N[ewman].

February 15

N[ewman]. Eye very bad. Dull day. Walk in p.m. See Miss H[ubbard?]. Mrs N. in eve. Queer time.

February 16

Mrs N[ewman]. eve. Felt better. Did errands. To Irving in eve. Saw Eugene Aram. A visible poem. Miss Rose.

February 17

Mrs N[ewman]. room. Out early. Got [undeciphered] for A[nna]. Come with L[ulu]. & K[ate]. at 3. Noisy time. Carnival in eve. Fine — & fun.

February 18

Mrs N[ewman]. Dressmaker. Fuss. Irving in eve. Much Ado [About Nothing].

February 19

Dr M[unroe]. in a.m. A[nna]. home. Rested. Mrs N[ewman]. in p.m. dined at P[arker]. House. W. S. in eve.

February 20

Dr M[unroe]. in a.m. feet. Better. Errands. flowers for J. Miss Whitney & J. E. M.[20] Read in eve. Pay Dr M. $6,50 to date.

February 21

Pay Mrs N[ewman]. $34.

February 22–25

[blank]

February 26

$2,00   Dr M[unroe].

February 27

To C[oncord]. Fixed stage. Cates came.[21] Play. Party. Bed late. Kept up well. So glad.

February 28

Home to B[oston]. very tired.

March.

Mrs N[ewman]. says "you've got it!" but she deceives herself for I have lost my faith & never feel any better after a sèance. Try Miss Adams as Mrs N. says she herself is "too powerful" for me.[22] Miss N. made no more impression on me than a moonbeam. After 30 trials I give it up. No miracle for me. My ills are not imaginary, so are hard to cure.

A. B. Warren comes & does me good, she is so sensible & happy & queer.[23] Talked much of the year we spent in Europe with May.

Vertigo, ill for ten days. Dr W[esselhoeft].

March 1

Rested.

March 2

N[ewman]. Lovely day. Felt well. Out in a.m. & p.m. Mrs N. says "I've got it." Hope so. Read in eve. J[ohn]. 3,00.

March 3

Mrs. G[iles]. A[nna]. & L[ulu]. Errands.

March 4

Mrs. N[ewman]. A[nna]. & L[ulu]. go home. Rest. J[ohn]. Not much. Pay N. 4,00.

March 5

Errands. Dine with S. E. S[ewall].

March 6

N[ewman]. pd — Errands in a.m. F. L. in p.m. Read Hawthorne in eve. Boys home to ball.

March 7

Read & wrote in a.m.

March 8

Rested & read.

March 9

Mrs N[ewman]. Got papers & shopped. Felt poorly. J[ohn]. 3,00.

March 10

Mrs N[ewman]. pd 4,00. Papers &c.

March 11

Mrs N[ewman]. Not a good one. Play in p.m. Sieba.[24] Read in p.m.

March 12

Mrs N[ewman] pd 4,00. Bad one. On sofa all day poorly in head & ear. teapot, cut up paper cards, 1.47.

March 13

Rain. Poorly. Kept in & lay on sofa. T, 1,50.

March 14

A[nna]. & L[ulu]. for the day. Birfday, good time. Read in eve. 1,25 flowers. N[ewman]. in eve.

March 15

Read & rest. Write letters in eve & put papers in order.

March 16

Miss A[dams]. Errands. Sewed. Booth in eve. Buy Bks. Dall. Miss A. sleepy

March 17

Out errands. T. N[iles]. got $48 cashed. A[nna]. R[icketson]. in eve.

March 18

Miss A[dams]. $4,00. No good. Head ached badly all day. Out. To Kings Chapel at noon. Got bonnets. Wrote in the eve to Miss Adams.

March 19

A[lice]. B[artlett]. comes. Very jolly. Talk &c. Mr W. Read S's book on Saxon.

March 20

To church in a.m. Errands in p.m. Home in eve with A[lice]. B[artlett]. Box home by J[ohn].

March 21

Cold. In house all day with A[lice]. B[artlett]. Very cold, no voice.

March 22

Cold. no voice. Read & keep warm. Wrote to A[nna].

March 23

See Mrs Pitts. Like her. Will come May 1st. A[lice Bartlett]. W[arren]. goes. Do errands in p.m.

March 24

To C[oncord]. at 3. Fixed dresses & sew falls. L[ulu]. naughty.

March 25

Fussed for eve. Went with A[nna]. Pretty good time. Got cold.

March 26

Home at 1 p.m. Very tired. Rested.

March 27

To Dr M[unroe]. but he could not attend to me till next day. Rested. Very poorly.

March 28

Dr M[unroe]. pd. 5,00. F[red]'s 22ond birthday. Lovely. Got a cake & gifts for him. A[nna]. & L[ulu]. came in for the day. Very tired. to bed at 9.

March 29

Snow. Wrote letters & read.

March 30

Dr M[unroe]. Send A[nna]. $100 for house.

March 31

Hot. Errands. Rest in p.m. Read in eve.

April.

11th   Home to C[oncord]. with boys. On the whole a good winter. They have been well & happy, & I have rested. Sorry not to be better. Voice gone, head bad, & spirits low, being tired of the long fight for health. The hospital experience was a costly one for me. Never well since. Yet it turned the tide & brought success.

19th   An oldfashioned party in an old time house. All in antique costume. Lulu very pretty in hers. Country kitchen & country fare. Spinning &

weaving. Old songs & dances. Tally ho coach with P[itts?]. as an ancient Weller.[25] Very funny.

April 1–18

[torn out]

April 19

Warm. L[ulu]. a better. P[itts]. stupid. Tired & worried.

April 20

Sewed. Party with L[ulu]. in p.m. Party in eve. Rather dull.

April 21

Sewed & ran after L[ulu]. Party in eve. Sing.

April 22

Hot. Sewed. A[nna]. to party in eve. Read & rested. Smelting Mills $12.[26]

April 23

Cooler. Sewed.

April 24

Spite. Sewed. Poorly.

April 25

Dr. M[unroe]. 4,00. To B[oston]. Errands. Saw boys, B[ond?].s & R[icketson?]s. Got 50 from P[rovident]. Bank & cashed 12. R. Mills.

April 26

Wrote letters. Took care of L[ulu]. & fixed papers.

April 27–30

[blank]

May & June.

Tribulations with nurses & maids. Mrs Giles comes for father & H[atty]. H[askell]. for Lulu.[27] Peace falls upon our troubled souls. Voice & pipes in misery. Try inhaling oxygen. Helps a little.

20th   To N[onquitt]. with H[atty]. & Lulu.

Settle in my little cottage & rest. Lulu happy with her mates. A quiet place, good for weary souls & bodies. Dont care much for the people.

Read Life of St Elizabeth by D'Alembert.[28] Quaint & sweet. Also French novels.

Write out the little tales I tell Lulu for a new Xmas book, having nothing else. Send one "The Candy Country" to St N.[29]

Tale for St N. $100

May 1

Mrs Giles comes in p.m.

May 2

Mrs G[iles]. goes.

May 3

[blank]

May 4

Go to B[oston]. Get City of C. & St L[ouis?]. dividends $103. Pay bills. Mrs Pitts goes.

May 5

Give A[nna]. $125 for house. Sew. New girl comes at 5,30. Alice.

May 6

Sew. New girl went at 6. Queer, too lonely. Didnt like her.

May 7

Sewed. L[ulu].

May 8

Sewed. Took care of L[ulu]. No sensations. Inhaled once.[30] *2 minutes.*

May 9

New girl came at 5,30. Hatty Haskell. Looks good. Pa rode with H[atty]. Care of L[ulu]. To town. Inhaled once.

May 10

H[atty]. begins. 3 minutes. A little feeling in the bottom of lungs.

May 11

Pipe. Feel rather smart & want to take long breaths. Nose better. S. E. S[ewall]. auction[.] H[atty]. does well. To town.

May 12

Pipe. Fine. To town. Felt pretty well.

May 13

Pipe.

May 14

Pipe.

May 15

Pipe.

May 16

No pipe. To B[oston]. shopping. Go to play with F[red]. Very funny.

May 17

H[atty]. 1 week. Pipe. Dr B. & L[ulu].[31] Care of L[ulu]. See Dr B. early. Write letters. Warm. Sore spot no better, nor voice.

May 18–21

[blank]

May 22

To B[oston]. with L[ulu]. Get $20 of T. N[iles]. as mine gave out.

May 23

Silver Wedding.[32]

May 24

H[atty]. 2 weeks pay. 8,00[.] Pipe.

May 25

Pipe. Dr B[lake].

May 26

Pipe. Sew.

May 27

Pipe. A[nna]. to B[oston].

May 28

Pipe in a.m. To B[oston]. errands. Voice better. Head dizzy at times. Sore spot in throat better.

May 29

Pipe. Sewed.

May 30

Pipe in eve. Decoration Day. To S. H. in a.m. Sewed in p.m.

May 31

Pay G[iles]. $40 for one month.

June 1–17

[pages torn out]

June 18–19

[blank]

June 20

To N[onquitt]. with F[red]. L[ulu]. & H[atty]. Supper at hotel. Put beds in order & cleaned up. Very tired. $4 for hack. 1,00 for trunk.

June 21

Up early & worked round all a.m. Rested in p.m. F[red]. put up doors & c. L[ulu]. happy. H[atty]. not very well.

June 22

Mrs H. 50 cts. Got ready for woman. Kitchen cleaned & carpet down. Very tired, but head feels better. Hoarse.

June 23

Baker 30 cts. Rested. Called on A[nna] R[icketson]. F[red]. went home. Cold. L[ulu]. happy.

June 24

Fussed round. L[ulu]. & H[atty]. out all day. Made couch. Mr B. lent a bed. Very nice in dining room now.

June 25

Sewed & read & rested. Mrs C. called & lent me a stove.[33] Getting all fixed. Bundle from A[nna].

June 26

Cleaned windows. Letter from A[nna]. Nice party. Get stove. Write to A[nna]. Miss L. in eve. Letter from A[nna].

June 27

Washed & ironed. Began to keep house. Made custard & got in berries milk &c. Read & rested. Rain.

June 28

Rain & gale. Read.

June 29

Rainy & cold. Dull day. Read.

June 30

Dr R.s in eve. Music.

July

Boys come up & down Sundays & enjoy bathing & fun.

My voice no better. Dyspepsia to add to my woes. Sea air not good for me I fear though Dr A[ngell?]. said, "Go."

Some pleasant musical evenings at the B[ound]s. F[red]. plays flute or organ & I am proud of his skill. A manly fellow, quiet, upright & intelligent. Promises well. Both boys great favorites, & A[nna]. & I are always so pleased & proud when men & women say "The Pratts are so talented & so *good.*" Nan has done well.[34]

July 1

Cold. Fire all day. F[red]. went home. Walk with A[nna] R[icketson]. Miss C. called. Read French & sewed.

July 2

Walked to Round Hills 4 miles with H[atty]. & L[ulu]. Nice time. Not very tired. L[ulu]. danced in eve.

July 3

Sewed read. Saw A[nna]. R[icketson]. Letters from A[nna]. Wrote to A[nna].

July 4

L[ulu]. had her first bath. Took care of her all a.m. Nap & bath at home in p.m. Fireworks in eve.

July 5

Wrote to A[nna]. Read Life of St Elizabeth by D'Alembert. Very quaint & sweet. French.

July 6–17

[pages torn out]

July 18

Very hot. Read, copy & lie round. L[ulu]. cross. Boys come at 6. Bathe & rest. Party in eve at M. C.s.

July 19

Boys bathe, talk & have a good time. Cooler. Walk. A[nna]. R[icketson]. & Bound's music in eve. Write to A[nna].

July 20

Boys go.

July 21–23

[blank]

July 24

Party at Mrs P.s in N[orth]. B[oston?]. No go for me.

July 25

Hoarse & pain. Pay bill from 1 to 25 for boys & all $110.20. just what my little tale earned. See Miss Chapman. Sew & write.

July 26–29

[blank]

[pages torn out]

August.

8th   Go home & A[nna]. goes to N[onquitt]. Take care of father, arrange the little tales & look at houses in B[oston]. Have a plan to take a furnished house for the winter & all be together. A. is lonely in C[oncord]. Boys must be near business. I want Lulu, & father will enjoy a change.

Sorted old letters & burned many. Not wise to keep for curious eyes to read, & gossip-lovers to print by & by.[35] Lived in the past for days, & felt very old recalling all I have been through. Experiences go deep with me, & I begin to think it might be well to keep some record of my life if it will help others to read it when I'm gone. People seem to think our lives interesting & peculiar.

Life rather a burden.

Write a tale for book, "How They Ran Away."[36]

August 1–16

[pages torn out]

August 17

Sewed, & fixed little tales for T. N[iles]. Proof came. Boys home at night. letters from A[nna].

August 18

Began to fix papers. Wrote letters, read & sewed. Boys to B's in eve.

August 19

Write to A[nna]. Girl about tale & men about houses. To town. Pa to drive with H[atty]. Letter from A[nna].

August 20

Drive Harris.[37] Write a tale for book.

August 21

To B[oston]. to see houses. Lost No 10.[38] Shopped a little. Very tired. See T. N[iles]. Rain in eve. F[red]. to N[onquitt].

August 22

Drive. J[ohn]. to N[onquitt]. for plays. Sew & rest.

August 23

Very warm. Felt very poorly. Slept & tried to forget. Life a burden when it should be all happy work.

August 24

Sorted old letters & lived in the past all day. Want to leave in order. Boys at night.

August 25

Put letters & papers in order. Mine for a life if I ever do it, & burn many from the people who write to me. A nice rainy day.

August 26

To B[oston]. to see house in M. St. Liked it.

August 27

A[nna]. telegraphed "take the house."

August 28

Went to B[oston]. & took the house in M. St. Telegraph in eve that we could have No 10 L[ouisburg]. Sq. Good.[39]

August 29

To B[oston]. about the L. Sq. house. Boys to N[onquitt].

August 30–31

[blank]

September.

After a lively time with house brokers I take a house in Louisburg Sq. for two years, Rent $1650. Seems a great deal after paying no rent for twenty-five years, but it is a large house, furnished, & well suited to our needs. Sunny, trees in front, good air & friends near by. All are pleased & we prepare to move Oct. 1st.

12. 250th anniversary of settlement of C[oncord].[40] Grand rally. Dinner & reception. Lowell, Curtis, Evarts, Gov. Robinson & the town dignitaries out in full force. I wished thier manners & grammer better, but beside Lowell & Curtis few would shine.

Curtis called on father. Outsiders asked why Miss A[lcott]. was never invited to sit among the honored ones at such times? C[oncord]. cant forgive her for not thinking it perfect.

September 1–3
  [blank]

September 4–9
  [pages torn out]

September 10–11
  [blank]

September 12
  250th celebration in C[oncord]. Lowell, Curtis, Evarts &c. Go to dinner & reception. Dr B[lake]. comes for my lungs.

September 13
  Curtis calls. Mrs Porter.

September 14–15
  [blank]

September 16–27
  [pages torn out]

September 28–29
  [blank]

September 30
  To B[oston]. with boys & Kate to open house No. 10 Louisburg Sq. Hard work all day.

October

  To B[oston]. with boys & K[ate]. to open our new house. Hard week. Things left dirty & in disorder. Shiftless cook & careless man in charge. General rummage & settling.

  Family came later. Father drove down very nicely. Pleased with his new room. Lulu charmed with her big, sunny nursery & the play house left for her. Boys in clover, & Nan ready for the new sort of housekeeping.

  I shall miss my quiet, care free life in B[oston]. but it is best for all so I shall try to bear the friction & the worry many persons always bring me.

264

It will be an expensive winter but T. N[iles]. tells me the books never sold better so a good sum in Jan. will make all safe. [41]

"Lulu's Library" as a little pot boiler will appease the children & I may be able to work on "Jo's Boys".

October 1

Getting things to rights. Get china &c.

October 2

Errands & fixing. F. E. calls.

October 3

Rain. Work & rest. F[red?]. & N. & S. & W. in eve. Mary Hogan, cook, comes in a.m.

October 4

Rest & fix papers.

October 5–11

[blank]

October 12

F[red]. to N.Y. at night with B. Club. Give J[ohn]. 5,00 for lectures.

October 13

Errands in a.m. Rested in p.m. To bed early. Rain.

October 14

To Dr M[unroe]. for head & foot. Errands. Rained hard. Sewed in p.m. F[red]. home from N.Y.

October 15–16

[blank]

October 17

Errands. Got teapot cake &c.

October 18

Pay G[iles]. Pay H[atty]. H[askell].

October 19–21

[blank]

October 22–December 31

[pages torn out]

SOURCE: Manuscript, Houghton Library, Harvard University.

1. Emma Nevada performed in Gaetano Donizetti's *Lucia di Lammermoor* (1835), based on Sir Walter Scott's *Bride of Lammermoor*, on 3 January.

2. The practitioners of the mind cure believed that since the spirit was superior to the body, cleansing one's mental state would result in a corresponding improvement in one's physical state. LMA's unsuccessful visits to Anna B. Newman at 17 Boylston Street in Boston are reported in "Miss Alcott on Mind-Cure" in the 18 April 1885 *Woman's Journal* and in her letter of 15 March [1885] to Maggie Lukens, in *SL,* pp. 287–288.

3. LMA is probably using "run" to indicate a walk or some other outdoor activity.

4. Anna and Walton Ricketson were the children of Daniel Ricketson of New Bedford, a longtime friend of the Alcotts; LMA's cousin Elizabeth Sewall Willis Wells.

5. Miss Hubbard assisted LMA with Lulu and general housekeeping chores.

6. LMA's cousins Elizabeth Wells and her daughter, Ruth Lyman Wells.

7. Dion Boucicault's *Colleen Bawn* (1859).

8. Dr. Milbrey Green specialized in botanic remedies.

9. Maria S. Porter was friendly with LMA during the last twenty years of her life (see *SL,* p. 190n).

10. Possibly Kate, who would help LMA in the running of the Boston house.

11. William Henry Channing had died in Britain on 23 December 1884. The memorial service for him, attended by Edward Everett Hale, Samuel May, and James Freeman Clarke, was held at the Arlington Street Church on 24 January, with its minister, Brooke Herford, officiating.

12. LMA called J. W. Cross's edition of *George Eliot's Life as Related in Her Letters and Journals* (1885) "wonderfully interesting" (letter of 16 February [1885] to Maggie Lukens in *SL,* p. 285; see also her comments in a letter of [February? 1885] to Thomas Niles, in *SL,* pp. 286n–287n).

13. Possibly Dr. W. H. Munroe on 19 Milford Street, Boston.

14. A Dickens carnival was performed on 17 February as a benefit for the Women's Educational and Industrial Union.

15. A stage adaptation of Edward George Bulwer-Lytton's *Eugene Aram* (1832).

16. LMA's cousin Louisa Wells Wendte; Mrs. Giles helped LMA to take care of Bronson.

17. LMA wrote Laura Hosmer on 16 May 1886: "The McGiheney family of 12 children & Pa & Ma send me tickets & a carriage to come & hear em" (Louisa May Alcott Collection, Barrett Library, University of Virginia).

18. Possibly "Baa! Baa!"; this appeared in the 15 and 22 September 1885 issues of *Harper's Young People.*

19. Possibly Dr. H. C. Angell, at 16 Beacon Street in Boston, an oculist and homeopathic physician.

20. The sculptor Anne Whitney had studied under William Rimmer with her friend May Alcott.

21. Jessica Lilian Cate (b. 1862), to whom Fred Pratt would propose on 1 January 1887 (see *SL,* p. 335n, for more information).

22. Miss Adams substituted for Mrs. Newman during the latter's absence. LMA called her "the wonderful-care girl" (letter of [16 March 1885] to Laura Hosmer, *SL,* p. 288n).

23. Alice Bartlett Warren had accompanied May and LMA to Europe in 1870.

24. The Kiralfy brothers' *Sieba and the Seven Ravens*.

25. Samuel Weller, Mr. Pickwick's valet in Dickens's *Posthumous Papers of the Pickwick Club* (1837).

26. LMA held stock in the Boston and Colorado Smelting Company.

27. Hatty Haskell helped LMA with Lulu and running the Boston house.

28. Charles de Montalembert's *Life of St. Elizabeth* (1870).

29. The first volume of *Lulu's Library* was published by Roberts Brothers in November 1885; "The Candy Country" appeared in the November 1885 *St. Nicholas*.

30. LMA was taking some sort of inhalation therapy for her lungs.

31. LMA refers to a female Dr. Blake in a letter to Laura Hosmer of [11 May 1886?], but no woman physician of that name is listed in the Boston directories (Louisa May Alcott Collection, Barrett Library, University of Virginia).

32. Anna Pratt would have been married twenty-five years had not John died. This was also the anniversary of LMA's parents' wedding; as she wrote Mary Stearns, it was rather "sad for both mateless ones; but we have done our best to cheer them up, and the soft rain is very emblematic of the memories their own quiet tears keep green" (23 May [1885], Cheney, p. 359).

33. LMA's neighbors, the Crapo family.

34. LMA wrote: "A[nna]. comes down & I go home" and then canceled it.

35. In a note dated February 1878, LMA wrote: "These journals are kept only for my own reference, & I particularly desire that if I die before I destroy them that they may *all* be *burnt* unread or copied by any one" (Houghton Library, Harvard University).

36. "How They Ran Away" appeared in vol. 1 of *Lulu's Library*.

37. Probably William Torrey Harris.

38. See the entry for 28 August.

39. LMA leased a house at 10 Louisburg Square, Boston, from a Mr. Morse for two years, beginning in October 1885, for Anna, Fred, John, Lulu, and herself.

40. At the celebration, James Russell Lowell spoke on "the connection of Concord with our national literature"; George William Curtis, then the editor of *Harper's Weekly*, gave a "very polished" speech on "patriotism and piety"; William M. Evarts, the U.S. senator from New York, "praised Concord as the boy's paradise and made fun of the self-esteem of her people"; and George D. Robinson, governor of Massachusetts, gave a talk that "captivated" the audience by its "intrinsic merit" and "high key of patriotism" (see the report in the *Concord Freeman*, 18 September, pp. 1, 4; partially reprinted in *Celebration of the Two Hundred and Fiftieth Anniversary of the Incorporation of Concord, September 12, 1885* [Concord: The Town, 1885]).

41. In 1885, Roberts Brothers printed 62,840 copies of LMA's works.

1886

January. 1886

Roberts Bros. for six months	$7591.00
St N. for "Look."	125.00
Harper Xmas tale	100.00 [1]

January 1

Find this journal at my place at table from Fred. Year opens brightly for all. Together in B[oston]. I am better. Lulu well, & Father comfortable. To a child's party at Mrs Waters in p.m. A[nna]. & boys to a party at Brooke Herford's in the eve. Kind letter from T. N[iles]. with 1000 on account.

January 2

Lovely day. Wrote letters. Went to find a nurse as G[iles]. goes next week. Busy day in horse cars. Got M. Carlsen. Gave A[nna]. for house 150.00. To the Symphony Concert in the eve with Miss A. Whitney. Very fine. Mendesohn, Shubert & Beetehoven. A Reception for the p.m. but didn't go.

January 3

F. E. E. came from N.Y. full of plans & spirit. J. E. M. & Clara with M. W. to dinner. Very tired but tried to be jolly. F[red]. brought me a pretty bronze seal of his own make.

January 4

Mrs G[iles]. left. I took care of father. Read & sat with him. L[ouisa]. W[endte]. & Mr Bowin & A[nna]. R[icketson]. called. Dull day. A[nna]. got a new nurse.

January 5

Rain. Took care of father.

January 6

Errands. Paid bills & got money. Took care of Pa in p.m. A[nna]. & boys to Cambridge in eve. Mrs Clark & the R's called.

January 7

Very cold. Dressmaker & L[ulu]. to school. Wrote letters & fixed accounts.

January 8

Felt poorly. To A[deline]. M[ay]s' in p.m. Cab.

January 9

Great storm & cold. Read.

January 10

Very cold, Blizzard.

January 11–17

[blank]

January 18

Fine day. Out shopping. Got 30 yds sheeting, hose for L[ulu]. &c. In p.m. went to see Dr. Said, "Take care." Made calls on Mrs Whipple, Mrs Wadsworth, Miss Bartol & Mrs Bollen. Read in eve "Cleopatra" by Greville.[2]

January 19

Kindlings. Snow. Wrote & rested, feeling poorly.

January 20–30

[blank]

January 31

Wrote, read papers & dawdled. R[icketson?]'s in eve.

February.

————

Try massage & feel better, thank God! It is tiresome to be always aching. Why cant people use their brains without breaking down?

February 1

Run in p.m. Fine day. sewed. Wrote a little & fussed round. Felt better.

February 2

Out doing errands. Rested in p.m. To L[ouisa]. W[endte].s in eve to a tea party. Dress &c. for L[ulu]. Dr L[awrence]. in eve.

February 3

Very cold. Out paying bills. S[ophy]. Bond & Mabel called.[3] Gas better. Carbo. Got Phosphates & Beef Extracts to try.

February 4

Party for Freda. Get a gift for her   1.25.

February 5

Out, did errands.[4] Read & rested in p.m.

February 6

Hatty's birth day. Give her six books. Go shopping. Get L[ulu]. a dress &c. Candy. Hose, drawers, &c. Miss Whitney called & Miss Bartol. Took care of L. all p.m. Dr L[awrence]. in eve.

February 7

Read papers & wrote up diary & accounts.

February 8

[blank]

February 9

To Concord & paid taxes for all. $243.70. Saw L[aura]. H[osmer]. Had a drive. Got book for Pa &c. Home at 4,30. Mrs L[awrence]. in eve. Feel better.

February 10

Wrote letters. Went for L[ulu]. To see "Jilt" in P.M.[5]

February 11

Rain. Took care of L[ulu]., wrote & read. J[essica]. C[ate]. in eve. A[nna]. & F[red]. & J. C. to opera. 7 autograph fiends.

February 12

Letters from F. Willard to write tales on the Social Purity question.[6] Also from the Brooklyn Magazine to write my views on "How Early should our girls marry?"[7] Will try to do both.

February 13

[blank]

February 14

Dr L[awrence]. Read & wrote. Rs to tea. To see the flood. Left food for the inundated people. Curious sight.

February 15

Fine. Out shopping. Got dress &c. for Lulu. Ballet suit. Sewed in p.m. A[nna]. & J[ohn]. to play in eve. Mrs [Maria] Porter with tickets to the Blind Asylum affair Mar. 5th.

February 16

Fine. Out on errands.

February 17

[blank]

February 18

Port Royal Lunch at Brunswick. Pleasant time.

February 19

Errands. Read Geo Meredith's books.[8] Queer & Richterish. Wrote a little tale for Lulu. All I dare to do.

February 20

Sewed & drove with Pa in a.m. To Mrs Heminway's in p.m. to hear Snider on the Illiad.[9] A good company & a pleasant time. Read 8 Cousins in eve & liked it. L[ulu]. to a party. Snow.

February 21

Tried to fix accounts but got my head in a muddle very soon & had to give it up. 4 little girls called making 16 in all.

February 22

Out with Lulu. Music Hall & children dancing.

February 23

Out for girls all day. Got L. Kimball.

February 24

Tired. Sewed & rested. F[anny?]. Lombard called.

February 25

Shopping. Blanket &c for Lulu. Things for house. F[red]. to N.Y. Gave him for trip. — 20.00.

February 26

[blank]

February 27

Had a dizzy turn on waking & kept [to] my bed. Sent for Dr W[esselhoeft]. Much discouraged. Lay still & helpless.

February 28

Ill. No sleep, dizzy head, weary & low in mind.

March.

16th A[nna]'s birthday. Give her a 1000 Bond. Put 1000 in bank for F[red]. & one for J[ohn].

Get up slowly from illness. Try to write as Dr W[esselhoeft]. thinks my "rebellious brain" will behave better if it is allowed a vent.

Pay taxes in C[oncord]. $243.70.

Miss F. Willard asks me to write tales on the Social Purity question. Brooklyn Mag. wishes to know, "How Early Shall Girls Marry?"

13th Great inundation at South End.

Port Royal lunch at Brunswick.

To Mrs Heminways to hear Mr Snyder read the Illiad. Enjoyed it.

16 little girls call, & the autograph fiend is abroad.

27th Another attack of vertigo. Ill for a week. Sleepless nights. Head worked like a steam engine & would not stop. Planned "Jo's Boys" to the end & longed to get up & write it. Told Dr W[esselhoeft]. that he had better let me get the ideas *out* then I could rest. He very wisely agreed & said, "As soon as you can write half an hour a day & see if it does you good. Rebel-

272

lious brains must be attended to or trouble comes." So I began as soon as able, & was satisfied that we were right for my head felt better very soon, & with much care about not over doing I had some pleasant hours when I forgot my body & lived in my mind.[10]

March 1

Ill.

March 2

Ill.

March 3

Ill.

March 4

Ill. Fainting at 11. p.m. sent for Dr W[esselhoeft].

March 5

Better. Dont eat enough Dr says. Must try chops &c.

March 6

A little better. Dr says I may write next week & get my head free from stories that haunt me & keep me awake. Wise man.

March 7

Sit up a little. A[nna] reads to me.

March 8

Up. Weak but pretty well. Read a little.

March 9–10

[blank]

March 11

Out for a walk.

March 12

Rested in a.m. Took F. H. Burnett to drive in p.m.

March 13

Rain. Sewed & read. Nap. R's to tea.

March 14

Fine. Saw the R's house. Wrote in poetry book in p.m. Dr W[esselhoeft]. came.

March 15

Out shopping. Got a nice chair for A[nna]. & many useful things for the dear soul. Out with Lulu in p.m. Got a big dolly & shoes &c. Read in eve. Dizzy in head.

March 16

Anna's 55th birthday. Gifts & kisses. Sewed & dressed the new doll.

March 17

Walked in a.m. Sewed & read.

March 18

11 calls. A[nna]. to C[oncord].

March 19

Shopping. A[nna]. home. Wrote in a.m. of "Jo's Boys." To J[ohn]. for bycle [bicycle] $50.

March 20

Made a gay dress for L[ulu]. to play in. Wrote up old journal.

March 21–31
[blank]

April.

Went on writing one or two hours a day & felt no ill effects.

April 1–3
[blank]

April 4

Write, walk with L[ulu]. Call on A[deline]. M[ay]. & Mrs Lovering. Read in p.m.

April 5

Shopping. Wrote an hour. Give A[nna]. for house. 50. Pay Geo. 10. Lulu had cold.

April 6

Lulu ill with cough. Dr A[ngell?]. comes. Croupy. Take care of her.

April 7

Lulu. Errands & toys for my baby.

April 8

Lulu.

April 9

Lulu.

April 10

Lulu better but cannot go out.

April 11

Dr. L[awrence]. Read to L[ulu].

April 12

Sewed. Feel much better.

April 13

Shopping. Feel better.

April 14

A[nna]. to C[oncord]. to see about the work. Quiet day. feel free & as if my ways did not annoy anyone. L[ulu]. good, cough better. Boiler cleaned out & stove.

April 15

Out in a.m. Errands.

April 16

Tell A[nna]. to stay. All well here, & she not needed.

April 17

A[nna]. home at noon, tired. Walls &c. being done in C[oncord].

April 18

Dr L[awrence]. Drove with Pa & L[ulu]. round the city. Pa enjoyed seeing the old places. Masonic Temple &c.[11] Rested in p.m.

April 19

Mrs. M. is to go.[12] Too much company & too little help. T. N[iles]. says the letters wont do. Mrs Cummings in eve. Call on Whitney & Drummond.

April 20

Out at 12. Errands for L[ulu]. Rested in p.m. Mrs Hall came.[13] Engaged her at 7 per week. B. Herford called. E[lizabeth]. W[ells]. & J. M. in eve.

April 21

Sewed for L[ulu].

April 22–30
[blank]

May

Begin to think of Concord & prepare to go back for the summer. Father wants his books, Lulu her garden, Annie her small house, & the boys thier friends. I want to get away & rest.

Anna goes up the last of the month & gets the house ready. We send Lulu & Father later & the boys & I shut up No 10.

Glad to be done with the winter experiment. It has worked as well as I expected but [has] been costly & hard with our mixed family of ten, invalids, nurses, maids boys & babies. My illness a great trial to all.

May 1–31
[blank]

June.

Home in C[oncord]. sunny clean & pleasant. Put Lulu in order, & get ready for a month in Princeton with Mrs H[all].[14] Very tired.

A quiet three weeks on the hill side, a valley pink with Cousel[?] in front, Mt Wachuset behind us, & green hills all round. A few pleasant people. I read, sleep, walk, & write. Get 15 chapters done to T. N[iles].s great joy.

Instinct was right, after seven years of rest the old brain was ready for work, & tired of feeding on itself, since work it must at something.

Enjoyed Hedge's Hours with German Classics, & "Bal[d]win" by Vernon Lee. [15]

Home in time to get Anna & Lulu off to N[onquitt]. for the summer. A[nna]. needs the rest very much, & Lulu the freedom. I shall revel in the quiet, & finish my book.

June 1–30

[blank]

July.

The sea shore party get off & peace reigns. I rest a day & then to work. Finish "Jo's Boys" & take it to T. N[iles]. on the [blank] Much rejoicing over a new book, 50,00[0] to be the first edition. [16] Orders coming in fast. Not good, too great intervals between the parts as it was begun long ago. But the children will be happy & my promise kept. Two new chapters were needed, so I wrote them, & gladly corked my inkstand.

What next? Mrs Dodge wants a serial & T. N[iles]. a novel. I have a dozen plots in my head but think the serial better come first. Want a great deal of money, for many things. Every poor soul I ever knew comes for help & expenses increase. I am the only money maker & must turn the mill for others though my grist is ground & in the barn.

The school begins. Father feeble but goes, for the last time I think.

July 1–3

[blank]

July 4

Ellen paid up to date. [17]

July 5–14

[blank]

July 15

Wrote letters, read Baldwin & slept. Rain. Called on Hortons in eve.

July 16

Arrange papers, write diary & look over some Mss. Want to go on writing as my head is full. Plenty of quiet now.

July 17

Boys to N[onquitt]. for Sunday.

July 18–22

[blank]

July 23

To B[oston]. Saw T. N[iles]. & picture for book. Pretty good. Did errands. To No 10. All right. Home at 3. Packed F[red]'s trunk. Boy to tea. German in eve.

July 24

Got boys off to N[onquitt]. F. B. at noon. Miss P. called. Rested in p.m. Read in eve. Wrote to Miss Hubbard about L[ulu].

July 25

Wrote to A[nna]. & L[aura]. H[osmer]. Read.

July 26

[blank]

July 27

Quiet days, nothing to record. Head full of plans. Very happy to feel well, & ask for nothing more.

July 28

A. Wilkinson dead.[18] Relief to all.

July 29

Last day of School. Pa went. I also. Very hot. Mrs Howe on the "Women of Plato's Republic."[19] Good. Talk afterward. Pa very tired. E. P. P[eabody]. kept popping up. A soul wished to read a paper. Queer people. Glad its done.

July 30

Mrs H[all]. to town. Sat with Pa all day. Read & sewed. Little girl called, wept & wailed because I could not see her.

July 31

To B[oston]. Saw T. N[iles]. about book & Low. May have to go to Canada for copyright.[20] Did errands & home at 11.

August 1

Wrote a little & fixed papers. Want to do something but dont know which of many things to take care of.

August 2

To town, sewed & read. Miss Ware &c called in p.m. F[red]. home in eve. No special news, but seemed happy. A[nnie]. & L[ulu]. well.

August 3

To town, lovely day, Felt smart. To Lancaster at 12. Saw the W.s library & called on R's. Quiet little trip. Country beautiful. Wrote to Miss Hubbard to come for L[ulu]. in Sept.

August 4

Pay bills. Potter 2.00 Milk 22.45 Ice 4.00 Ellen 16. to Aug. 1st. Wheeler & wood. Market & grocer $39.30. Lovely day. To town in a.m. Drove in p.m. Wrote to L[ouisa]. W[endte?]. Mrs Somme & L[aura]. H[osmer]. & A. P.[22]

August 5–17

[blank]

August 18

To B[oston]. Give T. N[iles]. $858 to invest for A[nna]. Do errands. Send W. R. $50 for the picture & sake of peace.[23]

August 19

Taxes for all came. 253.00. John's first poll tax. Go to town. See Dr B[lake?]. Liver out of order. Write to A[nna].

August 20–29

[blank]

August 30

To B[oston]. saw J[ohn]'s room & did errands.

August 31

A[nna]. & L[ulu]. return from N[onquitt]. All well.

September 1

Enjoyed my girl. Grows pretty & good. Happy & hearty, & so fond of Aunt Wee it is delicious to have her run to hug me at all times.

September 2

Dizzy in a.m. Sent for Dr B[lake?]. & stayed in bed. Much discouraged. Worked too hard & got cold.

September 3

In bed. Head bad.

September 4

Bed till p.m. Feeble & blue. Head & eyes in pain.

September 5

Up & about, but felt poorly.

September 6

H. H. goes & J. H. comes.[24]

September 7–11

[blank]

September 12

Head still dizzy. No strength. Much discouraged. Life a burden with constant pain & weariness. After my fine taste of health in July it is doubly hard to fall back in this way. A summer of rest would have built me up, but the everlasting home cares spoil it all.

September 13–26

[blank]

September 27

To B[oston]. Bad turn in p.m.

September 28

Rainy dull day. Poorly. Faint till I ate. Dr W[esselhoeft].

September 29

J[ohn]. cashes the $900 check give him 5.00. & Miss H[ubbard]. to use for Lulu 5.00. Better & out. Carriage an hour. 1.50 Haggerty & man for moving us. 16.00 Old Penny from Pa   5.00.

September 30

Miss H[ubbard]. shops for me.

October 1

Pretty well. Out. very hungry. Food not right. Busy. Awake till 1.

October 2

Surprised to feel better. Ate chop & oatmeal. Worked till 11. Lunch & out with L[ulu]. Pay rent. Give A[nna]. $100 for house.

October 3–8

[blank]

October 9

Get J[ohn]. his watch & chain. Much pleased. Good lad. love to make him happy. Mr N[iles]. thinks him very bright & quick. Wrote a notice of Lord Fauntleroy for The Book Buyer. $25.[25] Nap & sun with L[ulu]. in p.m. Dr L[awrence]. in eve.

October 10

Lovely day. Pretty well except headache. Go to drive with Pa & L[ulu].

October 11–14

[blank]

October 15

Pay 2,00 for a month board at Nursery for litle Kanagua boy. Dress $10. Shopping for poor. 5.00.

October 16–19

[blank]

October 20

Dr L[awrence]. Out with A[nna]. & bought a dress. 20.00.

October 21

Out twice. Fine day.

October 22

Sewed in a.m. To Aunty Bond's with L[ulu]. in p.m. Lovely day.

October 23

To dancing school at 9 — 30 with L[ulu]. Errands afterward.

October 24

[blank]

October 25

Pay Miss H[ubbard]. her first quarter $100. $25 paid before but added now to the $75 just paid. Paid up to Jan. 6th. Get rubber bottle & sundries for L[ulu].

October 26–30

[blank]

October 31

Rain. Read Dr Mitchell's book.[26] Not very good. Call on Mrs Burnett. Fix acts. with J[ohn].

November 1

Rain. G. sews. Cough. Pay girls Mrs H[all]. Ask T. N[iles]. for $5,00 for bills &c. Write a little. To see Hamlet. Fine time. Behind the scenes to meet W. Barret.[27]

November 2

Out in a.m. Nap. Pay coal bill. Get boots &c.

November 3

To Concord. Saw to apples & doors. Mrs H. ill. Very tired. Cough bad.

November 4

Cough all night. Out with L[ulu]. Play "Harbor Lights" with F[red]. & J[ohn].[28] Bad head ache & cough. Shopping for L[ulu]. &c.

282

November 5

Up late. For plays 10.00. Pay Sullivan for Oct. 17.00.

November 6

Saw Chatterton.[29] Very fine. Took Miss Hubbard.

November 7

Rested in a.m. Wrote in p.m.

November 8

My dear Lulu's 7th birthday. Kisses early in the a.m. & cuddles on my bed. Then a table full of gifts & a happy day for the precious child. God bless my darling baby.

November 9

Claudian. Splendid.[30]

November 10

Errands. Cough.

November 11

Out a good deal. A. to play.

November 12

Read in a.m. Called on Dr W[esselhoeft]. & paid his bill. A small one. 3.00. He was glad I was so well. In the eve with boys to see Clito.[31] A splendid spectacle. Saw B[arrett]. after it.

November 13

Rainy. Tired. Rested & played with L[ulu]. who was not very well.

November 14–19

[blank]

November 20

Pay Miss King one month to date for little boy at Home in Blossom St. 2.00.[32]

November 21–28

[blank]

283

November 29

Father & my birthday 87 & 54. Quiet day. Gifts. Take care of L[ulu]. Men call on Pa.

November 30–December 1

[blank]

December 2

Cold. Errands & writing in a.m. Wrote in p.m. Fairy tale. Have done three lately, besides two stories & a sketch of self.

December 3

Blizzard. Pain in side. Wrote & kept warm. Jessie to tea.

December 4

Cold & dull. Errands. Wrote on tale, "Ivy". [33]

December 5

Snow storm. Wrote, & took care of L[ulu].

December 6

Dr C. in p.m. [34] So used up with worry in stomach. Fine sunset. Like Rome.

December 7

Storm. H[atty]. in a fuss. Tears & tempest in teapot. Blessed state of things when we can do without strangers in the house! So tired of worrying with nurses, cooks & governesses.

December 8

Lulu all day. Shopping in a.m. Coasting with Emil in p.m. Bed in eve. Dr L[awrence].

December 9

Tired. Wrote up diary &c. Lonely. Calls in p.m.

December 10

Fine. Wrote in a.m. Calls in p.m. Lots to make. Xmas flurry begins.

December 11

[blank]

December 12

Sick all day.

December 13

Poorly. Rain, sewed & moped. Fair in eve.

December 14

Fair. Out at 10 Xmas shopping. & Fair till 1. Nap, H. B. in p.m. Editor of Transcript for a Xmas tale.[35] Got shelves; trunk &c.

December 15–31

[blank]

SOURCE: Manuscript, Houghton Library, Harvard University.

1. "The Blind Lark" appeared in the November 1886 *St. Nicholas*; "A Christmas Turkey, and How It Came" appeared in the 22 December 1885 *Harper's Young People*.

2. Gréville's (pseud. Alice Marie Céleste Durand) *Cleopatra* (1886).

3. Probably Mabel Allen, whom LMA hoped John Pratt would marry (see her letter of 12 February [1888] to Laura Hosmer, in *SL*, p. 336).

4. Before this paragraph, LMA wrote: "Sophy B[ond]. called." and then canceled it.

5. Dion Boucicault's *Jilt* (1885).

6. The reformer Frances Willard explained the social purity question as raising the age-of-consent laws, ensuring that men and women alike were punished for acts of prostitution, and strengthening and enforcing the laws on rape.

7. "When Shall Our Young Women Marry?" appeared in the April 1886 *Brooklyn Magazine*.

8. George Meredith's *Ordeal of Richard Feverel* (1859).

9. Probably Mrs. Harriet Lawrence Hemenway; Denton J. Snider, a St. Louis philosopher who knew Bronson, published *Homer's Iliad: A Commentary* in 1887.

10. Many of the events LMA records in this March entry actually took place in February.

11. Bronson's Temple School had been held in the Masonic Temple.

12. LMA's account book notes that ten dollars was paid in May 1886 to Mary McManus for labor (Houghton Library, Harvard University).

13. Mrs. Hall helped with running the Boston house.

14. Princeton, Massachusetts, where LMA often vacationed.

15. Frederic Henry Hedge's *Hours with German Classics* (1886); Vernon Lee's (pseud. Violet Paget) *Baldwin* (1886).

16. Roberts Brothers printed 10,000 copies of *Jo's Boys* in July and added two 10,000-copy printings in August.

17. Ellen helped LMA in running the Boston house.

18. Alfred Wilkinson, cousin Charlotte's husband, died on 7 July 1886.

19. Julia Ward Howe gave a lecture entitled "Woman in Plato's Republic" at the Concord School of Philosophy's morning session on 29 July.

20. A Canadian publisher had suggested that LMA travel to Canada on the day that her

book was published so she could secure copyright in the British empire (see Dawson Brothers to Roberts Brothers, 29 July 1886, with a postscript from Roberts Brothers to LMA, Houghton Library, Harvard University).

21. There are no more entries in LMA's journal volume for this year, even though she wrote in the heading for August. She did, however, continue to keep her daily diary.

22. Possibly the reformer Aaron Powell, whose name is among a list of addresses at the back of the 1887 diary.

23. LMA said of the bas-relief of her done by Walton Ricketson as the frontispiece for *Jo's Boys* that "Mr R. prefers softness to strength so has missed what I like best, but the old lady looks young & amiable, & as she was ten or fifteen years ago" (letter of 26 December [1885] to Florence Phillips, *SL*, p. 299n).

24. Possibly Hatty Haskell and Julia, who helped LMA in running the Boston house.

25. LMA reviewed *Little Lord Fauntleroy* in the December 1886 *Book Buyer.*

26. J. A. Mitchell's *Romance of the Moon* (1886).

27. Wilson Barrett was performing Shakespeare's plays at the Globe Theatre on 1–3 November.

28. Henry Alfred Pettitt and George Robert Sims's *Harbor Lights* (1886).

29. Henry Arthur Jones and Henry Herman's *Chatterton* (1886).

30. Henry Herman and William Gorman Willis's *Claudian* (1886).

31. Sydney Grundy and Wilson Barrett's *Clito* (1886).

32. Probably either the West End Nursery and Child's Hospital at 37 Blossom Street or the New Day Nursery at 35 Blossom Street.

33. "An Ivy Spray" appeared in the October 1887 *St. Nicholas.*

34. Possibly Dr. Conrad Wesselhoeft.

35. No such work has been located in either the *Boston Evening Transcript* or the *Holiday Transcript.*

1887

January 1

Saint's Rest

A sad & lonely day. Feeble & sick, away from home & worn out with the long struggle for health. Have had many hard days but few harder than this. Say my prayers & try to see many mercies. Fred & his happy love, A[nna]. & her pride in her good boys, Lulu well & good & happy. Father comfortable, & plenty to make all safe & easy. More courage & patience are all *I* ask.

January 2

Sick day. Lay quietly & lived in my mind where I can generally find amusement for myself. Planned Fred's wedding, took Lulu to Boston, & went on with my novel.[1] Dr W[esselhoeft]. came as my head was bad. Said rest, food & time were all I needed. A[nna]. in p.m. Very cold. Rubbed & made cosy & slept all night. Thank God for the blessing of sleep!

January 3

Lay late & forgot my woes in my story. A happy world to go into when the real one is too dull or hard. Tried broth & enjoyed it after much gruel. Set well. Had a nap.

January 4

Bad night. Brain too active, wont stop thinking when I want it to. A[nna]. came with letters from Boston & pleasant news of boys & all. Broth at noon. Set well. Nap in p.m.

January 5

Mild day. Pretty well for me but weak. Lulu & H[atty]. come. L. not well. Needs her "Mother Auntie" to brood over her. Said she cried for me

287

at night. It is very hard to keep away from my baby. L[ouisa]. W[endte?]. called & Dr W[esselhoeft]. Didn't say much but thought me doing well. Nux.[2] Read a little & rested. Tired with seeing people.

January 6

Rested all day. Poorly. Looked at the fine pictures Dr W[esselhoeft]. brought me. Vedder's Persian Poet.[3]

January 7

Drove in town at 10. Air felt lovely. Glad to see my people. L[ulu]. a bad cold. Picked up duds, saw A[nna]. & rested. Home at 3 with S. K. & L[ulu]. Felt better. Had nightmare. Too many [undeciphered] excite me, & any sudden noise startles my poor shattered nerves. Now I know what *fear* is. Never did before. See ghosts, & quake at shadows. Lord keep my wits!

January 8

Cold.[4] Rather poorly. A short walk at noon. Tried to sleep but couldnt. Injection & felt better. Tired & blue.

January 9

very cold. Slept well & felt better.

January 10

Sick & blue. Do nothing but knit, be still, & try to be patient.

January 11

Ditto.

January 12

Ditto.

January 13

Ditto.

January 14

Patience is having her perfect work. Hope she likes the job better than I do.

January 15

Snow. Poorly. Head bad. Dr W[esselhoeft]. came. Laid still all day.

January 16

Fair day. Head rather light. Kept still. Dr L[awrence]. read to me. Bath at night. Slept finely. F[red]. came in a.m. A[nna]. & L[ulu]. in p.m. H[atty]. ill.

January 17

Rain. A quiet day. Ate 3 oysters & they hurt me. Knit a little. Dr L[awrence]. read to me. Letters in eve from A[nna]. & J. B. O'Reilly's four little girls.[5] Slept well.

January 18

Fair. Felt nicely. Wrote to A[nna]. & others. Took a walk.

January 19

Fine. Very cold. Up at 9. Sewed & wrote.

January 20

Good day. Ate geum[6] & cream & they set well. Wrote a little on "Barker", & read some.[7] Head & eyes better.

January 21

Warm. Home for an hour. No trouble but a red cheek in p.m. Got yarn & saw Papa. Drove out with L[ulu]. & H[atty].

January 22

Rested. So little strength everything tires me.

January 23

Warm. Read & wrote. L[ulu] & Miss H[ubbard]. in p.m. Went to walk. Felt nicely. Bath in eve. Supper worried me a little. Geum & cream.

January 24

Rain. Much better. Slept well. Geum & cream for breakfast. Wrote letters, read & knit.

January 25

Not so well. Food wrong. Rode to town & back & did one errand. Rested in p.m. Bath in eve. Stomach bad.

January 26

Snow. Wrote to A[lice]. Warren & Lulu & A[nna]. Took a run. Baked apples for dinner & so go in p.m. Snowstorm. Low in mind. So tired of such a life!

January 27

Food didn't suit. Go back to gruel & wait for the poor worn out stomach to get tone again. No power now to digest solid food or take water. A nice tale!

January 28

Poorly all day. Very blue. Stomach bad. Tried Capsicum[8] & magnesia. Helped some. Read & [i.e., a] little. & sewed.

January 29

Mild. J[ohn]. came with check book &c. Did accounts &[c]. Took a run. A[nna]. in p.m. A pleasant call. Felt better. Bath in eve. Slept well.

January 30

Rain. Dull day. Read, knit, dozed & dawdled. Felt better. Massage in eve & an enema. Good.

January 31

Fine. To town at 10 a.m. House, then with J[ohn]. to Bank & Vault. Drew two checks. $30 for J[ohn]. & 400 for family use. Also two coupons for self $65. Drove back to R[oxbury]. Not tired. Felt better. Bath in eve. Pd Miss J. 20.[9]

February 1

Nothing happened. Pretty well. Stomach better. No solid food but geum. Had my walk.

February 2

Dull day. Head ached. Took a walk. Very cross.

February 3

Wrote a little. Read a little. Knit & lay down. Dull day. L[ulu]. came out. Sent J[ohn]. check for $5000 to invest for himself & F[red].

February 4

Fine. To town & saw A[nna]. & L[ulu]. Got duds. Drove out. Felt very well, & no worse for the trip. Bath in eve. Slept well.

February 5

Wrote a little. Took a run. Read in p.m. Rub at bed time. Did not sleep well. Head full of plans. Going home is too much for my weak head, much as I enjoy it.

February 6

Read & wrote a little. Had a X.[10] No good. Rather dull for want of sleep.

February 7

Fine. To town & did some shopping. Nice day & I felt well. A[nna]. in p.m. Pleasant talk. An X. in eve. Slept well. Pay Miss Joy $20.

February 8

Snow. Read a little & wrote a little. Well but cross. Bath.

February 9

Home in a.m. To T. N[iles]. saw boys. Got books. All well. Did not sleep very well. Planned a play "Boston Balls."[11]

February 10

Fine. Run in a.m. Read & sewed. A[nna]. & L[ulu]. in p.m. Bath in eve. Good. Slept well.

February 11

Rain. Read, sipped for Mrs L[awrence]. Wrote on Play. X in a.m. Good.

February 12

Ate too much gruel. Stomach out of order. H[e]ad dizzy &c. A[nna]. & L[ulu]. & K. M. called. Bath, slept well.

February 13

Head bad. Lay on the sofa all day. Dr L[awrence]. read Whipple to me.

February 14

Poorly. Lulu came with flowers. Dr L[awrence]. read to me. A dull day. Pay Miss J[oy]. $20. Bath.

February 15

Cross & blue. Liver stirred up. Rub.

February 16

Blue. A[nna]. came. Read & dawdled. Bath.

February 17

Lulu & H[atty]. called with Pa in a.m. Took a ride. X. Felt better. But head ached. Mrs L[awrence]. read in p.m. *Rub.* Put on a Liver Pad at night. X.

February 18

Rain. Thunder. Put on Liver pad. *Bath* in eve. Poorly. Head ached. Mrs L[awrence]. read to me & was very kind. L[ulu]. blue & cross.

February 19

Fine. *Job.*[12] Out for a drive at 11. Took a walk. Rested, & sewed on new dress. A[nna]. & L[ulu]. at 4. A pleasant call. Food did not set well all day. *Rub* at night.

February 20

Fine. Slept well. Cross. Read & wrote in a.m. Pain in back of head. *Bath.* Broiled squab for dinner. Only to chew, with geum & cream.

February 21

Miss Joy $20. Job. Cross. Read & sewed. Dr L[awrence]. saw Dr W[esselhoeft]. Got dose for head. Head better. *Rub.* Pigeon *to chew* at dinner with geum. J[ohn]. in eve with book.

February 22

Snow. Woke at 4 a.m. & had porridge. Up early. No hot stuff on liver. Took a little hot lemonade. No trouble. Oysters to chew at 12, & geum.

February 23

Rain. A[nna]. came. Good spin. Walk. Sew, read. *Bath.* Slept well.

February 24

Wind. Giles here. Sewed read. Called on Mrs Reed in p.m. *Rub* at night. Clams at noon. Earthquake in Italy.

February 25

Cold. Did not sleep well. Fussy. Head ache & liver. Sewed & wrote a little.

February 26

Snow. Read & wrote. Dull day.

February 27

Wrote & read. J[ohn]. came out. Head ached. Hot face. Short nap. Bath in eve.

February 28

Fine. Home at 10 a.m. Sat with A[nna]. till 12. Back with H[atty] & L[ulu]. Head ache & hot face. Dont amount to much yet.

March 1–2

[blank]

March 3

To Miss Rose. Very tired. Rested in p.m.

March 4

Read & wrote a little. A[nna]. in p.m.

March 5

Walk in a.m. Wrote letters. A[nna]. in p.m.

March 6

Snow. Headache. Did nothing. Dr read. F[red]. came in p.m. Better in p.m. Sewed a little.

March 7

Miss Joy $20. A[nna]. came out. Read & wrote a little. Pretty well.

March 8

To B[oston]. & got a dress &c. Not tired. Short nap in p.m. Read a little.

March 9

To Miss Rose. Pretty well till p.m. L[ulu]. & H[atty]. came. Note from A[nna]. Worried about C. Too much supper. Heart bumped in eve. Aconite. [13]

March 10

Flutter, feverish & blue. Slept pretty well. Poorly all day. Read, sewed a little, & tried not to think. Book from A[nna]. Wrote to Dr S. & Mr Kallad. [14]

March 11

Fair. Wrote till 11. Walk. Nap. A[nna]. came in p.m. Job. Oysters. Worry. Rub at night. Sleep well.

March 12

Fair. Read till 11. Walk. Nap. Read in p.m. Flutter a little. Beef to chew. Bath.

March 13

A[nna]. & W[alton]. R[icketson]. & F. E. & N in p.m. Rather tried. Pretty well except the flutter. White of egg in a.m.

March 14

Walk, read, sew. A[nna]. & A[nna]. R[icketson]. in p.m. Pleasant call. Flutter, but well otherwise. Chew beef & like it.

March 15

Dr W[esselhoeft]. Bath. Cold. Went to see Dr W[esselhoeft]. in p.m. Glad to see me better. Gave me medicine. Sleep well.

March 16

Rub. Hack to town. A[nna]'s birthday. Up early to greenhouse. Home at 9, with gifts & flowers. Pass a.m. with A[nna]. L[ulu]. & H[atty]. drive out with me. *Flutter better.* Pa in a fuss. Slept well.

March 17

To see *Dr E.* about bunch on neck. [15] Swelling of gland. To try rock salt & white of egg on it. *Dr W[esselhoeft].* called. Said trouble was not catarrh in stomach but nervous. Flutter better. Read. Nap.

March 18–19

[blank]

March 20

J[ohn]. comes. Poorly. Give J[ohn]. 5,00 for Lulu & H[atty]. to go to play.

March 21–22

[blank]

March 23

Poorly. See C. W[esselhoeft]. in p.m. Ordered to go to L. S. Have flutter pills. Cross & blue. Read & rest & sew. $100 to J[ohn]. to get a watch for F[red]. on his birthday.

March 24

Began to inhale C. O. twice a day. Good X in a.m. Felt better till p.m. Went home for an hour. All well. A[nna]. R[icketson].

March 25

Inhale. Bad night. Hot, nervous & blue. *Worry*. Fine day. Good X in a.m. A little better but sore & pains here & there, left as well as right.

March 26

Lucy. All night. A[nna]. in p.m. Read. To town.

March 27

Read Balsac.[16] J[ohn]. & L[ulu]. came. Wrote on "Bud" new tale for L.[17] Flax seed.

March 28

[blank]

March 29

Home to B[oston]. took food & stayed till 3 p.m. Looked over L[ulu]'s duds. Saw A[nna]. & boys. Back all right. Not very tired. Much stronger. Bath & flax seed.

March 30

Cold. At home. Wrote arti[c]le on The Ballet & read. Signed lease of Mrs M's furniture for a year.[18] Flax seed.

March 31

To town in a.m. Saw T. N[iles]. & boys. Got books $3,87 at Cupples.[19] A[nna]. & L[ulu]. in p.m. Read "Looking Glass." Very good. Bath. Flaxseed. Wrote E. P. R. Article came out.

April 1

Dr W[esselhoeft]. All well. Read new books. Wrote article about self for Advertizer man. Mon. Rub & Flaxseed. Oil bath & forment in a.m. Met M. Peabody & Helen B. Snow. A little sprite. X.

April 2

Great Snow. Wrote "Sofa Society" & Nile Bride.[20] Very good. Oil bath in a.m. Slept well.

April 3

Fine. Wrote in a.m. Read "Type". A[nna]. & L[ulu]. in p.m. Rode in with them. Late home. Slept well. Bread at dinner. 5 checks to A[nna]. & a coupon.

April 4

Fine. Wrote letters. To town at 11. Shopping. Dress &c. Felt well. Oil bath. Slept well. Pay Miss J[oy]. Chop.

April 5

Weighed — 143. One pd less than a month ago. But am much better. Sleeping well, eat bread & butter, some meat, & take water. Hooray! Cut out my dress, took a walk. Headache discharged & felt better.

April 6

Wrote & sewed. L[ulu]. & H[atty]. H. in a fuss for L. is saucy. Needs more freedom & she shall have it. A fine active girl shut up too much with quiddly old people. I know how she feels.

April 7

Wrote in a.m. Cut out wrapper. A[nna]. to M[elrose]. to see house. Fast Day. With Miss Mary [Joy] to hear the Baboo Mohini at Mr Hale's church.[21] Very good on Brotherhood.

April 8

Wrote & sewed in a.m. To look at rugs & shop in p.m. Lovely day. Felt well & enjoyed my trip. Bath of soap & water, compress & gruel. Slept well.

April 9

L[aura]. H[osmer]. called. Home early for the day with my [undeciphered]. Talk with A[nna]. & plan to see M[elrose]. house. Mrs B[ond?]. comes & we dont go. Mrs P. A[nna]. R[icketson]. & K. M. call. Rest, get papers & talk with L[ulu]. Poor dear in woe with her little faults. Home at 5.

April 10

Easter Sunday. Lovely day. Wanted to go to King's Chapel but was too tired. Wrote. Slept well.

April 11–13

[blank]

April 14

Sewed in a.m. Home to dinner. Made calls on E[lizabeth] W[ells?]. Mrs Underhill & Mrs Wadsworth. Cates & costumes. Home late. Rub.

April 15

Read in a.m. Kinners in p.m. Bath in eve.

April 16

Rain. Home all day resting. Read & sewed. A run for a book. X in eve. A good clearing out. Sleep late.

April 17

Fine. Read Chunder.[22]

April 18

Snow. Home. Check for 500. Pay Miss Joy $20. Get dividend 94. Dine at home. L[ulu]. hurt. Bath. Miss H[ubbard]. goes for 2 week[s]. Eva comes. Drove home at 4 p.m. 4 months today since I came. Oh me!

April 19

Fine. Slept well. Stiff in leg. Water acid. Sewed.

April 20

Fine. To town & home. Got L[ulu]. hat &c. Very tired. Head dizzy & queer. Bath. Did not sleep as well as usual. Scared feeling. Said good bye to L[ouisa]. W[endte?].

April 21

Fine. Wrote on "Virginia", & sewed in a.m.²³ Cleared up. L[ulu]. in p.m. Wrote letters. Head better. Took Dr W[esselhoeft].s stuff for flutter. L[ouisa]. W[endte?]. & R's sailed.

April 22

Fine. Poorly. Lay down & knit & read a little. Ate only my gruel. Soured of course. Solid food would have done better. No one came. A bad day. Not sick but blue & cross. So tired! Bath in eve.

April 23

Cloudy. Slept well. Head heavy. Geum. Knit & looked over tale for Harper.²⁴

April 24

Sent tale to "Young People" by J[ohn]. who came out in p.m. from Melrose where he & A[nna]. had been. Liked the new house. All looks well. Wrote on a new tale "Polly's Pious Wooing."²⁵ Read Mrs Camerons book on Work women. Very good.

April 25

Fine. Home at 11. Shopped & got sash &c. for self, & a dress for Lulu. Trimmed her hat. Got duds, & at 2½ drove to R[oxbury]. with Pa. Well all day. Letter from Miss. N. of England about book for the blind. Rub, good night.

April 26

Rain. Up early. Felt well. Wrote a little on "Anna" as I felt like it.²⁶ Head full of stories. Several ordered. $100 for one column in Ladies Home Journal.²⁷ Sew on dress.

April 27

Home at 11. Shop by the way. Plans & see to L[ulu]'s things. Dine at home. A[nna]. & L[ulu]. go back with me. Felt strong & well. Universal Food stays by better than the other. Bath & Flaxseed.

April 28

To B[oston]. with coat. Home at 10½. Read & rested. Sewed. Rain.

April 29

[blank]

April 30

Home at 9. Sewed for L[ulu]. fixed duds. Rested. Drove out at 4. Tired but none the worse. Rub & bed.

May 1

Wrote on article for Womans Mag $100 for one column.[28] A[nna]. & L[ulu]. came in a.m. Rode in with them. J[ohn]. & Pa came in p.m. Well but sleepy.

May 2

Weighed 145. Gained 2 pd since April 4th. Very well for porridge & geum. L[ulu]. came out with flowers. Took some in to L. S. Errands & rest in p.m. Rub & bed at 9.

May 3

Kitty killed. Home at 11. L[ulu]. & H[atty]. came out to R[oxbury].

May 4

Read in a.m. & sewed. Drive in p.m. with L[ulu]. & H[atty]. Rub. Headache.[29]

May 5

Wrote on Ivy in a.m. & went out with L[ulu].[30] L[ulu]. & A[nna]. to B[oston]. in p.m., sewed & read. Bath in eve.

May 6

To Concord at 10. Got clothes at house with A[nna]. Saw L[aura]. H[osmer]. & home at 4. Bore the trip very well. Glad & surprised to be so strong. Cars[,] tired head but otherwise not much fatigued.

May 7

Rested & wrote on "Ivy". Read a little. Took a run in p.m. L[ulu]. to dancing school. Very good. Pleasant to have her. T. N[iles]. wants to reissue M. M. with name.[31] Say, yes.

May 8–9

　[blank]

May 10

　Home. Hot & tired, packed & fussed.

May 11

　Home to pack & fix. Shop with A[nna]. Home in p.m. Felt strong & well. Rub. Slept till 6½.

May 12

　Sewed, finished the Pansy tale, & read "A Week From Time."[32] Poor. L[ulu]. & H[atty]. a fuss. Row in eve. Bad night. Flutter & sleeplessness. Bath.

May 13

　Mrs Giles sews. Hard day, sewing & taking care of L[ulu]. H[atty]. struck work, & was very foolish & rude. Bad temper & pride hurt. Cant whip L. & drive her.

May 14

　Home at 11. L[ulu]. to dance in p.m. Too shaky to go to the theatre as I hoped. A[nna]. went. Rested & home at 4. Cold. Saw Miss Rose.

May 15

　Head bad with a cold & ear ache. L[ulu]. & H[atty]. to church & a ride. On the sofa all day. Bath & slept well.

May 16

　Head better. Keep quiet. L[ulu]. & H[atty]. to town. Write to A[nna]. Finish Pansy & Ivy tales. Miss Joy $38.

May 17

　[blank]

May 18

　Sick.

May 19

　Sick.

May 20

Sick.

May 21

Sick. H[atty]. & L[ulu]. to M[elrose]. for Sunday. Glad to have two cares gone.

May 22

Sick. John came. Glad to see my boy.

May 23

Sick.

May 24

Better a little. Faint & weak. Bad turn in bath. Take Murdock & feel better.[33] Slept pretty well. Rain. Glad. L[ulu]. & H[atty]. at eve.

May 25

Stronger but still flutter & weak. Murdock & gruel. L[ulu]. & H[atty]. go in town. *Hack.* Pack up for M[elrose]. Must have quiet. Sorry! My one joy must go.

May 26

Get L[ulu]. & H[atty]. off with much fuss. Worn out. Bad time. H[atty]. stupid!

May 27

Rest.

May 28

Rain. Sew a little, write letters & read "Katia" by Tolstoi.[34] Dull day. No head ache. Bath at night. Dont sleep well. J[ohn]. comes with book. Glad to see him.

May 29

Better but feeble. Read Meredith & write to Plummer.[35]

May 30

Fine. Coupe. Pretty well. Drove to Miss K. & tried dress. Had a nap. Read a little, & knit. Walked a short way in p.m. Air did me good. *Bath.*

May 31

Knit. Dr read to me. Out a short way. Very weak. Rub at night. Slept well.

June 1

Rain. Bad day. Lay down. Dr L[awrence]. read to me. Dr W[esselhoeft]. in p.m. gave me something to strengthen stomach. *Bath.* Nightmare & bad night.

June 2

Rain a.m. Feeble. Geum hurt me. Brandy & hop tea. Lie all a.m. Two letters from A[nna]. Write a line to her. Send 42 00 for house bills &c.

June 3

Rain. Wrote a little. Weak & sad. Dr read. Bath. Hack late, so no ride. Good day.

June 4

Ride in town with Miss J[oy]. see T. N[iles]. & Boys. H[atty]. comes in a.m. Hack. Headache at night. Rub. Dream & dont sleep well. Much water. Dr W[esselhoeft].

June 5

Coupe 1 hour. Cold & dull. Bad head ache. Wrote a little. Dr read. Wrote to A[nna]. & L[ulu]. & Mrs Dodge. Bath & Clom.[36] felt better at night.

June 6

Weighed 140. Lots of letters. Good day. Slept without dreams from 9 to 6. Ride in car a.m. & p.m. Felt better for it. Geum & bath at noon. Beef Ex. & Clomonilla. No head ache. Rub.

June 7

Answered letters. A[nna]. Mrs C. L[aura]. H[osmer]. J[ohn]. P[ratt]. & T. N[iles]. $10 to the Fresh Air Fund.

June 8

Cool. To B[oston]. at 10½. Met A[nna]. got dresses. Poorly in a.m. Better in p.m. Dr read. Sewed. Gruel all day & beef juice.

302

Pay Miss J[oy]. 3 week[s]	60.00
Dr L[awrence].	10.00
Con. of Music for \87	2.00

June 9

Hot. Got up dizzy. Took a ride but run made head ache. Better in p.m. Dr read. sewed & cleaned up. People kept me awake. Fair night. K. M. called.

June 10

Cool. Woke feeling well. Ate geum, took a ride at 8 & did errands. Fine day, air lovely. Felt much better. Sewed & wrote letters.

June 11

To B[oston]. at 10½. Met A[nna]. & packed trunk. Home at 12½. Not very tired. Rested. Sewed & read. Dr W[esselhoeft]. gave me cubes[?] for pain in side.

June 12

Move up stairs. Glad to be more private.

June 13

Good day. Run in a.m. Wrote, read & sewed. Bath. good sleep all night. Bowels moved right.

June 14

Run in a.m. Sewed, read, wrote a little. Felt well. Jessies birthday. Sent a ring.

June 15

Run & errands at 8. Sewed. A[nna]. at 1 — sat till 3. Rather tired but glad to see the old dear. Slept well.

June 16

To B[oston]. shopping. Good ride. Rested till dinner. Read & wrote in p.m. Letters. *Bath.*

June 17

Sewed & read. *Rub.*

June 18

Read & sewed & fussed over duds. *Bath.*

June 19

Quiet day. Read & wrote. A walk at eve. Pretty well. Raisins dont suit. Wind & pain in side. *Rub.*

June 20

To town in a.m. did errands. L[ulu]. & A[nna]. in p.m. *nice call.* L. sweet & A. *dear* as ever. Sorry to have em go. *Good bath.* Slept well.

June 21

Town in a.m. Saw T. N[iles]. Took "Pansies." New idea about adopting John to secure copyrights.[37] Love to do it. Tired in p.m. Took a run. Bath. A little head ache. Rub.

June 22

Hot, foggy a.m. Read paper about Jubilee. Wrote an hour. Sewed.

June 23

[blank]

June 24

John's birthday. Give him $100. Pack & rest.

June 25

Pack & rest in a.m. To C[oncord]. at 3. Good trip. Go to Mrs Wheeler's.[38] Rest & bed. Good night. Glad to be on the way to the hills, "whence cometh strength".

June 26

Woke at 5. Took a walk after [undeciphered]. To old house. Saw L[ulu?]. Rested all p.m. L[ulu?]. called. J[ohn?]. came.

June 27

Up early. Felt well. To old house & looked over papers till 10. Home to rest & read till 3½ when H[enry]. H[osmer]. took us [on] a nice drive. H. B. in eve. Judge B. with papers to adopt John.[39]

June 28

Up at 7. felt well. Lovely day. To old house at 10. Wrote letters. Drove with L[aura]. H[osmer]. Very tired. Good rub. Slept well & dreamed of my Lulu.

June 29

Hot. Felt better. To house early. A[nna]. at 10 with five roses. Talked & made a sheet. Rested. A[nna]. to house. Letter from L[ouisa]. W[endte?]. & Mrs Dodge. Wrote to Lulu.

June 30

Very Hot. Bad day. Tried to go & couldn't get an answer to my message. Hot night. Packed for P[rinceton]. Rub & slept well.

July 1

Rested, very hot. Off at 12. for P[rinceton]. Hot journey, waited for carriage at W. Long drive, but cool air revived us. Good rooms. Arrived at 5 p.m. Bath & bed. Slept well.

July 2

Settled. Wrote letters, read, & sewed a little. Shower in p.m. Mrs L. to P[rinceton]. shopping. Feel well. Head steady & food no trouble. Letter from & to A[nna]. Carriage & Express.

July 3

Quiet day. Read & wrote. Walked. Cool.

July 4

Gay day. Read & sewed. Letter from A[nna].

July 5

Cool, walk early & feel well. Write on "Lilies".[40] Rain in p.m. Write to A[nna].

July 6

Rain all day. Finish Lilies. Sew & Mr L reads to me. Dull day. Letter from A[nna].

July 7

Fine. Early walk. Begin "Mignonette."[41] Write to A[nna]. & J[ohn]. & H[enry]. H[osmer]. Rather poorly. Need food but cant eat it. Color in face.

July 8

Wake dizzy. Very mad. Kept still all day, hot & feeble. Dr read. Took Nux. Rub & hot water at night. Slept well. Letters from A[nna].

July 9

A little better. Kept still. Dr read to me. Sad & lonely day. John & Emily came at 6 p.m.[42] H[enry]. B[ullard]. & Mr L. at 9. Slept well. Proof &c. Letters from home.

July 10

Head better. Got up & dressed. Signed Will & adoption papers. Helen B. & Mr Shepherd & Mrs L. witnessed.[43] Rested & read. Very tired. Head dizzy.

July 11

Woke at 4. Got J[ohn]. off at 5 a.m. Laid late. Head steady. Dr read. Lay down a good deal, & did nothing but knit a little. H[elen]. B[lanchard]. went in p.m. Rain.

July 12

Kept quiet & did not try to do any thing. No spirits or strength. Hope & patience seem in vain.

July 13

Lonely day, felt pretty well again. Lay on the hay in a.m. & p.m. Wrote to Pa & Lulu. Sewed. Nightmare.

July 14

Cool. Lie out till 10. Head queer. Lie down. Write to A[nna] & Bok.[44]

July 15

A little better. Too much meat juice. Head ache but felt stronger. Sew & read. Letters.

July 16

A dull day. Read & sewed & wrote letters. Sad & feeble. No staying up long. So I dont hope much.

July 17

Foggy. Reading, Pretty well, wrote a little on "Poppies".[45] Begun it. Read & sewed. Alone all day. Run at a.m. & eve. In parlor an hour. Slept well.

July 18

Rainy. A good day. Busy & happy. Wrote 10 pages, sewed & read. Felt stronger, but dont feel right yet in' stomach. Run at eve in fog. Girls came. Sitz bath.

July 19

Fine. Wrote to L[aura]. H[osmer]. Slept well. Blue when I woke. Had breakfast & a walk. Cool & clear. Wrote 3 pages & gave up for fear of a headache. Read a little & sewed.

July 20

Poorly. Sew a little & read a few pages. Shut in on all sides by infirmities. Small dark world to live in after so much freedom & strength all these years. Ah me!

July 21

Poorly. Sew & read.

July 22

Poorly. Sew & Dr reads.

July 23

Rain all day. Sew a little. Dr read. J[ohn]. came at eve. Head light. Rain in night.

July 24

Rain. Wrote on Poppies. Read a little. Saw J[ohn]. Dr read.

July 25

Fine. J[ohn]. went at 6 a.m. Felt well. Wrote, sat on porch, read, nap, & walk. Wind. Began Phosphites.

July 26

Brash.[46] Wrote some & sewed.

July 27

Hot. Sewed. Did not write. Got a room for J[ohn]. Also bill $11,45. Short drive. "Sir Peter" in eve. Slept well.

July 28

Brash. Early walk. talk with T & on piazza. Very pleased to be among people again. Wrote to A[nna]. Lovely cool day.

July 29

Sewed, wrote a little & read. Pretty well. Hot day. Drove with E. [Shepard].

July 30

Good day. J[ohn]. at 6. with box of letters books & s'prises from my dear A[nna]. & L[ulu]. So glad to get my boy cool. Mr M. read "Morlett" in eve.[47] Lay awake. So fine!

July 31

Hot. Read & wrote letters. Felt well. Drove with E[mily]. Nap in p.m. Enjoy my boy. Reading at Hotel in eve. Sit & talk & enjoy it. Pay Mrs L[awrence]. $50.

August 1

Cool. Up early. *Felt well.* Walked *a mile.* Got berries & saw Monadnoch. Wrote a little. New month begins well. May it end so!

August 2

Cool. Wrote in a.m. Drove in p.m. Talk with Mr M[urdoch]. in tent. Wrote to A[nna]. Good letters from home. J[ohn]. happy & well.

August 3

Fish dinner for J[ohn]. Good time 8 went. I was at home resting. $6,00. Walked & read & sewed. Head not right. Tired, so keep still. Peaches from F[red].

August 4

Cool. Poorly. Head ached & stomach bad. Lay down & Dr read to me. Nux. Better in p.m. Made birch baskets. read & drove to P[rinceton]. Walk in eve, saw [undeciphered], early to bed. Stomach bad. 136 pds.

August 5

Cool. Better. No brash in a.m. Ate geum, gluten & broth. Stomach quieter. J[ohn]. to L. Girls from C[oncord]. in p.m. (Peachs Miss J[oy].) Lost 4 pds last month. But feel better.

August 6–7

[blank]

August 8

J[ohn]. home better.

August 9

Stomach bad.

August 10

[blank]

August 11

Talk & sew with E[mily]. Sensible sweet girl. Fresh & unspoiled.

August 12

E[mily]. & Mrs F. to C[oncord].[48] Quiet day.

August 13

J[ohn] came up for Sunday. Rested.

August 14

Quiet day. J[ohn]. off to B[oston]. in p.m.

August 15

Fine day, dressed room for Jessie. She & F[red]. came at 3. Happy souls! young *well* & in love. Try to make a pleasant visit for them.

August 16

[blank]

August 17

Talk with J[essica]. Fine girl. Fred is lucky to find so sweet & sensible a mate. "God bless em!" says old Aunty.

309

August 18–19

[blank]

August 20

F[red]. & J[essica]. went at 7 a.m. Had a good time. All went well & both felt better. Rested. J[ohn]. came at night to hotel. Pa M[urdoch]. read at P[rinceton]. Dance at hotel. Looked a bit & to bed.

August 21

Rested, wrote & read. J[ohn]. & E[mily]. drove. Pretty well, all *but legs*. Very spotty & stiff. Dr fears an abcess. I dont care. No brash.

August 22

Rain. Dull day. Sewed, read, picked up duds. Games in eve. Legs queer & stiff & blue. Sleep well. No gas or brash.

August 23

Rain & fog. Read & sewed & packed. Games in eve. Back & legs queer. Sleep well. No gas. Brash at eve.

August 24

Fog, cold & dull. Write to A[nna]. & quiddle about. Tired of P[rinceton].

August 25

Pack up & decide to go home. Fine day. Walk. Pa M[urdoch]. reads in eve. All very kind. Sleep well.

August 26

Home. Tiresome journey. Rest in p.m. Sleep well.

August 27

Rest. A[nna]. & L[ulu]. came. Good time. Order furniture. Sleep & read in p.m. *Bath* at night.

August 28

Go to M[elrose]. & see my dear people. [49] A very pleasant home. All well. Pa feeble but happy. L[ulu]. rosy & restless. A[nna]. sweet & tired. Sewall's very kind. C's come. Home *very* tired. Slept like a log.

August 29

Rested well & feel all right except legs very stiff & back lame. To corner in car & got a table &c. Furniture came. Dr E[stabrook]. came. Says take baths & pine water for kidneys, & poor blood. Raw meat also. *Bath.*

August 30

Very stiff. Lump under knee. Cross & blue. Read. To No 10 in p.m. & get table. Hack. Back very bad. Lie down in p.m. Begin Nitre for kidneys.[50] *Bath.* Sleep well.

August 31

Very lame, back bad. Take Nitre, water better. Eat a mouthful of raw beef at 9. Read & sew. Very blue & cross. Dr E[stabrook]. hopeful. Try Nitre, beef, pine & milk, eggs & oysters. All a mistake.

September 1

Bath. A[nna]. came in a.m. Dear soul so anxious & loving. She did me good. Sent my things. Dr W[esselhoeft]. very kind but not encouraging. On this day Sept 1st I make a prophesy. The end is not far off. The Drs see it, & I feel it. Amen.

September 2

Too lame to get up in a.m. Lie & read. Letters from A[nna]. & L. S. Mrs G[ardner]. comes, engage her as nurse, too helpless now to be left alone. Dr L[awrence]. to a clairvoyant. A wonderfully true report. "Enlarged spleen, torpid liver, tired brain, worn out stomach, bad legs. Trouble humor all over." Just what the Dr says.

September 3

A[nna]. came & spent the day. Did me good. Dr W[esselhoeft]. said "Eat or die." So I eat & suffer. Might as well die. Mrs G[ardner]. began. Bed came, moved in. Mrs G. to nurse me. F[red]. in eve. Very tired. Bad night. Bath, pine pack.

September 4

Tired, food worried me. Read, wrote to A[nna]. & E[mily]. S[hepard]. Lay down to rest in a.m. John & F[red]. & J[essica]. came in p.m. Sweet to see youth *health* love & happiness! Did me good.

375 to Morse rent.[51] (100 to A[nna]. coal.) Bath, & pine pack, legs.

September 5

Fine. Slept well. 2 geum, egg — meat & onion, rennet[52] egg, gruel, meat gruel. Leg a little better. Packed in p.m. legs cold. Read & knit & sewed. *Bath.*

September 6

Bath. Poorly every way all day. Stomach in torment with nerves, legs very sore, spirits all gone. A hard hard day. A[nna]. & L[ulu]. came with flowers. E[mily]. & J[ohn]. also. All kind & sweet. Bad time in bath. Slept better. Worn out.

September 7

Lived on gruel to rest. Rennet once nothing else. Much easier, tho very blue & weak & stomach worried. So tired! A[nna]. to C[oncord]. I hope.

September 8

Dr E[stabrook]. & Dr G[reen]. came & looked me over. Starved nerves & poor blood. Liquid food & malt &c. every 2 hours. Liked Dr G. Brain all right but starved like the rest. Baths, packs of pine for legs which are doing well. Hope it is a wise move. Dismiss Dr W[esselhoeft]. Too slow & behind in methods. No time to lose. Suspect he thinks no help possible. So do I, but for A[nna]'s sake will try anything. *Furniture* came $6,00. Begin thin gruel & malt & Nux. Sets pretty well. Bath.

September 9

Bad day. Head ache. Gas & leg stiff. Wrong stuff. Bath. Try Lobelia for leg at night.[53]

September 10

Head better. Wrote & read. A[nna]. came in p.m. Gas at night. Try Lobelia for legs. Sleep well & stew. Bath.

September 11

Bath. Very feeble. Cramp. Dizzy & queer. Able to do nothing, but lie still & wait for help. Wake in night with the Malt worrying me. Food set well, 3 hours.

September 12

Kept in bed all day [due] to some pain in leg. Packed it with lobelia. Read, wrote knit & got on well. Head better. Stomach a little riled.

September 13

Bad day. Malt upset stomach in night. A[nna]. & L[ulu]. Legs too painful to sit up. In bed all day. Very hard time in bath with cramp. Woke often with back & worry. Dr G[reen]. Bath. Try sitz.

September 14

Rainy. In bed, read proof & tried to rush along. Back sore, legs stiff, head dizzy. Lonely & sad. Dr G[reen]. came. Like him. Pulse better. Legs also. Phosphites & Gel.[54] No bath for a time.

September 15

Slept well. Rub in a.m. & pack legs. Dr G[reen]. all doing well. Good movement. Ly. acting on liver. Felt better. No head ache. Take Gel. knit & keep quiet. 2 Rubs. Slept badly.

September 16

In spite of a wakeful night felt nicely in a.m. Note from Miss N.[55] Go in parlor to see A. Spirits good. A ray of hope! A[nna]. in p.m. & Jess with roses. A good day. Did not sleep very well. 2 rubs.

September 17

Felt pretty well. Fine day. Try to be happy. Ought to be with so much love & care. Wrote letters, knit, & lay on couch. Head in p.m. Dr came. All well *he says*. Rub. sleep pretty well.

September 18

Wake cross. Rub &c. Stay in bed all a.m. Nap. Head dont ache till late in p.m. Read a few minutes, knit, lie still & try to see *why* things are so hard. F[red]. calls, dear lad. Rub & bed.

September 19

Fine. Little sleep. Cross as a bear. Head in a snarl. Gas. Rub &c. Try to sleep. A[nna]. & L[ouisa]. in p.m. Very tired. Bath & bed. Slept well. Dr G[reen]. Bath.

September 20

Fine. *Try beef.* Felt better. Wrote letters, read a little, knit & sat up on couch. "L's L." came.[56] Pretty. J[ohn]. came in eve with flowers & books. Dear lad! Bath. Slept well.

313

September 21

Dr G[reen]. Pretty well. Dr said all going right. Read & sewed & wrote letters. Nap. Wedding in C[oncord].[57] A[nna]. & L[ulu]. & boys went. Bath. Slept pretty well.

September 22

Rain. Good day. No head ache. read sewed had a nap, & got on pretty well. Dull day, but not as long as usual. No pain anywhere only weak & tired & leg stiff. Bath.

September 23

Fair. Good day. Slept well, woke feeling pretty amiable. Rub. Read & knit & write letters. Take oyster juice. Set well. Chair came. Bath.

September 24

Dr G[reen]. Pretty well. Dr not coming till sent for. 7 calls, $21. Glad. Read, wrote to A[nna]. & T. N[iles].

September 25

Dr G[reen]. No call. Up late. Pretty well but blue. Read Atlantic & wrote to A[nna]. J[essica]. at noon with pictures. Comfortable day, read & knit. Bath.

September 26

Slept till 5 a.m. Pretty well. Read & wrote letters. Sewed & knit. Dr read. Bath. Slept well.

September 27

Good day. Ate 5 oysters. No trouble. Tried Pepsin. Very nasty, made me ill. Read & sewed wrote letters. F[red]. in eve, books. Bath.

September 28

Slept well. Read, sewed & wrote letters. Dr read to me. Letters from A[nna]. Mrs G[ardner]. Bath.

September 29

Rain. Slept pretty well. Wrote A[nna]. read & sewed. Dull day. Old lady failing next door to me. Letters.

September 30

Dull day. Pretty well. Fixed papers & sewed. Sent E. E.s book.[58] Dr G[reen]. called on me. Legs doing *very* well. Change in food Gluten, & in the *taking* of Laptondrin.[59] Bath.

October 1

Dull. Fuss with enema. Slept pretty well. Sew, cut out a nightgown. Write to A[nna]. Wont come in today I fear. Letter from A[nna]. Oxygen came & a bill for chair $23. Two rubs. Bath.

October 2

Pretty well. Read, wrote. J[ohn]. came. "Dean's Daughter."[60]

Pay Miss Joy	$122.50
Dr L[awrence].	$33.73
Mrs G[iles].	60.00
J[ohn?]. for Ropes	30.00
Keeler	60.50
	306.63[61]

Chew steak. Rub & bath.

October 3

Pretty good day. Steak, beef, egg, gruel. Sew read write. Bath & rub.

October 4

Fair day. Mrs E. died.[62] E[mily]. S[hepard]. called. Read & sewed. Sent flour &c. to poor. Mrs D[aniels]. by G[iles]. $10. Cant eat myself so take comfort in feeding those who can.

October 5

Fair. Cross. Read too much. Wrote letters & sewed. A[nna]. at 5. dear soul! So good to see her again. *Bath* & rub. Brash & worry.

October 6

Dr G[reen]. Slept pretty well. No medicine. *Dr G.* changed things. Very pleasant & kind. Felt better. Legs better. Read & wrote letters, knit & sewed. *Bath* & *rub.*

October 7

Bad day. Head & stomach upset by medicine. Lie still & am blue. J[ohn]. came for a visit with cards. Bath & rub.

October 8

Dear Marmee's birthday. Wish I could take her flowers & red leaves as usual. No! A[nna]. & L[ulu]. came. E[mily]. S[hepard]. with flowers. Quiet day, read & sewed. Bath & rub.

October 9

No medicine & food set well. Wrote to L[ulu]. & French people. Read & rested. J[ohn]. came for an hour with letters &c. began R. W. E[merson].[63] So good! Food worried at night & head ached. *Bath & rub.*

October 10

A better day. Took Kis[64] & Phos. Read, sewed & wrote one letter. Nap before dinner. Tried to stand on crutches. Too weak. May try magnetism. Dr E[stabrook]. called. Queer old man. *Bath.* Pretty good day. Slept well.

October 11

Rain. Finished night dress. Wrote on "Trudel"[65] & read R. W. E. Head ached. Put away pen. Cant work yet. Read R. W. E. enjoy it *much*. Bath & rub.

October 12

Good day. Felt pretty well. Sewed read, played Solitaire. Jessie came with roses. Murdoch sisters made a pleasant call. Read R. W. E. lovely life! Bath & rub.

October 13

Fine. Note from A[nna]. Read R. W. E. A[nna]. coming with L[ulu]. in p.m. Dr G[reen]. A[nna]. & L[ulu]. John in eve with Jess & book. A good day. Bath & Rub.

October 14

Very well in a.m. Tired in p.m. Read, knit & wrote 3 letters. Miss N[ewman]. mind cure for me. Sent Mrs D[aniels]. meat &c. $1,00. B[ath] & R[ub].

October 15

Mrs G[ardner]. paid to today. Bowels *natural*. Pretty well. Read, knit & write ½ an hour. A[nna]. & L[ulu]. to C[oncord]. Bath & rub.

October 16

Quiet day. Better. Bath &c.

October 17

Comfortable. B[ath]. & R[ub].

October 18

Good day. B[ath] & R[ub].

October 19

Good day. B[ath] & R[ub].

October 20

Dr came. All going well. Try Milk & pancreative. B[ath] & R[ub].

October 21

Rainy quiet day. No worry. Trim sash & read. Write to A[nna]. Try the Milk & it sets well. Good job. Head ache in p.m. Bath & rub.

October 22

Fine. Pretty well. Go on with milk twice a day. Write to A[nna]. L[ulu]. & F. E. came.

October 23

Went to drive to please Dr L[awrence], & had a bad time. Back in agony & legs too. No use. Done up in half an hour. To bed at once. Sick & cross.

October 24

Sick & blue. Back very lame & legs worse.

October 25

Poorly.

October 26

Poorly.

October 27

Dr G[reen]. in a.m. Doing well but slowly. Egg troubled me. Lulu in p.m. Very good. Read & sewed. Not very well.

October 28

Read & sewed. A[nna] in p.m. Poorly. Legs stiff & bad.

October 29

Read & sewed. Dull day. Slept better. Good *clearing up*.

October 30

Last day of my two sad hard months. Hope the next will go better. J[ohn]. came with lease of No 10. Write to Mr R[opes]. about it. Bath &c.

October 31

Pretty well. Sew & write. *Dr W[esselhoeft]. calls.* A[nna]. to C[oncord]. Fix things for L[ulu]. Who comes in pm. Lovely & gay. Bath &c.

November 1

Good day. Sew & read. A[nna]. in p.m. Dr G[reen]. Says all goes well. Try tincture of Lobelia on legs. No gruel at bed time. Slept well. Bath &c.

November 2

Good day. Sew, read & write letters. No calls. Stomach bad in eve. No gruel at bed time. Bath, & rub.

November 3

Vacation. Sewed & read. J[ohn]. in eve with papers &c. Miss M. called. No bath &c.

November 4

Wrote to Ropes & M[orse?]. A[nna]. came. Nap. dressed dolls for L[ulu]. Stomach bad. Slept well. Bath & rub.

November 5–7

[blank]

November 8

Lulu's birthday 8 years old. Sent note & love. The dear had many gifts & a fine time. Emile & fun in eve. Hard not to go to my baby!

November 9

Sewed & read. A[nna]. in p.m. Stomach bad, New Phosphites dont suit at all. Bad night. A[nna]. in p.m. Last time for [blank].

November 10

Restless night. Stomach bad. Took Nux. Sewed & read. Mrs G[ardner] goes to see Dr G[reen]. Get orders. Nux, less food & rest. Fred in eve.

November 11

Better but tired. So write a little on "Trudel" & then knit & rest.

November 12

Dizzy in a.m. Dr G[reen]. Abed all day. Done too much. Lulu, Laura & E[mily]. S[hepard]. No bath.

November 13

Sick, in bed. Cross & blue. Head dizzy & stomach bad. Oh dear.

November 14

Bad day. Head ache & sad. Weak & disappointed. Legs better. Stand up, walk a few steps. K. M. Bath.

November 15

Dr G[reen]. Headache & blue. Do nothing.

November 16

Poorly. Lie & rest. Dr reads to me.

November 17

Dr G[reen]. No change except Phosphites again. Knit & Dr reads to me. Weak but stomach better. Go back to Bartlett's Food.

November 18

Better.[66] Head light but tum quiet. Read Mr W.s Mss. Poorly in p.m.

November 19

Better day. Read & sew.

November 20

Dr G[reen]. Better, food sets well & head aches less. Read Pundita Ramahai. Very interesting! Must do a tale for St N.

November 21

Fair. X. Begin milk for Mrs Daniels. Good day. Wrote 5 letters to P[rinceton]. & M[elrose]. Read & sewed. No bath.

November 22–23

[blank]

November 24

Thanksgiving. Alone in my room. A cloudy sad day. Tried to think of my blessings & be grateful. Flowers & kind notes from A[nna].

November 25

Better. Sew & knit but no hard work. Long day. Several letters from my girls.

November 26

Good day. Made skirt for poor Mrs D[aniels?]. Read a bit in Crawford's book.[67] Wrote to A[nna]. Dr G[reen]. came & was very hopeful & kind. Thanked the Lord & went to bed cheerful.

November 27

John's death. Sent lilies to dear A[nna]. Read & wrote.

November 28

Rainy. Quiet. A[nna]. R[icketson]. & L[ulu]. came with some of the birthday. Pay G[reen]. $40.

November 29

Father's & my day.[68] No one but L[ulu]. came. Loads of gift[s] & good wishes. 40 gifts. A good day. Grateful for all my dear friends & their love. 6 boxes of flowers 2 baskets & 3 plants.

November 30

Fine. Pretty well. Kept still & enjoyed my pretty things. Pay G[reen]. 39.

December 1

First day of winter. Lord grant it is a happier one than last year. Rested all day. Pretty well in spite of flurry on 29th. Feel stronger in many ways, so hope & wait. Pay Dr L[awrence] $73.

December 2

Dr G[reen]. Head a little light. Wont read at all, but rest.

December 3

Sewed & Dr read to me. Head rather shaky. Stomach calm. Letters &c.

December 4

Quiet day. Rather blue. Wrote letters & read. Mrs B[ond?]. send[s] some lovely books & I enjoyed em much. Views of Europe & Art book. Very kind.

December 5

Good day. Sewed wrote a little, read. Mrs B[ond?]. drew the funny Hooper for me.

December 6

Good day. Wrote 3 pages of "Jino",[69] read & sewed. Dr G[reen]. Walked a good deal. Slept well. No pack for legs.

December 7

Good day. Read "Royal Girls",[70] sewed & walked a little. Wrote to Low & others.

December 8

Good day. Head better.

December 9

Comfortable. Head all right.

December 10

Sewed & read. Rested.

December 11

Quiet day read & rested.

December 12

Letters to poor children. Sew & read. Dr G[reen]. all well. Very happy. Head clear. Stomach quiet, strength & color slowly coming back. Thank the Lord!

December 13

Good day. Sew, read. Fix old cloak & hood to give away.

December 14

Watch for Dr $50. Nice letters from A[nna]. Read Bubbling Teapot for Lulu. Lulu poorly. Anxious.

December 15

Went down stairs easily. Legs all right but stiff. Got pin for Dr 6,50. Made a bonnet for poor old soul. *Lulu sore throat.* Dr G[reen]. sees her. Long for my baby.

December 16

Busy on sewing. Wrote a little on T[rudel's]. S[iege]. for St N.

December 17

Well & busy. Went to drive for half an hour. Walked down & in & out. No trouble, enjoyed drive much. Rested all p.m. Glad to be able to do it after much long helplessness & pain.

December 18

Wrote an hour. Read & sewed. Felt well. First snow.

December 19

Felt very well in a.m. Finished "Trudel," & dolls gowns. Wrote to A[nna]. & rested all p.m. Two drops tonic. Red cheek. Stop it.

December 20

Rode an hour & enjoyed it. Some head ache as I was cross & sad. Rested all p.m. Scolded Dr. Did not sleep well. Hungry.

December 21

Six weeks today since I saw A[nna]. Hard times. Sew & read a little. Sad. Pretty well but mind suffering for food.

December 22

Sewed & read a little. Sent off cards & tale to St N. Very blue & lonely. Tried to be good. Dreamed of lovely white flowers.

December 23

Ear ache. Sad day. Cleaned about, sent gifts to home by S. $100 to Aunt B[ond].

December 24

Dr G[reen]. All well but gas. Took Nux & more Bic[arbonate]. No Lulu. Got cold. Very sorry not to see my baby. Worried along & was glad to go to bed & forget.

December 25

Snow. Xmas. Blue. Gifts come at 10. Lots. all pretty. Felt cheered up. Read & rested. Dull day. Gas all gone.

December 26

Felt better wrote letters. Read Browning[71] & made a basket for N.Y.

December 27

[blank]

December 28

Not seen A[nna]. for 7 weeks.

December 29

Good day.

December 30

Wrote on my Stolen[?] story. Dressed L[ulu]'s doll & read a little. A good day & night. Happy. My Lulu came looking well. Lots of gifts to show.

December 31

Dr G[reen]. All well. Lulu nicely & I all right. Thank the Lord for all his mercies. A hard year, but over now. Please God the next be happier for us all. Wrote letters. Good bye 1887!

SOURCE: Manuscript, Houghton Library, Harvard University.
    1. Fred Pratt would marry Jessica Cate on 8 February 1888.

2. Nux vomica, the seed contained in the pulpy fruit of an Asiatic tree, from which strychnine is obtained. LMA's "My Medicine Book" contains this prescription for its use: "Nux. dil[ute] 6 drops in 3 table spoons of water, four times a day" (Houghton Library, Harvard University).

3. Probably a reference to Elihu Vedder's illustrations to *The Rubaiyat of Omar Khayyam* (1884).

4. LMA often begins an entry with a weather report.

5. John Boyle O'Reilly, president of the Papyrus Club.

6. The common term for geum rivale, a plant used as an astringent and tonic for dyspepsia.

7. "Barker" is unlocated.

8. Cayenne pepper, used as a stimulant to aid digestion.

9. Mary Joy, Dr. Lawrence's sister and the housemother at Dunreath Place. LMA called her "the house-mother At Saint's Rest" (undated letter to Mary Joy, Fruitlands Museums).

10. LMA is undoubtedly using the "X" as a code for some sort of treatment, most likely enemas.

11. "Boston Balls" is unlocated.

12. LMA is probably using "job" to describe a bowel movement.

13. A plant extract used in ointments and in laxative enemas. LMA's "Medicine Book" gives this prescription for its use: "Aconite dil[uted]. 5 drops in ⅓ glass water. Palpitation. Dose tea spoon every 15 min or half hour" (Houghton Library, Harvard University).

14. Probably Dr. G. R. Starkey of Philadelphia, whose name appears in a list of addresses written at the back of LMA's 1887 diary.

15. Dr. C. H. Estabrook on Shawmut Avenue, Boston, whose name appears in a list of addresses at the back of LMA's 1887 diary.

16. The French novelist Honoré de Balzac.

17. "Little Bud" appeared in vol. 2 of *Lulu's Library*, published in October 1887 by Roberts Brothers.

18. Possibly Mrs. Morse, from whose husband LMA had leased the Boston house.

19. The bookseller and publisher Cupples, Upham Company, at 283 Washington Street, Boston.

20. "Sofa Society" and "Nile Bride" are unlocated.

21. Babu Mohini M. Chatterji spoke on human brotherhood at the South Congregational Church, where Edward Everett Hale was minister.

22. Possibly a work by Pratap Chunder Mozoomder.

23. "Virginia" is unlocated.

24. LMA's next contribution to *Harper's Young People* was "The Silver Party," which appeared on 22 November 1887.

25. "Polly's Pious Wooing" is unlocated.

26. "Anna: An Episode" was never finished; see LMA's letter of 7 May 1887 to Thomas Niles, in *SL*, p. 311.

27. "Early Marriages" appeared in the September 1887 *Ladies' Home Journal*.

28. "Early Marriages."

29. At the beginning of this entry, LMA wrote: "Wrote on Ivy all a.m. sewed in p.m. & read. Run with L[ulu]. L. & H[atty]. to be in p.m. Bath in eve." and then canceled it, since the same information begins the entry for the next day.

30. "An Ivy Spray" appeared in the October 1887 *St. Nicholas*.

31. *A Modern Mephistopheles and A Whisper in the Dark* was published, with LMA's name on the title page, in 1889 by Roberts Brothers. "A Whisper in the Dark" was included as an example of Jo March's "necessity stories." For more information on this book, see *A Modern Mephistopheles and Taming a Tartar*, ed. Madeleine B. Stern (New York: Praeger, 1987).

32. "Pansies" appeared in the September 1887 *St. Nicholas*.

33. Murdock's Liquid Food was a homeopathic remedy. According to an advertisement,

four tablespoons taken daily "will make eight per cent. new blood weekly" (*Boston Evening Transcript*, 27 October 1886, p. 3).

34. Leo Tolstoy's *Katia* (1878) was first published in English in 1887.

35. The British novelist George Meredith; Miss Plummer of England had corresponded with LMA about May's death.

36. In "My Medicine Book," LMA writes that a "tincture of Clomonilla on cotton" should be used for an earache (Houghton Library, Harvard University).

37. LMA legally adopted John, who changed his name to John Sewall Pratt Alcott, in June 1887 so that he could assume her copyrights. She also gave him and Fred $25,000 apiece.

38. Mrs. B. F. Wheeler's in Concord, where LMA was staying.

39. George M. Brooks, probate judge in Concord.

40. Probably "Water-Lilies," which appeared in *A Garland for Girls* (Boston: Roberts Brothers, 1888).

41. "Mignonette" is unlocated.

42. Emily Shepard, accompanied by her mother, was at Princeton for her health, under the care of Dr. Lawrence.

43. LMA's will was witnessed by Helen Blanchard, Otis Shepard, and Dr. Lawrence.

44. Edward William Bok, writer of a syndicated literary column, in 1889 became editor of the *Ladies' Home Journal*. This letter might be related to LMA's of 16 June [1887], in *SL*, pp. 313–314.

45. Probably "Poppies and Wheat," which appeared in *A Garland for Girls*.

46. An ailment often described as heartburn or a short, severe attack of illness.

47. LMA wrote Laura Hosmer that "old James Murdoch the actor elocutionist is here with his daughters, & very entertaining as he gives readings, & tells jolly tales of his life" ([19 July 1887], Louisa May Alcott Collection, Barrett Library, University of Virginia; and see the photograph of him with LMA in *SL*, following p. 264).

48. Possibly Mrs. F. L. Fynes of Roxbury, whose name appears in a list of addresses at the back of LMA's 1887 diary.

49. Samuel E. Sewall and his family had lived in Melrose, Massachusetts, since 1846.

50. A treatment involving inhalation of natron, a sodium carbonate.

51. For the house in Louisburg Square.

52. Rennet is added to milk to form a curd, or custardlike substance.

53. An emulsion used for the suspension of powders.

54. Gelsemiums, the root of the yellow jessamine, were used externally for rheumatism and arthritis, internally for headache and as emetics. According to LMA's "Medicine Book," they were used for "vertigo & dizziness" by putting "10 drops in half glass water. 1 tea spoon every ½ hour if bad" (Houghton Library, Harvard University).

55. Probably Miss Norton, one of LMA's charities, who is discussed in a letter of 19 January [1887] to Anna Ricketson in *SL*, p. 329n.

56. The second volume of *Lulu's Library*.

57. Herbert W. Blanchard married Julia S. Wood in Concord on 21 September 1887.

58. *The Frost King*, vol. 2 of *Lulu's Library*, reprinted material from *Flower Fables*, originally narrated to Emerson's daughter Ellen; hence the new volume was appropriately dedicated to her. LMA's letter of 24 September [1887] to Ellen is in *SL*, p. 320; her inscribed copy of the book is at the Houghton Library, Harvard University.

59. Laptondra was used as a cathartic and an emetic.

60. Possibly Catherine Gore's *Dean's Daughter* (1853).

61. J. C. Ropes apparently supplied LMA with coal; her letter of 25 September 1885 to him is in the Louisa May Alcott Collection, Barrett Library, University of Virginia, and his name is among those listed at the back of her 1887 diary.

62. A Cordelia Eliot of Roxbury is listed in the Boston papers as dying on 4 October at the age of eighty-one; possibly she was a neighbor of LMA's near Dr. Lawrence's.

63. LMA was reading James Elliot Cabot's *Memoir of Ralph Waldo Emerson* (1887). Her comments on this book are in her letter of 13 October [1887] to Bronson, in *SL*, p. 321.

64. Possibly Kissinger Salt, a preparation of potassium chloride, sodium chloride, magnesium sulfate, and sodium bicarbonate, added to water to simulate Kissinger spring water.

65. "Trudel's Siege" appeared in the April 1888 *St. Nicholas*.

66. LMA wrote: "Dull day stomach bad." and then canceled it.

67. Francis Marion Crawford published *Marzio's Crucifix* and *Paul Patoff* in December 1887.

68. LMA's extended account of her last birthday celebration is in her letter of 29 November [1887] to Anna Pratt, in *SL*, pp. 325–326.

69. "Jino" is unlocated.

70. M. E. W. Sherwood's *Royal Girls and Royal Courts* (1887).

71. No fewer than twenty volumes by Robert and Elizabeth Barrett Browning were published in 1887.

1888

January 1

A happy day & great contrast to Jan. 1st of last year. Then I was ill & hopeless & sad. Now though still alone & absent from home I am on the road to health at last & feel hopeful after much tribulation & pain for two years. Very grateful for my many mercies, & better for my trials I trust. Read & wrote letters. L[ulu]. brought a box of gifts from home & I have not seen any one but Lulu for 8 weeks. A vase, cherub's head, & "Daily Strength" from my son. Sent my little gifts back, & enjoyed my sweet book. Rain outside but peace within.

January 2

Headache. In bed & on sofa all day. L[ulu]. came. Very pale. Pretty gifts. Dull day.

January 3

Better, but pain in chest & sore throat. Write to A[nna]. & pay bills.

January 4

Poorly. Throat & head. Wrote to A[nna].

January 5

Poorly. Head & cold. Knit & dawdled.

January 6

Dull day. Made a basket & knit. Cross & blue. Sweet letter from Peddy.[1] Also Jess & Jacks.

327

January 7

Rain. Cross & blue like the day. No Lulu. Wrote letters, made a gay basket & tried to *live*.

January 8

Snow. Bad cold. Wrote letters, & lay still all a.m.

January 9

My Lulu came & was very sweet. Sewed, knit & amused myself as well as I could. Cold a little better but spirits low.

January 10

Snow. Dull day. Knit, pasted pictures & Dr read Higginson to me.[2]

January 11

Lay a bed till ten as I had nothing to do. Dosed & tried to shorten the long day. Wrote to A[nna]. & a little of tale. Sent A[nna]. $100. The $300 check being lost.

January 12

Cold & Fine. Dr G[reen]. Gave me an Inhaler. Said I could drive in tomorrow & see father who is feeble. Glad! Cant have callers yet, nor eat. Must wait. No freedom yet. (Had drive out & play all I can to keep jolly.)

January 13

Job. Snow. Dull day. Sewed & Dr read to me.

January 14

Job. Fine. Drove in & saw Pa & A[nna]. for 15 minutes. All quiet & well. Not tired at all. Rested all p.m. Dr. G[reen]. came.

January 15

Rain. Well. L[ulu]. came. Wrote letters, read a little, made a basket. Rested.

January 16

Fair. Well. Job X. Wrote to A[nna]. T. N[iles]. & A[nna]. R[icketson]. Good day.

January 17

Snow. Busy day. Felt well. Job X. Sewed, wrote on tale & several letters. Paid Vault bill. $30 & $2,00 for the year to U. E. for Women.[3]

January 18

Fine. Dr G[reen]. Write to A[nna]. & Dr Hunt.[4] Make a basket & read a little.

January 19

Fine. Go at 7½ to Dr H[unt]. about eyes. Have to have new glasses. Good drive & call. Eyes ache all p.m. so lie & doze & knit. G[ardner?]. gets hot[?] & sees A[nna?]. Takes baskets in &c.

January 20

Fine. Rest, paste pictures & keep eyes quiet for tomorrow. Good J[ohn]. Write to A[nna].

January 21

Fair. Dizzy, did not go to Dr H[unt]. Lay & shut my eyes & planned "Madge".[5] Sorry not to go in & see boys but dared not. Cold wind & I felt poorly. Flutter & weak & head light. [undeciphered] at home. Took Gel.

January 22

Very cold. Pain in chest. Keep warm & still. Dr G[reen]. Begin "Madge" 14 pages, in 1½.

January 23

Cold. Kept warm & still. Not very well, but chest better. Sew & Dr reads Thoreua [sic]. Nice book.[6]

January 24

Drive in & see Boys & T. N[iles]. Snow hurts my eyes. Lie still from 1 to 3. Sew a little. Sleep well. Get books. Give J[ohn]. my 6,700. check to invest. A[nna]. R[icketson]. pays the 42 00 I lent em & brings flowers.

January 25

Fine. Pretty well. Write to A[nna]. T. N[iles]. & Mr H[osmer?]. Sew on baby things.

January 26–27

[blank]

January 28

Wrote in a.m. Smoke all a.m. & at 1 found floor on fire under fire place. Still alarm. Men came pulled up floor & found beams burning. Put it out. Shoddy work & dangerous. Not upset. Kept cool. Long awake, silly women kept up such a fuss all night.

January 29

Kept still, wrote a little & Dr read to me. All right, tho I expected to be upset by the flurry. Slept poorly. Head full of a story that wont let me alone till writ. Miss J[oy]. $100.

January 30

X. Warm. To Dr H[unt]. at 1. Had eyes looked at again. Went to oculust for glasses in Winter St.[7] Glad to see Boston again. Rested two hours & felt all right. Cut out dress for my poor baby. No bath. Slept well.

January 31

Pay G[ardner]. to Feb. 11th $40. Write & sew. Feel well & do a good deal. Make a warm wrapper for a poor baby & work on "Sylvester" which possesses me strongly.[8] Queer idea. Miss J[oy]. towels $6,00.

February 1

To town with Dr L[awrence]. Got silver. Meet A[nna]. & F[red]. A lively time for a few minutes. Home & rest. No harm but riding jars head & back. Take Bell[9] & sleep it off.

February 2

Dr G[reen]. ordered Gel. to make me sleep. Sewed & dawdled round resting. Head tired, but not used up. Much stronger. So glad. Dr L[awrence]. $100

February 3

Kept quiet feeling rather shaken up by my trip to B[oston].

February 4

Dr G[reen]. about Pa. Failing fast. I am gaining fast. So keep still & wait. Make a scrap book & sew. Hope L[ulu]. will come.

February 5

Go in to see father who fails fast. Say good by as he seems nearly gone. In a stupor half the time. Opened his eyes & smiled at me. No pain but so weak. The oil is nearly gone.[10] A sad p.m. Lay still & Dr read Coleridge, Wordsworth to me so I should not think of sad things. Slept well. Made a poem.

February 6

Fine. A good day. Write letters, sew & read a little. Well & happy as Pa is better & all going smoothly at home. Copied poem on Papa.[11] Flowers & towels to A[nna].

February 7

Go to Dr H[unt]. Fine. Good letter from A[nna]. Pa better. All going well. Gifts flowing in fast. Dear A[nna]. with a heart full of love & pride over her good & happy boy. Poor old father just giving out of life, Fred just entering its sweetest part, & I standing on the brink to know my fate. God be with us all!

February 8

Fred's Wedding Day[12]

Foggy but cleared at night. Sewed & read & had 2 letters from A[nna] to keep me posted. All went well. A pretty wedding, many gifts & friends, good wishes & a merry send off. A[nna]. & L[ulu]. came safely home after a happy time. $500 worth of silver.

February 9

Mrs [sic] & Mrs F. A. Pratt to N.Y. this a.m. Family to see them off at 10 a.m. Sewed & read. Lulu came in p.m. Very well.

February 10

Cold. In town to see father. In bed, failing, we think. Heavy cold, fever, no appetite, no strength. Time to go. A[nna]. & L[ulu]. well. Rested & Dr. read to me. Made dust bags. Very well.

February 11

Dr G[reen]. Snow. Sewed & read. Good day. Dr in p.m. to say father was failing fast. Bath, slept well. Dr G. much pleased with my progress. Feel as if I *was* really better.

February 12

Fine. A lonely day. Drove in at 10 alone. Dr G[reen]. at house. Saw A[nna]. J[ohn]. & L[ulu]. Poor Papa so feeble but sweet & knew me. Will soon go I think. Peace be with him! Had a nice call & took L. & J. for a drive. Nap, read & rested. Felt nicely.

February 13

Fine. To town with Dr L[awrence]. Got curtains and rug for A[nna]. Good drive, nap & rest. Sewed & read. *Very well.*

February 14

Fine. Home to see father. Going fast, wanders, but knew me & smiled. Happy & calm. No pain. A natural & sweet end. Said, "Most people buy religion, I have it." Also "Come, read me your book." I spoke of being well. "I shall not see it," he said. Kissed him good bye if he gone when met again.

February 15

Fine. Drive out to J[essica]. P[ratt?]. with Dr L[awrence]. Air is so good. Sleep well & feel so well I rejoice & give thanks every day. Write a little on Madge & to A[nna]. Read "Queen Money." Very good.

February 16

Cold. Slept quietly, sewed wrote an hour, read a little & got thro the day. Did not feel very well. Head sore, & after no *bismuth* for 2 days stomach rather qualmish. Cross. Rode too often. G[reen?]. said go if tired, so I went 4 days. Too much.

February 17

Poorly & blue. Father drifting away fast. Hears music & talks to mother. Happy & quiet, No pain. Go tomorrow to see him if he is here. A[nna]. busy & quiet. Ready for F[red]. & J[ohn]. Eyes bad so dawdle & feel cross. 2 checks.

February 18

Go in town. Say Good bye to Father whose last day has come. Lies dreaming peacefully away. Said "Good bye." to me dimly conscious of "Weedy". "God bless & be with him. He goes to mother."

February 19

Dr G[reen]. came. Pa better. Read & rested.

February 20

Head poorly. Kept quiet, sewed & wrote a little. Madge.

February 21

Head better. Sewed & took a drive out of town. Fine day.

February 22

Fine. Better, sewed, read a little. F[red]. & J[essica]. came.

February 23

Finished Madge. Pay Mrs G[ardner]. $20 to the 25th of Feb. Sew & read 15 minutes. Pretty well. Write letters.

February 24

Fine. Lonely day. Go in to 10 & see A[nna]. Papa very much changed. So old & wasted & weak. A mere wreck of the beautiful old man. Sorry he did not slip away sooner. Hate to have him linger so. Rested 2 hours. Saw T. N[iles]. & boys. Got books. Sewed. Not tired. Head better.

February 25

[blank]

February 26

To town & saw F[red]. & J[essica]. & the wedding things. Very pretty. Rested & wrote letters & knit. Dr read.

February 27

Fine. Wrote on "Sylvester." Paid Miss Joy $100. Walked to store & was weighed. 113 pds. 136 last Sept. Lost 23 pds in six months. Now we will see how much I gain in the next 6. Cut out night gowns for my poor baby.

February 28

Sew, write letters & Dr reads. Dull & blue. Food not right.

February 29

Cold. Blue. Read a little. Write on Lu Sing an hour.[13] Sew. Send A[nna]. $200 for house.

March 1

Fine. In to see Papa. Very sweet & feeble. Kissed me & said "Come soon." Smelt my flowers & asked me to write him a letter. Nearly gone. A[nna].

very dear. Jess came for a moment. Met Mrs P[orter].[14] Saw "Leif" on the way home.

Pay rent.	375,00
Dr L[awrence]	51,20
Milk Mrs D[aniels].	2,32
Hack	29,30

March 2

Fine. Better in mind but food a little uneasy. Write letters. Pay Ropes $30, Notman 4. Sew. Write a little. L[ulu]. to come.[15]

SOURCE: Manuscript, Houghton Library, Harvard University.

1. Peddy, LMA's nickname for Fred Pratt.

2. Thomas Wentworth Higginson's *Women and Men* (1888).

3. The Massachusetts Society for the University Education of Women, founded in 1876.

4. Probably either Drs. David, Israel, or L. J. Hunt of Boston.

5. Possibly *Marjorie's Three Gifts* (Boston: Little, Brown, 1899).

6. *Winter: From the Journal of Henry D. Thoreau*, ed. H. G. O. Blake (1888).

7. The opticians John W. Sanborn & Company were at 3 Winter Street, Boston.

8. "Sylvester" is unlocated.

9. Possibly belladonna.

10. Probably a reference to the bay rum that Mary Stearns provided as rubbing oil for Bronson; see LMA's letter of 31 May [1883?] to her, *SL*, p. 270.

11. Possibly "Dear Pilgrim" (dated 29 November 1885) in Cheney, p. 387.

12. For a description of Fred's wedding, see LMA's letter of 8 February 1888 to Laura Hosmer, in *SL*, pp. 333–335.

13. "Lu Sing" appeared in the December 1902 *St. Nicholas*.

14. Above the initial, in a different hand, is: "(Porter)."

15. This is the last entry in LMA's hand. After it, a line is drawn across the page, under which is written the following: "The last entry. Died the following Tuesday. (Anna Alcott Pratt's Memo) Loaned by Mrs F. A. Pratt." The family also noted Bronson's death and the funerals on 4 March ("A. B. A. died about 11 o'clock in the morning at 10 Louisburg Sq. Boston. Mum & John at Roxbury, with L. M. Alcott, dying. Fred, Jessica, Mrs Hall at home with A. B. A."), 6 March ("L. M. A. died at Roxbury in the morning early on March 6. A. B. A. funeral at 10 Louisburg Sq. at 11 A.M."), and 8 March ("Funeral of L. M. Alcott at 10 Louisburg Square Boston at 11 A.M.").

Appendix A:

Mrs. Jarley's Waxworks

LOUISA MAY ALCOTT'S delight in the writings of Charles Dickens and her stage mania were combined in *Mrs. Jarley's Waxworks*, her dramatization of Chapter 27 from *The Old Curiosity Shop*. Her monologue proved especially suitable for amateur theatricals, and, arrayed in her old green dress with a large calash, or hood, on her head, clutching an umbrella and a basket, Alcott impersonated "the genuine and only Jarley" in performances in the Concord Town Hall to raise funds for the Concord Lyceum, or in Boston for the benefit of the New England Hospital for Women and Children. Jarley was Alcott's star role. It is interesting to note that George B. Bartlett, her fellow Concordian and member of her dramatic troupe, later compiled *Mrs. Jarley's Far-Famed Collection of Waxworks* for the drama publisher Samuel French. Alcott also dramatized scenes from *Oliver Twist, David Copperfield,* and *Martin Chuzzlewit;* manuscripts of her adaptations are preserved at the Houghton Library of Harvard University.

Wax Work

Mrs Jarley — advancing.

Ladies & gentlemen, I have the honor to present to you the finest collection of wax-work in the known world. The selection of figgers is elegant & instructive, classical & calm. They are fitted to instil moral lessons into the mind of infancy to warm the burnin heart of youth & cheer the eye of totterin age. Wax-work is the friend of man, it refines the soul, it cultivates the taste, it enlarges the sphere of the human understanding. Therefore cherish it.

Points to the figures.

This ladies & gentlemen is the unfortunate Maid of Honor of the time of Queen Betsey, who died from prickling of her finger in consequence of working on the Sabbath day. You may observe the blood a tricklin from her finger, also the gold eyed needle of the period.

335

This is Jasper Packle, merchant of atrocious memory, who married 14 wives & destroyed them all by ticklin the soles of their feet when they were sleepin in the consciousness of innocence & virtoo. On being brought to the scaffold & asked if he warnt sorry, he said "Yes, he was sorry for havin let em off so easy, & hoped all Christian husbands would forgive him the offence." Let this be a warning to all young misses to be particular in the character of the gentlemen of their choice & learn their little domestic amusement beforehand. You may percieve that his fingers is curled as if in the act of ticklin & that his eye is represented a winkin as he appeared when committing his barbarious murders.

The next is the famous Welch dwarfess "Morgan of Kerrich Vic-ian-nor Erin go brah" in the 99th year of her age. Her height was two feet three inches, of a mild disposition, deeply religious, bland, passionate & serene, & died at 110 from partaking copiously of "clam-mac-nea-maw" — the national dish of her native land.

Here is Captain Kyd the great nautical highwayman who scuttled 94 ships, murdered 16 innocent babes, 10 lovely women & 97 galliant men during the course of his sinful career which was brought to a providential terminus in a conflict with the natives of Patagonia during the last election riots. He is here represented as spilling the highly connected blood of Lady Boadicea Fitz battle axe, an heroic miss who fell a victim to his sanguinary sword because with Spartanian firmness she refused to betray the hiding place of her venerable parient Lord Coriolanious Herculeneum who with the usual courage of his sex retired behind a hen coop[1] leaving his daughter to enjoy that one of women's right which they are always permitted to enjoy, namely that of martyrdom.[2]

This is the striking likeness of Martha Bang the mad maid servant who poisoned 14 families with pickled walnuts. Her brain having become saturated with the fumes of biling vinegar she became a lunacy & spread desolation far and wide as she went from one home to another beholding parients, aged beings, & tender babes fall before the power of the pestilential pickle, till she was discovered[,] when she instantly recovered her reason & died calmly penitent in fierce convulsions.

This I hardly need to say is a speaking image of Lord Beron as he appeared when composing the third chapter of his great novel of Infant Harold. This has been pronounced by many more natural than life. The moral religious & social characteristics of the great & unhappy bard render him a noble object for the instruction & admiration of an enlightened public.

My last & *greatest* work of art is the well known instructer of the youth of Chinese persuasion — Ching-chang-do-ong-po-po-catte pattle. His name was rendered famous by the introduction of Arts & Sciences into Pekin where he established a Li-book-sob or Seminary & a Hi-fun-see or Theatre for the representation of Chinese life & manners, which labors still render his memory verdant in the hearts of his country men & gave the "queue" for farther improvements. This great Panjandrum died in his 353 year & was interred with eastern splendor in a Pagoda which was considered a triumph of Chinese architecture, on which was this inscription. "Hi man see sky" "He had not far to go" — a graceful allusion to his height & consequent nearness to Heaven.

I am in the habit of exhibiting a feat which no other wax-work show ever equalled or can ever surpass. It is the winding up of the figgers when, such is the miraculous extent to which machinery has been fetched each figger immeadiately makes some graceful & appropriate gesture with a naturalness which utterly deceives the eye & caused her Majesty to exclaim "Almighty Science! they live, they move, they have a bein!"

After the winding up is over —

Ladies & Gentlemen, allow me to thank you for your genteel & respectful attention during the Exhibition & to solicit your distinguished patronage for the futer in behalf of Jarley's Unsurpassed Wax work.

Bows & curtain falls.

SOURCE: Manuscript, Houghton Library, Harvard University.
1. LMA wrote: "to the privacy of a sugar hogs head" and then at a later date canceled it, inserting: "behind a hen coop."
2. LMA wrote: "her rights of self defense" and then at a later date canceled it, inserting: "that one . . . martyrdom."

Appendix B: Early Sketches by the Alcott Sisters

THE INFLUENCE of Dickens, especially of *The Posthumous Papers of the Pickwick Club*, is paramount in the early Alcott family newspaper. Just as the voluminous transactions of the Pickwick Club included observations, narratives, and adventures of club members, the Alcott girls' paper — variously styled the *Olive Leaf*, the *Pickwick Portfolio*, and *The Portfolio*, running from about 1849 to about 1853 — contained romances, autobiographical narratives, and poetry by the Alcott sisters. Of special interest are the contributions, usually unsigned, by Louisa May Alcott, for these included forerunners of her sensational tales as well as forerunners of her great domestic novel, *Little Women*. Among the former was "The Masked Marriage," which was later actually revamped and used in *Little Women*, where one issue of the *Pickwick Portfolio* dated "May 20, 18 — " was printed. Among the latter is the example presented here, "Two scenes in a family." Alcott recalled with fondness "the dear little Pickwick Portfolio of twenty years ago" when in 1873 she wrote to the Lukens sisters about a similar enterprise of theirs (*SL*, p. 176). Also printed are two sketches by May and Anna Alcott, both showing the same youthful, moralistic didacticism of their sister's work.

Two scenes in a family.

The night was dark and windy the wind whistled mournfully over the barren hills and leafless trees.

In a small humble house round a bright fire sat a group of happy faces, the room was simply furnished though here and there some small object showed that they had seen better days; A well stocked bookcase a few rare pictures and more than all the countenances on which the fire fell brightly round the table sat five person[s]. the pale anxious face and busy fingers that plied the needle so swiftly could be mistaken for none but the mother. sitting at her feet was a child who was fondly watching over the pussy that lay purring in her lap   beside her sat another some years older   a book lay on her knee but she was looking up at the others.

the quiet little form with an air of such perfect repose and contentment about it that few would not envy it   the fire light seemed to linger lovingly on the rosy cheek and bright locks.

Beside the mother sat two more daughters   one in whose gentle face and quiet eyes shone a good and happy spirit, the perfect neatness of the dress and the taste with which the sunny brown hair was parted back and lay in a shining crown above contrasted strongly with the face beside her so thin dark and restless yet not without a certain beauty in the small deep eyes and finely formed head betokening will and strength of mind   one hand was hidden in the disordered hair that fell over it. the other tossing over some papers that lay before her and listening carelessly to a clear musical voice near her. The speaker was a face seldom seen in our land, the thin grey hair fell over a high full forehead   the[re] was a soft holy light in the eyes and about the whole person something pure and sacred that brought to the mind the faces of the old philosophers so strongly beautiful in their grace and simplicity   in low ernest tones he said Why should we be troubled   rich and poor have there cares and sorrow but the hearts of the poor warmed and purified by their own griefs feel for others and their few joys are shared freely with those less fortunate   wealth brings selfishness and the love and care of the poor and lowly is forgoten. then are we not happier than they and can we wish for riches if they take from us the quiet joy and contentment that now are ours.

But father it is so pleasant to be rich and not be troubled with debts. to leave in ease and comfort and enjoy all the lovely things money can give us   people must be so happy   I think I should be as kind to the poor or perhaps kinder if I could help them more   is it wrong to wish to be rich asked the child with the book.

No Lizzie   I think nothing could harden your gentle little heart but time alone will show, the darkness of the world can dim even the brightest spirit[,] can take from it all it loved or cared for said the father with a sigh   I *know* I should be better happier and of more use if I had money   every body must be. The world need not hurt us if we have strength enough not to let it. money cannot hurt us I think[,] not me at least   the power of doing good always makes people happy. wouldn't you like to be rich Annie broke out[,] the brown girl   think how good it would seem to have all we want and not be doomed to pass our lives doing what we hate   I dont know said the sister looking into her wild face   I should like it for the many pleasant things I could do with it yet I am not sure but the little we can do while poor brings a truer joy than the careless alms of the rich   What do you think mother   I cannot decide answd the mother   the moral and social laws are entirely false   while the rich waste the poor will want   while there is no sympathy and love there will be sin and misery   when the rich will give their abundance wisely and kindly will the poor live virtuously and happily   It is not only what we give but how we give it   a gentle word enriches a generous action. the wounds made by cruelty cannot be healed by money but truthful kindness can restore joy and peace to the loneliest hearts   wealth may be made a source of true happiness to high and low but I fear that time will never come   It never will said

339

the Father till a greater event has taken place[,] till charity is a principle not a task. Not till men feel deeply and truely that it is better to give than to recieve will pove[r]ty cease and equality appear

Let us wait till we are tried for we may be found wanting   wealth is a greater trial than poverty for the golden walls it builds around our hearts, we love not to break,   We are dazzled by the bright bars that shut out love and Charity and we do not feel that more we seek and honor it higher grows the wall till the sweet virtues are cast away leaving the soul they would purify to wear its golden fetters
but the cold dark stones that in poverty lie before us in keeping from us what we need we eagerly seek to pass over them to the rest beyond and as we suffer and hope feel for those like ourselves   then let us strengthen ourselves in humility that pride shall not cast us down.

[Louisa]

SOURCE: *The Portfolio*, no. 7, 18 November; manuscript, Houghton Library, Harvard University.

Biography

There was once a little girl who lived in Groton Street   she was not a very good girl and used to trouble her three sisters and was very bad then,   her father & mother were very nice people & did all they could to make folks good,

This little girl went to school & took music lessons   her school mistress was very kind to her & did not speak cross to her at all,

She had ever so many little girls & boys to play with & did have nice times in the snow with her sled,

And this little girl used to read & sew & write notes to her friend Mary Park, & her name was

Abba Alcott.

SOURCE: *The Portfolio*, no. 5, 26 November; manuscript, Houghton Library, Harvard University.

Words from an elder sister

There is nothing so sad and troublesome as a little girl who is always fretting & crying about little things   she makes herself unhappy and troubles every one about her,   now if this child would like to [be] happy & loved she should leave off this naughty habit & if any thing vexes her she should try to be cheerful about it & listen to the little voice in her own heart and do as it tells her, then she will be happy again & little things will not trouble her so much, for the gentle voice comes from a good little spirit who stays there to keep the child from going from the narrow path of its duty,   Then listen to it my little sisters & it never will lead you astray, but will make the world a pleasant home where nothing evil can come to disturb you.

Annie

SOURCE: *The Portfolio*, no. 5, 26 November; manuscript, Houghton Library, Harvard University.

Index

343

348

352

Trevor, Richard, 115, 122n
Trowbridge, John Townsend, 160n
Tsalter, Miss, 190n
Tuckerman, Salisbury, 94, 96n
Turner, J. M. W., 179, 181n, 189, 191–193

Underhill, Mrs., 297
United States Sanitary Commission, 135n
United States Service Magazine, 122, 126n, 127,
134n, 135n, 152; works by LMA in,
139

Vassar College, 196, 198n
Vedder, Elihu, 288, 324n
Verne, Jules, 225, 230n
Victoria, Queen, 149
Von Arnim, Bettina, 60, 60n

Wadsworth, Mrs., 269, 297
Walker, Wise, and Company, 131, 132,
136n
Walpole, Horace, 160n
Wansey, Miss, 116
Ward, Samuel Gray, 96n
Warren, Alice Bartlett. *See* Bartlett, Alice
Warren, William, 74, 76n
Warren family, 178, 181n
Wasson, David Atwood, 119, 123n, 130
Waters, Mrs., 268
Waterston, Mr., 132, 136n
Waterston, Mrs., 132
Wayside, 59n, 89, 93n
Webster, Daniel, 65, 65n
Weiss, John, 167, 169n
Weld, Anna, 141, 142, 144, 145, 147n,
148n, 149–151, 154
Weld, George, 141, 143–145, 147n
Weld, William Fletcher, 33, 141, 147n,
148n, 152, 155
Wells, Eliza, 156n
Wells, Eliza May, 117, 123n, 153, 156n
Wells, Elizabeth Sewall Willis, 123n, 159,
161n, 205, 228, 230n, 248–250, 266n,
276, 297
Wells, Ruth Lyman, 248, 249, 266n
Wells, Thomas Goodwin, 123n
Wendte, Louisa Wells, 266n, 268, 270, 288,
298, 305
Wendte, Louisa Wells Willis, 279
Wesselhoeft, Conrad, 191, 194n, 205, 213,
236, 248, 253, 272, 274, 280, 283,

286n, 287, 288, 292, 294, 296, 298,
302, 303, 311, 312, 318
Wheeler, Charles P., 133, 137n
Wheeler, Mrs. B. F., 304, 325n
Whipple, Eddie, 69
Whipple, Edwin Percy, 14, 81, 83n, 130,
247, 248, 251, 291
Whipple, Mrs., 250, 269
Whiting, Annie, 98, 102n
Whiting, William, 102n
Whitney, Anne, 252, 266n, 268, 270, 276
Whittier, John Greenleaf, 135n
Wilbur, Hervey B., 75, 77n, 100
Wilkinson, Alfred, 124n, 278, 285n
Wilkinson, Alfred, Jr., 124n
Wilkinson, Charlotte Coffin, 119, 285n
Wilkinson, Charlotte Coffin May, 124n
Wilkinson, Marion, 124n
Willard, Frances, 271, 272, 285n
Willard, Mrs., 43, 52n
Williams, Charles H. S., 218, 222n
Willis, Benjamin, 75, 76, 76n
Willis, Dr., 90
Willis, Elizabeth May, 76n
Willis, Hamilton, 52n, 74, 76, 76n, 80,
117, 129, 134, 211, 212n
Willis, Helen Phillips, 129
Willis, Louisa, 47, 52n, 74, 76, 79, 80, 83n,
84, 90, 94, 95, 106, 111, 112n
Willis, William Gorman, 286n
Windship, Charles May, 74, 76n, 78, 80,
99
Windship, Charles W., 52n
Windship, Martha Ruggles, 52n
Windship family, 117
Winslow, John, 115–117, 122n
Winthrop, Theodore, 129, 135n
Wisniewski, Ladislas, 33, 144, 145, 148n,
149, 151, 153, 154
Wolcott, Mrs., 216, 221n
Wollstonecraft, Mary, 13, 213, 220n
Woman's Journal, works by LMA in, 198n,
211, 212n, 221n, 230n, 233, 236n,
266n
Wordsworth, William, 331
Wright, Henry, 4

Youth's Companion, 159, 161n, 162, 221n;
works by LMA in, 148n, 173n, 185n,
190n, 194n, 195n, 199n, 202n, 208n,
234, 236n